Energetics of Human Activity

W.A. Sparrow
Deakin University,
Melbourne, Australia

Editor

Human Kinetics

Library of Congress Cataloging-in-Publication Data

Energetics of human activity / W.A. Sparrow, editor.
    p. cm.
    Includes bibliographical references and index.
    ISBN 0-88011-787-7
    1. Human locomotion. 2. Energy metabolism. 3. Human mechanics. I. Sparrow, William Anthony, 1955-
    QP301 .E568 2000
    612.7'6--dc21   99-059623

ISBN: 0-88011-787-7
Copyright © 2000 by William A. Sparrow

Acquisitions Editor: Loarn D. Robertson, PhD
Managing Editor: Coree Schutter
Copyeditor: Arlene Miller
Proofreader: Andy Smith
Indexer: Marie Rizzo
Permission Manager: Heather Munson
Graphic Designer: Fred Starbird
Graphic Artist: Tara Welsch
Cover Designer: Jack W. Davis
Illustrator: Tom Roberts
Printer: Versa Press

Printed in the United States of America   10 9 8 7 6 5 4 3 2 1

Human Kinetics
Web site: http://www.humankinetics.com/

United States: Human Kinetics, P.O. Box 5076, Champaign, IL 61825-5076
1-800-747-4457
e-mail: humank@hkusa.com

Canada: Human Kinetics, 475 Devonshire Road Unit 100, Windsor, ON N8Y 2L5
1-800-465-7301 (in Canada only)
e-mail: humank@hkcanada.com

Europe: Human Kinetics, P.O. Box IW14, Leeds LS16 6TR, United Kingdom
+44 (0)113-278 1708
e-mail: humank@hkeurope.com

Australia: Human Kinetics, 57A Price Avenue, Lower Mitcham, South Australia 5062
(08) 82771555
e-mail: liahk@senet.com.au

New Zealand: Human Kinetics, P.O. Box 105-231, Auckland Central
09-523-3462
e-mail: humank@hknewz.com

This book is dedicated to Alan, Alma, Helen, Nicola, and to my friends at the University of Illinois in the early 1980s, especially John. I sincerely thank the book's contributors for their efforts, and we are all grateful to the scientists whose work is cited in the chapters.

Contents

Preface

Collectively, the chapters in this book address whether the learning and control of motor skills is underpinned by one expedient, namely, to execute motor actions in such a way that the metabolic energy cost of coordination and control is minimised. Casual observation of individuals performing a variety of everyday motor tasks invariably leads to the hypothesis that an attempt is being made to meet the task requirements with the least amount of energy expenditure. From a movement science perspective, the metabolic cost of performing mechanical work in order to interact with the environment describes the "efficiency" or "economy" of movement. The chapters in this book provide a detailed, contemporary discussion and definition of economy and efficiency from a multidisciplinary movement science perspective.

Economical movements are those that meet the task demands with relatively low metabolic energy expenditure. "Relative" in this sense implies comparisons between individuals performing the same task, intraindividual changes in energy expenditure as a function of practice, or differences between alternative coordination and control options, or "solutions," at a particular point in time. Thus, individual differences, motor learning, and the control of action are three topics of interest from a movement economy perspective. In addition, the related concepts of metabolic energy expenditure and the mechanical work demands of motor task performance can be addressed from a variety of movement science sub-discipline perspectives. The mechanics of human motion, the physiological cost of meeting task demands, and the effects of practice on performance are three scholarly domains that, in the chapters in this book, are brought to bear on a single, fundamental movement science issue. The broad aim of the book, therefore, is to present various approaches to the study of motor learning and control; these approaches have examined the hypothesis that minimisation of metabolic energy expenditure is a universal constraint on the structure of emerging movement patterns. Each chapter provides a systematic principled basis for examining metabolic energy expenditure, presents research findings that address the issues outlined above, and makes valuable suggestions for future research.

Metabolic Energy Expenditure and Accuracy in Movement: Relation to Levels of Muscle and Cardiorespiratory Activation and the Sense of Effort

Nicholas J. O'Dwyer

School of Physiotherapy, The University of Sydney, Australia

Peter D. Neilson

Cerebral Palsy Research Unit, Institute of Neurological Sciences, The Prince Henry Hospital and Neuroengineering Laboratory, School of Electrical Engineering and Telecommunications, University of New South Wales, Australia

In this chapter, we consider two important issues in the study of movement, namely, metabolic economy and movement accuracy. A key issue concerning the optimisation of metabolic economy in movement is the fact that signals of global metabolic energy expenditure have not been identified in the central nervous system (CNS). Since everyday movements appear to be constrained by the imperative to optimise metabolic economy (see Sparrow and Newell 1998 for review), the source(s) of sensory information by which metabolic energy expenditure is regulated remains a crucial, unresolved question. A key issue concerning the optimisation of movement accuracy is the observation that the noise in motor output increases with the magnitude of the force or muscle output (e.g., Schmidt et al. 1979; Carlton and Newell 1993). This suggests that minimising noise by minimising muscle output should maximise movement accuracy. We review the literature on these two key issues and conclude that the optimisation of both metabolic economy and movement accuracy are linked via the process of minimisation of muscle activity.

1

The chapter is divided into three main sections. In the first section, we focus on local muscle activity and consider the possible signals available to the CNS to provide information relevant to movement economy. Pertinent literature is reviewed concerning the perception of centrally generated motor commands, which gives rise to a *sense of effort* associated with muscle activation and on cardiovascular and respiratory responses to muscle activation. We conclude that the sense of effort and cardiorespiratory activity are linked, not directly by global metabolic energy expenditure, but by the relative level of activation of muscles, regardless of their mass.

In the second section, we consider the levels of muscle activation and how they change with practice and level of skill. We relate this issue to impulse variability theory (Schmidt et al. 1979), which proposes that the noise in motor output increases with the magnitude of the force or muscle output. This relationship between magnitude of muscle activation and motor output noise underscores the importance of motor accuracy to the level of muscle activation. In both these sections of the chapter, therefore, the relative level of muscle activation is identified as a critical variable in movement; this variable thus unites the optimisation of both metabolic economy and movement accuracy. Furthermore, the sense of effort appears to reflect both the relative level of muscle activation and the level of metabolic energy expenditure. Accordingly, the sense of effort may provide a primary perceptual mechanism whereby both metabolic economy and movement accuracy may be optimised. This mechanism appears to operate at a local muscle level rather than a global output level, consonant with the fact that reductions in energy expenditure must ultimately be implemented via reductions in the activity of specific muscles.

Finally, in the third section of the chapter, we consider the question of coordination between the motor commands to the skeletomotor and the cardiorespiratory systems and propose that both types of commands be considered to form part of the planning processes for movement.

Metabolic Energy Expenditure in Movement

In static exercise, contraction below 15% of maximum is reported to be nonfatiguing, as evidenced by ventilatory and cardiovascular parameters rising to a steady-state level that is maintained until the contraction ceases (Monod and Scherrer 1965; Muza et al. 1983). Beyond approximately 15% of maximum contraction, therefore, fatigue is a potential threat to sustained performance of static exercise, and ventilatory and cardiovascular responses rise accordingly. Compared with sustained exercise, therefore, metabolic energy expenditure may not be an important consideration in movements that recruit only low levels of muscle activity, are isolated, are infrequent, or are of short duration. Performance of infrequent movements is also unlikely to be refined in the same way as sustained exercise or everyday movements, so that the energy expenditure associated with these movements is less likely to be minimised with practice. Conversely, the more frequently we carry out a movement, the more important it is that the associated energy cost is minimised, hence our ability to walk and speak for prolonged periods.

The primary consideration in the execution of any movement is the fulfilment of the purpose or task goal. In the early stages of acquiring a new skill, meeting the demands of the task probably outweighs other considerations, and in subservience to these demands, energy expenditure may be high. However, in the longer term and in the later stages of skill acquisition, as desired movements are executed more accurately and the demands of the task are more successfully met, energy expenditure may be reduced. Thus, energy efficiency is one of the characteristics commonly attributed to skilled movements. Such a changing relationship between movement accuracy and energy expenditure as a function of skill acquisition suggests that subjects vary their behaviour by altering the compromise between energy expenditure and movement accuracy. Sparrow and Newell (1998) considered the question of how organisms regulate metabolic energy expenditure to perform work to meet task demands. From their extensive review of the literature pertaining to this question, they provided convincing evidence that performance of everyday motor skills is constrained by the imperative to optimise the metabolic economy of movement. They considered the propensity to minimise the metabolic cost of everyday actions to be a natural consequence of evolutionary adaptation.

Motor behaviour was described by Sparrow and Newell (1998) as "the process by which organisms convert chemical energy, through the metabolism of foodstuffs, to mechanical energy, in order to interact adaptively with their environment" (p. 174). This mechanical energy is provided by muscle activation; therefore, muscle is the primary site of the energy transaction in movement. In considering control of metabolic energy expenditure in movement, we therefore focus on muscle and on the potentially relevant muscle-related signals that are available to the CNS. This focus is important because, as indicated below, the muscle mass that is mobilised for a specific task appears to be a less significant control consideration than the intensity of activation of the participating muscles or muscle groups. Walking and handwriting, for example, mobilise muscles of markedly different mass and entail different global metabolic energy expenditure. Sustained performance of either walking or handwriting may be threatened, not by generalised exhaustion, but by the onset of fatigue in any of the participating muscles. This is because the kinetic chain is only as strong as its weakest link, and the weakest link is the muscle or muscle group that is under greatest strain, meaning that it is activated at the highest level relative to its maximum. Consequently, local muscle energy expenditure rather than global expenditure appears to be the more important consideration in controlling movement.

Muscle activation is necessarily correlated with metabolic energy expenditure. Strasser and Ernst (1992), for example, measured oxygen consumption, heart rate, and electromyogram (EMG) in seven chest, upper arm, and shoulder muscles during a repetitive lifting task performed in a seated position. The seven muscles recorded appeared to provide a representative sample of muscles participating in the lifting task, apart from postural muscles involved in maintaining upright sitting, which would not be expected to vary markedly between the lifting conditions. They examined three lifting conditions that imposed different workloads on the subjects. The study showed that global physiological cost, demonstrated by oxygen consumption and heart rate, correlated significantly with local physiological cost, demonstrated by the magnitudes of EMG activity (expressed as percentages of maximal voluntary contraction). Furthermore, the strength of the correlation generally increased with increasing workload; this is consistent with the finding that the rate of energy expenditure of muscle increases markedly as more motor units are recruited (Goldspink 1981). Therefore, the conclusion from the Strasser and Ernst study, not surprisingly, is that ensemble levels of muscle activity provide a measure of the metabolic energy expended in performance of a motor task. If muscular energy can be minimised, metabolic energy will also be minimised. The CNS has at its disposal multiple channels of information about muscle activity, and we consider next the signals that might facilitate control of metabolic energy expenditure.

The Informational Basis for Regulation of Metabolic Energy Expenditure

Sparrow and Newell (1998) examined the sensory regulation of metabolic energy expenditure and concluded that the most important available information is that from *interoceptors*. They considered interoceptors to be the source of "the information from internal organs that provides some of the sensory stimulation concerning metabolic energy expenditure" (p. 174). The term interoceptors apparently refers to all the receptor organs of the digestive tract, the cardiovascular and lymphatic systems, and the internal organs (Chernigovskiy 1967). While the cardiovascular system will figure prominently in the following discussion, our emphasis throughout is on muscle as the primary site of the energy transaction in movement. Since the CNS directly controls muscle activity, muscle is also the primary site where metabolic energy expenditure can be regulated. Accordingly, in searching for potential sources of sensory information concerning metabolic energy expenditure, the link with local muscle activity will be uppermost in our minds. We will examine both the skeletomotor and the cardiovascular systems.

Skeletomotor Signals

In both this section and the subsequent section on cardiovascular and respiratory signals, we will consider separately the signals of peripheral muscular origin and the command signals of central origin. We are looking particularly for a signal that provides a measure of the level of muscle activation.

Muscle Signals

Golgi tendon organs have received considerably less attention than muscle spindles, but they are plentiful in striated somatic muscles and might be expected to assume a preeminent role in providing information about muscle activation and, hence, energy expenditure. Accordingly, we here summarise the most pertinent findings concerning the activity of this receptor as reviewed by Hasan and Stuart (1984). Golgi tendon organs are found near aponeuroses (fibrous membranes formed by the expansion of tendons) of the origin and insertion of muscles. They are also found deep in some muscles if an aponeurosis extends there. Few Golgi tendon organs are found in the tendon proper. They are not connected in series with the whole muscle; rather, each tendon organ is connected in series with only 5 to 25 (mean about 10) muscle fibres (and in parallel with the remainder). Each of these muscle fibres typically belongs to a different motor unit. Bearing in mind that the territory of single motor units is relatively widespread throughout a limited cross-section of the muscle, each Golgi tendon organ appears to provide a sample of forces from a cross-section of muscle occupied by about 10 motor units of differing motor unit types. The sample is essentially random and, therefore, may be representative of the muscle as a whole.

The Golgi tendon organ is a particularly low-threshold force detector with a sensitivity to muscle force that is at least on a par with the sensitivity of muscle spindles to muscle length. Passive muscle stretch, however, is a relatively ineffective stimulus to the Golgi tendon organ and must be substantial in order to reach the force threshold of receptor response. On the other hand, the contractile force of only a single in-series muscle fibre (as little as 4 mg wt) is sufficient to excite the receptor. The output of the receptor is related to the force in a more or less linear, nondynamic fashion, at least to a first approximation, since nonlinearity of response and sensitivity to derivatives of force are modest. Tendon organ discharge can signal moment-to-moment changes in localised, active, intramuscular force; and the summed responses of all tendon organs in a muscle should provide a better estimate of total muscle force than the responses of any single receptor (Hasan and Stuart 1984).

It is evident, therefore, that Golgi tendon organs are the primary source of signals concerning muscle force or tension that is available to the CNS. However, muscle metabolic activity is determined by the level of muscle activation. Do tendon organs signal the level of muscle activation?

The best measure of the level of excitatory drive to muscle, reflecting the contribution of both central motor commands and reflex input, is the EMG. EMG activity is functionally related to muscle tension, although it has been shown to correlate linearly with tension only under isometric conditions or during contractions with constant velocity (Inman et al. 1952; Lippold 1952; Bigland and Lippold 1954; Gottlieb and Agarwal 1971; Lindström, Magnusson, and Petersén 1974; Milner-Brown and Stein 1975; Hof and van den Berg 1977). Under dynamic conditions, the level of tension generated at a given level of muscle activation is significantly affected by a number of factors such as muscle length, rate of change of length, and whether the muscle is shortening or lengthening. When, for example, the same level of drive, measured by EMG activity, is directed to homologous adductor pollicis muscles, the tension generated is equal in both muscles when they are at the same length, but less in one of the muscles if placed in a shortened position (Cafarelli 1982). Again, it is well known that the same level of muscle tension can be generated at a lower level of muscle activation (Komi 1986) and with lower oxygen uptake (Asmussen 1953) through eccentric rather than concentric muscle contraction. The relationship between level of muscle activation and achieved tension is also significantly altered by fatigue. In order to maintain the same level of tension as a muscle undergoes fatigue, additional motor units must be recruited, and metabolic activity is consequently increased. Therefore, due to these functionally significant dissociations between muscle tension and muscle activation, the level of muscle tension signaled by the Golgi tendon organs cannot provide an unequivocal signal of the level of activation of muscle, or of metabolic energy expenditure.

Central Command Signals

Having discounted peripheral information from Golgi tendon organs, at first sight the most likely candidate to provide signals related to muscle metabolism, we now consider a potential central source of information concerning muscle metabolism. Activation of motoneurons is preceded by motor commands generated within the CNS; psychologists, physiologists, neurologists, and even philosophers have long wondered whether signals related to such motor commands directly evoke sensation. In his review of the literature on this question, McCloskey (1981) presented convincing evidence for the intrusion of centrally generated motor commands into perceptual processes. This view was reiterated by Gandevia (1987), who noted that while it is usual to emphasise tangible feedback signals in motor control, there is a considerable body of evidence that perceived signals of centrally generated motor commands have important roles in directing, quantifying, and timing the outputs to muscles. McCloskey (1981) defined any neural signal derived from motor commands that remains wholly within the CNS as an *internal command collateral*. Noting the considerable inconsistency in this context in historical use of the terms *corollary discharges* and *efference copy*, he proposed that corollary discharges be confined to internal command collaterals that affect sensation. He also noted that electrophysiological evidence for internal command collaterals abounds, although only some of this evidence concerns the involvement of these collaterals with sensory processing.

Most of the evidence concerning the roles of perceived signals of centrally generated motor commands has been derived from experiments in human subjects on weight matching and perceptions of force or weight. The perception of force and weight has a long history in both experimental psychology and physiology dating back to Weber (1834/1978). The results of many studies since Weber's work indicate that sensations of force and heaviness are derived from centrally generated motor commands, rather than from afferent discharges arising peripherally in various sensory receptors (see reviews by McCloskey 1981; Jones 1986; and Gandevia 1987).

Typically, in these experiments the normal relationship between motor commands and evoked muscular tension was disturbed in a variety of ways, such as by partial neuromuscular paralysis or altered reflex assistance, or by inducing fatigue. Whenever this is done, the perception of muscular force or heaviness maintains, at least qualitatively, its relationship to the motor command rather than to the tensions and pressures generated. One of the key experiments providing evidence in support of this view was that of McCloskey, Ebeling, and Goodwin (1974). Subjects were asked to support a weight with one arm (the reference arm), and at various intervals they were required to match this weight with weights lifted by the other arm (figure 1.1). When the reference arm was rested between trials, subjects chose weights close to the reference weight when attempting to match it. When the reference arm supported the weight continuously, the arm became fatigued; as this fatigue progressed, successively larger matching weights were chosen, showing that the perceived heaviness of the continuously supported weight did indeed increase.

The role of afferent input from the periphery in the perception of increased weight described by McCloskey, Ebeling, and Goodwin (1974) can be excluded on the basis of results from experiments using high-frequency muscle vibration. When vibration is applied over the tendon of a muscle, it powerfully excites spindle primary afferents and increases the discharge of spindle secondary afferents and Golgi tendon organs (Burke et al. 1976a,b). An involuntary reflex contraction, known as the

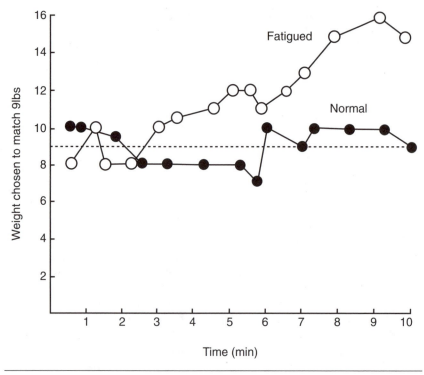

Figure 1.1   The subject was given a 9-lb (4.09-Kg) weight to support with one arm (the reference arm) and was to match this with weights supported in the same way by the other arm. These matching weights are shown here. When the reference arm was rested between matching trials, subjects chose weights close to 9 lbs (closed circles). When the reference arm supported the weight continuously, it became fatigued and progressively larger matching weights were chosen (open circles), showing that the perceived heaviness of the continuously supported weight increased.

Adapted, by permission, from McCloskey, D.I., P. Ebeling, and G.M. Goodwin, 1974, "Estimation of weights and tensions and apparent involvement of a 'sense of effort,'" *Experimental Neurology* 42: 220-232.

tonic vibration reflex, is evoked in the vibrated muscle and has been attributed to spindle excitation (De Gail, Lance, and Neilson 1966; Hagbarth and Eklund 1966). When a given tension is achieved in this way with the assistance of a tonic vibration reflex, subjects perceive themselves to be exerting a smaller than normal muscular force (McCloskey, Ebeling, and Goodwin 1974) and, indeed, they get "a feeling of relief or lessening of tension which seems to counteract the feeling of fatigue" (Hagbarth and Eklund 1966, p. 179). This perception of reduced tension occurs because the reflex assistance provided by vibration permits a reduction in the central motor command that is required to achieve the given tension. This finding also argues against the role of spindles or tendon organs in the sensation of muscular force, since their firing was increased, not decreased, by vibration.

The common experience that an object lifted by a fatigued muscle feels heavy is now accepted to result from the increased central command required to lift it, rather than from changes in peripheral sensation. The same explanation accounts for the experience of weakened limb muscles in patients with CNS lesions and in experimental subjects following partial neuromuscular paralysis (McCloskey 1981). Both groups report that objects feel heavier, their limbs feel heavy, and great effort is required to lift objects. Since the muscle force necessary to lift a given object is constant, and since sensory receptors in skin, joints, tendons, and muscles continue to provide accurate information on pressure and force generation, muscle afferents could not provide a signal related to a sense of increased heaviness or effort. The central motor command required to provide sufficient force to maintain the weight would, however, increase as muscles are weakened and so would provide a signal related to the perception of increased heaviness or effort. Indeed, the view that the perceived heaviness of an object reflects the magnitude of the centrally generated motor command required to lift it has been sufficiently well established that perceptions of heaviness are used experimentally in order to study changes in motor command (e.g., Gandevia and McCloskey 1977a,b).

It is evident, therefore, that information concerning the magnitude of centrally generated motor commands is available to sensory centres and gives rise to a perception for which McCloskey, Ebeling, and Goodwin (1974) coined the term "sense of effort." The evidence from experiments on weight matching described above shows how central motor commands can be reliably compared between different muscles or muscle groups. Gandevia and Rothwell (1987) demonstrated the precision of control with which central commands can be directed to particular sets of motoneurons without afferent feedback. They showed that subjects could quickly learn to focus their internal motor command upon one of two intrinsic hand muscles. The muscle on which they focused could selectively be brought closer to threshold for activation, but without actual recruitment of the muscle or movement of the hand. It would appear that central motor commands and, therefore, the accompanying sense of effort, can be fractionated with regard to muscles.

We stated at the outset that we were looking particularly for a signal that provided a measure of the level of muscle activation. If the magnitude of centrally generated motor commands properly reflected the magnitude of muscle activation, the sense of effort would provide such a measure of muscle activation and hence would also reflect the muscle metabolic energy expenditure. The relationship between central commands and muscle activation, however, is altered by reflex assistance to the voluntary drive to alpha motoneurons. Macefield et al. (1993) have shown that muscle afferents provide a net facilitation to the motoneuron pool, reflexly increasing motor output at all levels of voluntary neural drive by approximately one third. This reflex assistance was explicitly manipulated in the study of McCloskey, Ebeling, and Goodwin (1974) cited above. They showed that for a given level of muscle tension, when reflex assistance was increased by vibration of the agonist muscle, the central command was reduced; whereas when reflex assistance was reduced by vibration of the antagonist muscle, the central command was increased. Sense of effort was modulated according to the size of the central command, but the level of muscle activation remained unchanged. Therefore, the sense of effort does not appear to reflect the level of muscle activation directly, but, rather, only the component of activation due to the central drive. The peripheral afferent input to muscle activation, although it can affect the sense of effort in the manner described above, is not reflected in the sense of effort.

Calibration of the sense of effort.   While acknowledging the contribution to muscle activation from afferent input, it is clear that the magnitude of centrally generated motor commands is nevertheless correlated with the magnitude of muscle activation, and hence with muscle metabolic energy expenditure. The calibration of the relationships between these signals is an important issue that requires further study. Both McCloskey (1981) and Gandevia (1987) pointed to the complexity of the quantitative relationship between motor commands and perceived force. For example, even when maximal voluntary tension is reduced to less than 20% of normal by partial neuromuscular paralysis, perceived force rarely exceeds twice control levels; and the situation is apparently similar in fatigue and after motor stroke (McCloskey 1981). Gandevia (1987) noted that the nonlinearity of the relationship between motor commands and perceived force is supported by classical psychophysics, while McCloskey (1981) suggested that the nonlinearity may partially reflect nonlinearities in the relationship between command and achieved tension. Both authors proposed a role for afferent inputs in calibrating the signal of perceived central command. Noble and Robertson (1996) also assigned to afferent signals the role of scaling and calibrating the central motor commands according to the size and strength of the contracting muscle. Since skilled motor performance suggests that the nonlinear relationship between motor commands and achieved muscle tensions can be mastered by the CNS, there seems little reason to doubt that the relationship between signals of motor command and perceived force can also be learned with experience. We have previously outlined possible neural circuitry for learning such nonlinear dynamic relations (Neilson, Neilson, and O'Dwyer 1992).

Perception of tension versus effort.   The many demonstrations of an association between motor commands and perceived muscular force should not be taken as evidence that actual achieved muscular tension cannot be perceived. It has been shown that subjects are able to distinguish the centrally mediated sensation of effort from the peripheral sensation of achieved muscular tension (McCloskey, Ebeling, and Goodwin 1974; Gandevia and McCloskey 1977b; Roland and Ladegaard-Pedersen 1977), but when judging the weight of an object, they usually attend to the effort put into lifting the object in preference to the muscular tension required to lift it (McCloskey, Ebeling, and Goodwin 1974; Gandevia and McCloskey 1977b). Feedback from the periphery cannot therefore be disregarded as a source of sensory information about the muscle state, but feedforward mechanisms appear to play a primary role in signaling information concerning the magnitude of motor commands, the extent of muscle activation, and the level of muscle metabolic activity. As outlined below, further light will be shed on metabolic activity by considering signals related to the cardiovascular and respiratory responses to exercise.

Neurophysiological Basis for Perception of Motor Commands

In concluding that internal collaterals from centrally generated motor commands, through corollary discharges, are responsible for the perception of muscular force or effort, McCloskey (1981) stated that the simplest explanation for this association between motor commands and perceived muscular force is that motor commands irradiate sensory centres. In other words, the signal that evokes sensation arises merely as a collateral of the motor command. He noted that numerous possible sites for such irradiation between major motor and sensory centres have been shown by electrophysiological and anatomical studies; he suggested that the motor signals for force arise relatively late in the command sequence between volition and execution, but before the spinal motoneurons. Gandevia (1987) proposed that neural traffic reaching or leaving the motor cortex via the internal capsule (which carries most of the axons running to and from the cerebral hemispheres) provides a critical component of the signal required for sensation of motor command, implicating both the motor cortex and a subcortical input; but he excluded the pons, midbrain, and cerebellum from the latter.

Cardiovascular and Respiratory Signals

Muscle contraction increases the metabolic rate and this leads to coordinated increases in blood pressure, heart rate, and ventilation (Paterson 1928). Indeed, the primary metabolic function of the cardiovascular system in responding to exercise demands is widely accepted (Sherwood et al. 1986). At workloads below the anaerobic threshold, linear dynamic relationships between work rate, ventilation, heart rate, oxygen consumption, and carbon dioxide production have been demonstrated (Casaburi et al. 1977). The dynamics of ventilation were found to be closely correlated with carbon dioxide production in a manner that suggested a cause and effect relationship, while the considerably faster dynamics of heart rate and oxygen consumption were also closely correlated. It has been suggested that the physiological advantage of the cardiovascular responses to exercise is the increased flow that is possible in the contracting muscle group when the blood pressure rises (Humphreys and Lind 1963). Obviously, the higher the contraction level, the more crucial this becomes.

Historically, there have been two main hypotheses regarding control of these ventilatory and circulatory changes that accompany increased metabolic rate (Eldridge et al. 1985). The first proposes control via peripheral sensory feedback, either chemical or mechanical, from working muscles; the second hypothesis is that of feedforward control from supraspinal centres. As in the previous section on skeletomotor signals, we will consider separately signals of peripheral muscular origin and command signals of central origin.

Muscle Reflex Signals

In their review of the literature on muscle receptors, Hasan and Stuart (1984) examined the role of undifferentiated, free nerve endings in muscle. These receptors are more plentiful than spindles and Golgi tendon organs and are supplied predominantly by groups III and IV afferents. Indeed, the majority of receptors in muscle are those innervated by groups III and IV afferents. Hasan and Stuart considered the possibility that some of these muscle receptors might have an "ergoreceptive" function, such as contributing to exercise-related rises in blood pressure and ventilation rate. Potential candidates included those receptors (particularly with group III afferent innervation) that respond to nonnoxious warming, touch, pressure, and contraction. They noted that the response latency of these receptors to mechanical stimuli is much longer than that of spindles and tendon organs, but suggested that this slowness and the tendency for the discharge to outlast the stimulus might have a particular significance during ongoing exercise. As shown by Paterson (1928), cardiovascular and respiratory responses are delayed with respect to both onset and offset of exercise.

That fibres within groups III and IV (small myelinated fibres and unmyelinated fibres) mediate reflex cardiovascular and respiratory responses originating in exercising muscle has been demonstrated by McCloskey and Mitchell (1972). Working with decerebrate cats, they showed that isometric exercise elicited by stimulating spinal ventral roots produced a rise in arterial blood pressure, with small increases in heart rate and pulmonary ventilation. Cutting the dorsal roots receiving afferents from the exercising muscle abolished these responses, while selective blocks of dorsal roots indicated that it was groups III and IV fibres that mediated the responses. Large myelinated afferents from either Golgi tendon organs or muscle spindles did not appear to have been involved in the responses. McCloskey and Mitchell concluded that the reflex responses were mediated by muscle chemoreceptors and perhaps also mechanoreceptors.

Therefore, afferent input from contracting muscle signals information pertaining to the level of metabolic activity that affects breathing and circulatory adjustment. Such afferents have not been studied in the same detail as muscle spindle or tendon organ afferents, so their characteristics are not as clearly understood. For example, two types of contraction-sensitive group III and IV afferents were recorded in cats by Mense and Stahnke (1983), but while the mechanism of activation was mechanical for one, it remained obscure for the other. Furthermore, the ergoreceptive function of these afferents has not been firmly established. Finally, the importance of peripheral reflex signals during actual exercise has proved difficult to quantify (McCloskey and Streatfeild 1975; Eldridge et al. 1985; Gandevia and Hobbs 1990).

Central Command Signals

As early as 1913, Krogh and Lindhard had proposed that during muscular exercise there is "irradiation of impulses from the motor cortex" (p. 132) to the cardiovascular and respiratory control centres. Eldridge et al. (1985) provided impressive experimental evidence in support of this proposal. Again working with cats, their preparations included anaesthetised animals with intact brains and unanaesthetised decorticate (hypothalamic) and decerebrate (mesencephalic) animals. Actual treadmill locomotion and fictive locomotion (i.e., locomotory activity in the motor nerves to the legs in paralysed animals) were studied, being elicited either spontaneously or by electrical or pharmacological stimulation. In fictive locomotion, muscular contraction and limb movement were absent, and there was no change of metabolic rate. In all cases studied, however, whether actual or fictive, respiration and arterial pressure increased together in proportion to the level of locomotor activity. Eldridge et al. (1985) concluded that neural signals emanating from the hypothalamus were primarily responsible for the proportional driving of locomotory, respiratory, and circulatory adjustments during exercise. They also noted that, consequently, stimulation of more peripheral structures such as muscles, motor nerves, or ventral roots (as in the study by McCloskey and Mitchell 1972) does not duplicate the mechanism of true locomotor exercise.

Evidence for the central command, feedforward hypothesis concerning control of the ventilatory and circulatory response to exercise has also been provided in humans. Goodwin, McCloskey, and Mitchell (1972) performed an intriguing study of cardiovascular and respiratory responses to changes in central command during prolonged isometric exercise. They had subjects generate a sustained isometric contraction (20-50% of maximal voluntary contraction for 2-8 minutes) of the biceps or triceps muscles. They applied vibration to the biceps tendon during the contractions, thereby providing powerful excitation of spindle primary afferents. During biceps contraction, this increased afferent input provided an element of reflex excitation to biceps, thereby assisting the voluntary contraction so that less central command was required to achieve a given tension. During triceps contraction, vibration of the antagonist biceps muscle produced disynaptic inhibition of triceps, so that more central command was required to achieve a given tension. The subjective sense of effort associated with a given tension was greater when an increased central command was required to achieve that tension in the presence of vibration of the antagonist muscle. Blood pressure, heart rate, and ventilation always increased during isometric effort; but the responses were graded according to the central command signal rather than to the tension actually achieved, which remained constant across experimental conditions. Since reflex cardiorespiratory effects from the working muscle were similar, because the level of tension was constant, the authors concluded that the central command from higher centres to the exercising muscles provides an input for cardiovascular and respiratory control during voluntary movement. In addition, it may be noted that since the level of tension was constant, signals from Golgi tendon organs also would have been constant. This fact is consistent with the finding that tendon organ input does not affect the cardiovascular responses that are mediated by other muscle afferents (McCloskey and Mitchell 1972).

More recently, Gandevia and Hobbs (1990) showed that the grading of heart rate, but not blood pressure, with level of central command was maintained during attempted contraction of acutely paralysed muscles. The paralysis in this experiment was induced by local infusion of lignocaine distal to a sphygmomanometer cuff inflated above systolic pressure. Hobbs, Rowell, and Smith (1980) trained baboons to hold constant load contractions with or without neuromuscular blockade and showed that both heart rate and blood pressure increased with the central command signal. They suggested that the central command signal thus normally reflects "the extent of motor unit activation" (p. 120). In a later intrepid experiment, Gandevia and colleagues studied cardiovascular responses following the induction of total neuromuscular blockade in three subjects by infusion of atracurium, at a dose fivefold greater than that used for 'surgical paralysis' (Gandevia et al. 1993). It had been shown previously that subjects remain able to sustain and grade their effort during muscular paralysis (Gandevia and Hobbs 1990; Gandevia et al. 1990). Under these conditions of complete whole body muscular paralysis while fully conscious, attempted contractions of arm, leg, and trunk muscles increased heart rate and blood pressure; and the increases were graded according to the intensity of effort over a range from 0-100% of maximum (figure 1.2). For attempted handgrip contractions, the increases

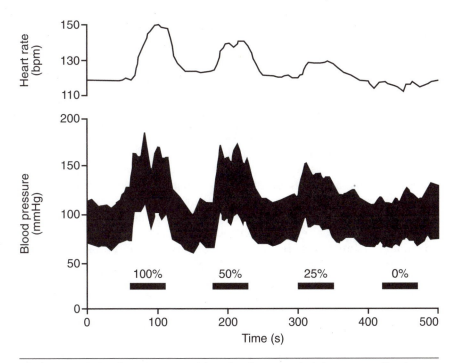

Figure 1.2   Blood pressure and heart rate records taken every 5 s in one subject during an uninterrupted sequence of attempted contractions of ankle dorsiflexors during complete whole body muscular paralysis. Bars indicate the duration of each test period and the percentage of maximal effort attempted, including a sham manoeuvre (0%, no attempted contraction).

Reproduced, by permission, from Gandevia, S.C., K. Killian, D.K. McKenzie, M. Crawford, G.M. Allen, R.B. Gorman, and J.P. Hales, 1993. "Respiratory sensations, cardiovascular control, kinaesthesia and transcranial stimulation during paralysis in humans." *Journal of Physiology* 470: 85-107.

were similar to those observed with actual contractions immediately before paralysis. Since there were no metabolic or mechanical consequences in any muscle, the command signals to the cardiovascular system could not have arisen from feedback from the periphery, but must have been feedforward control signals from the CNS.

Characteristics of Cardiorespiratory Control

It is clear therefore that both feedforward and feedback control mechanisms contribute to the cardiovascular and respiratory responses to exercise. Regarding feedback mechanisms, Eldridge et al. (1985) proposed that while not required for driving the respiratory and circulatory adjustments, they may be involved in their fine control. Gandevia and Hobbs (1990) concluded that the cardiovascular response to moderate intensities of static contraction can be produced primarily by motor command, but that both motor command and muscle chemoreflexes contribute at higher intensities of exercise.

A number of important characteristics of the cardiovascular response to isometric exercise must be noted. The muscular reflex drive of the cardiovascular response has been shown to be proportional to the mass of contracting muscle (McCloskey and Streatfeild 1975). Thus, when handgrip contractions and flexion contractions of the little finger were examined at comparable proportions of maximal tension, the handgrip contractions produced a greater reflex drive than the finger contractions. The actual cardiovascular response to isometric exercise is, however, determined by the relative tension at which the muscles contract, not by the mass of the contracting muscles or the absolute tension achieved (Lind and McNicol 1967; McCloskey and Streatfeild 1975). Thus, when two or more muscle groups contract at the same proportion of their maximal tension, the increases in heart rate and blood pressure are the same whether the muscle groups contract separately or together; again, when two or more muscle groups contract simultaneously at different proportions of their maximal tension, the increases in heart rate and blood pressure are the same as when the muscle group at the higher proportion of maximum contracts alone at that tension (Lind and McNicol 1967). Even when the muscle groups involved are of quite different total mass, these findings still apply. The study of Gandevia et al. (1993) added to this picture. They found that cardiovascular responses were graded with the level of motor command or intensity of motor *effort*, rather than with the size of the muscle group, viz., handgrip contractions, ankle dorsiflexion, contractions of all limb muscles, or maximal inspiratory efforts. These findings suggest that maintaining blood flow in the most strongly contracting muscle group, regardless of muscle mass, may be the most important physiological advantage of the cardiovascular responses to exercise, in line with the suggestion of Humphreys and Lind (1963).

When Krogh and Lindhard (1913) put forward the proposal of 'central irradiation' of the cardiovascular and respiratory control centres by elements of the command signal descending from higher centres to the contracting muscles, they were influenced by the fact that one of their subjects had shown a marked increase in ventilation when the subject anticipated the application of a heavy load on the bicycle ergometer, but then actually started pedalling without any brake load. Normally, cardiovascular responses are initiated only at the onset of muscle contraction (Iwamoto et al. 1987) and reach a peak after about 10 to 15 seconds (Gandevia et al. 1993). Nevertheless, both the cardiovascular and respiratory responses evoked by the central command actually *anticipate* the metabolic energy demand that will be imposed by the muscle activity being commanded. The notion that cardiovascular mobilisation is a motor preparatory response—a state of behavioural readiness for physical exertion—has been suggested by Sherwood et al. (1986). Nowhere is this anticipation more obvious than in attempted contractions during whole body paralysis, as illustrated in figure 1.2, where no muscular energy cost is actually incurred. Furthermore, the anticipated energy cost is tied to the sense of effort that accompanies the attempts.

Sensitivity to Metabolic Cost

There is, therefore, a clear link between the sense of effort, the magnitude of central command, the cardiovascular and respiratory responses, and the actual or anticipated metabolic energy cost. These variables appear to be linked to *the proportion of maximum activation of the muscles*, in other words, the extent of motor unit activation. Sense of effort necessarily increases with increased drive to muscles, with, by definition, maximum central command or effort required to maximally activate all of the motor units in any given muscle. Cardiovascular and respiratory responses increase with increased central drive to muscles in accordance with the proportion of maximal activation commanded, not with their mass nor their absolute tension. And as noted earlier, metabolic energy expenditure shown by oxygen consumption is correlated with the magnitude of activation of individual muscles shown by EMG activity, the strength of this correlation increasing with the level of muscle activation (Strasser and Ernst 1992).

The study of perceived exertion provides support for this interpretation. Noble and Robertson (1996) posed the question whether an "effort sense" (p. 45) can be said to exist analogous to the basic sensory modalities or to the sense of movement or *kinaesthesia*, for which nervous system structures have been identified. They noted that effort or exertion is a complex sensory experience that has not been directly connected to a unique receptor or nervous system structure. Nevertheless, they tied the perception of physical exertion to corollary discharges of central motor commands—the greater the magnitude of the corollary signals, the more intense the perception of physical exertion.

Perceived exertion is most frequently measured using rating scales such as the Borg Scale; such ratings of perceived exertion have been shown to correlate well with heart rate, thus showing a fundamental relationship between a physiological indicator of physical stress and a psychological indicator of perceived exertion (Borg 1973). The time course and magnitude of subjects' perceived sense of effort during static handgrip exercise has been shown to closely resemble the time course and magnitude of the ventilatory response (Muza et al. 1983). At the same exercise intensity, perceived exertion is less during eccentric than concentric contractions; also when compared at equal oxygen consumption levels, eccentric contractions produce greater ratings of perceived exertion (Henriksson, Knuttgen, and Bonde-Peterson 1972). Again, at the same absolute exercise intensity, perceived exertion is lower when a larger muscle mass (viz., two limbs versus one limb) is employed; at the same relative intensity, however, there is no difference in perceived exertion (Sargeant and Davies 1973). These results suggest that perceived exertion, signaled by corollary discharges of central motor commands, is also tied to the proportion of maximum muscle activation. The studies of Henriksson, Knuttgen, and Bonde-Peterson (1972) and Sargeant and Davies (1973) in particular suggest that perceived exertion is not coupled to total metabolic energy expenditure, as measured by level of oxygen consumption, but instead is tied to local muscle cost and output relative to maximum. A signal of global or total metabolic energy expenditure does not appear to have been identified, even in psychological ratings of perceived exertion.

Summary

The studies reviewed above suggest that both the sense of effort and the cardiorespiratory response to exercise are linked to the level of motor unit activation of the contracting muscles. The sense of effort measures the central drive to the muscle, not the muscle tension, and is thus correlated with the energy expenditure of the muscle. Therefore, during concentric, isometric, and eccentric contractions and during muscle fatigue, the sense of effort would appear to provide a reliable indicator of local metabolic load in the participating muscles. It appears to be possible to fractionate the sense of effort with regard to muscles, so that perception of energy expenditure may also thereby be fractionated. In the planning of movement, the coupling between the magnitude of the central command and the magnitude of activation of the participating muscles may be the most important consideration for the imperative to optimise the metabolic economy of movement. Ultimately, it seems likely that if the sense of effort is reduced, global metabolic energy expenditure will also be reduced. In the next section we will outline evidence suggesting that reduction of effort and energy expenditure may also be directly related to increased movement accuracy and stability.

Movement Accuracy and Level of Muscle Activation

Thus far we have highlighted the relative level of activation of muscles as central to the sense of effort associated with movement and as important from the perspective of metabolic energy expenditure for the movement. In the second part of this chapter, we will examine evidence that the relative level of muscle activation is also important from the perspective of movement accuracy and stability and so is relevant to information-processing issues in the control of movement. In the first instance, we wish to consider how the level of muscle activation observed in performance of movement alters as a function of practice and skill.

Effect of Practice on Muscle Activation

There is conflicting evidence in the literature from EMG studies of the effect of practice on magnitude of muscle activation. Some studies have reported a decrease in muscle activity after practice (Kamon and Gormley 1968; Herman 1970; Payton 1975); other studies have reported an increase in activity (Finley, Wirta, and Cody 1968; Vorro, Wilson, and Dainis 1978; McGrain 1980; Vorro and Hobart 1981a,b); yet other studies have reported no change in activity (Hobart and Vorro 1974; Payton 1975; Payton, Su, and Kelley 1976); while other studies have reported, for different muscles, an increase, a decrease, or no change in activity (Payton and Kelley 1972; Hobart, Kelley, and Bradley 1975). A shortcoming of most of these studies is that a limited number of muscles were monitored. Many of the studies investigated a ball-tossing task (Payton and Kelley 1972; Hobart and Vorro 1974; Hobart, Kelley, and Bradley 1975; Payton 1975; Vorro, Wilson, and Dainis 1978; Vorro and Hobart 1981a,b), and only the study of Kamon and Gormley (1968) looked at multijoint movements. The divergent results are further complicated by changes with practice in the variables of movement time and movement speed, which usually decreased and increased, respectively. As has been shown in running, swimming, and kicking (Asami et al. 1976), an increase in speed requires an exponential increase in energy. McGrain (1980) concluded that if task performance demands an increase in joint angular velocity, then both agonist and antagonist muscle activity at the joint will increase. It is likely that an increase in speed of movement associated with a reduction in movement time after practice accounts for the increases in magnitude of muscle activity reported in the studies cited above.

The level of muscle co-contraction may be more clearly associated with level of skill. Humphrey and Reed (1983) noted that increased tonic coactivation of agonist and antagonist muscles may be prominent in the early stages of learning skilled movements, thereby increasing the stiffness of body segments and stabilising the movement or posture against disturbances. Abbs and Gracco (1984), for example, reported an overall increase in lip muscle activity in anticipation of expected (although not unexpected) external perturbations. As noted by Humphrey and Reed (1983), however, the strategy of increased co-contraction need not be confined to external perturbations but may be employed to reduce the magnitude of movement errors that are produced by inappropriate commands. Such a situation may apply, for example, in the dysfluent utterances of stutterers, where increased levels of muscle activity are observed (Guitar et al. 1988). Inappropriate commands would also be expected in the early stages of skill acquisition, perhaps accounting for increased co-contraction. With improvement in skill, however, several studies have observed a reduction in muscle co-contraction (Person 1958; Finley, Wirta, and Cody 1968; Kamon and Gormley 1968; MacConaill and Basmajian 1977).

Cerebral Palsy

Another approach to the question of the level of muscle activity in skilled versus unskilled movements is to examine the relative level of muscle activation in cerebral palsy, since persons with this syndrome exhibit many of the characteristics of unskilled movement. Although symptoms such as spasticity and involuntary movements have traditionally commanded most of the attention in cerebral palsy, a number of studies have indicated that the primary disability in this syndrome is a disruption of the physiological mechanisms that subserve acquisition of motor skills (Neilson and O'Dwyer 1981, 1984; O'Dwyer and Neilson 1988; Vaughan, Neilson, and O'Dwyer 1988; Neilson, O'Dwyer, and Nash 1990).

Neilson and O'Dwyer (1984) conducted a study of adult athetoid cerebral palsy subjects with unintelligible or nearly intelligible dysarthric speech. Since the acoustic signal is determined by the shape of the vocal tract as a function of time, the dysarthric speech is a reflection of abnormal kinematics of the articulatory structures. Athetoid cerebral palsy is characterised by the presence of involuntary movements, although abnormalities of stretch reflexes are also well documented (Neilson and Andrews 1973; Milner-Brown and Penn 1979). EMG activity was recorded intramuscularly from two lip, two tongue, and two jaw muscles during 20 recitations of a test sentence. In the athetoid subjects the articulation of the test sentence was disrupted intermittently and irregularly by involuntary activity, so that the timing of their total motor output for the sentence was both prolonged and variable compared with normal speakers. On detailed analysis of the patterns of EMG activity, however, it was found that the involuntary activity usually occurred in the time intervals *between* the syllables in the test sentence, such that speech output was often halted transiently. During articulation of the syllables themselves, however, the pattern of muscle activity employed for any one syllable by any one subject was very similar from one repetition of the syllable to the next. When the EMG activity (rectified and low-pass filtered) was averaged across the 20 recitations, the test sentence and partitioned into its reproducible and variable components, the ratios of the mean square value of the reproducible ('signal') component to the mean square value of the variable ('noise') component was not significantly different between normal and cerebral palsy subjects. The grand mean signal-to-noise ratios for the normal and athetoid subjects were 19:1 and 16:1, respectively. Thus, despite the presence of variable involuntary muscle activity between syllables, this finding indicated that there was a significant degree of underlying voluntary control.

O'Dwyer and Neilson (1988) carried out a detailed analysis of this re-producible component of the muscle activity in the athetoid subjects. The analysis showed that voluntary control in these subjects consisted of grossly abnormal temporospatial patterns of muscle activity (figure 1.3). Peak levels of speech muscle activity in normal subjects varied between 5 to 50% of maximum voluntary contraction, whereas in the cerebral palsy subjects the range was 30 to 100% (Neilson and O'Dwyer 1981). When the muscle energy, defined as the integral of the squared EMG waveform, was computed, a striking difference between the cerebral palsy and normal groups was apparent. The athetoid subjects employed on average about 20 times as much energy in lip muscles and nearly 30 times as much energy in tongue muscles in order to articulate the sentence (figure 1.4). The energy cost in jaw muscles was not as high, about a fivefold increase. This difference in muscle energy expenditure could be readily appreciated by observation of the subjects articulating the sentence, since they displayed exaggerated facial movements and grimacing that is characteristic of this population. This exaggeration of movement was such that we may safely assume that the subjects performed more mechanical work when attempting to speak compared to normal subjects. Thus, excessive muscular energy expenditure was a major component of the disorder of voluntary movement in these subjects.

The exaggerated energy expenditure could not in this instance be attributed simply to uncontrolled muscle activity, since the cerebral palsy subjects could relax muscles during ongoing speech and could modulate the level of activity in a reproducible way. The increased magnitude of muscle activity appeared to be a strategy to resist or at least minimise the deviations from their intended movements arising from their own involuntary and/or inappropriate voluntary activity. Since satisfactory task performance (viz., clearly intelligible speech) was never achieved by these cerebral palsy speakers, it would appear that the exaggerated expenditure of energy could not be reduced despite years of practice at the task.

This finding during speech in adult subjects is consistent with studies of walking in children with cerebral palsy, where both energy expenditure (Campbell and Ball 1978; Rose et al. 1994; Unnithan et al. 1996) and muscle activity (Csongradi, Bleck, and Ford 1979; Rose et al. 1994) have been shown to be exaggerated relative to normal. The increase in energy expenditure appears to be related to the degree of disability (Rose et al. 1990). Increased coactivation of agonist and antagonist muscles has been noted as a prominent feature by Unnithan et al. (1996), who demonstrated that agonist-antagonist co-contraction of both lower leg and thigh muscles was significantly correlated with oxygen consumption in cerebral palsy children, but not control children. Since this feature accounted for about 50% of the variance in oxygen consumption in these children, it appeared to be a major factor responsible for the higher energy cost. Moreover,

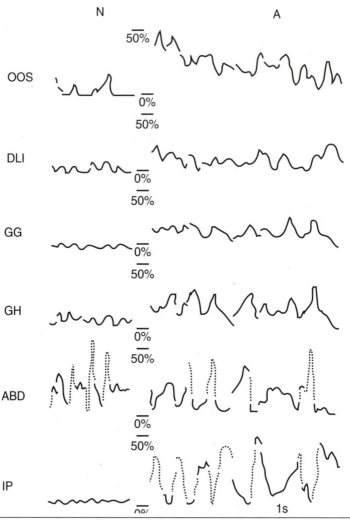

Figure 1.3 Activity of lip (OOS: orbicularis oris superior; DLI: depressor labii inferior), tongue (GG: anterior genioglossus; GH: geniohyoid), and jaw (ABD: anterior belly of digastric; IP: internal pterygoid) muscles averaged over 20 recitations of the test sentence "Do all the old rogues abjure weird ladies," from a normal (N) and an athetoid dysarthric (A) subject. The 10 syllables in the sentence were analysed separately, and the resultant average waveforms have been concatenated to form each muscle trace shown here. Calibrations indicate 0-50% of maximal voluntary contraction for each muscle.

Adapted from original publication: O'Dwyer, N.J., and P.D. Neilson, 1988, "Voluntary muscle control in normal and athetoid dysarthric speakers," *Brain* 111: 877-899. Used with permission of Oxford University Press.

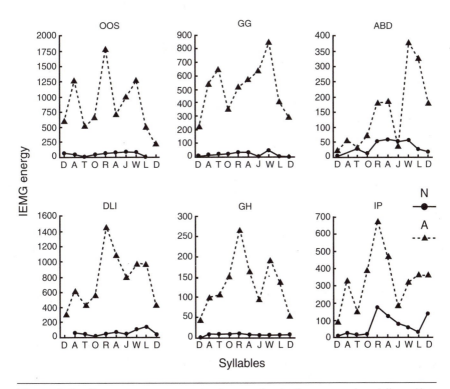

Figure 1.4 Group mean energy in six muscles in five normal and five athe-toid subjects for 10 syllable waveforms. Abbreviations for the 10 syllables are the first letter of each syllable, indicated by capital letters as follows: Do All The Old Rogues Abjure Weird Ladies. Other abbreviations as in figure 1.3. Energy is defined as the integral of the squared EMG activity in units of % EMG relative to maximum voluntary contraction for each muscle.

Reproduced from original publication: O'Dwyer, N.J., and P.D. Neilson, 1988, "Voluntary muscle control in normal and athetoid dysarthric speakers," *Brain* 111: 877-899. Used with permission of Oxford University Press.

children with cerebral palsy have been reported to become exhausted while walking even at moderate speeds (Berg 1970; Dahlbäck and Norlin 1985). Since the children were working at less than 50 to 60% of their maximal oxygen uptake, Dahlbäck and Norlin (1985) concluded that the exhaustion may have been due to local muscle factors rather than cardiopulmonary factors, a conclusion also reached by Unnithan et al. (1996). Therefore, this may be a case, as suggested at the outset, of task performance being compromised by local muscle fatigue, rather than by global metabolic energy expenditure.

The question of the potential effects of motor learning in cerebral palsy was taken up in a study by Neilson, O'Dwyer, and Nash (1990). Normal and cerebral palsy subjects were compared on their ability to track a continuously moving target via a response cursor that they controlled by varying the level of isometric contraction of elbow flexor muscles between 10 and 40% of maximal voluntary contraction. The EMG activity was again rectified and low-pass filtered in order to provide a relatively smooth signal related to the muscle contraction level. The target provided a visual representation of the required muscle activity, while the response cursor provided a representation of the actual muscle activity. If the subjects could control the EMG feedback, they could track the target. The task was a relatively simplified one, because control of only the flexor muscle group was required; and abnormal coordination between other muscles, such as antagonists, or inappropriate contraction or movement in adjacent or distant body segments could not interfere with performance of the task. The objective was to discover whether practising this novel but simple task could produce improved performance at that task, regardless of any transfer of learning to other situations.

From the standpoint of whether a residual potential for motor learning persists in adult cerebral palsy, the results of this study were disappointing. The subjects performed to their maximum potential within the first few minutes of the first day of practice and then did not improve further. The subjects' muscle response was partitioned into two components, termed the "appropriate" and the "inappropriate" responses. The appropriate response was the component of the response that was linearly correlated with the target, and the inappropriate response was the remainder that was not linearly related to the target. Obviously, the task required that the appropriate response be maximised and the inappropriate response be minimised. Whereas in normal subjects the majority of their responses were appropriate, the reverse was the case in the cerebral palsy subjects. The variance of their appropriate response reached a plateau within the first few minutes of practice, and then they could only maintain that level of performance over the ensuing 18 hours of practice conducted over a period of 12 weeks.

From the standpoint of the muscular energy expended in this task, this study provided one interesting outcome. On the first day, with one exception, the variance of both the total muscle response and the inappropriate muscle response generated by the cerebral palsy subjects was greater than in the normal subjects. Furthermore, the poorer the task performance, the greater were these variances. Over 36 days of practice, the variance of the inappropriate response (and hence the tracking error) decreased significantly in the subjects with the poorest performance (figure 1.5). Since the total response was dominated by the inappropriate response in these subjects, this meant that the variance of their total muscle response, and therefore of the muscular energy expended, also decreased with practice. At the kinematic level, a similar reduction in inappropriate response output with practice has also been observed (Neilson and McCaughey 1982). Therefore, with practice at a task, it appears that cerebral palsy subjects reduce their excessive energy expen-

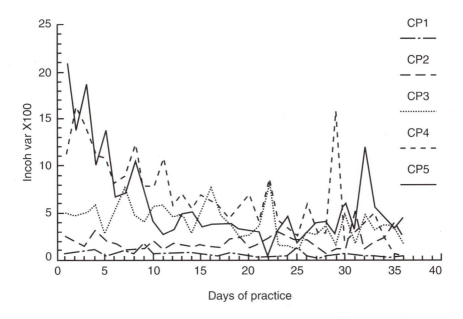

Figure 1.5   Variance of inappropriate component of response plotted against days of practice for five cerebral palsy subjects. Variance (incoh var = incoherent variance) plotted in arbitrary units proportional to variance of deflection on tracking display screen (mm²).

Reproduced by permission from original publication: Neilson, P.D., N.J. O'Dwyer, and J. Nash, 1990, "Control of isometric muscle activity in cerebral palsy," *Developmental Medicine and Child Neurology* 32: 778-788.

diture to some degree, despite the fact that there is little concomitant improvement in overall task performance.

Effect of Practice on Energy Expenditure

An alternative to examining the effects of practice and skill acquisition on muscle activity is to examine their effects on global energy expenditure, since this will reflect aggregate muscle activity. Abitol (1988) compared energy expenditure at rest and during bipedal and quadrupedal stance and locomotion in early infant walkers (aged 12 to 15 months) and adults. They found that the adults had lower energy consumption for all postures except quadrupedal locomotion (walking on hands and knees), at which the infants could be considered to be more skilled. An important factor here is whether the amount of work is constant among the performances being compared. This was not addressed in the Abitol study. Durand et al. (1994) studied energy expenditure in a task where the amount of work increased with skill. Subjects were required to make rhythmic oscillatory movements on a slalom ski simulator; the amplitude and frequency of the movements increased with practice. In this task energy expenditure also increased with practice. Asami et al. (1976) had skilled and unskilled soccer players kick a ball at a target and examined the relationship between energy expenditure and ball velocity. At a given ball velocity, they found that skilled players had lower energy expenditure than unskilled players, and the rate of increase of energy expenditure with ball velocity also appeared less in the skilled players. Work rate was held constant in studies by Sparrow and Irizarry-Lopez (1987) and Sparrow and Newell (1994) of subjects who practised creeping (walking on their hands and feet) on a treadmill driven at a constant speed. Metabolic energy expenditure was shown to reduce with practice in accordance with the *principle of least effort*, whereby organisms adapt movements in order to achieve a goal using the least amount of physical energy (Tolman 1932).

These studies indicate that movement economy is greater after practice and in more skilled performers and, consequently, aggregate muscle activity must be reduced. Furthermore, in parallel with the reduced energy cost, subjective ratings indicate reduced exertion and increased ease of performance. For example, in the study by Sparrow and Irizarry-Lopez (1987), the subjects' reports that the task became easier with practice paralleled the reduction in energy expenditure. This is supported by a recent study by Sparrow and Hughes (1997) where, again with task demands fixed, perceived exertion was shown to decrease reliably and systematically over days of practice in line with decreased energy expenditure.

In addition to metabolic energy expenditure, the related issue of mechanical efficiency (the ratio of work done to energy used) was also examined in some of these studies. Sparrow and Irizarry-Lopez (1987) found that mechanical efficiency tended to increase with practice, but the change was not statistically significant. Durand et al. (1994) found that 'movement cost' (the ratio of oxygen intake to the product of movement amplitude and frequency) generally decreased across learning sessions, indicating an increase in efficiency with practice. Asami et al. (1976) found that mechanical efficiency varied with ball velocity, increasing to a maximum at about 80% of maximum velocity and then decreasing according to a bell-shaped quadratic relationship. The skilled subjects were more efficient than the unskilled subjects at all ball velocities. Of particular interest, however, was the finding that both unskilled and skilled subjects achieved their highest kicking accuracy at the velocity at which they attained the highest mechanical efficiency. Across the eight subjects (four skilled, four unskilled), they found a very high correlation ($r = 0.96$) between maximum mechanical efficiency and accuracy. On the basis of this finding, Asami et al. concluded that the degree of mechanical efficiency can be used as an indicator of skill.

Muscle Activation and Performance Accuracy

We now return to the specific question of the relationship between level of muscle activation and performance accuracy. The studies reviewed in the previous sections indicate that, at least when work rate is taken into account, aggregate muscle activity, metabolic energy expenditure, and the sense of effort associated with a given motor task all decrease with increasing skill. That performance accuracy may also be systematically related to these variables is suggested by the findings of Asami et al. (1976). The accuracy of rapid movements is well known to be inversely related to their speed (Fitts 1954; Fitts and Peterson 1964), and such movements have been the subject of considerable study in the field of motor performance, which has established the robustness of this relationship. The most important explanatory principle that has been proposed for this speed-accuracy trade-off in movement is that there is variability, or 'noise,' in motor output, and that the magnitude of this noise increases with the magnitude of the output. This proposal is best exemplified by the impulse-variability theory of the speed-accuracy trade-off presented originally by Schmidt et al. (1979) and subsequently, using more stringent theoretical derivations, by Meyer, Smith, and Wright (1982). Rapid movements are generated by brief "impulses" of force, each impulse being the area under the force-time curve for acceleration. As speed of movement increases, the magnitude of the impulse required to rapidly accelerate the limb must increase. Hence the magnitude of the noise increases, and this leads to greater errors that must be traded against speed in order to maintain accuracy.

As noted by Carlton and Newell (1993), the proposals of Schmidt et al. (1979) were the first attempt to directly associate variability at the kinematic and kinetic levels. Carlton and Newell (1993) likewise assumed that a complete description of variability in force production could explain movement space-time variability. Based on a synthesis of a number of experiments, they presented a description of force variability that accounted for variability in peak force, impulse, and rate of force production across a range of force production conditions. Their prototypic force-time function, showing the various parameters of force that have been studied, is presented in figure 1.6a, and their proposed relationship between standard deviation of peak force and level of peak force is shown in figure 1.6b. Contrary to earlier proposals of Schmidt et al. (1979) and Meyer, Smith, and Wright (1982), their own studies and those of others reviewed by Carlton and Newell (1993) indicated that the relationship between impulse magnitude and impulse variability is not proportional. In other words, the relationship does not appear to follow Weber's law, which posits a proportional relationship, but is more in line with Stevens' power law, which has been shown to apply to many different sensory

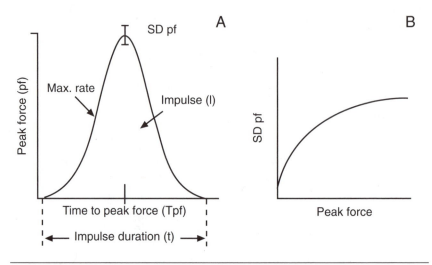

Figure 1.6   (A) Prototypic force-time function produced by subjects attempting to match a criterion peak force, showing the various parameters of force that have been studied. Max. rate is the maximum rate of force produced between the initiation of force and peak force, impulse is the area under the force-time curve, and SD_{pf} represents the standard deviation of the peak force over a series of trials. (B) Proposed square-root relationship between standard deviation of peak force and level of peak force.

Adapted, with permission, from Carlton, L.G., and K.M. Newell, 1993, "Force variability and characteristics of force production." In *Variability and motor control,* edited by K.M. Newell and D.M. Corcos (Champaign, IL: Human Kinetics), 15-36.

dimensions (Stevens 1957). By also incorporating temporal parameters into their description, Carlton and Newell (1993) developed the following general force variability equation that provided an accurate fit to data from a number of experiments covering a wide range of force levels and times to peak force:

$$SD_{pf} \propto PF^{1/2} / T_{pf}^{1/4}$$

where PF = peak force, T_{pf} = time to peak force, and SD_{pf} = standard deviation of peak force.

The studies on which Carlton and Newell (1993) based their force variability description involved brief pulses of force, while studies of the speed-accuracy trade-off more generally have also involved rapid and usually discrete movements. Recently, O'Dwyer and Neilson (1998) have examined the issue of force variability in a task that involved sustained, slowly changing, isometric force production. Visual pursuit tracking was employed with two types of motor output—isometric EMG activity from the upper lip (EMG tracking) and isometric elbow flexor torque (force tracking). The experimental setups were as illustrated in figure 1.7. The subject controlled a response cursor on a computer monitor via either

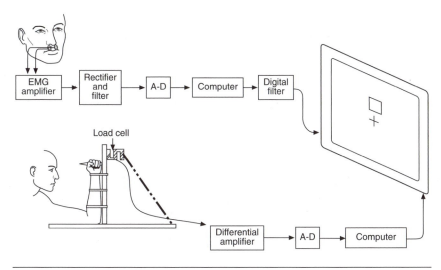

Figure 1.7   Schematic illustration of EMG and force tracking setups, showing visual display screen with target (square) and response (cross) cursors and subject with electrodes placed on the upper lip or with arm in frame.

type of motor output and was required to track the movement of a target cursor so as to maintain the response cursor aligned with the target. The target moved vertically on the screen in a slow sinusoidal fashion at 0.3 Hz. This meant that it took 1.67 seconds for the target to move through the full range of the screen from top to bottom or vice versa.

Four experimental conditions were employed to compare proficiency of control at two average levels and two amplitudes of motor output. In condition one (average level: 15%, amplitude: 30%), the subject had to vary the motor output (force or muscle activation) in the range of 0 to 30% of maximum in order to track the target. For example, if the output was exactly 30%, the response cursor was located at the top of the display; if the output was exactly 0%, the response cursor was located at the bottom of the display; if the output was exactly 15%, the response cursor was located at the middle of the display. In condition two (average level: 15%, amplitude: 10%), the output range was 10 to 20% of maximum; in condition three (average level: 45%, amplitude: 30%), the output range was 30 to 60% of maximum; in condition four (average level: 45%, amplitude: 10%), the output range was 40 to 50% of maximum. The display range and hence the required visual accuracy was the same for all tracking conditions, but the required accuracy of force/muscle control varied between the two amplitude conditions.

Ostensibly, this was a very easy tracking task, due to the slow and highly predictable nature of the target, but an unexpected finding emerged. Of no surprise, force tracking was shown to be superior to EMG tracking overall, due to the inherently noisy character of EMG signals.

However, the variations in performance at different levels and amplitudes of motor output were very similar for both types of tracking. The salient findings are illustrated by the force tracking data in figure 1.8. Consistent with the impulse-variability theory and the findings of Carlton and Newell (1993), tracking performance deteriorated when the average level of force or muscle activation required to track the target was increased. This is shown by the increased noise (and tracking error) in the response at 30 to 60% compared with 0-30%. However, performance also deteriorated when the amplitude of force or muscle activation available to track the target was reduced, hence requiring finer gradations of control. This is shown by the increased noise in the response at 10 to 20% compared with 0 to 30%. The unexpected finding was the response at 40 to 50%, which combined increased level with reduced amplitude. The effect of this combination was greater than the sum of the level and amplitude effects, leading to a marked deterioration in performance. Due to the increased noise at high levels of output, fine motor adjustments became practically unrealisable. Clearly, therefore, the grading of motor output

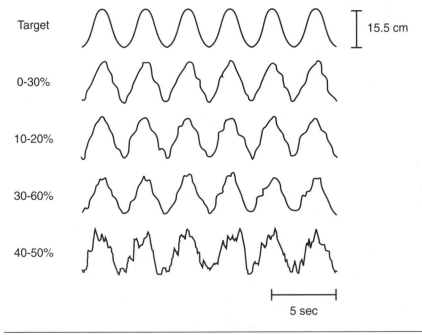

Figure 1.8   Sample target and force tracking response traces from one subject for the four experimental trials. The samples show the same 20-second segment from the one-minute trials and were chosen from a subject whose error scores for each trial were close to the group mean. Vertical calibration shows deflection on tracking display screen. Percentages are relative to maximum voluntary elbow flexor force.

is not uniform throughout its operational range. The hitherto unrecognised functional consequence of this is that the same level of accuracy cannot be maintained if the same task is performed using higher levels of force or muscle output. The clear implication is that superior accuracy and control should be attainable at lower levels of force or muscle output.

Information and Energy

The findings in this area suggest that both consistency and accuracy of motor control are enhanced at lower levels of force and muscle output. Furthermore, this principle appears to apply to slow and sustained motor outputs as well as to rapid and discrete outputs. Since metabolic cost can be equated with global levels of muscle activity and force, lower levels of muscle activity mean both lower metabolic cost and lower noise in motor output. Thus, there appears to be a direct link between energy cost and information processing in control of movement, whereby reduced energy cost can be expected to be associated with superior performance accuracy. This is consistent with the evidence reviewed above showing decreasing energy expenditure with increasing movement skill. However, more direct support for this link is provided in a study by Holt et al. (1995). They found that minimal metabolic cost during walking at preferred stride frequency compared with nonpreferred frequencies was associated with maximal stability of the head and joints (figure 9.2, Holt et al. 1995, this volume). These authors proposed "a complementary relationship between energetic (physiological) and stability constraints" (p. 164). The evidence reviewed here suggests that the relative level of activation of participating muscles could be an important variable underpinning this relationship. The sense of effort would also be expected to exhibit a similar relationship with stability. Muza et al. (1983) observed increased breath-to-breath variability in tidal volume during static handgrip exercise compared with rest, suggestive of control instability. This increased variability coincided with an increase in the subjects' perceived effort.

An additional finding by Holt et al. (1995) was that greater instability was observed at higher frequencies of walking than at lower frequencies (figure 9.2, Holt et al. 1995, this volume). Again, this may be at least partially explained in terms of levels of muscle activation and force. Increasing the frequency of movement necessarily requires increasing force and muscle activation, and the inertial loads on limb muscles increasingly dominate the movement. For purely inertial loads (neglecting stiffness and viscous elements), the torque required to accelerate the limb would increase with the square of the movement frequency. The required muscle forces and the magnitudes of muscle activation will increase in parallel with the torques. Empirical studies confirm that a rapid rise in

EMG activity occurs with increasing movement frequency (Cathers, O'Dwyer, and Neilson 1996); and studies of both orofacial and limb muscles in normal, hemiparetic, and cerebral palsy subjects have shown that the variability of EMG activity increases at higher levels of muscle activation (Tang and Rymer 1981; Neilson and O'Dwyer 1984; Gielen, van den Oosten, and Pul ter Gunne 1985; O'Dwyer and Neilson 1988). Consequently, the motor output noise will increase in parallel with the movement frequency. Since the accuracy requirements of a given task normally do not change as the frequency of movement increases, the absolute accuracy required of the controlling force 'signal' does not change. However, the magnitude of the 'noise' that is superimposed on the force signal does increase (see figure 1.8), so that the same level of absolute accuracy cannot be maintained. Furthermore, this difficulty will be exacerbated by the increase in required temporal accuracy that is engendered by the increase in frequency. For instance, the rate of force generation must increase with increased movement frequency and so the time to peak force must reduce, a factor noted above that also increases the output variability or noise (Carlton and Newell 1993). This interpretation is supported by the finding of Cathers, O'Dwyer, and Neilson (1996) that during rhythmic elbow flexion-extension movements, the consistency both of movement and of flexor and extensor muscle activity decreased sharply with increasing frequency.

Recent evidence indicates that the level of muscle activation may also affect proprioception and hence have an important bearing on performance accuracy. Wise, Gregory, and Proske (1998) have recently reported that the threshold for detection of imposed elbow movements is increased during co-contraction of flexor and extensor muscles at 15 to 20% of maximum, compared with the relaxed forearm. Their subjects reported that during a co-contraction there seemed to be more 'noise in the system,' which made it more difficult for them to detect the direction of imposed movement. However, Taylor and McCloskey (1992) reported greatly enhanced proprioceptive performance during elbow flexor contraction (as opposed to co-contraction) compared with the relaxed condition, possibly because of increased discharge from muscle spindles. The contractions studied (about 5N and 20N) were of smaller magnitude than those studied by Wise, Gregory, and Proske (1998). These apparently conflicting results raise the important questions of how proprioception varies as a function of increasing levels of contraction and co-contraction and how this variation affects performance accuracy.

Summary

In this section, changes with increasing skill in levels of muscle activity and muscle co-contraction were reviewed in studies of normal subjects and persons with cerebral palsy, the latter deemed to provide a model of unskilled motor performance. While some of the evidence is equivocal, these studies are consistent with a decrease in muscle activity and co-contraction with increasing skill if changes in movement time and speed are taken into account. A more reliable decrease with increasing skill has been reported, however, for the global metabolic energy cost of movement, which may be taken to reflect ensemble muscle activity. The reduction in energy cost is taken as evidence of increased efficiency. The sense of effort associated with the movement reduces concomitantly with these changes. Hence, muscle activity and the sense of effort are not minimised early in skill learning, the achievement of the task goal presumably being of overriding importance. The increase in accuracy and stability of movement with increasing skill appears to be linked to the level of muscle activation and force employed, since accuracy and stability of control appear to be enhanced at lower levels of muscle activity. Ensemble muscle activity, via the sense of effort, may guide the search for greater accuracy and dynamic stability with practice.

Cardiorespiratory-Skeletomotor Coordination

In the previous section we outlined the changes in muscle activation, metabolic cost, and the sense of effort that occur with increasing skill. In this section we consider whether cardiorespiratory command signals may be considered to form part of the planning for a movement and, consequently, may also be modified as a function of skill learning. It is clear that the voluntary movement system and the cardiovascular and respiratory systems operate in a coordinated fashion, and that command signals to the cardiovascular and respiratory systems are closely linked to the central command signals for movement. Indeed, Gandevia (1987) noted that the central signals used in cardiovascular control are often tacitly assumed to be the same as the perceived signals of central motor command or effort (although he pointed to evidence from subjects with spinal cord transection of a dissociation between these signals). Cardiovascular and respiratory responses are greater when the motor command increases, even when achieved muscular work does not change; these effects can be confidently ascribed to 'central irradiation' (McCloskey 1981). This demonstrable involvement of the motor commands in evoking autonomic responses indicates, at least to some extent, that somatic and autonomic control mechanisms overlap within the CNS. The ability to control autonomic response voluntarily (Smith 1974) can be explained by this.

In light of these overlapping CNS mechanisms, it is not surprising that coupling of both respiratory and cardiac activity to skeletal movement has been shown to occur during sustained exercise. Jasinskas, Wilson, and Hoare (1980) observed entrainment of breathing rate to cycle ergometer pedal movement in the majority (= 87%) of their subjects working at their preferred pedaling frequency. There was a trend toward increasing entrainment for a higher intensity workload. Bramble and Carrier (1983) noted that phase locking of limb and respiratory frequency has been recorded during locomotion in jackrabbits, dogs, horses, and humans. They showed that human runners employ several phase-locked patterns (4:1, 3:1, 2:1, 1:1, 5:2, and 3:2 strides per breath), although a 2:1 coupling ratio appeared to be favoured. Of particular interest in the present context was their observation that the coupling increased with skill—experienced runners exhibited the phase locking within the first four or five strides, less experienced runners required somewhat longer for coupling to occur, and inexperienced runners typically showed little or no tendency to synchronise gait and respiration.

Coupling of heart rate and cadence was studied by Kirby et al. (1989). They recorded coupling in most of their subjects at one or more speeds of treadmill locomotion (walking and running). Locomotor-respiratory coupling was also observed. One possible mechanism considered by these authors for the coupling of heart rate and cadence was that the vertical movement of the heart and abdominal viscera during running might mechanically enhance blood flow to or from the heart. Therefore, these investigators also studied pedaling on a bicycle ergometer, since the thorax moves much less during pedaling than during running. Again in most subjects, however, coupling was also recorded between heart rate and pedal rate.

There appear to be sound biomechanical reasons for the coupling of both respiratory and cardiac activity to skeletal movement. The general principle here is one of preventing antagonistic interactions. Bramble and Carrier (1983) proposed that the nature of locomotor-respiratory coupling was determined by biomechanical constraints, so as to avoid antagonistic interactions between inhalation and expiration and the cyclic loading and unloading of the thoracic complex during locomotion. In all cases it was evident that breathing was entrained to gait and not vice versa, because breathing often remained locked to body motion for variable periods of time when runners slowed to a walk at the end of a run. Kirby et al. (1980) noted that during repetitive exercise of moderate intensity, oxygenated blood may flow only while the muscle is relaxed or contracting minimally. This situation has been documented in skeletal muscle, diaphragm, and myocardium. They speculated that if peak intra-arterial pressure due to cardiac contraction occurred at the lowest phase of the intramuscular pressure cycle, then cardiac-locomotor coupling should permit increased muscle blood flow and reduced cardiac load. Obviously, this would provide improved metabolic support for the muscles. However, they acknowledged the complexity of multiple muscles being involved at different phases of the exercise cycle and emphasised that more direct measurements in animals were required to substantiate their hypothesis. In light of the studies reviewed earlier, we might specu-late that peak intra-arterial pressure due to cardiac contraction would be coupled to the lowest phase of the intramuscular pressure cycle of the muscle or muscle group that is under the most strain, i.e., contract-ing at the highest relative tension.

These studies provide clear instances of coordination between the voluntary movement system and the cardiorespiratory system. Most importantly, the degree of coordination appears to increase with level of skill. The prevention of antagonistic interactions suggested by Bramble and Carrier (1983) would appear to provide a plausible principle accord-ing to which skill might develop. However, a more positive interpreta-tion of this principle would be akin to that proposed by Turvey and Fitzpatrick (1993) of exploiting reactive forces, or what might otherwise be described as promoting synergistic interactions. This brings to mind the statement by Bernstein (1967) that the "secret of co-ordination lies not only in not wasting superfluous force on extinguishing reactive phe-nomena but, on the contrary, in employing the latter in such a way as to employ active muscle forces only in the capacity of complementary forces" (p. 109).

The available data concerning both central control of the cardiorespi-ratory response to exercise and cardiorespiratory coupling to skeletal movement indicates that cardiorespiratory command signals may indeed be considered to form part of the planning for a movement, and that they show modifications as a function of skill learning. This incorpora-tion of cardiorespiratory commands into the planning of movement ex-pands the scope of movement planning as conventionally viewed in the literature on motor control. Nevertheless, it is consistent with the sug-gestion by Sherwood et al. (1986) that cardiovascular mobilisation is a preparatory response for motor activity.

The changes in muscle activity that occur with motor learning and skill acquisition appear certain to be accompanied by parallel changes in the cardiorespiratory command signals. However, the precise nature of this parallelism remains to be elucidated. For example, the relation-ship between heart rate and oxygen consumption (and hence, aggregate muscle activity) has been shown to differ between static and dynamic exercise, the regression showing a steeper slope and lower intercept for static exercise (Carroll, Turner, and Rogers 1987). Furthermore, increases in cardiac activity that are surplus to metabolic requirements have been reported in some circumstances, such as psychological challenge (e.g., Obrist 1976; Sherwood et al. 1986; Turner, Carroll, and Courtney 1983). Therefore, the cardiorespiratory-skeletomotor linkage is not immutable. Learning-related changes in voluntary and cardiorespiratory commands clearly merit further investigation, but it seems likely that corollary dis-charges of central motor commands and the sense of effort play a pre-eminent role in guiding these changes.

Conclusion

That humans are sensitive to metabolic cost is indicated by the finding that minimal metabolic cost occurs at preferred frequencies of movement in various tasks (Sparrow 1983; Cavanagh and Kram 1985; Holt et al. 1995). It is undeniable that, via performance errors and inaccuracies, humans are also sensitive to noise in their motor output. We propose that minimising the levels of activation of individual muscles provides a means by which both metabolic energy expenditure and motor output noise may be minimised during movement. The sense of effort provides a perceivable signal to guide the process of energy expenditure reduction with increasing skill. The sense of effort is determined by the central command to muscles, and this command, in turn, is graded according to the extent of motor unit activation. It is the intensity of the motor effort that determines the cardiorespiratory response to motor activity, being especially sensitive to muscles activated at high proportions of their maximum, rather than muscle mass. Precision of control and accuracy of motor performance decrease as the relative level of muscle activation increases, due to increasing noise in the motor output. With acquisition of skill, metabolic economy and accuracy of control increase and the sense of effort reduces, consonant with the subjective experience of motor learning.

Acknowledgments

The authors are grateful to Simon Gandevia and Louise Ada who provided helpful comments on an earlier version of the manuscript.

References

Abbs, J.H., and V.L. Gracco. 1984. Control of complex motor gestures: orofacial muscle responses to load perturbations of lip during speech. *Journal of Neurophysiology* 51: 705-723.

Abitol, M.M. 1988. Effect of posture and locomotion on energy expenditure. *American Journal of Physical Anthropology* 77: 191-199.

Asami, T., H. Togari, T. Kikuchi, N. Adachi, K. Yamamoto, K. Kitagawa, and Y. Sano. 1976. Energy efficiency of ball kicking. In *Biomechanics V-B*, ed. P. Komi, 135-140. Baltimore: University Park Press.

Asmussen, E. 1953. Positive and negative muscular work. *Acta Physiologica Scandinavica* 28: 364-382.

Berg, K. 1970. Effect of physical training of school children with cerebral palsy. *Acta Paediatrica Scandinavica* 204 (Suppl. 204): 27-33.

Bernstein, N.A. 1967. *The co-ordination and regulation of movements*. Oxford: Pergamon.

Bigland, B., and O.C.J. Lippold. 1954. The relation between force, velocity and integrated electrical activity in human muscles. *Journal of Physiology* 123: 214-224.

Borg, G.A.V. 1973. Perceived exertion: a note on "history" and methods. *Medicine and Science in Sports* 5(2): 90-93.

Bramble, D.M., and D.R. Carrier. 1983. Running and breathing in mammals. *Science* 219: 251-256.

Burke, D., K.E. Hagbarth, L. Löfstedt, and B.G. Wallin. 1976a. The responses of human muscle spindle endings to vibration of noncontracting muscles. *Journal of Physiology* 261: 673-694.

Burke, D., K.E. Hagbarth, L. Löfstedt, and B.G. Wallin. 1976b. The responses of human muscle spindle endings to vibration during isometric contraction. *Journal of Physiology* 261: 695-711.

Cafarelli, E. 1982. Peripheral contributions to the perception of effort. *Medicine and Science in Sports and Exercise* 14: 382-389.

Campbell, J., and J. Ball. 1978. Energetics of walking in cerebral palsy. *Orthopedic Clinics of North America* 9: 374-377.

Carroll, D., J.R. Turner, and S. Rogers. 1987. Heart rate and oxygen consumption during mental arithmetic, a video game and graded static exercise. *Psychophysiology* 25(1): 112-118.

Carlton, L.G., and K.M. Newell. 1993. Force variability and characteristics of force production. In *Variability and motor control*, eds. K.M. Newell, and D.M. Corcos, 15-36. Champaign, IL: Human Kinetics.

Casaburi, R., B.J. Whipp, K. Wasserman, W.L. Beaver, and S.N. Koyal. 1977. Ventilatory and gas exchange dynamics in response to sinusoidal work. *Journal of Applied Physiology* 42(2): 300-311.

Cathers, I., N. O'Dwyer, and P. Neilson. 1996. Tracking performance with sinusoidal and irregular targets under different conditions of peripheral feedback. *Experimental Brain Research* 111: 437-446.

Cavanagh, P.R., and R. Kram. 1985. Mechanical and muscular factors affecting efficiency of human movement. *Medicine and Science in Sports and Exercise* 17(3): 326-331.

Chernigovskiy, V.N. 1967. *Interoceptors.* Washington, DC: American Psychological Association.

Csongradi, J., E. Bleck, and W.F. Ford. 1979. Gait electromyography in normal and spastic children, with special reference to quadriceps femoris and hamstring muscles. *Developmental Medicine and Child Neurology* 21: 738-748.

Dahlbäck, G.O., and R. Norlin. 1985. The effect of corrective surgery on energy expenditure during ambulation in children with cerebral palsy. *European Journal of Applied Physiology* 54: 67-70.

De Gail, P., J.W. Lance, and P.D. Neilson. 1966. Differential effects on tonic and phasic reflex mechanisms produced by vibration of muscles in man. *Journal of Neurology, Neurosurgery, and Psychiatry* 29: 1-11.

Durand, M., V. Geoffroi, A. Varray, and C. Préfaut. 1994. Study of the energy correlates in the learning of a complex self-paced cyclical skill. *Human Movement Science* 13: 785-799.

Eldridge, F.L., D.E. Millhorn, J.P. Kiley, and T.G. Waldrop. 1985. Stimulation by central command of locomotion, respiration and circulation during exercise. *Respiration Physiology* 59: 313-337.

Finley, F.R., R.W. Wirta, and K.A. Cody. 1968. Muscle synergies in motor performance. *Archives of Physical Medicine and Rehabilitation* 49: 655-660.

Fitts, P.M. 1954. The information capacity of the human motor system in controlling the amplitude of movement. *Journal of Experimental Psychology* 47: 381-391.

Fitts, P.M., and J.R. Peterson. 1964. Information capacity of discrete motor responses. *Journal of Experimental Psychology* 67: 103-112.

Gandevia, S.C. 1987. Roles for perceived voluntary motor commands in motor control. *Trends in Neurosciences* 10: 81-85.

Gandevia, S.C., and S.F. Hobbs. 1990. Cardiovascular responses to static exercise in man: central and reflex contributions. *Journal of Physiology* 430: 105-117.

Gandevia, S.C., K. Killian, D.K. McKenzie, M. Crawford, G.M. Allen, R.B. Gorman, and J.P. Hales. 1993. Respiratory sensations, cardiovascular control, kinaesthesia and transcranial stimulation during paralysis in humans. *Journal of Physiology* 470: 85-107.

Gandevia, S.C., and D.I. McCloskey. 1977a. Effects of related sensory inputs on motor performances in man studied through changes in perceived heaviness. *Journal of Physiology* 272: 653-672.

Gandevia, S.C., and D.I. McCloskey. 1977b. Changes in motor commands, as shown by changes in perceived heaviness, during partial curarization and peripheral anaesthesia in man. *Journal of Physiology* 272: 673-689.

Gandevia, S.C., and J.C. Rothwell. 1987. Knowledge of motor commands and the recruitment of human motoneurons. *Brain* 110: 1117-1130.

Gielen, C.C.A.M., K. van den Oosten, and F. Pul ter Gunne. 1985. Relation between EMG activation patterns and kinematic properties of aimed arm movements. *Journal of Motor Behavior* 17: 421-442.

Goldspink, G. 1981. Design of muscle for locomotion and the maintenance of posture. *Trends in Neurosciences* 4: 218-221.

Goodwin, G.M., D.I. McCloskey, and J. H. Mitchell. 1972. Cardiovascular and respiratory responses to changes in central command during isometric exercise at constant muscle tension. *Journal of Physiology* 226: 173-190.

Gottlieb, G.L., and G.C. Agarwal. 1971. Dynamic relationship between isometric muscle tension and the electromyogram in man. *Journal of Applied Physiology* 30: 345-351.

Guitar, B., C. Guitar, P. Neilson, N. O'Dwyer, and G. Andrews. 1988. Onset sequencing of selected lip muscles in stutterers and nonstutterers. *Journal of Speech and Hearing Research* 31: 28-35.

Hagbarth, K.E., and G. Eklund. 1966. Motor effects of vibratory muscle stimuli in man. In *Muscular afferents and motor control,* ed. R. Granit, 177-186. New York: Wiley.

Hasan, Z., and D.G. Stuart. 1984. Mammalian muscle receptors. In *Handbook of the Spinal Cord,* ed. R.A. Davidoff, 559-607. New York: Marcel Dekker, Inc.

Henriksson, J., H.G. Knuttgen, and F. Bonde-Peterson. 1972. Perceived exertion during exercise with concentric and eccentric muscle contractions. *Ergonomics* 15: 537-544.

Herman, R. 1970. Electromyographic evidence of some control factors involved in the acquisition of skilled performance. *American Journal of Physical Medicine* 49: 177-191.

Hobart, D.J., D.L. Kelley, and L. Bradley. 1975. Modifications occurring during acquisition of a novel throwing task. *American Journal of Physical Medicine* 54: 1-24.

Hobart, D.J., and J.R. Vorro. 1974. Electromyographic analysis of the intermittent modifications occurring during the acquisition of a novel throwing skill. In *Biomechanics IV,* ed. R.C. Nelson and C.A. Morehouse, 559-566. Baltimore: University Park Press.

Hobbs, S.F., L.B. Rowell, and O.A. Smith. 1980. Increased cardiovascular responses to voluntary static exercise after neuromuscular blockade (NMB) in baboons. *The Physiologist* 23(4): 120.

Hof, A.L., and J. van den Berg. 1977. Linearity between the weighted sum of the EMGs of the human triceps surae and the total torque. *Journal of Biomechanics* 10: 529-539.

Holt, K.G., S.F. Jeng, R. Ratcliffe, and J. Hamill. 1995. Energetic cost and stability during walking at preferred stride frequency. *Journal of Motor Behavior* 27(2): 164-178.

Humphrey, D.R., and D.J. Reed. 1983. Separate cortical systems for control of joint movement and joint stiffness: reciprocal activation and coactivation of antagonist muscles. *Advances in Neurology* 39: 347-372.

Humphreys, P.W., and A.R. Lind. 1963. The blood flow through active and inactive muscles of the forearm during sustained handgrip contractions. *Journal of Physiology* 166: 120-135.

Inman, V.T., H.J. Ralston, J.B de C.M. Saunders, B. Feinstein, and E.W. Wright. 1952. Relation of human electromyogram to muscular tension. *Electroencephalography and Clinical Neurophysiology.* 4: 187-194.

Iwamoto, G.A., J.H. Mitchell, M. Mizuno, and N.H. Secher. 1987. Cardiovascular responses at the onset of exercise with partial neuromuscular blockade in cat and man. *Journal of Physiology* 384: 39-47.

Jasinskas, C.L., B.A. Wilson, and J. Hoare. 1980. Entrainment of breathing rate to movement frequency during work at two intensities. *Respiration Physiology* 42: 199-209.

Jones L.A. 1986. Perception of force and weight: theory and research. *Psychological Bulletin* 100: 29-42.

Kamon, E., and J. Gormley. 1968. Muscular activity pattern for skilled performance and during learning of a horizontal bar exercise. *Ergonomics* 11(4): 345-357.

Kirby, R.L., S.T. Nugent, R.W. Marlow, D.A. MacLeod, and A.E. Marble. 1989. Coupling of cardiac and locomotor rhythms. *Journal of Applied Physiology* 66(1): 323-329.

Komi, P.V. 1986. The stretch-shortening cycle and human power output. In *Human Muscle Power,* ed. N.L. Jones, N. McCartney, and A.J. McComas, 27-39. Champaign, IL: Human Kinetics.

Krogh, A., and J. Lindhard. 1913. The regulation of respiratory and circulation during the initial stages of muscular work. *Journal Physiology* 47: 112-136.

Lind, A.R., and G.W. McNicol. 1967. Circulatory responses to sustained handgrip contractions performed during other exercises, both rhythmic and static. *Journal of Physiology* 192: 595-607.

Lindström, L., R. Magnusson, and I. Petersén. 1974. Muscle load influence on myo-electric signal characteristics. *Scandinavian Journal of Rehabilitation Medicine* 6 (Suppl. 3): 127-148.

Lippold, O.C.J. 1952. The relation between integrated action potentials in a human muscle and its isometric tension. *Journal of Physiology* 117: 492-499.

MacConaill, M.A., and J.V. Basmajian. 1977. *Muscles and movements: a basis for human kinesiology*. Huntington, NY: Krieger.

Macefield, V.G., S.C. Gandevia, B. Bigland-Ritchie, R.B. Gorman, and D. Burke. 1993. The firing rates of human motoneurons voluntarily activated in the absence of muscle afferent feedback. *Journal of Physiology* 471:429-443.

McCloskey, D.I. 1981. Corollary discharges: motor commands and perception. In *Handbook of Physiology*, ed. Brookhart, J.M., V.B. Mountcastle, V.B Brooks, and S.R. Geiger, 1415-1447. Bethesda: American Physiological Society.

McCloskey, D.I., P. Ebeling, and G.M. Goodwin. 1974. Estimation of weights and tensions and apparent involvement of a "sense of effort." *Experimental Neurology* 42: 220-232.

McCloskey, D.I., and J.H. Mitchell. 1972. Reflex cardiovascular and respiratory responses originating in exercising muscle. *Journal of Physiology* 224: 173-186.

McCloskey, D.I., and K.A. Streatfeild. 1975. Muscular reflex stimuli to the cardiovascular system during isometric contractions of muscle groups of different mass. *Journal of Physiology* 250: 431-441.

McGrain, P. 1980. Trends in selected kinematic and myoelectric variables associated with learning a novel motor task. *Research Quarterly for Exercise and Sport* 51(3): 509-520.

Mense, S., and M. Stahnke. 1983. Responses in muscle afferent fibres of slow conduction velocity to contractions and ischaemia in the cat. *Journal of Physiology* 342: 383-397.

Meyer, D.E., J.E.K. Smith, and C.E. Wright. 1982. Models for the speed and accuracy of aimed movements. *Psychological Review* 89: 449-482.

Milner-Brown, H.S., and R.D. Penn. 1979. Pathophysiological mechanisms in cerebral palsy. *Journal of Neurology, Neurosurgery, and Psychiatry* 42: 606-618.

Milner-Brown, H.S., and R.B. Stein. 1975. The relation between the surface electromyogram and muscular force. *Journal of Physiology* 246: 549-569.

Monod, H. and J. Scherrer. 1965. The work capacity of a synergic muscular group. *Ergonomics* 8: 329-338.

Muza, S.R., L-Y. Lee, R.L. Wiley, S. McDonald, and F.W. Zechman. 1983. Ventilatory responses to static handgrip exercise. *Journal of Applied Physiology: Respiratory, Environmental and Exercise Physiology* 54(6): 1457-1462.

Neilson, P.D., and C.J. Andrews. 1973. Comparison of the tonic stretch reflex in athetotic patients during rest and voluntary activity. *Journal of Neurology, Neurosurgery, and Psychiatry* 36(4): 547-554.

Neilson, P.D., and J. McCaughey. 1982. Self-regulation of spasm and spasticity in cerebral palsy. *Journal of Neurology, Neurosurgery, and Psychiatry* 45: 320-330.

Neilson, P.D., M.D. Neilson, and N.J. O'Dwyer. 1992. Adaptive model theory: application to disorders of motor control. In *Approaches to the study of motor control and learning*, ed. J.J. Summers, 495-548. Amsterdam: Elsevier.

Neilson, P.D., and N.J. O'Dwyer. 1981. Pathophysiology of dysarthria in cerebral palsy. *Journal of Neurology, Neurosurgery, and Psychiatry* 41: 1013-1019.

Neilson, P.D., and N.J. O'Dwyer. 1984. Reproducibility and variability of speech muscle activity in athetoid dysarthria of cerebral palsy. *Journal of Speech and Hearing* 27: 502-517.

Neilson, P.D., N.J. O'Dwyer, and J. Nash. 1990. Control of isometric muscle activity in cerebral palsy. *Developmental Medicine and Child Neurology* 32: 778-788.

Noble, B.J., and R.J. Robertson. 1996. *Perceived exertion.* Champaign, IL: Human Kinetics.

Obrist, P.A. 1976. The cardiovascular-behavioral interaction—as it appears today. *Psychophysiology* 13: 95-107.

O'Dwyer, N.J., and P.D. Neilson. 1988. Voluntary muscle control in normal and athetoid dysarthric speakers. *Brain* 111: 877-899.

O'Dwyer, N.J., and P.D. Neilson. 1995. Learning a dynamic limb synergy. In *Motor control and sensory motor integration: issues and directions,* eds. D.J. Glencross, and J.P. Piek, 289-315. Amsterdam: Elsevier.

O'Dwyer, N.J., and P.D. Neilson. 1998. Motor output variability: variation with average level and range of force. *Australian Journal of Psychology* 50 (Suppl.): 8.

Paterson, W.D. 1928. Circulatory and respiratory changes in response to muscular exercise in man. *Journal of Physiology* 66: 323-345.

Payton, O.D. 1975. Electrical correlates of motor skill development in an isolated movement: the triceps and anconeus as agonists. *World Confederation for Physical Therapy. Proceedings of the Seventh International Congress,* 132-139. London: The Confederation.

Payton, O.D., and D.L. Kelley. 1972. Electromyographic evidence of the acquisition of a motor skill. A pilot study. *Physical Therapy* 52: 261-266.

Payton, O.D., S. Su, and D.L. Kelley. 1976. Abductor digiti quinti shuffleboard: a study in motor learning. *Archives of Physical Medicine and Rehabilitation* 57: 169-174.

Person R.S. 1958. An electromyographic investigation on coordination of the activity of antagonist muscles in man during the development of a motor habit. *Pavlovian Journal of Higher Nervous Activity* 8: 13-23.

Rose, J., J.G. Gamble, A. Burgos, J. Medeiros, and W.L. Haskell. 1990. Energy expenditure index of walking for normal children and for children with cerebral palsy. *Developmental Medicine and Child Neurology* 32: 333-340.

Rose, J., W.L. Haskell, J.G. Gamble, R.L. Hamilton, D.A. Brown, and L. Rinsky. 1994. Muscle pathology and clinical measures of disability in children with cerebral palsy. *Journal of Orthopaedic Research* 12(6): 758-768.

Sargeant A.J., and C.T. Davies. 1973. Perceived exertion during rhythmic exercise involving different muscle masses. *Journal of Human Ergology* 2: 3-11.

Schmidt, R.A., Zelaznik, H., Hawkins, B., Frank, J.S., and Quinn, J.T. 1979. Motor-output variability: a theory for the accuracy of rapid motor acts. *Psychological Review* 86: 415-451.

Sherwood, A., M.T. Allen, P.A. Obrist, and A.W. Langer. 1986. Evaluation of beta-adrenergic influences on cardiovascular and metabolic adjustments to physical and psychological stress. *Psychophysiology* 23(1): 89-103.

Smith, O.A. 1974. Reflex and central mechanisms involved in the control of the heart and circulation. *Annual Review of Physiology* 36: 93-123.

Sparrow, W.A. 1983. The efficiency of skilled performance. *Journal of Motor Behavior* 15: 237-261.

Sparrow, W.A., and K. Hughes. 1997. Minimum principles in human learning: the effects of practice and non-preferred work rates on metabolic energy expenditure and perceived exertion. *Australian Journal of Psychology* 49 (Suppl.): 23.

Sparrow, W.A., and V.M. Irizarry-Lopez. 1987. Mechanical efficiency and metabolic cost as measures of learning a novel gross motor task. *Journal of Motor Behavior* 19(2): 240-264.

Sparrow, W.A., and K.M. Newell. 1994. Energy expenditure and motor performance relationships in human learning a motor task. *Psychophysiology* 31: 338-346.

Sparrow, W.A., and K.M. Newell. 1998. Metabolic energy expenditure and regulation of movement economy. *Psychonomic Bulletin and Review* 5(2): 173-196.

Stevens, S.S. 1957. On the psychophysical law. *Psychological Review* 64: 153-181.

Strasser, H., and J. Ernst. 1992. Physiological cost of horizontal materials handling while seated. *International Journal of Industrial Ergonomics* 9: 303-313.

Tang, A., and W.Z. Rymer. 1981. Abnormal force-EMG relations in paretic limbs of hemiparetic human subjects. *Journal of Neurology, Neurosurgery, and Psychiatry* 44: 690-698.

Taylor, J.L., and D.I. McCloskey. 1992. Detection of slow movements imposed at the elbow during active flexion in man. *Journal of Physiology* 457: 503-513.

Tolman, E.C. 1932. *Purposive behavior in animals and men.* New York: Century.

Turner, J.R., D. Carroll, and H. Courtney. 1983. Cardiac and metabolic responses to "Space Invaders": an instance of metabolically-exaggerated cardiac adjustment? *Psychophysiology* 20(5): 544-549.

Turvey, M.T., and P. Fitzpatrick. 1993. Commentary: development of perception-action systems and general principles of pattern formation. *Child Development* 64: 1175-1190.

Unnithan, V.B., J.J. Dowling, G. Frost, and O. Bar-Or. 1996. Role of cocontraction in the O_2 cost of walking in children with cerebral palsy. *Medicine and Science in Sports and Exercise* 28(12): 1498-1504.

Vaughan, C.W., P.D. Neilson, and N.J. O'Dwyer. 1988. Motor control deficits of orofacial muscles in cerebral palsy. *Journal of Neurology, Neurosurgery, and Psychiatry* 51: 534-539.

Vorro, J., and D. Hobart. 1981a. Kinematic and myoelectric analysis of skill acquisition: I. 90cm subject group. *Archives of Physical Medicine and Rehabilitation* 62: 575-582.

Vorro, J., and D. Hobart. 1981b. Kinematic and myoelectric analysis of skill acquisition: II. 150cm subject group. *Archives of Physical Medicine and Rehabilitation* 62: 582-589.

Vorro, J., F.R. Wilson, and A. Dainis. 1978. Multivariate analysis of biomechanical profiles for the coracobrachialis and biceps brachii (caput breve) muscles in humans. *Ergonomics* 21: 407-418.

Weber, E.H. 1978. *The sense of touch*, ed. and trans. H.E. Ross. London: Academic Press. (Original work published 1834.)

Wise, A.K., J.E. Gregory, and U. Proske. 1998. Detection of movements of the human forearm during and after co-contraction of muscles acting at the elbow joint. *Journal of Physiology* 508: 325-330.

2

Factors That Have Shaped Human Locomotor Structure and Behavior: The 'Joules' in the Crown

Aftab E. Patla

Neural Control Laboratory, Department of Kinesiology,
University of Waterloo, Canada

W.A. Sparrow

School of Health Sciences, Deakin University, Australia

$\mathbf{F}$or all animals the fundamental survival needs of feeding and avoiding predators require that they transport their body from one location to another. It is, therefore, not surprising that evolutionary pressures have ensured that the energy cost of locomotion has been minimized through changes in both the organism's structure and behavior. The evolutionary legacy clearly confers energy efficiency in locomotion for all animals, irrespective of their size, structure, and mode of travel. Our purpose in this chapter was to determine the extent to which local (step cycle) and global (route selection) human locomotor behavior is constrained by the requirement to minimise metabolic energy expenditure. Studies showing structural and behavioral properties of the bipedal locomotor system that minimizes energy cost per stride are presented. Structural properties include skeletal muscle characteristics and intersegmental dynamics. Behavioral properties relate to the selection of a particular gait pattern to accommodate specific environmental demands such as changing speed and negotiating obstructions. The effects of pathologies on the adaptability of the locomotor system are also considered. Evidence that energy cost considerations does not explain all the features of specific locomotor patterns or behavior are discussed. These include: a) higher energy cost for human bipedal locomotion compared to energy cost for a quadruped of similar size; b) the inability of oxygen cost studies to predict the exact speed of locomotion that will minimize energy consumption; and c) the failure of single-cost function optimization models to predict all aspects of locomotor patterns, and the choice of travel path. Among other factors that shape locomotor behavior, the influence of maintenance of dynamic stability on gait patterns is discussed. It is concluded that human bipedal locomotor structure and behavior emerges from the competing demands of several constraints rather than a single objective based on the metabolic energy costs of locomotor coordination and control.

Evolutionary Constraints on the Energetics of Human Bipedal Locomotion

Sea squirts have a lazy existence, spending their adult life more or less stationary and feeding by filtering out food particles brought to them by water currents (Corlett 1992). For most animals feeding and evading predators requires that they transport their bodies from one place to another; survival depends on this ability. Depending on the habitat and the availability of food, the distance traveled and maximum speed vary considerably. Wildebeest and caribou, which are migratory animals, travel large distances in search of food and water, while other species such as giraffe confine themselves to a relatively small area (Dagg 1977). Depending upon the habitat, the requirements for speed differ. Cursorial animals that do not have a specialized habitat travel over open terrain and require fast speeds to evade predators or catch prey. Animals such as impala have developed interesting locomotor strategies to evade predators, such as erratic high jumps and changes in direction of travel (Dagg 1977).

It is, however, interesting that the energy cost of such gait or "transport" activities appears to have been minimized through evolutionary changes in structure and behavior. High energy cost associated with the activities of hunting and gathering food would be self-defeating from an evolutionary perspective (Alexander 1989). The dromedary, which wanders in the Sahara Desert, exemplifies the energy efficiency of locomotion, because it can travel extraordinarily long distances without replenishing its fuel sources. In contrast, a biped robot built by the Honda motor company could travel for only approximately 15 minutes before it had to be recharged. While it is true that the inability to carry more fuel (battery) is what limits the robot's ability to function for a longer time, increasing the efficiency of the motors and the battery can extend travel time. The fuel sources and motors that make it possible for humans and animals to travel have evolved to ensure long distance travel without refueling.

The metabolic energy used by animals to move is dependent on their structure, size, and locomotor mode. Animals have, of course, adopted characteristically different locomotor modes to suit the medium of their existences, with specific adaptations made to water, air, and various types of terrain (Schmidt-Nielsen 1972; Fedak and Seeherman 1979). In order to make comparisons across species and transport media, researchers have expressed the cost of travel in terms of metabolic cost per unit mass and distance traveled, a type of "weight-adjusted mileage rating," which is a familiar specification for automobiles (Taylor, Heglund, and Malloy 1982).

For a given speed, swimming is more efficient than flying, which, in turn, is more efficient than terrestrial locomotion (Schmidt-Nielsen 1972). Compared to flying and terrestrial locomotion, travel through water is very efficient, because the animal does much less work to support its weight against gravity. Impact with the ground and requirement to accommodate the energy demands of surface characteristics such as compliance and grade make terrestrial locomotion the least efficient transport mode. But, as would be expected, this is true for animals whose habitual medium of travel is water. Humans are not designed to be efficient swimmers, nor can they fly (Schmidt-Nielsen).

For terrestrial locomotion, studies show that the larger the animal the lower the normalized energy cost expressed as a plot of rate of oxygen consumption per unit body mass versus speed of travel (Taylor, Heglund, and Malloy 1982a). Hill (1950) pointed out that all vertebrate striated muscle will produce the same maximum force per cross-sectional area, the same maximum work per unit mass of muscle, and have the same maximum efficiency for converting chemical energy to mechanical work. Given these properties, when compared to larger animals, small animals moving at the same speed will have higher step frequency and will therefore utilize energy at higher rates. Energy consumed during a stride per unit mass for a given speed has been found to be similar (5-6 Joules; Taylor, Heglund, and Malloy). Once the effects of the animal's size on energy cost for travel are taken into account, the next question is whether the form of locomotion for a given medium (terrestrial locomotion) has any effect on energy cost.

There has been debate about whether bipedal locomotion consumes more energy than quadrupedal locomotion. Early studies suggested that bipedal locomotion in birds was more energy costly than quadrupedal locomotion in animals of similar size and at similar speed, and it was suggested that this difference would be more pronounced in larger animals (Fedak and Seeherman 1979). Later studies on larger animals showed similar energy cost of locomotion for an ostrich and a horse of similar size (Fedak and Seeherman). A study by Taylor and Rowntree (1973) was particularly interesting in comparing the metabolic cost of bipedal and quadruped locomotion in the same species. In their study chimpanzees and monkeys locomoted on a motor-driven treadmill at speeds from 1 km/hr to 7 km/hr and 1 km/hr to 10 km/hr, respectively. The slopes of the linear regression lines for oxygen consumption against running velocity were not statistically different; indicating that the oxygen cost per unit time in the two gait modes was essentially identical. Clearly these animals were equally well-adapted to either gait mode. When Sparrow and Newell (1994) compared the oxygen consumption for humans in either a normal upright bipedal gait or a four-limbed hands-and-feet gait (creeping), the oxygen cost for the creeping gait was approximately three times greater than for upright bipedal walking at the same treadmill speed (2.4 km/hr). Clearly, therefore, the relative metabolic cost of two-limbed and four-limbed locomotion in primates (including humans) depends on their specific anthropometric and other physical and physiological constraints.

The primary focus of Taylor and Rowntree's (1973) paper, discussed above, was the question of, as the author's phrased it, ". . . the energetic price of freeing the hands" (p. 186). They concluded that, from an evolutionary perspective, the energy cost of adopting a bipedal gait could not be used in arguments concerning the costs and benefits of bipedalism. In other words, on the assumption that our ancestor who made the transition to bipedalism was equally well-designed (in terms of its structural anatomy) for bipedal and quadrupedal gait, the relative energy cost of the two modes would not serve as an evolutionary pressure. The flip side to the freeing of the forelimbs (hands) during the transition from quadrupedal to bipedal locomotion is whether the feet have been slaved exclusively to the task of locomotion. If that were the case, the central nervous system would have had to develop a separate set of control signals for the muscles of the lower limb. This is clearly not the case. We are able to use our lower limbs for variety of movements and postures. As has been pointed out by many researchers (see Bernstein 1967), the central nervous system has multiple options at both the sensory and motor level as it executes most movements.

Consider first the redundancy in sensory systems. Both the visual and kinesthetic sensory modalities have the potential to provide similar information for the control of locomotion, providing stimuli concerning either whole-body self-motion or movements and posture of body segments. Utilizing multiple sources of the same informational support for action insures against failure and can be used by the control system to cross-check and validate the information it is going to use. There are no models for the control of locomotion that use the processing of sensory information to explain the observed locomotor patterns. For example, during walking body orientation with respect to gravity can be obtained from kinesthetic input. Control of the head in the gravito-inertial frame is perhaps not a critical source of sensory support (Dunbar and Badam 1998). In contrast, during the free-flight phase in running, head stability in the gravito-inertial frame is more important to extract body orientation information from the vestibular and visual inputs.

Next we turn our attention to the redundancy in the motor system, the subject of much research. It is known that many muscles can produce the same torque at a given joint, and there are many degrees of freedom in the skeletal system that allow one to move from one spatial location to another through various paths involving different joint motions (Rosenbaum et al. 1995). Given the options available to the central nervous system in coordinating and controlling the mechanical degrees of freedom alone (defined solely in terms of the constraints on the limb segments' spatial coordinates), many investigators have been tempted to decode the principles governing the planning and control of movement by proposing energy cost as the central nervous system's prime objective.

In the next section we will consider human bipedal locomotion in more detail to see how at the "local" level of step cycle measures and the "global" level of route or path selection, the choice of gait control strategy is constrained by energy minimization considerations.

The Energetics of Human Bipedal Locomotion

We begin this section of the chapter with a review of evidence about the structural and behavioral properties of bipedal locomotion that serve to minimize energy cost. In the following major section we evaluate the evidence for other factors, primarily dynamic stability, which influence the expression of locomotor pattern. It is argued here that the 'Joules' costs in the walking crown are necessary but not sufficient for the expression of the human bipedal locomotor pattern. We conclude the chapter by proposing that human locomotor patterns emerge from competing demands of several objectives rather than from a single objective.

Muscle Mass Distribution and Force Modulating Properties

Let us consider first the influence of muscle morphology on the energetics of locomotion. The more massive muscles such as the gluteus maximus are located in the proximal joints closer to the body's center of mass. As one moves distally from the body center of mass, the muscle mass in general reduces. This is seen not only in the lower limbs but also in the upper limbs. One effect of this fundamental design principle is to reduce the moment of inertia by reducing the mass distribution. This will result in lower torque requirements for a given angular acceleration, and movements of the limbs will cost less energy. These energy-saving characteristics of body form are similar in principle to the shape of the fish that allows it to move through water without costly turbulence.

Vertebrate striated muscles provide an unrivaled power-to-weight ratio, and no person-made motor comes close to achieving the energy-converting efficiency of muscle. Consider the ankle plantarflexors that can produce peak power of over three-quarters of a horsepower and yet weigh less than one kilogram. Match these to the weight of the electric motor that powers a household vacuum cleaner and the advantages become clear. This high power production to low weight ratio means that the cost of carrying these motors as we move around is reduced. Next we turn our attention to the properties of muscle that make it such a remarkable energy saver. The impressive elastic properties of the muscles and the tendons and their force-length and force-velocity relationships for a given activation have been shown to provide unique cost-saving features that the nervous system exploits.

Researchers have shown that the spring-like properties of the musculo-tendon complex can be utilized effectively to store energy in one phase of the movement and release it in another, resulting in energy savings (Alexander 1990). The kangaroo, for example, exploits this mechanism very effectively, resulting in a dip in oxygen consumption at the same time as the speed is increased (Alexander 1989). Recently, Roberts et al. (1997) measured muscle force and length changes directly in running turkeys and showed that muscles served to hold the end of the tendon springs rigid so that they could store energy during landing; this energy can be subsequently recovered to minimize work. While there is some debate about how much energy is saved by this mechanism in humans (see van Ingen Schenau, Bobbert, and de Haan 1997), there is no doubt that these "springs" contribute to movement control in other ways besides energy minimization. This will be discussed later.

Other properties of muscles that are often overlooked by students of motor control, are their force-length and force-velocity relationships, as shown in figure 2.1. The complex nature of the muscle actuator is seen in these properties. Activation, but also muscle length and muscle velocity, does not only modulate muscle force even when the neural activation is held constant. The force-length relationship shown in figure 2.1 indicates that for a given activation level, muscle produces variable force, and a nonlinear increase in force is seen as the length of the muscle is increased. Part of the increase is due to cross-bridge dynamics (more cross-bridge formation between the actin and myosin filaments), and part of it is due to the passive elastic component. This spring-like property can provide resistance and hence maintain stability without active involvement of the muscle. The force-velocity relationship provides a variable viscosity that can also be suitably exploited to dampen perturbations and control movement trajectories. Any function that can be derived without resorting to energy-costly changes in muscle activation is clearly desirable.

Recently, researchers have begun to realize how these complex properties can simplify movement control and provide efficiencies. Gribble et al. (1998) have shown how complex muscle properties simplify the command signals needed to control arm movements. Young, Scott, and

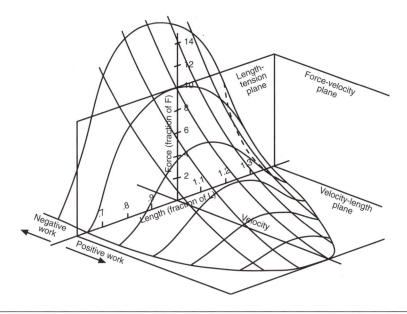

Figure 2.1   Force, length, and velocity characteristics for a muscle (Winter 1991).

Loeb (1992) have argued that joint-angle-dependent moment-arm length changes provide an intrinsic mechanism for stabilization. Carrier, Heglund, and Earls (1994) have shown how movement of the center of pressure under the feet during running in humans provides variable gearing for the ankle extensors. As in automobile engines, this variable gearing allows the motor (muscle) to operate in the limited range of speeds where the efficiency is at its peak.

Energy Saving Due to Passive Intersegmental Dynamics

The theoretical principles of pendulum dynamics have been used to model lower limb control in human locomotion. Pendulum motion, once initiated and assuming no friction, can in theory continue without any external energy input; the interchange between potential and mechanical energy provides the mechanism, and the movement trajectory is thereby passively specified. Many researchers have pointed out that the body and the limb movements can be modeled as compound pendulum and have suggested that similar mechanisms can simplify control and provide efficiencies in limb movements for locomotion (Alexander 1982; McGeer 1990; Mochon and McMahon 1980, 1981; Zernicke and Smith 1996). In fact, McGeer built a passive bipedal robot that can walk downhill with gravity providing the only source of energy (figure 2.2). The motion of the body and limbs are not planned and generated but rather

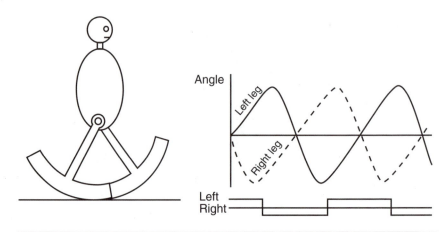

Figure 2.2   A passive mechanical robot designed by McGeer (1990).

emerge from the interaction of the multi-body system operating in the gravito-inertial environment. Thus, when an organism is "designed" in such a way that it can take advantage of various energy-conserving mechanisms, the metabolic cost of transport is considerably reduced. We explore other energy-saving mechanisms further in a later section; for now we focus on the contribution of intersegmental dynamics to energy conservation.

During human locomotion, the movements of body center of mass show the interchange between potential and kinetic energy (Elftman 1939). This exchange conserves energy, and while this mechanism is now understood, two other related energy-saving mechanisms are less well-appreciated. The first of these is the exchange of energy between body segments as described by Winter and his colleagues (see Winter and Robertson 1978). When one considers energy balance of a given segment, one has to consider all sources of energy flowing into and out of the segment (figure 2.3). As seen in figure 2.3, muscles acting on the segment can produce a change in energy of that segment. In addition, the energy flowing into the segment from an adjoining segment can also alter the energy of the segment. The best illustration of this is the various contributions to swing-limb elevation when stepping over an obstacle (Patla and Prentice 1995). We see that the vertical translational power at the hip joint is highly correlated with limb elevation, and this provides a major source of energy that is transferred to the swing limb.

The second mechanism that is often overlooked is the role of torques generated by the motion-dependent terms (Zajac and Gordon 1989; Zernicke and Smith 1996). Torques arising from mechanical interaction between segments can and do play an important role in shaping the swing phase trajectory. Mochon and McMahon (1981) clearly showed that the swing phase during normal locomotion can be passively generated; the initial conditions set up at the end of the stance phase are sufficient to

$$\frac{dE_s}{dt} = P_{jp} = P_{mp} + P_{jd} + P_{md}$$

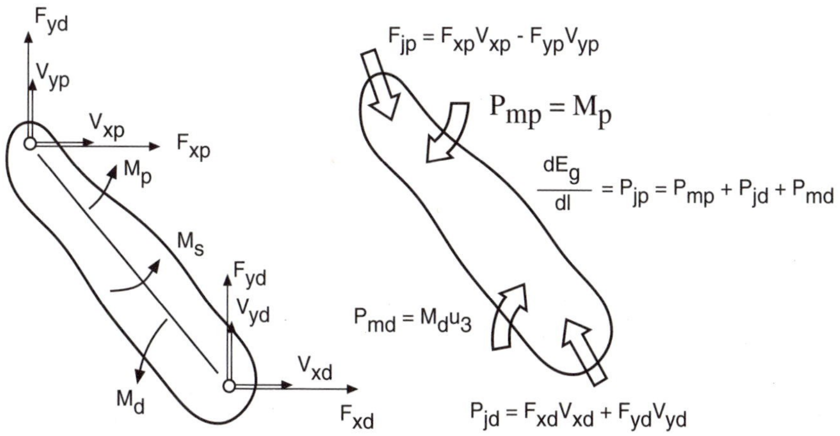

$$F_{jp} = F_{xp}V_{xp} - F_{yp}V_{yp}$$

$$P_{mp} = M_p$$

$$\frac{dE_g}{dl} = P_{jp} = P_{mp} + P_{jd} + P_{md}$$

$$P_{md} = M_d u_3$$

$$P_{jd} = F_{xd}V_{xd} + F_{yd}V_{yd}$$

Figure 2.3   Power balance within segments (Winter 1991).

uniquely specify the motion of the compound pendulum of the swing limb. There are, however, two caveats to this conclusion. The first is that the ankle joint has to be locked in the neutral posture (90 degrees). The second caveat is that dampers have to be introduced to slow the movement at the end of the swing phase. If either of these requirements are not met, it is impossible to generate the trajectory that produces adequate ground clearance and stable landing.

While passive dynamics have been shown to play an important role during normal locomotion, recently Patla and his group have also examined the role of intersegmental dynamics in the control of swing-limb trajectory over an obstacle (Patla and Prentice 1995). They found that modulation of the hip and ankle flexion needed for swing-limb elevation is not achieved by actively modulating the rotational energy at the swing-limb hip and the ankle joint. The rotational energy at the swing hip and the ankle joint show no modulation as a function of obstacle height (figure 2.4). The motion-dependent flexion torque at the hip and ankle joint that is modulated as a function of obstacle height is the mechanism by which hip and ankle flexion is increased (figure 2.4). This motion-dependent torque arises from active control of the knee joint and the translational power at the hip joint. Hip and ankle flexion does not, therefore, cost the system any energy. Interestingly, when we investigated the reason why the central nervous system might employ these strategies, we found that translational power at the hip joint is the most energy-efficient mechanism. This was followed by the rotational power at the knee joint, with the rotational power at the hip joint being the least efficient

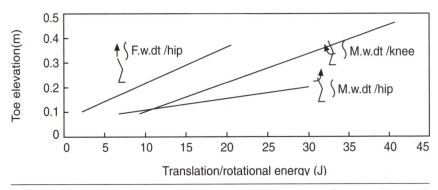

Figure 2.4 Toe elevation achieved by different sources of mechanical work (Armand et al. 1994).

(Armand et al. 1997). Figure 2.5 shows the results of the joint energy analyses from the Armand et al. study. It is not surprising, from an energy-conservation perspective, that the central nervous system uses translational power at the hip and rotational power at the knee joint to elevate the swing limb over the obstacle.

Having considered control of limb dynamics at the "local" level of lower limb modulations to accommodate environmental contingencies, we now extend the discussion of energy-saving mechanisms in gait by investigat-

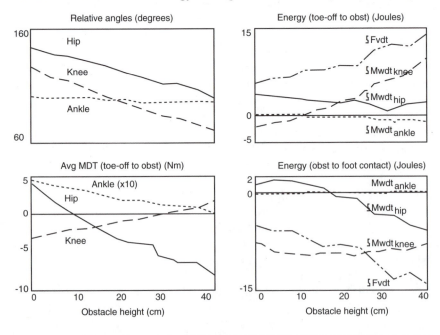

Figure 2.5 Contributions of intersegmental dynamics to the control of limb elevation during obstacle avoidance (Patla and Prentice 1995).

ing how the organism's selection of a particular speed and gait pattern (the inter-limb coordination characteristics of gait) also play a role in metabolic energy conservation.

Modulations of Speed and Transition in Gait

Terrestrial legged locomotion is characterized by different gaits. Alexander (1989) defines a gait as " a pattern of locomotion characteristic of a limited range of speeds described by quantities of which one or more change discontinuously at transition to other gaits." The influential paper of Hoyt and Taylor (1981) showed clearly that in ponies, the self-selected speeds of locomotion for a walk, trot, and gallop resulted in lower energy cost. Their data are presented in figure 2.6. This finding illustrates the first major point in this section that all animals are sensitive to the energy cost of locomotion and are able to "self-select" a speed that minimizes the metabolic cost of transport within a particular gait mode. At nonoptimal speeds for the same gait patterns the energy cost is substantially higher, and Hoyt and Taylor showed that when running unconstrained in a field there were locomotor speeds that were rarely adopted within a gait mode (walk, trot, or gallop). Once a certain critical speed is reached the animal will switch to another, more economical, gait mode rather than increase speed with the interlimb coordination pattern unchanged. Similarly, in humans, at a given speed of locomotion individuals select a stride length that results in lower energy cost, stride lengths larger or shorter than preferred considerably increase the energy cost (Cavanagh and Williams 1982).

In addition to speed selection as an energy minimization strategy in gait control, it is also possible to minimize the metabolic cost of transport (per unit distance traveled) by switching to a different gait pattern. Metabolic energy cost as a function of speed for walking and running show that energy savings can be achieved by switching to running from walking at a given speed (see data summarized in Minetti and Alexander 1997). Others have argued that the transition from a walk to run is guided by stability of gait patterns (Diedrich and Warren 1995).

Transition in gait patterns has been primarily studied while the speed of locomotion has been varied, but the terrain characteristics have not usually been manipulated in experimental studies of gait energetics. Changes in terrain characteristics do, however, require modifications to gait patterns. Warren (1984), for example, varied the riser height of stairs and showed that individuals make a transition from bipedal ascent to quadrupedal ascent at critical riser height. Recently, Patla examined the choices made by individuals when obstacles of varying heights are encountered in the travel path (Patla 1997). When the obstacle height reaches a critical size (equal to the lower leg length), individuals choose to go around rather than step over the obstacle. Such transition in ac-

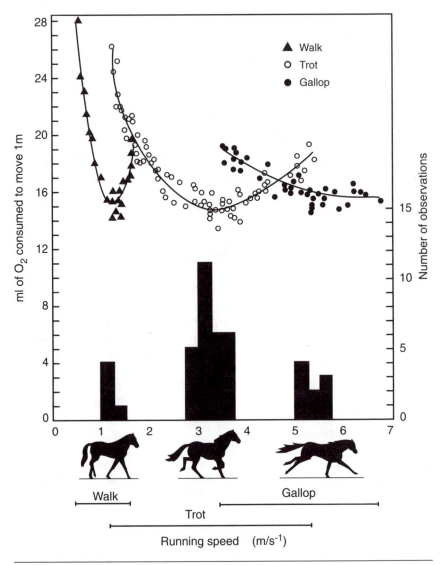

Figure 2.6 Oxygen consumption curves.

tion pattern can also be argued to be guided by energy cost; raising the center of mass against gravity for stepping over a very high obstacle may be more costly than a detour.

Energy Cost of Neuro-Musculoskeletal Pathologies

Given the evidence that normal locomotor patterns are indeed most efficient, it is reasonable to propose that any pathology that affects the control system or the musculoskeletal system imposes added demands on the cardiovascular system (Winter 1978). Patients who have suffered a stroke, for example, are not able to travel over large distances within a reasonable time frame. Spinal cord injured patients with a relatively intact musculoskeletal system show higher energy cost compared to healthy individuals while walking with an artificial control system (Massucci et al. 1998).

In summary, there are built-in mechanisms that the nervous system can and does use to save energy during the execution of locomotor patterns. The important question then is whether energy-cost considerations can fully explain locomotor patterns or whether there are other central nervous system "priorities" that may account for the observed pattern of human gait control. This question is explored in the following section.

Energy Costs Do Not Explain All Features of Locomotor Patterns

Human bipedal locomotion requires more metabolic energy than does quadrupedal locomotion for an animal of similar size at the same speed of locomotion. The energy cost for human running at a given speed is clearly higher than for a quadruped of similar size (see Taylor and Rowntree 1973). The transition from quadrupedal to bipedal locomotion, therefore, must offer humans advantages that outweigh the higher energy cost. Researchers have argued that changes in habitat from the tropical forest to the open grassland provided the impetus for change from quadrupedal to bipedal locomotion (Napier 1967). Open grassland provided new evolutionary opportunities and added dangers from predators. Napier (1967) has argued that the woodland savanna provided a transitional habitat between the tropical forest and the open grassland, where the primates could practice occasional bipedal locomotion to sample new foods, while the trees provided an escape route from predators and also supplied forest foods. He argues that the 'vertical clinging' seen in the primates, where the trunk was held vertical, was the transitional locomotor behavior from which striding habitual bipedal gait pattern emerged (Napier 1967). The freeing of the forelimbs from locomotor tasks allowed humans to carry food from one place to another for later consumption and develop tools to hunt prey at a distance. Researchers have argued that the accurate use of tools for hunting was the impetus for the development of larger brains.

It should be noted that even the allometric equation, predicting energy consumption at a given speed for animals of varying sizes, shows considerable scatter (Fedak and Seeherman 1979; Taylor et al. 1982a). For a given size animal there is almost a twofold variation in energy cost at a given speed. Researchers suggest that other factors such as "gracefulness" of certain animals may explain why they have lower energy cost than other animals of the same size (Fedak and Seeherman 1979).

Oxygen Consumption and the Selection of Speed and Form of Locomotion—Some Reservations

The pioneering studies by Taylor and his group (Hoyt and Taylor 1981) have often been cited to support the notion that energy cost plays a critical role in the expression of locomotor patterns. The fundamental thesis is that animals choose the speed of locomotion that is most cost-effective in terms of oxygen consumption, and they also choose the form of locomotion (walk, run, trot, gallop) that is most economical at a given speed. While it is hard to argue with the experimental data presented, it is worthwhile looking at this evidence in some detail.

First, the oxygen consumption curves versus speed of locomotion shown by Hoyt and Taylor (1981) do not show a unique and single minimum (see figure 2.6). The flattened U-shaped curve suggests there is more than one speed of locomotion where the oxygen consumption is similar (within measurement error). Therefore, although certain speeds of locomotion do result in lower oxygen consumption compared to other speeds, and animals generally operate in the region where the oxygen consumption is lower, this observation alone does not uniquely specify a speed of locomotion.

Second, measurement of oxygen consumption implies that anaerobic fuel is not a major factor during locomotion. This is by no means a given, particularly during running. Besides we have to recognize that oxygen consumption measure is an average over a cycle. Within a cycle of activity, there is no direct evidence that oxygen consumption is primarily fueling the muscle contraction. In cycling, for example, it is possible that during the propulsive phase (downward phase of the limb movement) the muscles are contracting and extracting fuel primarily anaerobically, and oxygen consumption represents the recovery phase (upward phase of the limb movement) of the cycle.

Third, consider the duration over which the oxygen consumption is measured. It makes intuitive sense to measure oxygen consumption while the individual is walking or running. This is precisely what is done and what is reported. But we also know that during whole-body movements such as locomotion, we incur energy debt that is repaid by the cardiorespiratory system following the cessation of activity. Anyone who is involved in sports or has even watched athletes can attest to this energy debt; individuals are often seen gulping for air following an event. Granted, when we talk about locomotion at normal speeds we are nowhere near the limits of the cardiorespiratory system to provide stable steady-state fuel aerobically. When, however, we consider running or walking at higher speeds, this energy debt cannot be discounted. Therefore, the anaerobic energy cost not accounted for by the oxygen consumption measure has to be taken into consideration; anaerobic energy cost leads to energy debt.

Fourth, efficiency of movements is implicit in the use of oxygen consumption as a measure in these studies. Minimizing oxygen consumption implies that the movement is more efficient. Oxygen consumption, despite the problems discussed above, represents only the denominator of the efficiency equation. The mechanical work output is the numerator of the equation. Mechanical work not only includes external work of moving the body center of mass from one point to another, but also internal mechanical work of moving the limbs cyclically. Since these energy cost studies generally involve individuals walking or running on a treadmill, we are not dealing with any external mechanical work (center of mass theoretically is not displaced); only internal mechanical work has to be considered in the numerator. The problem is that calculating the internal mechanical work is by no means easy, and there is no agreement among researchers on how best to account for this work (Winter 1979; Williams and Cavanagh 1983; Elftman 1939). We will return to this issue of internal mechanical work later in the chapter. For now consider the implication of only using the denominator of the efficiency equation as a determinant for locomotor patterns. One assumes that the internal mechanical work done at two different speeds of locomotion is not different; only the oxygen consumption changes. It is clear that this assumption is not tenable unless experimentally validated. One would predict, therefore, that energy cost alone would not be successful in accurately predicting specific muscle activity patterns. This prediction has indeed been shown to be true and is discussed next.

Optimization Models Do Not Predict Muscle Activity or Energy Cost

Single-cost function optimization models have been used to predict muscular activity patterns (see Pedotti, Krishnan, and Stark 1978; Penrod, Davy, and Singh 1974: Crowninshield and Brand 1981) with very limited success. Often visually compared, muscle activity patterns as revealed by electromyographic signals and muscle force predicted by the model carries out validation of the models. Crowninshield and Brand (1981) used energy cost minimization as the objective in their optimization model, but failed to predict the muscle activity patterns accurately. For example, models predict that the gluteus medius produces high muscle force during the whole of the stance phase, and yet the muscle activity is seen only during the early and late stance phase. Similarly, tibialis anterior activity during the swing phase should result in muscle force being generated, and yet the model predicts zero muscle force during midswing. It is not that the model completely fails to predict muscle activity, but that it is unable to account for all the characteristics of muscle activity. Note that in this discussion we along with the authors have focused on temporal correlation between observed muscle activity and predicted muscle force pattern. Lack of agreement between the shape of the profiles as seen may be partially accounted for by the different nonlinear EMG-to-force relationships for each muscle (Fuglevand, Winter, and Patla 1993). In summary, energy cost alone cannot account for the muscle activity patterns seen during locomotion.

Forward dynamic models of bipedal gait that use the energy optimization to predict the speed and form of locomotion, while predicting the general trend observed in the experimental data, greatly underestimate the energy cost of locomotion (Minetti and Alexander 1997). The authors state that the simulation results suggest "that the gaits we use may be a little different from those that would minimize energy expenditure."

More recently, Draganich et al. attempted to use energy optimization to explain locomotion over obstacles, but they were unsuccessful in matching the trajectory predicted by the model to the measured limb trajectory. This result was not surprising to us, because in contrast to normal level-ground locomotion when the ground clearance is relatively small (minimum less than 1 cm), toe clearance over an obstacle is on the average 10 cm (Patla and Rietdyk 1993). If energy cost were a critical constraint, the nervous system would be expected to reduce clearance, thereby lowering the energy needed to elevate the swing limb. As we have discussed, safety and not energy cost is more important during adaptive locomotion. An important point, however, is that although limb elevation is not constrained to reduce energy cost, limb elevation is achieved in the most energy-efficient way (Patla and Prentice 1995; Armand et al. 1997).

Travel Paths Chosen Between Two Locations Are Not Always the Shortest Paths

Our discussion so far has been restricted to local features of the locomotor pattern as revealed in the changing structure of the step cycle. Since locomotion involves repetition of this basic pattern, the assumption is that if the step cycle is efficient then travel from one location to another will also be efficient for metabolic energy expenditure. Recently researchers have looked at the evolution of human trail systems albeit on a small scale (Helbing et al. 1997). They examined the paths created in open green areas between buildings on a university campus. They found that the trails developed by everyday users were not the shortest route between two buildings. Thus, energy cost for travel between two buildings had not been minimized; they argued that the trails chosen were "more comfortable." Trails formed by passage of other individuals ensure that the ground affords locomotion, and therefore provide a sense of security.

This lack of correspondence between user preferences and the most direct route is, perhaps, not surprising. Anyone who has visited man-made or natural monuments such as the Mayan pyramids or Ayres Rock has witnessed a well-worn travel path created by other travelers that new visitors use. The paths created are not necessarily the shortest between two points; therefore, the energy cost would be higher simply based on the increased distance traveled. Researchers have argued that this behavior of following in other people's footprints is molded by evolution to ensure survival. Taking the paths traveled by others ensures that terrain traveled will support the individual; other paths may contain terrain that may be unstable or contain predators. It is, therefore, safer to travel the well-trodden paths.

Maintenance of Dynamic Stability

Quadrupedal locomotion is inherently stable with the wide base of support afforded by three limbs at any given time. This makes it relatively easy to ensure that the system is statically stable at all times (Ting, Blickhan, and Full 1994). Static stability implies that the position of the center of mass is within the base of support and the velocity of the center of mass is low so that it can be ignored. These requirements are satisfied in quadrupedal gait, while, in contrast, bipedal locomotion is statically unstable for the majority of the stride cycle (Winter 1991) because the body center of mass is outside the base of support (as defined by the feet) 80% of the time. Therefore, stability considerations are considerably more challenging. Because we are dealing with dynamic stability, we have to consider both the displacement and velocity of the body center of mass. It is not surprising that considerable resources of the sensorimotor system are devoted to the maintenance of dynamic stability. Structural evolutionary changes in musculoskeletal system have ensured that the large body mass of the trunk can be controlled both in the pitch and roll planes (Lovejoy 1988).

Consider the muscle activity patterns that can be directly attributed to the control of dynamic stability during locomotion. First the hip extensors and flexors during the stance phase provide control of trunk pitch motion (Winter 1991). The muscles around the knee joint fight gravity and prevent collapse. The hip abductors/adductors provide control of the trunk roll motion and through foot placement control the body center of mass in the mediolateral plane. The activation of the hamstring at the end of the swing phase provides deceleration of the lower leg, resulting in the lower foot contact velocity critical for slip avoidance. The activation of the tibialis anterior in the early swing phase ensures adequate ground clearance critical for trip avoidance, while activation later in the swing phase ensures proper foot position for stable landing. The trunk musculature dampens the acceleration felt by the head as a result of the hip acceleration and deceleration, ensuring a stable platform for the visual and vestibular systems. This cast of roles of muscle activity during a step cycle shows the tremendous influence of dynamic stability on locomotor patterns. Energy considerations have to take a back seat to the more urgent requirement of a stable and safe locomotor pattern.

So far, our discussion has focused on the maintenance of external stability to ensure that we do not fall as we move in our environment. Internal stability is equally important. The forces used during locomotion will put stress on various tissues. It is desirable that these forces do not damage the locomotor apparatus. Here the structural properties of various tissues play an important role in the expression of the locomotor patterns. For example, bones are able to withstand large compressive forces but are more susceptible to bending stress (Biewener 1990). Thus co-contraction that increases compressive stress and energy cost is preferred during locomotion, because it minimizes the bending moments on the bones (Winter and Scott 1993).

Conclusion—Multiple Objectives Are Optimized During Locomotion

This brings us to the central message of this chapter—that locomotor patterns emerge from competing demands of several objectives rather than the sole objective of minimizing metabolic energy cost. Optimization studies, which have used a single objective function to predict locomotion patterns have, not surprisingly, failed (Pedotti, Krishnan, and Stark 1978; Chow and Jacobson 1971: Crowninshield and Brand 1981; Collins 1995). No models have in the past used multiple objective optimization to predict locomotor patterns. Recently Patla and his colleagues have, however, focused on modeling the swing limb motion over obstacles (Armand, Huission, and Patla 1998).

We have used multiple objectives that included toe clearance (energy cost), stable landing (dynamic stability), and adequate stride length (stability and energy cost) to predict a set of control inputs that could generate the swing limb trajectory. The control inputs were the initial conditions at the end of the stance phase and activation of biarticular muscles during the swing phase. One of the key results is summarized in figure 2.7. When the control system optimizes only the energy cost (toe clearance and the location of the maximum toe elevation), the simulations show that the swing (trail) limb is able to step over the obstacle successfully. The landing is, however, severely compromised because the center of mass is ahead of the foot at landing and this is clearly undesirable. The simulations show a successful step over the obstacle only when the

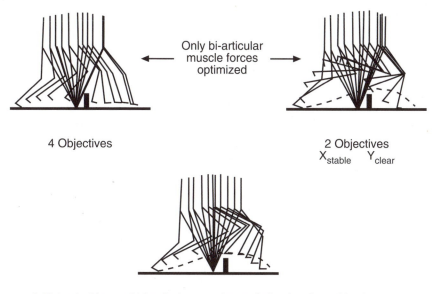

Initial velocities and bi-articular muscles optimized — four objectives

Figure 2.7   Results from multiobjective optimization on the limb trajectory over obstacles (Armand et al. 1998).

control system satisfies both energy-cost objectives and stability objectives. Similar results were seen for the lead limb.

What this first attempt showed us is that observed experimental patterns are needed to satisfy the different objectives during the swing phase. If the number of objectives to be satisfied are varied, the control inputs change along with the observed movement patterns. Therefore, accurate prediction of human locomotor patterns demand that the central nervous system consider more than one objective in its plan.

Future Research

Skilled locomotor behavior is critical for survival and has been shaped by evolutionary pressures. The challenge facing researchers is to uncover what is it that the nervous system tries to optimize. It is clear that a single objective does not explain the many unique features of bipedal locomotor behavior. More than likely, depending on the task, there is probably a continuous trade-off among competing objectives. Also, the time scale over which the objectives operate may vary; what is important for the long-term survival of the locomotor apparatus may be sacrificed in the short term. New experimental paradigms exploring locomotion over different terrains, combined with improved measures and analytical models, will be needed as we journey along this important research avenue.

Acknowledgments

Financial support by NSERC and MRC Canada are gratefully acknowledged.

References

Alexander, R. McN. 1982. Simple models of the mechanics of walking in neural prostheses. In R.B. Stein, P.H. Peckham, and D.P. Popovic, 191-201. London: Oxford University Press.

Alexander, R. McN. 1989. Optimization and gaits in the locomotion of vertebrates. *Physiological Reviews* 69: 1199-1227.

Alexander, R. McN. 1990. Three uses for springs in legged locomotion. *The International Journal of Robotics Research* 9: 53-61.

Alexander, R. McN., and H.C. Bennet-Clark. 1977. Storage of elastic strain energy in muscle and other tissues. *Nature* 265: 114-117.

Armand, M., J.P. Huissoon, and A.E. Patla. 1998. Stepping over obstacles during locomotion: Insights from multiobjective optimization on set of input parameters. *IEEE Transactions on Rehabilitation Engineering* 6: 43-52.

Armand, M., A.E. Patla, and J. Huissoon. 1994. Modelling of human swing leg motion during locomotion. *Proceedings of the 18th Biennial Conference of the Canadian Society of Biomechanics*, 94-95. Calgary, Canada.

Batty, M. 1997. Predicting where we walk. *Nature* 388: 19-20.

Bernstein, N.A. 1967. *The coordination and regulation of movements*. London: Pergamon Press.

Biewener, A.A. 1990. Biomechanics of mammalian terrestrial locomotion. *Science* 250: 1097-1103.

Carrier, D.R., N.C. Heglund, and K.D. Earls. 1994. Variable gearing during locomotion in the human musculoskeletal system. *Science* 265: 651-653.

Cavagna, G.A., N.C. Heglund, and C.R. Taylor. 1977. Mechanical work in terrestrial locomotion: two basic mechanisms for minimizing energy expenditure. *American Journal of Physiology* 233: R243-R261.

Cavagna, G.A., and P.R. Margaria. 1983. A model for the calculation of mechanical power during distance running. *Journal of Biomechanics* 15: 115-128.

Cavanagh, P.R., and K.R. Williams. 1982. The effect of stride length variation on oxygen uptake during distance running. *Medicine and Science in Sports and Exercise* 14: 30-35.

Chou, L., L.F. Draganich, and S.M. Song. 1997. Minimum energy trajectories of the swing ankle when stepping over obstacles of different heights. *Journal of Biomechanics* 30: 115-120.

Chow, C.K., and D.H. Jacobson. 1971. Studies of human locomotion via optimal programming. *Mathematical Biosciences* 19: 239-306.

Collins, J. 1995. Redundant nature of locomotor optimization laws. *Journal of Biomechanics* 28: 251-267.

Corlett, J. 1992. The role of vision in the planning and guidance of locomotion through the environment. In *Vision and Motor Control*, eds. L. Proteau and D. Elliott, 375-397. Elsevier Science.

Crowninshield, R.D., and R.A. Brand. 1981. A physiologically based criterion of muscle force prediction in locomotion. *Journal of Biomechanics* 14: 793-801.

Dagg, A.I. 1977. *Running, Walking and Jumping: the science of locomotion*. London: Wykeham.

Diedrich, F.J., and W.H. Warren Jr. 1995. Why change gaits? Dynamics of the walk-run transition. *Journal of Experimental Psychology: Human Perception and Performance* 21: 183-202.

Dunbar, D.C., and G.L. Badam. 1998. Development of posture and locomotion in free-ranging primates. *Neuroscience and Biobehavioral Reviews* 22: 541-546.

Elftman, H. 1939. Forces and energy changes in the leg during walking. *American Journal of Physiology* 125: 339-356.

Fedak, M.A., N.C. Heglund, and C.R. Taylor. 1982. Energetics and mechanics of terrestrial locomotion. *Journal of Experimental Biology* 79: 23-40.

Fedak, M.A., and H.J. Seeherman. 1979. Reappraisal of energetics of locomotion shows identical cost in bipeds and quadrupeds including ostrich and horse. *Nature* 282: 713-716.

Fuglevand, A.J., D.A. Winter, and A.E. Patla. 1993. Models of recruitment and rate coding organization in motor unit pools. *Journal of Biomechanics* 70: 2470-2488.

Gribble, P.L., D.J. Ostry, V. Sanguineti, and R. Laboissiere. 1998. Are complex control signals required for human arm movement? *Journal of Neurophysiology* 79: 1409-1424.

Heglund, N.C., G.A. Cavagna, and C.R. Taylor. 1982. Energetics and Mechanics of Terrestrial Locomotion. *Journal of Experimental Biology* 79: 41-56.

Heglund, N.C., M.A. Fedak, C.R. Taylor, and G.A. Cavagna. 1982. Energetics and mechanics of terrestrial locomotion. *Journal of Experimental Biology* 79: 57-66.

Helbing, D., J. Keitsch, and P. Molnár. 1997. Modelling the evolution of human trail systems. *Nature* 388: 47-50.

Hill, A.V. 1950. The dimensions of animals and their muscular dynamics. *Science Progress* 38: 209-230.

Hoyt, D.F., and C.R. Taylor. 1981. Gait and the energetics of locomotion in horses. *Nature* 292: 239-240.

Lovejoy, C.O. 1988. Evolution of human walking. *Scientific American* 259: 118-125.

Massucci, M., G. Brunetti, R. Piperno, L. Betti, and M. Franceschini. 1998. Walking with the advanced reciprocating gait orthosis (ARGO) in thoracic paraplegic patients: energy expenditure and cardiorespiratory performance. *Spinal Cord* 36: 223-227.

McGeer, T. 1990. Passive dynamic walking. *International Journal of Robotics Research* 9: 62-82.

Minetti, A.E., and R. McN. Alexander. 1997. A theory of metabolic costs for bipedal gaits. *Journal of Theoretical Biology* 186: 467-476.

Mochon, S., and T.A. McMahon. 1980. Ballistic walking. *Journal of Biomechanics* 13: 49-57.

Mochon, S., and T.A. McMahon. 1981. Ballistic walking: an improved model. *Journal of Mathematical Biosciences* 52: 241-260.

Napier, J. 1967. The Antiquity of Human Walking. *Scientific American* 217: 50-60.

Patla, A.E. 1997. Understanding the roles of vision in the control of human locomotion. *Gait and Posture* 5: 54-69.

Patla, A.E., and S.D. Prentice. 1995. The role of active forces and intersegmental dynamics in the control of limb trajectory over obstacles during locomotion in humans. *Experimental Brain Research* 106: 499-504.

Patla, A.E., and S. Rietdyk. 1993. Visual control of limb trajectory over obstacles during locomotion: effect of obstacle height and width. *Gait and Posture* 1: 45-60.

Pedotti, A., V.V. Krishnan, and L. Stark. 1978. Optimization of muscle-force sequencing in human locomotion. *Mathematical Biosciences* 38: 57-76.

Pennisi, E. 1997. A new view of how leg muscles operate on the run. *Science* 275: 1067-1068.

Penrod, D.A., D.T.O. Davy, and D.P. Singh. 1974. An optimization approach to tendon force analysis. *Journal of Biomechanics* 7: 123-129.

Quanbury, A.O., and G.D. Reimer. 1976. Analysis of instantaneous energy of normal gait. *Journal of Biomechanics* 9: 253-257.

Roberts, T.J., R.L. Marsh, P.G. Weyand, and C.R. Taylor. 1997. Muscular force in running turkeys: the economy of minimizing work. *Science* 275: 1113-1115.

Rosenbaum, D.A., L.D. Loukopoulos, R.G.J. Meulenbroek, J. Vaughan, and S.E. Engelbrecht. 1995. Planning reaches by evaluating stored postures. *Psychological Review* 102: 28-67.

Schmidt-Nielsen, K. Scaling in biology: the consequences of size. *Journal of Experimental Zoology* 194: 287-308.

Schmidt-Nielsen, K. 1972. Locomotion: energy cost of swimming, flying, and running. *Science* 177: 222-227.

Scott, W.H., and D.A. Winter. 1990. Internal forces at chronic running injury sites. *Medicine and Science in Sports and Exercise* 22: 357-369.

Sparrow, W.A., and K.M. Newell. 1994. Energy expenditure and motor performance relationships in humans learning a motor task. *Psychophysiology* 31: 338-346.

Taylor, C.R., N.C. Heglund, and G.M.O. Malloy. 1982. Energetics and mechanics of terrestrial locomotion. I. Metabolic energy consumption as a function of speed and body size in birds and mammals. *Journal of Experimental Biology* 97: 1-21.

Taylor, C.R., and V.J. Rowntree. 1973. Running on two or four legs: which consumes more energy? *Science* 179: 186-187.

Ting, L.H., R. Blickhan, and R.J. Full. 1994. Dynamic and static stability in hexapedal runners. *Journal of Experimental Biology* 197: 251-269.

van Ingen Schenau, G.J., M.F. Bobbert, and A. de Haan. 1997. Does elastic energy enhance work and efficiency in the stretch-shortening cycle? *Journal of Applied Biomechanics* 13: 389-415.

Warren, W.H. Jr. 1984. Perceiving affordances: visual guidance of stair climbing. *Journal of Experimental Psychology: Human Perception and Performance* 10: 683-703.

Williams, K.R., and P.R. Cavanagh. 1983. A model for the calculation of mechanical power during distance running. *Journal of Biomechanics* 15: 115-128.

Winter, D.A. 1978. Energy assessments in pathological gait. *Physiotherapy Canada* 30: 183-191.

Winter, D.A. 1979. A new definition of mechanical work done in human movement. *Journal of Applied Physiology* 46: 79-83.

Winter, D.A. 1991. *The biomechanics and motor control of human gait: normal, elderly and pathological.* Waterloo, Canada: University of Waterloo Press.

Winter, D.A., A.O. Quanbury, and G.D. Reiner. 1976. Analysis of instantaneous energy of normal gait. *Journal of Biomechanics* 9: 253-257.

Winter, D.A., and D.G.E. Robertson. 1978. Joint torque and energy patterns in normal gait. *Biological Cybernetics* 29: 137-142.

Young, R.P., S.H. Scott, and G.E. Loeb. 1992. An intrinsic mechanism to stabilize posture: joint-angle-dependent moment arms of the feline ankle muscles. *Neuroscience Letters* 145: 137-140.

Zajac, F.E., and M.E. Gordon. 1989. Determining muscles' force and action in multiarticular movement. *Exercise and Sport Sciences Reviews* 17: 187-230.

Zernicke, R.F., and J.L. Smith. 1996. Biomechanical insights into neural control of movement. In *Handbook of Physiology,* ed., 293-330.

3

Movement Proficiency: Incorporating Task Demands and Constraints in Assessing Human Movement

Graham E. Caldwell, Richard E.A. van Emmerik, and Joseph Hamill
Department of Exercise Science, University of Massachusetts, United States

Over the past three decades, movement scientists have applied the concept of "mechanical efficiency" to human performance in an effort to categorize skill level. "Efficiency" is a term borrowed from the world of mechanical systems and is defined as unit work output per unit energy cost. While efficiency is a useful method of comparing refrigerators or furnaces, its use in describing human motion has been less successful. Norman et al. (1976) illustrated the interpretative problems with efficiency calculations in their study on treadmill running. Metabolic and kinematic measurements were taken on three subjects running at the same speed and were used to calculate mechanical work output, metabolic cost, and mechanical efficiency. Runner A had a greater efficiency value than runner C, who was characterized by relatively low mechanical work output. One might conclude that runner A, with higher work output and efficiency values, was a more skilled runner than runner C. However, another interpretation could be that runner C was able to run at the same speed as runner A while performing less mechanical work, and that perhaps runner C was more skilled. Another shortcoming of using efficiency as an index of skill is apparent in this example; single efficiency or mechanical work 'scores' give us very little information regarding the actual performance itself and offer little insight as to the strengths and weaknesses of either runners' movement technique. In other words, the efficiency value does not suggest *how* the limb movements are controlled and coordinated to achieve an effective or 'efficient' performance. For movement scientists, knowledge of how one successfully performs a skilled motion is critical.

In the preface to this book, it was stated that "economical movements are those that meet the task demands with relatively low metabolic energy expenditure." In our view, the emphasis in this statement should be on task demands, which are inherently important in defining successful performance of any action. The emphasis on task demands necessitates that one explicitly recognizes important aspects of a particular movement performance. The recognition of these performance criteria is crucial before we can assess how effectively a given individual succeeds in meeting task demands. It is clear that a single value of a performance measure, such as mechanical efficiency or economy (a physiological measure of 'efficient' technique), is lacking in this regard. In this chapter we will focus our attention on the integration of task demands and constraints, and their role in shaping adaptive movement patterns. In our view, the skillfulness of a performance must be considered in light of the constraints that bound possible movement solutions. These constraints arise from both internal (performer-specific) and external (environmental- and task-specific) considerations of any given movement situation (Newell 1986).

In a task such as running, for example, let us consider the task demands and constraints faced by the individual performer. Although the basic running stride is used in all competitive races, the constraints that affect performance change greatly with different running events. In the 100 m track event, an individual's aerobic metabolic capacity is of little concern, while at longer distances such as 1500 m, the aerobic capability of the runner is of paramount importance. At intermediate distances, the metabolic system will constrain the performance to some extent, but at what distance does the aerobic metabolic system become unimportant? While sprinters and long distance runners do not use exactly the same running technique, to what extent does the metabolic demand overtly affect the choice one makes in choosing this technique? An alternative explanation for differences in technique between sprinters and distance runners is that the running velocity dictates the chosen technique. Another aspect of the running problem is apparent in cross-country events, where the uneven terrain adds a new constraint to the basic running motion. Under these conditions, external stability demands might be critical in establishing a certain running style or coordination pattern. It is apparent that running in different situations includes different environmental and metabolic constraints on the human system, yet the basic form of the running pattern is similar in all events (i.e., two alternating single-stance phases separated by a flight phase).

These different running scenarios exemplify the notion of task constraints put forth earlier by Newell (1986), who proposed three categories of constraint that interact to determine optimal patterns of coordination. These categories are organismic, environmental, and task constraints. Organismic constraints can be relatively time independent (such as body height, weight, or shape) or time dependent (such as changes in synaptic connections). Environmental constraints are external to the organism generally, can be either time independent (e.g., gravity) or change relatively quickly (e.g., temperature, wind, humidity), and are not manipulated by the experimenter. Finally, task constraints specify more specific goals, rules on response dynamics, and particular implements or machines that can constrain the response dynamics. It is clear from the above distinction that 'optimality' in movement is the result of the confluence of these three sources of constraint. An important consideration in many actions is the identification of the optimality criterion the performer is seeking.

In a paper on mechanical work in human locomotion, Caldwell and Forrester (1992) suggested the term "proficiency" as an alternative to the calculation of efficiency. In their view proficiency was a term directly related to task goals, and would be measured using variables that reflected the performer's ability to attain those task goals. Of central importance to the proficiency concept was the coordinated action of muscle force production and limb segmental motions. This approach addresses the issue of how an individual performs a successful movement pattern, a shortfall of the single value efficiency calculation. In the Caldwell and Forrester study, mechanical work, power production, and energy transfer mechanisms were used to discuss proficiency in walking and running. In this chapter, we will discuss proficiency and coordination from several different viewpoints, drawing on examples from both sporting and clinical situations, in an attempt to point out the importance of including task demands and constraints in any assessment of movement performance. The tools for such analyses are varied and range from traditional Newtonian mechanics to more contemporary dynamical systems theories. We will begin with a section on movement economy and efficiency, followed by a more detailed examination of movement proficiency. Our focus will then shift to the dynamical systems perspective of movement control, its contributions to the understanding of movement and task constraints, and the notion of system stability and variability with regard to energetics.

Movement Economy and Efficiency

The terms "economy" and "efficiency" are often used interchangeably, as if they represent the same concepts. However, this is not the case, as economy is a physiological measure that refers to the metabolic cost of a performance. It is obtained indirectly by measuring oxygen consumption ($\dot{V}O_2$). Economy is usually defined as the steady-state rate of oxygen consumption for a given submaximal effort. For example, Costill (1970) presented data on two runners with comparable values for $\dot{V}O_2$max. During submaximal runs, however, one runner consistently used less oxygen than the other. Clearly, while the $\dot{V}O_2$max values were the same, their energy requirements were different and this difference was attributed to a greater running efficiency. It may be surmised that "running" efficiency refers to mechanical efficiency. However, in this paper mechanical efficiency was not quantified.

Any discussion of the efficiency concept should begin at the level of the muscle, for it is the direct link between the metabolic and mechanical systems. The processes which result in the conversion of chemical energy to mechanical energy in the muscle are complex and are dictated by the laws of thermodynamics. While the scope of the present chapter precludes a detailed discussion of this energy conversion, a basic understanding can be gained by considering that there are two main steps involved. The first involves the conversion of chemical energy within food substrates into ATP (known as *phosphorylative coupling*), and the second the conversion of ATP into mechanical energy and force (*contraction coupling*). The phosphorylative coupling efficiency has been estimated at 60%, while the contraction coupling efficiency is thought to be about 40% (van Ingen Schenau, Bobbert, and de Haan 1997). This leads to a muscular efficiency value of approximately 25%, although this figure is not universally accepted (van Ingen Schenau, Bobbert, and de Haan). It should be noted that any value of whole-body mechanical efficiency in a particular movement would include the efficiency of these muscular processes.

In order to calculate efficiency of the whole body, two measures are required: energy input and energy output. In terms of human motion, efficiency is the ratio of mechanical work done to metabolic work expended, usually expressed as a percentage:

$$\% \text{ efficiency} = \frac{\text{Mechanical work done by muscles}}{\text{Metabolic cost of work done by muscles}} \times 100$$

There are a number of measures of mechanical and physiological work used in the calculation of efficiency, and thus it is difficult to compare efficiency values across studies. The major drawback in using this term is that the calculations of both the numerator and denominator of the above equation are flawed and often misunderstood.

The denominator of this ratio should be calculated from the caloric equivalent of $\dot{V}O_2$ using the nonprotein respiratory exchange ratio. However, oftentimes a conversion factor of 5 kCal $\cdot$ 1^{-1} oxygen consumed is used as a constant in this calculation. The energy expenditure calculated using this procedure represents the energy cost of the entire body and not necessarily the cost of skeletal muscle contractions only. This method is usually referred to as the gross metabolic cost, because it measures the metabolic cost of the total body and does not isolate the energy cost of the muscles doing work. Several different methods have been used to determine the metabolic cost of specific tasks (Donovan and Brooks 1977; Stainsby et al. 1980). Generally, these methods consist of some baseline subtraction from the gross measure of $\dot{V}O_2$. For example, another measure is called the net metabolic cost and is determined by subtracting a baseline resting metabolic measurement from the gross measure of $\dot{V}O_2$.

Using gross metabolic cost in an efficiency calculation would seem to overestimate the oxygen cost of performing the measured mechanical work and thus underestimate the resulting efficiency. Thus, it would appear that the net metabolic cost (gross metabolic cost – resting cost) is one method that would be effective in most calculations of efficiency. However, net metabolic cost is the increase in metabolism due to exercise and is not necessarily related to mechanical work. Increased muscular activity because of muscular co-contraction or stabilization functions would not be reflected in an increase in mechanical work. Thus, there appears to be little that can be done to partition out the work done solely by muscles accomplishing the mechanical work. Net metabolic cost is probably an overestimate of the actual muscular cost of accomplishing the task. The net metabolic cost therefore relates more to exercise efficiency than to mechanical efficiency.

It is the evaluation of the numerator of the efficiency calculation that has sparked the most controversy. Cavagna, Saibene, and Margarla (1963, 1964) used a point-mass model, that is, the whole-body center of mass, to represent the total body mechanical energy in an evaluation of the external sources of work in walking and running. The potential and kinetic energies of the center of mass were calculated, and the total mechanical energy or external work was defined as the sum of the forward speed changes and those due to vertical displacements. By summing the kinetic and potential energies, Cavagna (1964) acknowledged the possibility of exchanges between energy components. However, work is done to move the limbs during locomotion, and the internal mechanical work associated with moving the limbs was not included in these studies. The most common criticism of Cavagna and his associates' work is, therefore, their assumption that total body energy could be represented by the motion of the center of mass.

Mechanical work is acknowledged to consist of internal work, which is this work done to move the body segments, and external work by the body on an object (Winter 1979). External work is relatively easy to measure. For example, on a cycle ergometer the external resistance may be set; this constitutes the external work done by the body. External work is the product of the resistance setting in units of force and the distance over which that force was applied. In locomotion, external work is done when the subject does graded walking or running. In this case, external work is the product of the gravitational force (body weight) and the distance over which the body is raised. In uphill walking or running positive external work is done, while in downhill walking or running negative external work is performed. However, in level locomotion situations, no external work is done. This has led authors of level walking and running studies to use an estimate of internal work to quantify the mechanical work, and it is this area of internal work in which the calculation problems lie.

Several researchers have proposed methods of calculating internal work based on the calculation of the kinetic, potential, and rotational energies of the segments that were then summed to give a total body energy (for example, Norman et al. 1976, and Winter 1978, 1979). For example, total segment energy was calculated as:

$$TE_{segment} = KE + PE + RKE$$

where $KE = 1/2mv^2$, $PE = mgh$ and $RKE = 1/2\ I\ \omega^2$. Depending on whether or not the absolute or algebraic values of the individual energies are summed, transfer between energy sources was considered or not considered. Similarly, the segment energies were summed in one of two ways: to allow transfer of energy between segments (algebraically) or to allow no transfer (summing absolute values). Winter (1979) acknowledged that energy may be transferred between and within a segment, while Norman and associates did not. A further criticism of Norman and associates' work was that they equated positive and negative work. The metabolic cost of positive and negative work is not the same. The oxygen cost of doing positive work, that is, the mechanical work done by a muscle as it shortens under tension, is greater than when doing negative work. In fact, it has been shown that negative work costs approximately 1/3 that of positive work (Nagle, Balke, and Naughton 1965). Critical reviews of the various methods for calculating total-body mechanical work have been provided by Aleshinsky (1986d) and Caldwell and Forrester (1992).

One common criticism from Aleshinsky (1986d) and Caldwell and Forrester (1992) was that many estimates of work do not account for all possible sources of mechanical energy. For example, the elastic energy stored in passive tissues, the motion of segmental endpoints relative to the segment center of mass, and the transfer of energy through multi-articular muscles are often neglected. It is clear that the estimation of the mechanical work done must include all types of work done including the movement of the body segments (both positive and negative work), the exchange of energy both within and between segments, and the storage and reutilization of elastic energy. Williams and Cavanagh (1983) proposed a mechanical power model for running that incorporated coefficients to account for the factors identified above. The general equation that they proposed for calculating total body energy took the following form:

$$PTOT = (1 - a_i)\ (1 - b_j)\ TPOS + \frac{(c_k)TNEG}{d_l}$$

where TPOS = total positive energy; TNEG = total negative energy; a_i =

fraction of TPOS due to between segment energy transfer; b_j = fraction of TPOS due to elastic storage of energy; c_k = fraction of TNEG resulting from eccentric muscle contraction; and d_l = relative metabolic cost of negative to positive muscular power. Systematic variation of the coefficients resulted in efficiency values ranging from 31% to 197%. The authors concluded that more research was needed before confidence in mechanical power measures could be established because of the wide range of their efficiency values and the fact that some of the efficiency values were unrealistic.

Another calculation of mechanical work is often referred to as the mechanical power method. This involves the calculation of the net muscle moment and joint reaction forces using a rigid link analysis, for example, that requires anthropometric, kinematic, and kinetic data. The work done at a joint by muscles is calculated as the time integral of power:

$$W_m = \int M \, \omega \, dt$$

where M = net muscle moment and ω is the joint angular velocity. The transfer of energy through the joint center is evaluated by:

$$W_j = \int Fv \, dt$$

where F = joint reaction force and v = absolute velocity of the joint center. The total work done is simply the sum of these values for all joints. Equating the time derivative of segmental energy and the sum of all joint and muscle powers creates a link between the mechanical energy and mechanical power techniques (Robertson and Winter 1980).

The previous calculation was the basis of arguably the most complete analysis of segment energy proposed by Aleshinsky (1986a-e). He expanded the previous calculations, adding terms that explained sources of energy that were omitted from most other calculations of mechanical work. Aleshinsky's expanded model included work terms associated with the difference in velocity between the segment endpoints and the segmental center of mass as a result of the rotation of the segment. In the mechanical power model suggested by Robertson and Winter (1980), there were six power terms per segment, while Aleshinsky's model added an additional five terms. Aleshinsky's method was used in a study by Caldwell and Forrester (1992), who investigated the nonsupport phase of the lower extremity during walking and running. The papers by Aleshinsky (1986a-e) and Caldwell and Forrester demonstrated unequivocally therefore that mechanical work values calculated from energy models are not representative of actual mechanical work being done.

Unfortunately, efficiency is one of the most misused terms in the biomechanics and physiology literature. There is still considerable confusion as to what it means. Both the estimates of work in the numerator and the denominator are flawed in that they really do not measure either energy input or work output. Some of the efficiency calculations result in percent values greater than 100% (Williams and Cavanagh 1983) and some result in negative efficiency values (Gaesser and Brooks 1975), both of which are not theoretically possible and violate the laws of thermodynamics. Comparison of efficiency values across studies is, therefore, a tedious and often fruitless endeavor; it is safe to conclude, however, that it is not correct to assume that efficiency is simply a measure of how well the system converts biochemical energy into mechanical energy.

Movement Proficiency

One of the most common techniques for the study of human movement is the application of principles from Newtonian physics. In this approach a link is made between observed movements and underlying external and internal forces that are responsible for generating these motions. As described in the mechanical power model, it is possible to calculate the resultant forces and moments acting at individual joints of the body using a rigid link inverse dynamics approach. From these calculations, time series plots that detail the changes in segmental motion (kinematics) and forces (kinetics) may be constructed. This approach has been used to study coordination of segmental kinematics and kinetics in many different movement sequences (e.g., Bresler and Frankel 1950; Enoka 1988; Robertson and Winter 1980). By itself, the inverse dynamics approach is a useful tool for the description of motion patterns and for understanding the underlying forces behind these motions.

To gain maximum understanding of a movement performance, the results from inverse dynamics or any other type of analysis must be framed within the context of the motion being performed. Aside from the details of a specific individual's motion, the researcher must understand the goal of the desired movement in terms of the same Newtonian mechanics. For example, in a maximal effort standing vertical jump, the goal is to propel one's center of mass as high as possible. This performance goal must be achieved within certain constraints; in this case a major constraint is that the subject must start from a static position and is unable to generate useful mechanical energy through running prior to takeoff. Other constraints may be added by the researcher for experimental control; perhaps the motion must start from a certain position, with the arms held across the chest. However, vertical jumping demands a rather specific movement pattern, and such a simple statement of the performance goal is not easily accomplished in other more complex or less constrained movement patterns. For example, while many studies have speculated on the performance goal in human locomotion (Hardt 1978; Dul et al. 1984; Crowninshield and Brand 1981), it is unknown at this time exactly what goal or goals are sought by the human organism. It is possible to predict muscular forces associated with various movement criteria such as minimal energy expenditure, minimal muscular stress, or minimal joint torque, yet none of these criteria are entirely successful in correctly identifying active muscles (Collins 1995). In a later section on dynamical systems aspects, we will return to a discussion on possible optimality criteria in human locomotion.

When viewed in this light, it is clear that the effectiveness of a performance is not necessarily clearly assessed using the concepts of mechanical efficiency or economy. Efficiency calculations, irrespective of the problems noted in the previous section, deal strictly with mechanical work output as a function of metabolic cost, without telling the researcher if the mechanical work performed was useful to the completion of task goals. How would the calculation of mechanical efficiency help one to understand vertical jumping? Is the highest jumper necessarily the most efficient? In light of these considerations, the concept of mechanical proficiency has been suggested, in which the segmental motion of an individual is assessed in terms of its ability to contribute to successful completion of movement goals (Caldwell and Forrester 1992). This concept relies on several different analysis steps, which can be roughly described as follows:

1. **Identify the movement goal(s).** As outlined above, the goal of some movement sequences is unclear, and often a motion will be constrained by several independent and possibly conflicting objectives. To move beyond a mere description of the motion to understanding whether an individual's technique is "good," one must come to some level of comprehension concerning these movement tasks. But how does one gain this comprehension? In specific movement situations, the mechanics may dictate the objective so clearly that the goal is unequivocal (such as in the vertical jump). In more broadly defined motions such as locomotion the objectives are not as clear, making the identification of a movement goal difficult. Saltzman and Kelso (1987) have stressed the importance of defining movement goals in terms other than only mechanical. In their view, behavior of an effector system is controlled by a task-specific patterning of the system's dynamic variables (such as stiffness, damping, etc.). This so-called task-dynamic approach may be fruitful in identifying underlying movement goals not apparent using traditional Newtonian physics.

2. **Identify mechanical correlates of these goals.** Often the movement goal identified in step 1 must be reformulated into more specific mechanical terms. For example, the general goal in maximal effort vertical jumping is to attain the highest possible height for the body's center of mass (CM). However, because the body's airborne motion is projectile in nature, it is instructive to restate this objective as attainment of the highest possible CM vertical velocity at takeoff. This form of the goal focuses our attention on movement patterns during the jumping push-off that contribute to vertical velocity at takeoff. Which characteristics of the jump push-off contribute to the takeoff vertical velocity? Which push-off characteristics do not contribute to velocity and are

therefore unimportant features? Such reformulation of the mechanical goal of the jump would also lead one to study the important kinetic parameters that could influence takeoff velocity (i.e., generation of mechanical impulse on the ground prior to takeoff).

3. **Identify segmental movement patterns capable of fulfilling these goals.** The question now focuses on how the performer can attain the stated mechanical objective. In this light it is important to consider the biological nature of the human system. The inherent properties of the neuromuscular system will dictate the ability to produce the required movement objective and therefore the performer's level of skill. The metabolic system is another constraint in that it must supply the neuromuscular system with as much energy as is required. In some activities this metabolic constraint may dictate the form of the movement solution, while in others it may play a reduced role. In all movements the system will be constrained by both internal and external factors that ultimately shape the form of the movement patterns and the subsequent level of success in achieving the performance goal.

4. **Identify analysis techniques that will allow evaluation of how well the critical movement patterns are performed.** After identifying what the performer is attempting to do, and the critical parameters that will shape the degree of success, the researcher must decide upon the best set of tools to assess the performance. Due to the wide range of possible movement goals, not all performances will lend themselves to analysis using the same tools. Success can be achieved using kinematic, kinetic, or muscular variables, using either standard biomechanical techniques or dynamical systems analysis.

This approach is powerful because it marries a theoretical understanding of the motion being studied (steps 1 and 2) with experimental data analysis of specific movement performances (steps 3 and 4). It encourages modeling the movement on several levels and is not restrictive in that it does not explicitly define the required analysis tools. Indeed, with the many different types of movements and constraints found within the field of human movement research, it is expected that various movement goals are to be found and that various data analysis tools are needed to assess skillful performance. This should not, however, encourage researchers to use a "scatter-gun" approach by analyzing data sets in as many ways as possible. In contrast, the first two steps encourage scientists to use their experience and insight to understand the motion as much as possible before collecting or analyzing the data with any specific approach. In the following sections we will illustrate briefly the use of different types of variables (kinematic, kinetic, and muscular) in the search for proficiency. In each case the reader should note the tight link between theoretical background and the subsequent movement analysis. These brief examples will be followed by a lengthier example drawn from recent work in our laboratory on cycling.

Kinematic Analyses

Vertical jumping performance has been studied extensively, using both experimental (Bobbert and van Ingen Schenau 1988) and modeling (van Soest et al. 1993; Pandy et al. 1990; Pandy and Zajac 1991; Selbie and Caldwell 1996) approaches. As mentioned above, the goal in this ubiquitous movement is clear and easy to define, i.e., to raise the total body CM as high as possible. During the flight phase after pushoff, the CM behaves as a projectile under the gravitational pull of the earth; therefore, the goal of the push-off phase is to maximize the CM vertical velocity at takeoff. One method of studying the jumping motion during push-off is to examine the underlying segmental and joint contributions to the CM vertical velocity (Bobbert, Huijing, and van Ingen Schenau 1986). By contrasting the patterns of ankle joint and CM velocities, these authors were able to demonstrate the importance of plantarflexion in the last 100 meters of push-off prior to takeoff. In a similar manner, Jacobs, Bobbert, and van Ingen Schenau (1993) were able to demonstrate the contributions of different joints to the acceleration of the CM at the beginning of a sprint race. Again, note that the goal of a sprint start is clear: to maximize CM horizontal velocity change from its starting value of 0 m/s.

Striking and throwing skills are also movement patterns in which kinematic analysis has proven useful. In throwing for maximal distance or velocity, the rotational velocity of each involved body segment contributes to the linear velocity of the ball upon release from the hand (Herring and Chapman 1992). In racquet sports such as tennis, badminton, racquetball, and squash one goal is to generate as much racquet speed as possible as the racquet strikes the ball. During the impact this racquet speed will be translated into ball velocity as the ball's flight begins. Clearly, high ball velocity is desirable in these racquet sports; so the generation of high racquet speed, effected by rotation of the trunk, upper arm, and forearm, is important. A study by Sprigings et al. (1994) illustrated the three-dimensional nature of this rotation sequence and quantified the contributions of individual segments to the attained racquet velocity. These throwing and striking examples, like the aforementioned jumping and sprinting studies, illustrate the use of purely kinematic variables in understanding the essential elements of a performance. Comparison of different performances (pre-, mid-, and post-season) would help athletes monitor their progress and provide a basis for technique correction or performance improvement.

Kinetic and Muscular Analyses

While these kinematic analyses are useful for studying some movements in which CM velocity is a critical part of the performance goal, often other levels of analysis are needed. A good example in this regard is bicycling, an activity that has a number of conflicting performance goals. On one hand, a rider needs to maximize horizontal velocity, but because of relatively long race distances the metabolic requirements will place an exacting constraint on a cyclist's ability to maintain that velocity. From physiological considerations, it has been predicted that the optimal cadence in endurance cycling should be near 60 rpm (Coast and Welch 1985), but in practice we find that cyclists commonly choose preferred cadences near 100 rpm. Hull, Gonzalez, and Redfield (1988), using optimization techniques, found that this preferred cadence of 100 rpm is predicted by a model that attempts to minimize for muscular stress in the muscles of the lower extremities. These studies emphasize the need to understand the relative importance of different variables that are critical to performance goals.

Another example in which kinetic variables gave valuable information concerning performance was a study on the ability to attain maximal sprinting velocity (Chapman and Caldwell 1983). The running stride consists of a propulsive phase while the foot is in contact with the ground and a recovery phase in which the foot is airborne as it is brought forward for the next propulsive phase. As one nears maximal running velocity, the airborne phase becomes increasingly important because the time available for the recovery decreases. Inverse dynamics and power analysis of the recovery leg identified several key kinetic variables that were increased in magnitude as sprinting velocity increased up to the penultimate speed, but seemed to reach an upper limit as running speed increased to maximal (Chapman and Caldwell 1983). It is unclear if this limitation was an organismic constraint (i.e., related to the inherent muscular strength or force-velocity characteristics of the sprinters involved) or a task constraint directly related to the segmental motions necessary to complete a successful recovery phase at high velocity.

The calculation of muscular power sources and the generation, absorption, and transfer of energy are useful techniques for the assessment of human motion sequences because they link mechanical and muscular attributes of performance (Aleshinsky 1986a-e; Caldwell and Forrester 1992; Chapman and Caldwell 1983; Robertson and Winter 1980). Muscle power ($M\omega$) indicates whether the predominant muscle action at a joint is concentric (positive power) or eccentric (negative power). Joint force power ($F\,v$) indicates the magnitude and direction of energy transfer between adjacent segments. Together, these power sources dictate the flow of mechanical energy within individual and between connected body segments, and they can be calculated as time histories throughout a movement sequence. This allows one to link specific muscular energy modulations during the course of the motion with mechanical events important for successful task completion.

Limitations of the joint moment and power calculations are the underlying assumption that only single joint muscles are involved and that the amount of antagonistic co-contraction at a joint cannot be assessed. These limitations can be overcome in two ways. One way is by the use of electromyography (EMG) to assess the magnitude and relative timing of individual muscle usage and coordination during an activity (Pandy and Zajac 1991; Bobbert and van Ingen Schenau 1988). Second is by the use of models incorporating the mechanical properties of muscle (Hill 1938; Gordon, Huxley, and Julian 1966). Such muscle models allow the representation of specific muscles within the musculoskeletal system during a movement sequence (Bobbert et al. 1986; Caldwell and Chapman 1991; Davy and Audu 1987; Pandy and Zajac 1991; van Soest et al. 1993). These musculoskeletal models are extremely useful for identifying important muscles associated with proficiency within a movement, but unlike inverse dynamics solutions, which are determinate, musculoskeletal models with multiple muscles acting at each joint lead to an indeterminacy problem in that there are more unknown muscle forces than there are equations of motion (Crowninshield and Brand 1981). One must therefore specify constraints on the system in terms of neural control, either in the form of a neural control model (Pierrynowski and Morrison 1985; Caldwell and Chapman 1991) or by assuming an underlying optimization cost function (Seireg and Arvikar 1975; Pandy and Zajac 1991; Collins 1995). As previously stated, in many movement situations the goal of the motion is unclear and the underlying neural cost function is unknown.

Uphill Cycling—Why Stand?

An example of the proficiency approach is seen in recent work from our laboratory concerning uphill cycling (Caldwell et al. 1988; Caldwell et al. 1999; Li and Caldwell 1998). During level cycling, competitive riders adopt a streamlined seated posture in an effort to reduce their frontal area and therefore their air resistance, the major impediment to forward motion. While riding on an uphill grade, an additional resistance to overcome is that of gravity. On long and/or steep climbs, some cyclists will choose to stand on their pedals, bringing their trunk upward and forward which increases their frontal area. Other riders will choose to remain seated throughout the length of even long uphill climbs. However, if one were to find a hill with a constantly increasing slope, it is safe to say that all riders would reach a point where they deemed it necessary to stand to make further progress. Why do cyclists choose to stand while climbing steep hills, and how does standing increase their proficiency in performing the cycling task? One of the first thoughts might be that standing would give some type of metabolic advantage, as wind resistance becomes less of a factor at the slower velocities seen while climbing. However, the metabolic cost of climbing an 8% grade for 10 minutes with different postural strategies (seated, standing, or alternating between seated and standing) is invariant (Hagberg, Caldwell, and McCole, unpublished data).

To understand why a rider might choose to stand, we first must delineate the objectives involved in the movement. In competitive cycling, the goal is to maintain high forward velocity in the face of the resistance provided by the air, friction, and gravitational load. The total resistance faced by a rider can be written as a function that expresses the component loads in a quantitative manner:

$$\text{Total resistance force} = 0.5 \, C_d \, A \, \rho \, v^2 + \mu_k R + mg \sin \theta$$

In this equation, the three terms represent air resistance, friction, and gravitational loading, respectively. For the air resistance, C_d represents the drag coefficient, A the cyclist's frontal area, r the air density, and v the riding velocity. The frictional term includes a general coefficient of kinetic friction μ_k and normal force R to represent all frictional losses both within the bicycle (chain, crank, and wheel resistance) and between the tires and road. The final gravitational term uses m to represent the rider and cycle mass and θ for the slope of the terrain. The frictional resistance is quite small compared to the wind and gravitational terms. Note that in level cycling the gravitational term is zero, so air resistance provides the main load to overcome. However, while on an uphill climb the rider is subjected to substantial resistance by both the air and gravity. These two retarding forces must be overcome by the cyclist who wishes to maintain high forward velocity while on the hill.

For recreational cyclists on a steep hill, the ultimate goal is not high velocity, but maintaining forward motion of the bicycle at all times. In both competitive and recreational cases, a rider interacts with the environment through force and torque applied to the pedals and crank, and the cyclist's velocity (or ability to move forward) will be determined by the balance between resistive forces and the rider's applied crank torque, which is translated into an applied force at the tire/ground interface. The movement goals can therefore be restated in terms of torque applied by the rider on the crank, as the resistive forces are environmental and beyond the rider's immediate control (although riders have some influence on the air resistance through their posture / frontal area). The rider's goal is to provide enough applied crank torque to overcome the resistive forces acting to reduce forward velocity. If the rider's applied torque is less than the external resistance, forward velocity will decrease, and as the hill gets steeper the decrease in forward velocity can be such that forward progression stops (i.e., the bike and rider start to roll down the hill!).

Now we turn our attention to the rider's ability to produce crank torque throughout the pedaling cycle. For a variety of reasons (geometrical, anatomical, and muscular) a cyclist generates an uneven amount of crank torque as each foot spins through the cycle from its highest position (0 degrees or top-dead-center [TDC]) to its lowest (180 degrees or bottom-dead-center [BDC]) and back up to TDC as it completes the 360-degree cycle. In seated cycling, the strongest position (highest torque) occurs with one foot (e.g., the right) pushing downward around 90 degrees while the contralateral left foot is pulling upward near 270 degrees. In contrast, with one foot near TDC and the other near BDC the rider is in a relatively weak position to produce propelling crank torque. The crank torque pattern for uphill seated cycling is shown in figure 3.1. The weakest point in this crank cycle occurs with one foot (right) almost at BDC while the other (left) is nearly at TDC (just before 180° in figure 3.1). In this position the cyclist must pull almost straight back with the right foot and push straight forward with the left to produce propulsive torque. However, anatomically the lower right limb is almost fully extended and in a poor position to apply backward force, while the left is nearly fully flexed and in a poor position to apply forward force. Furthermore, prior to TDC, failure to pull up and forward on the pedal will cause a torque in the opposite direction. Once past this weak point at TDC, the rider can easily produce propulsive torque from the inertia and weight of the leg as it comes forward and down.

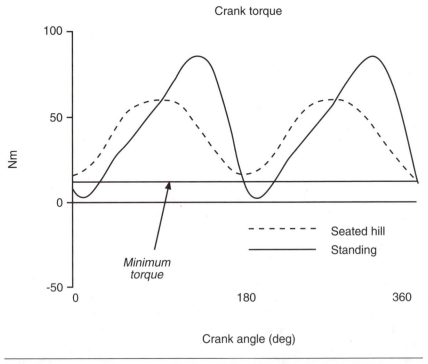

Figure 3.1 Crank torque profile in uphill cycling on simulated 8% grade, plotted as a function of crank angle from top-dead-center (TDC, 0°) through bottom-dead-center (BDC, 180°) and back to TDC (360°). Data represents the torque applied to the crank from both feet of the cyclist. The torque pattern for uphill cycling while seated is shown by the broken line, while data for uphill standing condition is shown by the solid line. The horizontal line represents a hypothetical minimum torque level (see text).

By combining the movement goal (crank torque production at a level needed to overcome air and gravitational resistance) with the cyclist's ability to produce crank torque throughout the crank cycle, we begin to understand the importance of the weak point in the crank cycle. Superimposed on the crank torque plot in figure 3.1 is a hypothetical minimum torque level, representing the smallest torque necessary to balance the external resistance and maintain the forward velocity. Application of torque above this level will increase the rider's velocity, while torque magnitudes below this level will result in a decrease in the rider's forward velocity. As one rides up an increasing slope, this minimum torque level will increase as the gravitational load (mg sin θ) increases. At some point the cyclist will no longer be able to provide enough crank torque during the weak part of the crank cycle (lower foot near 180 degrees), and therefore will be unable to maintain the same forward velocity during this portion of the crank cycle. This is especially crucial in the region just prior to BDC, for if the velocity drops too close to zero the upper foot will be unable to provide propulsive torque due to its position just prior to TDC. Note that this situation changes just after the upper foot passes TDC, for now the rider merely has to put weight onto the pedal to produce propulsive torque.

The strategy of standing during the climb can now be viewed in the preceding context of crank torque production and the movement goal of minimum necessary crank torque. As described previously (Caldwell et al., 1998) the standing posture changes the nature of force application on the pedal, and therefore the profile of crank torque production. Figure 3.1 also illustrates the crank torque profile for uphill cycling while standing. The standing torque pattern is quite different than that for seated cycling, with a larger peak that occurs much later in the crank cycle and a more exaggerated 'trough,' or minimum, again occurring later in the crank cycle just after TDC and BDC. It should be noted that the area under the torque profile (representing work done on the crank) is nearly identical for the seated and standing conditions. Thus, the difference between the two conditions is in the *pattern* of torque application, and not in the amount of torque applied. While standing, the shifting of maximum and minimum torque to points later in the crank cycle is important in that the weak point in the cycle is now shifted to *after* TDC / BDC. This torque pattern means the rider accelerates the bike to a greater degree in the late downstroke and shifts the weak point until after TDC / BDC when the rider is in a better position to apply propulsive torque. Because the rider is standing on the pedals, propulsive torque can be generated merely by leaning towards the side in which the foot has just passed TDC. Furthermore, the other ('back') leg is fully extended and just past BDC, and the rider's positioning is such that the extended arms form a rigid 'strut' over the handlebars. This allows the rider to pull upward with the back leg (using hip and knee flexors), using the extended arms to simultaneously push downward and provide support against the handlebars. Thus, the rider is in a strong position to pull the lower limb upward, providing a force and propulsive torque that will augment the torque being produced by the gravitational loading of the 'front' pedal by the contralateral downstroke leg.

More details on the proficiency of standing while cycling can be appreciated by examining the profiles of joint torques (Caldwell et al. 1999) throughout the crank cycle (figure 3.2). As with the crank torque patterns, the most distinctive changes in the joint torques are shifts in the profiles in the late downstroke phase around BDC. The knee joint demonstrates an extended period of extensor torque during late downstroke in the standing condition, in contrast to the seated condition in which the knee torque switches to flexor just after the 90-degree crank position, to help with pulling the leg and foot backwards. Also, in the standing condition the ankle joint shows a large plantarflexor torque that peaks just prior to BDC, in contrast to the seated condition, which demonstrates a peak at a much lower value near 90 degrees of crank rotation. Both of these torque changes in late downstroke are necessary to support the weight of the body pushing down on the pedal, as the rider shifts his or her weight onto one foot as much as possible to provide forward propulsion. Furthermore, the knee extensor torque can be used for propulsion just prior to BDC through the more angled position of the foot and pedal, permitting the delay of the weak point in the crank cycle until after BDC.

Further information concerning standing cycling can be found by examining the sources of energy generation through a power analysis (Caldwell et al. 1997). Figure 3.3 illustrates the joint powers at each of the three lower extremity joints, associated with work done by the muscles surrounding each joint (Robertson and Winter 1980; van Ingen Schenau et al. 1990). Also shown is the hip joint force power, which traces energy movement between the leg and pelvis through the hip joint, known as an energy transfer (Robertson and Winter 1980). The joint powers all show the shift in energy generation (positive power) to later in the downstroke, or past BDC into the beginning of the upstroke. The importance of the late downstroke is emphasized in the hip joint force power profile, as the standing condition demonstrates a large transfer of energy into the thigh that is nonexistent in the seated condition. This energy influx is associated with the shifting of weight onto the pedal and the freedom of the hip joint to move downward rather than being constrained by the bicycle saddle. This energy transfer is realized because of the contribution of the body weight and inertia afforded by the removal of the saddle as a base of support in the standing posture.

In summary, the kinetic analysis of the pedal, crank, and body motions has generated data that shows differences between the seated and standing conditions in uphill cycling. These differences can be best understood by beginning with an understanding of the requirements of the cycling task itself. By themselves the kinetic data merely offer a descrip-

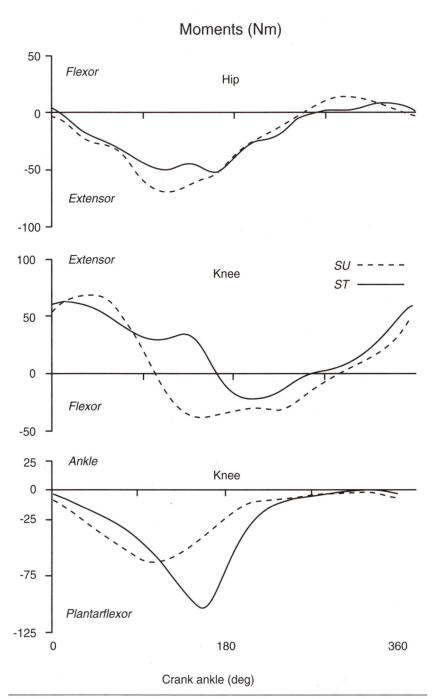

Figure 3.2 Moments for the lower extremity joints in uphill cycling, expressed as a function of crank rotation. Data are shown for uphill seated (SU, broken line) and uphill standing (ST, solid line) cycling conditions.

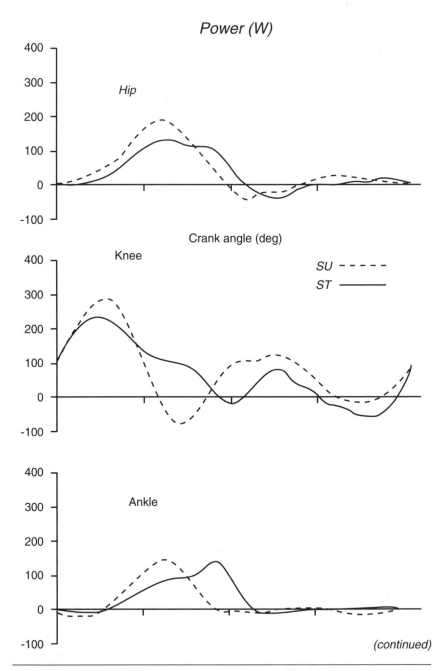

Figure 3.3 Power profiles for the lower extremity joints, expressed as a function of crank rotation. Data are shown for the uphill seated (SU, broken line) and uphill standing (ST, solid line) cycling conditions. Bottom panel (next page) illustrates joint force power at the hip, indicating energy transfer into the lower extremity.

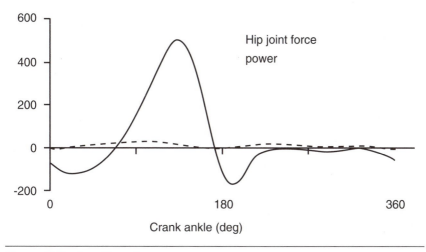

Figure 3.3   *(continued)*

tion of the cycling conditions, but when combined with an understanding of the task they offer insight into the proficiency of the changes involved when a rider chooses to stand.

Gait Transitions and Dynamical Systems Analysis

Here we turn to different constraints involved in gait transitions and discuss them from a dynamical systems perspective.

Energetics and Gait Transitions

Many studies on human and animal locomotion have suggested that gaits are selected on the basis of metabolic energy considerations (e.g., Margaria 1976; Hoyt and Taylor 1981). In their well-known paper, Hoyt and Taylor had horses walk, trot, and gallop on a treadmill at a variety of different speeds in each gait pattern. The authors observed U-shaped functions between speed and oxygen consumption per unit distance traveled. These data have provided clear evidence that oxygen cost is an important determinant in the selection of locomotory gaits and transitions between gait patterns. In human walking the metabolic cost of walking a unit distance reaches a minimum at about 1.2 m/s and then begins to increase. The transition to running occurs at about 2.2 m/s and at this point the energy costs for running and walking are roughly equal. At speeds after this transition point, the energy cost per unit distance remains the same or increases slightly in running but increases dramatically in walking. In walking there appears to be a minimum at around 1.2 m/s, above and below which there is an increase in energetic cost (e.g., Hreljac 1993).

If changes in gait patterns are dominated by metabolic energy-saving mechanisms, then it would be expected that transitions are always made at those points where energy expenditure is minimal. In the literature there is a growing body of evidence against this notion. Farley and Taylor (1991), for example, have shown that horses change from trot to gallop at a speed in which the gallop is less metabolically efficient than the trot. Hreljac (1993) found in human subjects that preferred transition speed from walking to running (on average 2.07 m/s) was generally lower than the energetically optimal transition speed (on average 2.24 m/s). Hreljac concluded on the basis of these findings that humans do not change gait patterns in order to minimize metabolic energy expenditure.

Selles et al. (submitted) examined energy expenditure in three different patterns of human walking. In the first condition subjects were asked to walk naturally in the range 0.2-1.2 m/s. In the second condition subjects were asked to synchronize their arms to the step frequency with an in-phase coordination pattern between the arms. In the third condition subjects were instructed to synchronize their arms to the stride frequency with an antiphase coordination between the arms. Even though these conditions created distinct coordination patterns, results from energy expenditure measurements revealed no significant differences between the three conditions. These findings demonstrate that in the human walking mode different patterns of coordination, as shown by different frequency and phase couplings between arms and legs, are not distinguished on the basis of energy expenditure requirements.

Locomotor Stability and Gait Transitions

From the examples above it appears that the minimization of metabolic energy expenditure might not be the only or primary mechanism underlying gait changes. Another possible factor driving gait changes is the stability of the coordination patterns. In the dynamical systems perspective on movement coordination and control, specific tools and methods have emerged to examine the role of variability and stability of movement patterns in transition processes (Haken 1977; Kugler and Turvey 1987; Kelso 1995; Schöner and Kelso 1988; Turvey 1990). Whereas from more traditional engineering viewpoints instabilities in patterns are regarded as noise to be eliminated, within the dynamical systems approach instabilities can provide a clear distinction between different behavioral patterns (Kelso 1995). These distinct behavioral patterns identify the collective variable or "order parameter." The order parameter reflects the coordinative or relational tendencies between the components (e.g., muscles, joints, limbs, etc.). Control over these order parameters rather than individual components may reduce the degrees of freedom problem in biological organisms, as originally proposed by Bernstein (1967). In other words, order parameters identify low-dimensional qualitative states of the system dynamics. The full identification of the order parameter dynamics can be obtained through manipulation of a control parameter, such as velocity or frequency of movement. In quadrupedal gait, for example, different gaits are identified by the specific pattern of coordination (phase relation) between the four legs. In the gallop of the horse the limbs of the front and hind girdles move (nearly) antiphase, whereas in the trot diagonally opposite limbs move in-phase. The order parameter captures and characterizes each of those different gait patterns. In addition, the stability aspects of these different gait patterns have been identified using dynamical systems principles (Schöner, Jiang, and Kelso 1990). Changes in gait patterns are brought about by manipulation of, for example, speed, which acts as a control parameter. By systematically scaling locomotor speed, the different patterns (walk, trot, gallop, etc.) emerge.

Phase relations or the relative phase between body segments have been considered as potential order parameters based on previous modeling and empirical data (e.g., Haken, Kelso, and Bunz 1985). Relative phase between segments or joints can identify different qualitative states of the system dynamics (e.g., in-phase and out-of-phase leg motions in the different gaits in quadrupedal locomotion) on which basic changes in coordination patterns can be evaluated. An important feature of these phase transitions is the emergence of variability in relative phase that occurs before the transition point. This instability can be measured by means of critical fluctuations (increase in standard deviation) in relative phase or the relaxation time after a transient perturbation (Kay, Saltzman, and Kelso 1991; van Emmerik 1992).

The paradigmatic example of these concepts can be seen in phase transitions in human finger movements (Kelso 1995). Subjects were asked to move both index fingers out-of-phase and then increase movement frequency. The result was a sudden transition in which the coordination pattern spontaneously shifted to an in-phase pattern. A critical feature of the observed transition was a loss of stability (increased variability) of the relative phase when the control parameter frequency was scaled. The central message from Kelso's research is that variability is a necessary ingredient for coordination change.

Diedrich and Warren (1995) recently used a dynamical systems approach to study the walk-to-run transition in human bipedal locomotion. Their analysis focused on within-limb joint angular transitions in the lower extremity. They used discrete relative phase as a measure of coordination and observed abrupt switches in ankle-hip and ankle-knee relative phase around the transition from walking to running. These transitions were also accompanied by increases in fluctuations in relative phase between joints of the lower extremity, with fluctuations occurring mainly for the coordination of contiguous segments, namely the ankle-knee relative phase. In both the transition from walking to running and from running to walking, there was a speed-related increase in standard deviation of relative phase, followed by a decline after the transition had been made.

These transitions and stability changes have not only been observed for the lower extremity. Van Emmerik and Wagenaar (1996) used this approach to examine the stability in the trunk during locomotion at a variety of walking velocities and showed that at low walking velocities the relative phase between pelvis and thorax was close to in-phase (about 20 degrees), but with increasing speed this phase relation changed to more out-of-phase (about 120-140 degrees; see figure 3.4 for an example). This counter rotation in the trunk is essential for maintaining stability at higher velocities and helps to avoid excessive left or right rotations in the entire upper body. Similar coordination changes have been observed in the relative phase and frequency coupling between the arms and legs (Wagenaar and Van Emmerik 1994). An important observation in the van Emmerik and Wagenaar study was that the variability of relative phase changed systematically as a function of walking velocity. This variability represents the within-subject coordination changes from stride cycle to stride cycle. In figure 3.4 the variability of relative phase between pelvic and thoracic rotation is highest at intermediate walking velocities (0.7-

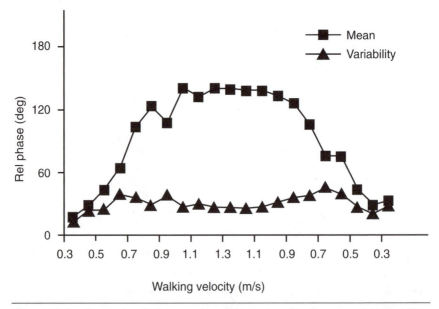

Figure 3.4 Example of changes in relative phase between pelvic and thoracic rotation for young healthy subject as a function of walking velocity. Relative phase of zero degrees indicates perfect in-phase coupling between pelvis and thorax. Relative phase of 180 degrees indicates perfect antiphase coupling. Also indicated is the change in stability of the relative phase coupling, as measured by the cycle-to-cycle variability in relative phase between pelvis and thorax.

0.9 m/s), and lower variability at speeds below and above 0.7-0.9 m/s indicates two more stable modes separated by a region of instability.

Using a similar relative phase analysis, Wagenaar and Van Emmerik (1994) also observed reduced ability to change the coordination pattern of pelvis and thorax in patients with Parkinson's disease. This reduced ability to change the relative motion between pelvis and thorax from more in-phase to out-of-phase, necessary to maintain overall body stability during gait, was accompanied by a reduced variability in this coordination pattern. Similar problems in switching patterns in the coordination between the arms and legs were also observed in these patients.

The above examples on healthy and pathological gait provide support for the hypothesis that the observed changes or transitions in movement patterns are effected to maintain or improve system stability. In disabled populations these stability considerations could become the most important optimization criteria. These stability considerations do give the same general message as the earlier reported data on uphill cycling. In addressing the question of "why stand?" it was described that in uphill cycling different postural strategies (i.e., seated versus standing) did not result in differences in metabolic cost. It was argued, however, that mechanically (in terms of the pattern of applied crank torque), the change from a seated to a standing position would allow the rider to either maintain or improve forward progression velocity. Collectively, these results show that an integration of task goals with the kinetic and kinematic aspects of the movement is essential in understanding the proficiency of the task at hand.

Locomotor Stability and Energy Expenditure

Very few studies in the literature have investigated the combined optimization of stability and energetic constraints. Holt et al. (1995) had subjects walk on a treadmill at a preferred constant speed. Subjects were required to walk at their preferred frequency as predicted by the resonance of a force-driven harmonic oscillator model, as well as at frequencies above and below this preferred frequency. The data showed that walking at the preferred and predicted frequencies resulted in minimal metabolic costs. In addition, Holt et al. (1995) also measured stability at the head and lower extremity joints, revealing a complementary relationship between head stability and metabolic cost. Head stability—as measured by the standard deviation of the head in the vertical (up-down) direction—was largest close to the frequency at which the metabolic cost was minimal. Although in the Holt et al. (1995) study metabolic and stability measures were closely related to each other, maximal head stability (minimal standard deviation) was obtained before reaching minimal energy expenditure.

As shown in figure 3.4, in human walking, coordination patterns involving the trunk (as well as the coupling of the arms and legs) indicate that there are more or less stable coordination patterns above and below speeds in the range 0.7-.0.9 m/s, implying the existence of multiple coordination patterns in walking. Figure 3.5 plots the changes in stability features of these patterns as well as energetic cost as a function of walking speed. As appears from figure 3.5, different trends are observed in that energetic cost per kg body weight per km traveled reaches a minimum around 1.0-1.2 m/s, whereas the coordination in the trunk shows maximum variability before the minimum metabolic energy velocity. This example shows that metabolic energy cost and stability measures can change in significantly different ways during walking. These different patterns need to be investigated in more detail with a specific focus on more specific manipulations of the system stability, for example, in the form of asymmetrical loading of the limbs.

As indicated earlier, findings from a number of studies suggest that energy-saving mechanisms might not be as strong a determinant of gait transitions as was once believed. Farley and Taylor (1991), for example, argue that peak bone forces might induce transitions from trot to gallop in the horse. The importance of stability measures as a constraint on pattern change could become even more prominent under conditions in which stability is challenged to a larger degree, such as during running over irregular terrain or walking with loads. In the experiments discussed above, animals or humans were required to locomote on a treadmill in

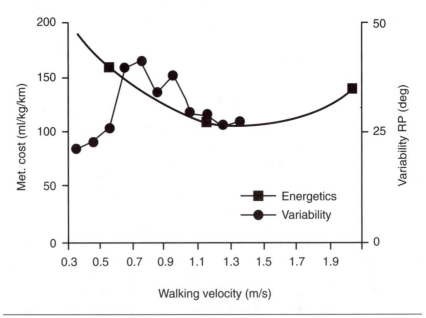

Figure 3.5 Changes in metabolic energy cost and stability of relative phase as a function of walking speed. Data on metabolic cost are derived from representative studies in the literature (e.g., Hreljac 1993). Relative phase variability represents coordination between pelvic and thoracic rotations.

which instabilities due to terrain were not imposed. Under those conditions significant shifts in the relative contribution of energy and stability optimization could occur. On the other hand, in most studies on energy consumption in human locomotion (e.g., Hreljac 1993) the time scale over which energy expenditure was investigated was relatively short (minutes). The relative contribution of energy expenditure and stability should be investigated under a variety of constraints, including the time scale over which this is measured. When taking this into account, the observed similarity between different gait patterns in energy expenditure in, for example, the Selles et al. (submitted) study on human walking might reveal that under certain task constraints the different coordination patterns in the human walking mode do differ in terms of their metabolic costs.

Summary

In this chapter we have argued that an understanding of the task demands and constraints of a specific movement are paramount in determining how well one can perform the movement. In some cases the metabolic system may play an important role, in which case mechanical efficiency or economy may be important optimizing variables. The importance of physiological constraints must, however, be viewed within the context of the overall demands of the movement task, and in some cases the metabolic requirements may be relatively unimportant, as in speed-related events like the 100-meter sprint. The concept of movement proficiency provides a framework for assessing the competency or skillfulness of a performance within the context of the task requirements. The emphasis on task demands dictates that one should consider the interaction of different movement subsystems (metabolic, mechanical, perceptual, etc.), and that no one analysis technique will be the proper tool for assessing and understanding all movement patterns. Answers to questions regarding human motion will be found by observing the movement system in different ways and with different analysis tools, but one should always consider the specific task goals and constraints in interpretation of experimental data.

References

Aleshinsky, S.Y. 1986a. An energy 'sources' and 'fractions' approach to the mechanical energy expenditure problem - I. Basic concepts, description of the model, analysis of a one-link system movement. *Journal of Biomechanics* 19: 287-293.

Aleshinsky, S.Y. 1986b. An energy 'sources' and 'fractions' approach to the mechanical energy expenditure problem - II. Movement of the multi-link chain model. *Journal of Biomechanics* 19: 295-300.

Aleshinsky, S.Y. 1986c. An energy 'sources' and 'fractions' approach to the mechanical energy expenditure problem - III. Mechanical energy expenditure reduction during one link motion. *Journal of Biomechanics* 19: 301-306.

Aleshinsky, S.Y. 1986d. An energy 'sources' and 'fractions' approach to the mechanical energy expenditure problem - IV. Criticism of the concept of "energy transfers within and between links." *Journal of Biomechanics* 19: 307-309.

Aleshinsky, S.Y. 1986e. An energy 'sources' and 'fractions' approach to the mechanical energy expenditure problem - V. The mechanical energy expenditure reduction during motion of the multi-link system. *Journal of Biomechanics* 19: 311-315.

Bernstein, N.A. 1967. *The coordination and regulation of movements.* London: Pergamon Press.

Bobbert, M.F., P.A. Huijing, and G.J. van Ingen Schenau. 1986. A model of the human triceps surae muscle-tendon complex applied to jumping. *Journal of Biomechanics* 19: 887-898.

Bobbert, M.F., and G.J. van Ingen Schenau. 1988. Coordination in vertical jumping. *Journal of Biomechanics* 21: 249-262.

Bresler, B., and J.P. Frankel. 1950. The forces and moments in the leg during level walking. *American Society of Mechanical Engineering* 48-A-62: 27-35.

Caldwell, G.E., and A.E. Chapman. 1991. The general distribution problem: a physiological solution which includes antagonism. *Human Movement Science* 10: 355-392.

Caldwell, G.E., and L.W. Forrester. 1992. Estimates of mechanical work and energy transfers: demonstration of a rigid body power model of the recovery leg in gait. *Medicine and Science in Sports and Exercise* 24: 1396-1412.

Caldwell, G.E., L. Li, S.D. McCole, and J.M. Hagberg. In press. Pedal and crank kinetics in uphill cycling. *Journal of Applied Biomechanics* 14: 245-259.

Caldwell, G.E., Hagberg, J.M., McCole, S.D., and L. Li. (1999). Lower extremity joint moments during uphill cycling. *Journal of Applied Biomechanics,* 15: 166-181.

Caldwell, G.E., D.G.E. Robertson, L. Li, and J.M. Hagberg. 1997. Lower extremity power and work in level and uphill cycling. In *Proceedings of the XVIth International Congress of Biomechanics*, eds. M. Miyashita et al., 226. Tokyo, Japan.

Cavagna, G.A., F.P. Saibene, and R. Margaria. 1963. External work in walking. *Journal of Applied Physiology* 18: 1-9.

Cavagna, G.A., F.P. Saibene, and R. Margaria. 1964. Mechanical work in running. *Journal of Applied Physiology* 19: 249-256.

Chapman, A.E., and G.E. Caldwell. 1983. Kinetic limitations of maximal sprinting speed. *Journal of Biomechanics* 16: 78-83.

Coast, J.R., and H.G. Welch. 1985. Linear increase in optimal pedaling rate with increased power output in cycle ergometry. *European Journal of Applied Physiology* 53: 339-342.

Collins, J.J. 1995. The redundant nature of locomotor optimization laws. *Journal of Biomechanics* 28: 251-267.

Costill, D.L. 1970. Metabolic responses during distance running. *Journal of Applied Physiology* 28: 251-255.

Crowninshield, R.D., and R.A. Brand. 1981. The prediction of forces in joint structures: distribution of intersegmental resultants. *Exercise and Sports Science Review* 9: 159-181.

Davy, D.T., and M.L. Audu. 1987. A dynamic optimization technique for predicting muscle forces in the swing phase of gait. *Journal of Biomechanics* 20: 187-201.

Diedrich, F.J., and W.H. Warren. 1995. Why change gaits? Dynamics of the walk-run transition. *Journal of Experimental Psychology: Human Perception and Performance* 21: 183-202.

Donovan, C.M., and G.A. Brooks. 1977. Muscular efficiency during steady-rate exercise II. Effect of walking speed and work rate. *Journal of Applied Physiology* 43: 431-439.

Dul, J., M.A. Townsend, R. Shiavi, and G.E. Johnson. 1984. Muscular synergism - I. On criteria for load sharing between synergistic muscles. *Journal of Biomechanics* 17: 663-673.

Enoka, R.M. 1988. Load- and skill-related changes in segmental contributions to a weightlifting movement. *Medicine and Science in Sports and Exercise* 20: 178-187.

Farley, C.T., and C.R. Taylor. 1991. A mechanical trigger for the trot-gallop transition in horses. *Science* 253: 306-308.

Farley, C.T., and T.A. McMahon. 1992. Energetics of walking and running: insights from simulated reduced-gravity experiments. *Journal of Applied Physiology* 73: 2709-2712.

Gaesser, G.A., and G.A. Brooks. 1975. Muscular efficiency during steady-rate exercise: effects of speed and work rate. *Journal of Applied Physiology* 38: 1132-1139.

Gordon, A.M., A.F. Huxley, and F.J. Julian. 1966. The variation in isometric tension with sarcomere length in vertebrate muscle fibres. *Journal of Physiology* 184: 170-192.

Hagberg, J.M., G.E. Caldwell, and S.D. McCole. Unpublished observations.

Haken, H. 1977. *Synergetics: an introduction. Nonequilibrium phase transitions and self-organization in physics, chemistry, and biology.* Heidelberg: Springer.

Haken, H., J.A.S. Kelso, and H. Bunz. 1985. A theoretical model of phase transitions in human hand movements. *Biological Cybernetics* 51: 347-356.

Hardt, D.E. 1978. Determining muscle forces in the leg during normal human walking—an application and evaluation of optimization methods. *Journal of Biomechanical Engineering* 100: 72-78.

Herring, R.M., and A.E. Chapman. 1992. Effects of changes in segmental values and timing of both torque and torque reversal in simulated throws. *Journal of Biomechanics* 25: 1173-1184.

Hill, A.V. 1938. The heat of shortening and the dynamic constants of muscle. *Proceedings of Royal Society London* B126: 136-195.

Holt, K.G., S-F. Jeng, R. Ratcliffe, and J. Hamill. 1995. Energetic cost and stability during human walking at the preferred stride frequency. *Journal of Motor Behavior* 27: 164-178.

Hoyt, D.F., and C.R. Taylor. 1981. Gait and the energetics of locomotion in horses. *Nature* 292: 239-240.

Hreljac, A. 1993. Preferred and energetically optimal gait transition speeds in human locomotion. *Medicine and Science in Sports and Exercise* 25: 1158-1162.

Hull, M.L., H.K. Gonzalez, and R. Redfield. 1988. Optimization of pedaling rate in cycling using a muscle stress-based objective function. *International Journal of Sport Biomechanics* 4: 1-20.

Jacobs, R., M.F. Bobbert, and G.J. van Ingen Schenau. 1993. Function of mono- and biarticular muscles in running. *Medicine and Science in Sports and Exercise* 25: 1163-1173.

Kay, B.A., E.L. Saltzman, and J.A.S. Kelso. 1991. Steady-state and perturbed rhythmical movements: a dynamical analysis. *Journal of Experimental Psychology: Human Perception and Performance* 13: 178-192.

Kelso, J.A.S. 1995. *Dynamic patterns: the self-organization of brain and behavior.* Cambridge, MA.: MIT Press.

Kugler, P.N., and M.T. Turvey. 1987. *Information, natural law, and the self-assembly of rhythmic movement.* Hillsdale, NJ: Erlbaum.

Li, L., and G.E. Caldwell. 1996. Muscular coordination in cycling: effects surface incline and posture. *Journal of Applied Physiology* 85: 927-934.

Margaria, R. 1976. *Biomechanics and energetics of muscular exercise.* Oxford: Claredon Press.

Nagle, F.J., B. Balke, and J.P. Naughton. 1965. Gradational step tests for assessing work capacity. *Journal of Applied Physiology* 20: 745-748.

Norman, R.W., M.T. Sharratt, J.C. Pezzack, and E.G. Noble. 1976. Reexamination of the mechanical efficiency of horizontal treadmill running. In *Biomechanics V-B*, ed. P. Komi, 87-93. Baltimore: University Press.

Newell, K.M. 1986. Constraints on the development of coordination. In *Motor development in children: aspects of coordination and control,* eds. M.G. Wade and H.T.A. Whiting, 341-361. Dordrecht, the Netherlands: Martinus Nijhoff.

Pandy, M.G., and F.E. Zajac. 1991. Optimal muscular coordination strategies for jumping. *Journal of Biomechanics* 24: 1-10.

Pandy, M.G., F.E. Zajac, E. Sim, and W.S. Levine. 1990. An optimal control model for maximum-height human jumping. *Journal of Biomechanics* 23: 1185-1198.

Pierrynowski, M.R., and J.B. Morrison. 1985. A physiological model for the evaluation of muscular forces in human locomotion: theoretical aspects. *Mathematical Biosciences* 75: 69-101.

Robertson, D.G.E., and D.A. Winter. 1980. Mechanical energy generation, absorption and transfer amongst segments during walking. *Journal of Biomechanics* 13: 845-854.

Saltzman, E.L., and J.A.S. Kelso. 1987. Skilled actions: a task dynamic approach. *Psychological Review* 94: 84-106.

Schöner, G., and J.A.S. Kelso. 1988. Dynamic pattern generation in behavioral and neural systems. *Science* 239: 1513-1520.

Schöner, G., W.Y. Jiang, and J.A.S. Kelso. 1990. A synergetic theory of quadrupedal gaits and gait transitions. *Journal of Theoretical Biology* 142: 359-391.

Seireg, A., and R.J. Arvikar. 1975. The prediction of muscular load sharing and joint forces in the lower extremities during walking. *Journal of Biomechanics* 8: 89-102.

Selbie, W.S., and G.E. Caldwell. 1996. A simulation study of vertical jumping from different starting postures. *Journal of Biomechanics* 29: 1137-1146.

Selles, R.W., J.M. Dirks, R.C. Wagenaar, R.E.A. Van Emmerik, and L.H.V. van der Woude. Oxygen cost and coordination in human walking. Manuscript submitted.

Sprigings, E., R. Marshall, B. Elliott, and L. Jennings. 1994. A three-dimensional kinematic method for determining the effectiveness of arm segment rotations in producing racquet-head speed. *Journal of Biomechanics* 27: 245-254.

Stainsby, W.N., L.B. Gladden, J.K. Barclay, and B.A. Wilson. 1980. Exercise efficiency: validity of base-line substractions. *Journal of Applied Physiology* 48: 518-522.

Turvey, M.T. 1990. Coordination. *American Psychologist* 45: 938-953.

van Emmerik, R.E.A. 1992. Kinematic adaptations to perturbations as a function of practice level in a rhythmic drawing movement. *Journal of Motor Behavior* 24: 117-131.

van Emmerik, R.E.A., and R.C. Wagenaar. 1996. Effects of velocity on relative phase dynamics in the trunk in human walking. *Journal of Biomechanics* 29: 1175-1184.

van Ingen Schenau, G.J., M.F. Bobbert, and A. de Haan. 1997. Does elastic energy enhance work and efficiency in the stretch-shortening cycle? *Journal of Applied Biomechanics* 13: 389-415.

van Ingen Schenau, G.J., W.W.L.M. van Woensel,. P.J.M. Boots, R.W. Snackers, and G. de Groot. 1990. Determination and interpretation of mechanical power in human movement: application to ergometer cycling. *European Journal of Applied Physiology* 48: 518-522.

Van Soest, A.J., A.L. Schwab, M.F. Bobbert, and G.J. van Ingen Schenau. 1993. The influence of the biarticularity of the gastrocnemius muscle on vertical-jumping achievement. *Journal of Biomechanics* 26: 1-8.

Wagenaar R.C., and R.E.A. van Emmerik. 1994. The dynamics of pathological gait: stability and adaptability of movement coordination. *Human Movement Science* 13: 441-471.

Williams, K.R., and P.R. Cavanagh. 1983. A model for the calculation of mechanical power during distance running. *Journal of Biomechanics* 16: 115-128.

Winter, D.A. 1978. Calculation and interpretation of mechanical energy of movement. *Exercise and Sports Science Review* 6: 183-201.

Winter, D.A. 1979. A new definition of mechanical work done in human movement. *Journal of Applied Physiology* 46: 79-83.

4

Movement Economy, Preferred Modes, and Pacing

W.A. Sparrow, K.M. Hughes, A.P. Russell, and P.F. Le Rossignol

School of Health Sciences, Deakin University, Australia

In the early 1970s Gavriel Salvendy at Purdue University and Nigel Corlett at the University of Birmingham engaged in a collaborative research venture to examine two related phenomena. The first was the effect of pacing on performance, in which Salvendy, Corlett, and their collaborators considered the effects of compelling individuals to perform activities at a pace either faster or slower than "preferred." Operationally preferred pace is the pace that an individual adopts when unconstrained by an outside agent (Salvendy and Piltisis 1971; Corlett and Mahadeva 1970). The second phenomenon of interest to this group were the effects of practice on performance; and, given their orientation, practice on industrial work tasks was of primary interest (Salvendy and Piltisis 1971). The most interesting feature of their research was the choice of dependent measures for examining the effects of pacing and practice. Rather than utilising the traditional measures of time and error, they chose to examine "physiological performance" by measuring the metabolic energy expenditure associated with work output using indirect calorimetry via measurements of oxygen concentration in expired air, techniques that are now commonplace in respiratory physiology.

With Salvendy's (1972) study a suitable starting point for our discussion, we will in this chapter consider the effects of preferred modes on metabolic energy expenditure. From time to time practice effects on metabolic energy expenditure will be briefly discussed. Practice effects on metabolic energy expenditure have, however, been reviewed recently in some detail by Sparrow and Newell (1998), and in this chapter more attention will, therefore, be given to our ideas concerning pacing and preferred modes. In addition, we will develop the concept of preferred modes in the context of contemporary theorising about motor coordination and control.

The chapter has been organised around five major themes, each comprising a major section of the chapter. The first addresses the definition of "economy" and related terms, and highlights differences in the economy of various everyday actions. For example, the metabolic costs of various modes of human transport, such as walking, running, and swimming, are compared. The second section introduces preferred modes and "pacing," providing a systematic review of studies showing the "self-organising" properties of motor responses in such a way that the cost of task-related work is minimised within a preferred action mode. The third section of the chapter discusses, briefly, the topical question of transitions in coordination and speculates as to whether transitions in coordination modes are underpinned by considerations of metabolic energy cost. In section four we have identified three "mechanisms" by which selection of preferred modes may be achieved and, in so doing, have attempted to suggest the processes underlying the "self-organising" phenomenon of preferred mode selection. In our final major section of the chapter, we extend the underlying processes idea and propose the sources of sensory information used to establish preferred coordination modes.

Quantifying the Economy of Action Modes

Economical movements are those that meet the task demands with relatively low expenditure of metabolic energy. The metabolic energy expended in meeting task demands can be described using the related concepts "efficiency" and "economy." Efficiency is calculated when power output and oxygen consumption associated with the task can be measured. One major problem, however, in defining efficiency, is calculating the work rate (power) associated with task performance. A standard laboratory ergometer (such as rowing or cycling) measures work rate as a function of the force exerted via the handle or pedals and the distance over which the force is applied in a given time. The apparatus does not measure how the limbs are moved to perform the task and, therefore, while the external work done to operate the ergometer can be determined, there is no measure of the associated internal work required to move the limbs. One of the major themes of this book is the observation that with practice movement patterns become more refined and the internal mechanical work required to coordinate and control the limbs may decrease. Changes in internal mechanical work result from changes in the contributions of one- and two-joint muscles and energy transfers between and within segments. It is, therefore, very difficult to measure the total power output of the body in motion, and for most practical purposes only external mechanical efficiency is measured.

Another influence on oxygen uptake variation during exercise is the oxygen consumption kinetics in relation to the onset and intensity of a regular rhythmic movement pattern. Appropriate measurement of efficiency requires that oxygen consumption be sampled during steady-state conditions at intensities below the anaerobic threshold. At constant power outputs up to three minutes is required for the oxygen consumption to plateau, such that all energy requirements are supplied aerobically. This plateau represents a steady state at intensities below the anaerobic threshold. At intensities above anaerobic threshold there is, however, a further increase in oxygen uptake over time. This increase in oxygen consumption beyond the anaerobic threshold, termed the "slow component" of oxygen uptake kinetics, causes mechanical efficiency to decrease over time, particularly during high to extreme work intensities.

With these caveats the efficiency of external power output or work rate is traditionally calculated using four different methods, as follows:

$$\text{Gross efficiency \%} = \frac{\text{Power output}}{\text{Energy expended}} = \frac{P}{E} \times 100$$

$$\text{Net efficiency \%} = \frac{\text{Power output}}{\substack{\text{Energy expended above} \\ \text{that at rest}}} = \frac{P}{E - e} \times 100$$

$$\text{Work efficiency \%} = \frac{\text{Power output}}{\substack{\text{Energy expended above} \\ \text{that in unloaded cycling}}} = \frac{P}{E_L - E_U} \times 100$$

$$\text{Delta efficiency \%} = \frac{\Delta \text{ Power Output}}{\Delta \text{ Energy expended}} = \frac{\Delta P}{\Delta E} \times 100$$

Where P = caloric equivalent of external power output

E = gross caloric expenditure including resting expenditure

e = resting caloric expenditure

E_L = caloric expenditure under load

E_U = caloric expenditure when unloaded

ΔP = caloric equivalent of increments in power output above a previous power output

ΔE = increment in caloric expenditure related to the two power outputs used in ΔP

The above four methods of defining efficiency have their advantages and disadvantages; some of these are pointed out briefly below. Gross efficiency, while simple to calculate, has the disadvantage of including resting oxygen uptake in the calculation because oxygen consumption at rest is not a component of exercise efficiency. Net efficiency is often considered a more appropriate measure than gross efficiency because the effect of resting metabolism is removed by subtraction. Resting metabolism is, however, difficult to measure as it is affected by the individual's posture, such as standing, sitting, or lying, and has inherent variability linked to diurnal and monthly human biorhythms.

Work efficiency is defined in such a way as to eliminate the internal work associated with moving the limbs while unloaded. In calculating the efficiency of cycling on an ergometer, for example, the internal work rate represented by the oxygen cost of unloaded cycling is subtracted from the oxygen consumption associated with loaded cycling. One limitation of this method, however, is that oxygen consumption when working unloaded does not only represent internal work, but also includes a small component of external work due to the residual friction associated with operating an unloaded ergometer. This additional workload cannot be eliminated and this nonmeasured component of external work becomes a small but significant error when calculating external work efficiency.

If oxygen consumption rises linearly with increasing work rate, efficiency can be represented by the slope of the regression function of power output with oxygen consumption, termed delta efficiency. Delta efficiency is likely to be a superior measure, as it eliminates the errors inherent in attempting to establish gross and net efficiency; but this method can be used only when there is a linear relationship between power output and oxygen consumption over the measured range of power outputs.

The above four methods result in different values being calculated for efficiency under the same experimental conditions on a bicycle ergometer. DeVries and Housh (1994) illustrated this point with gross efficiency showing a range of 7.5% to 20.4%, net efficiency of 9.8% to 24.1%, and delta efficiency of 24.4% to 34.0%. Work efficiency was not calculated in this study because of the difficulty in obtaining a true zero-work pedaling condition.

The above approaches to measuring the movement efficiency cannot be implemented when the task-related power output is either unknown or does not accurately reflect the internal and external work demands of the activity. The total power output of many "real skills," for example, mining, forestry, and other work skills is difficult to quantify. In this situation "economy," defined as the energy expenditure required in completing the task, can provide a suitable measure of the organism's capacity to convert chemical energy to mechanical work. The less energy required to perform the task, the more economical the movement.

Economy, as defined above, has often been used to quantify the metabolic cost of doing work in locomotor tasks. In order to standardise the economy measurement to take into account variations in speed, oxygen consumption can be divided by the speed of locomotion. The units for the two parts of this equation are selected so that time can be canceled out. For example, oxygen consumption is measured in $ml \cdot kg^{-1} \cdot min^{-1}$ and speed of locomotion is measured as $m \cdot min^{-1}$ or $km \cdot min^{-1}$. Consequently, the standard units for economy become millilitres of oxygen consumed per kilogram per distance traveled in meters or kilometers. Using a similar approach to the calculation of efficiency that we outlined above, the economy of locomotion can be calculated by the following three methods.

$$\text{Gross economy} = \frac{\text{Energy expended}}{\text{Speed}} = \frac{E}{S}$$

$$\text{Net economy} = \frac{\text{Energy expended above that at rest}}{\text{Speed}} = \frac{E - e}{S}$$

$$\text{Delta economy} = \frac{\Delta \text{ Energy expended}}{\Delta \text{ Speed}} = \frac{\Delta E}{\Delta S}$$

Where E = total $\dot{V}O_2$ including the resting $\dot{V}O_2$

S = speed

e = resting $\dot{V}O_2$

ΔE = increment in $\dot{V}O_2$ above that of the previous selected speed

ΔS = increment in speed related to the VO_2s selected in ΔE

Based on the previous discussion of efficiency, delta economy may be the most appropriate measure for estimating movement economy. As with delta efficiency its validity relies on a linear relationship between speed of progression and oxygen cost over the range of speeds for the particular action mode being considered. While a linear relationship with oxygen uptake is found over a wide range of speeds for running (Hreljac 1993), a linear function does not hold for walking. Walking presents a U-shaped relationship, with higher oxygen costs at speeds of locomotion both slower and faster than preferred.

Coupled with the oxygen-cost/speed relationship is the need to compare the different movement economies of action modes with standardised units. Since gross economy does not make an allowance for resting metabolism, net economy might be the most appropriate standardised method for comparing movement economy across a variety of action modes. Table 4.1 demonstrates some of the variability in net economy both within and between the action modes of walking, running, creeping on all fours, and swimming.

When comparing the four locomotor actions in table 4.1, it is evident that walking is the most economical form of locomotion. As pointed out in our earlier comment on the U-shaped oxygen-consumption/speed function for walking, economy of walking (shown in the table) varies considerably across a range of speeds with minimum cost occurring at approximately 75 m·min^{-1} (4.5km·hr^{-1}) (Hreljac 1993). The quadratic model that best fits the data of individual oxygen-consumption/speed relationships for walking predicts that slower and faster speeds than the optimal 4.5km·hr^{-1} will increase the net oxygen cost per kilometer of walking and, therefore, decrease economy of movement. Alternatively, running is reported to have a relatively constant metabolic cost per kilometer across a wide range of running speeds. The cost of running is reported to average approximately 200 ml of oxygen consumed per kilogram body mass for each kilometer traveled in active fit subjects (Hreljac 1993). Trained runners have lower metabolic costs of transport compared to individuals of average fitness, and there is also variability in net economy between athletes. Data from a study by Joyner (1991), for example, with 12 well-trained marathon runners, revealed an 18% difference between the least and most economical athletes.

Freestyle swimming is not only a less economical form of locomotion than running, but also the economy of the action is considerably more variable between individuals. Costill, Maglischo, and Richardson (1992)

Table 4.1   Net Economy of Human Walking, Walking on Hands and Feet (Creeping), Running, and Swimming

	Speed (m·min^{-1})	Mean net economy (ml·kg^{-1}·km^{-1})	Authors
Slow walking	40	120	Sparrow and Newell 1998
Fast walking	124	173	Hreljac 1993
Ideal walking	75	110	Hreljac 1993
Slow running	124	201	Hreljac 1993
Best running	268	162	Joyner 1991
Worst running	268	192	Joyner 1991
Creeping	40	450	Sparrow and Newell 1998
Best swimming	66	300	Costill et al. 1992
Worst swimming	66	820	Costill et al. 1992

demonstrated a 270% difference between the least and the most economical swimmers. This variability in the economy of trained swimmers compared to trained runners is likely to be associated with the ongoing practice effects on the skill of swimming.

A further interesting comparison from the data in table 4.1 is between the gait modes of creeping and normal upright walking. Comparing the same individuals, Sparrow and Newell (1998) revealed approximately a 400% lower net economy between normal upright walking and creeping on a horizontal treadmill at the relatively slow speed of 40 m·min⁻¹. The considerable oxygen cost of locomotion per kilogram per kilometer traveled for creeping illustrates the relatively inefficient nature of this novel complex skill. One interesting speculation is the extent to which this difference is likely to be attributed to practice effects or due to the inherently less well-adapted physical constraints of hands-and-feet walking. With respect to the contribution of practice the individuals in Sparrow and Newell's (1998) study undertook only 16 three-minute trials at creeping. It would be interesting to know, when compared to almost a lifetime of practice at upright gait, what the potential contribution of practice would be to the locomotor economy of this task.

At the beginning of this section we used the term "relative" to convey the idea that "economy" is a qualitative concept, and there is no easy distinction between "economical" and "uneconomical" movements. In this paper we suggest, for example, that early in practice individuals perform relatively less economically than they would later in practice. Similarly, as we have seen above, some action modes, such as swimming, are much less economical than others. In the following section the first of our major topics is addressed, that of movement economy, pacing, and preferred modes. The fundamental observation here is that relative to externally paced conditions self-paced, or "preferred" modes, are more economical of energy expenditure.

Preferred Modes and Pacing

It is interesting to observe that across a wide range of motor activities, when unconstrained by an outside agent, individuals naturally adopt a preferred mode or "comfort mode." The propensity to adopt preferred modes has also been referred to as "self-optimising" (e.g., Cavanagh and Kram 1985) to suggest that preferred modes are both self-selected, in that augmented feedback is not required, and optimal with respect to variables such as work, time, or energy. While preferred modes have most commonly been operationalised in terms of preferred rate, in which the number of repetitions or cycles per unit time is the independent variable, preferred modes have also been examined in relation to other optimum criteria, such as optimum bicycle seat height (Nordeen-Snyder

1977). Despite the variety of ways in which preferred modes have been operationalised, with few exceptions the common finding has been that at preferred mode metabolic energy expenditure is minimised relative to performing under nonpreferred conditions. The early work by Salvendy (1972), for example, revealed the characteristic inverted U-shaped relationship between preferred rates of movement and economy. As shown in figure 4.1 freely chosen work rate during cycle ergometry, when using a hand-operated pump and stepping up and down on a bench (Harvard Step Test), was associated with the lowest physiological cost and, therefore, highest efficiency relative to work rates faster or slower than freely chosen or "preferred."

More recent work has shown the relationship between preferred rate and movement economy in human walking and running (Gotshall, Bauer, and Fahmer 1996; Cavanagh and Williams 1982; Martin and Morgan 1992; Redfield and Hull 1984). Studies of stride- length variation have shown that an optimum stride length can be located with either an increase or decrease in length resulting in an increase in metabolic energy expenditure (Heinert, Serfass, and Stull 1988; Högberg 1952; Hreljac 1993). In order to explain the stride- length/economy relationship it has been suggested that walking more slowly than preferred (with a relatively short stride length) causes the elastic energy stored in the muscles to be wasted in static components of muscle activity. In addition, at a slow gait speed, body weight is supported for a long time relative to the useful work done to propel the body in the direction of travel. Traveling at rates faster than preferred causes the energy consumption to increase more rapidly than the useful work done and economy again falls off, presumably because of the disproportionate increase of energy wasted in accelerating and decelerating body parts.

Cavanagh and Williams (1982), for example, observed that a preferred stride rate was evident for 10 trained male runners when running at a 7 minute-per-mile pace. The preferred stride length was established as the stride length that minimised oxygen consumption. After establishing their most economical stride length as a percentage of leg length the runners then performed tests at a 7 minute-per-mile pace at stride lengths 20% longer and 20% shorter than their preferred stride length. The results indicated that oxygen consumption increased by 2.6 and 3.4 ml·kg^{-1}·min^{-1} at the shorter and longer stride lengths, respectively. Similar relationships between running economy and stride length were reported by Heinert, Serfass, and Stull (1988) when preferred stride length was manipulated. They revealed that 16 male distance runners running with stride lengths 8% longer and shorter than preferred resulted in oxygen consumption increases of 3.8% and 2.1%, respectively. To show the association between stride length and oxygen consumption, figure 4.2 reproduces the best-fit curves for two subjects in the Cavanagh and Williams (1982) study.

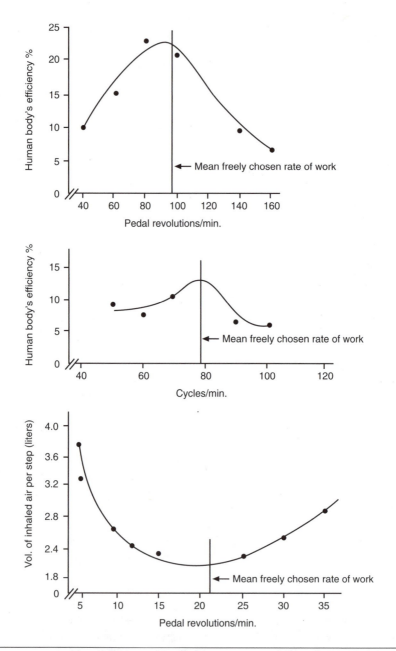

Figure 4.1 Effect of paced and unpaced work on efficiency of the human body. Top: bicycle ergometer; Middle: pump ergometer; Bottom: Harvard Step Test.

Reprinted, by permission, from G. Salvendy, 1972, "Physiological and psychological aspects of paced and unpaced performance," *Acta Physiologica Academiae Scientiarum Hungaricae* 42: 267-275.

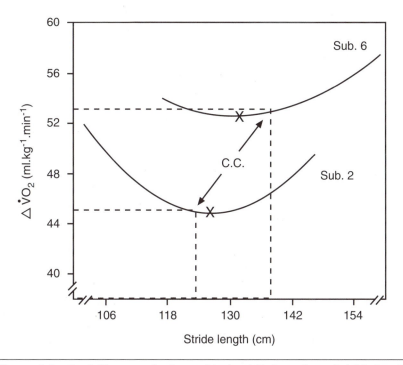

Figure 4.2 Best-fit curves for two subjects at their preferred stride lengths and at stride lengths longer and shorter than preferred. The cross on each curve corresponds to the stride length that would confer lowest oxygen consumption. The dashed lines show the stride length chosen by the subjects as optimal (C.C.). Subject 2 has a shorter stride length and lower oxygen uptake than subject 6.

From Cavanagh and Williams, 1982. Used with permission.

In addition to the work on preferred modes in gait, there has also been interest in preferred modes in cycling, and from time to time other tasks have been investigated from a preferred-mode perspective. Studies of cycling with power output held constant have, interestingly, sometimes observed that the most economical pedal rate is slower than the preferred pedal rate (Patterson and Moreno 1990; Marsh and Martin 1993). Marsh and Martin, for example, showed that preferred rate was significantly higher than the most economical rate in both trained and untrained cyclists, as shown in figure 4.3. It was concluded that the disadvantage of higher aerobic demand at the preferred rate is outweighed by the need to enhance muscular power production and minimise peripheral stress. In addition, it has been observed that pedaling rates that produce a minimal neuromuscular fatigue coincide with the subject's preferred rate (Takaishi et al. 1996). This observation suggests that faster pedal rates are related to increasing muscular power and minimise peripheral stress rather than increasing metabolic economy.

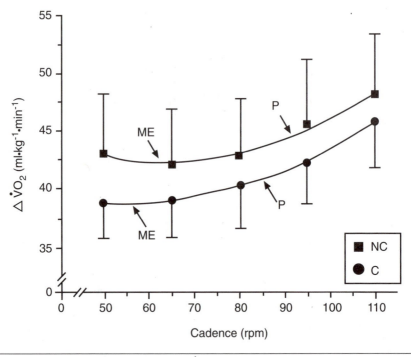

Figure 4.3 Oxygen consumption ($\dot{V}O_2$) for cyclists (C) and noncyclists (NC) pedaling at 50, 65, 80, 95, and 110 rpm at a power output of 200 Watts. The most economical (ME) and the preferred (P) cadences are identified on the oxygen consumption curves.

Reproduced from original publication: Marsh, A.P. and P.E. Martin, 1993, "The association between cycling experience and preferred and most economical cadences," *Medicine and Science in Sports and Exercise* 23: 186-192. Used with permission.

Takaishi et al. observed that the pedaling rate that minimised neuromuscular fatigue did not produce the minimal oxygen cost that was, however, associated with the preferred rate of cycling. This study also indicated that the increase in pedal rate from 40 rpm to 80 rpm decreased the pedal force, causing recruitment of a greater percentage of slow-twitch muscle fibers. Slow-twitch fibers have been shown to possess a greater oxidative capacity and mechanical efficiency than fast-twitch fibres (Coyle et al. 1992). This observation suggests higher pedal frequency associated with lower pedal forces should be more economical of energy expenditure if a greater proportion of slow-twitch fibers is recruited.

Cyclists could minimise peripheral muscle fatigue by pedaling at a rate that produces a higher than optimal oxygen cost, but which lowers crank forces. This upper limit for pedaling rate would be influenced by the cyclist's ability to direct the pedaling force perpendicular to the crank. If, however, the pedal forces were poorly directed as pedal rate increased, the pedal forces may increase. Coyle et al. (1992) showed that their "force effectiveness index" decreased in a linear manner as pedaling rate increased from 0.46 to 0.16 at a power output of 100 W and from 0.53 to 0.26 at 200 W. This finding indicates that the ability to effectively direct pedal forces decreases when pedal rate increases at a constant power output. The authors speculated that pedaling rate might increase until there is no further reduction in the resultant force on the pedals. This rate should minimise fatigue by operating at lower percentage of the subject's maximum strength and only slightly increasing oxygen cost.

The proposition that optimal pedaling rate depends on the cyclist's ability to apply forces to the pedals in a direction perpendicular to the crank arm is consistent with the finding that trained cyclists are more effective than recreational riders at directing pedal forces perpendicular to the crank arm. They can pedal at higher rates without power or economy decrements, suggesting that there are practice-related mechanisms underlying movement economy at preferred rates.

Effects of rate on wheelchair propulsion have also been examined, with increases in velocity causing increases in cycle frequency (Vanlandewijck, Spaepen, and Lysens 1994). With respect to an optimal frequency, it was concluded that road-racing wheelchair cyclists have higher pedaling frequencies because they train using high rates and, therefore, perform more efficiently at faster rates. On the other hand, novice performers have lower freely chosen lower pedal rates and lower optimal pedal rates. As wheelchair speed increases wheelchair users have to adapt their movement patterns in order to maintain the higher cycle frequency. As with cycling, this process of adaptation is learned and with practice not only does performance become more economical, but the preferred mode may also change.

In a recent study (Sparrow, et al. in press), unpracticed individuals had to row at preferred and nonpreferred rates (20% faster "+20%" and 20% slower "-20%") with a fixed power output. It is important to note that we were careful to ensure that preferred rate effects were examined independent of variations in power output. The study confirmed that performance at preferred rate is more economical in terms of oxygen consumption relative to power output than at rates faster or slower than preferred. The data suggested, however, that the traditional U-shaped relationship between oxygen consumption and work rate, with the bottom of the function representing the most economical rate, may, to some extent, be a function of changes in work rate combined with variation in power. While we found that at +20% of preferred rate performance was least economical, the -20% preferred rate condition was very similar in metabolic demands to the preferred rate condition. We attributed this finding to the fact that for this task a slower-than-preferred mode is closer to optimal, and so by setting a slower stroke rate we were assisting the participant to adopt a more economical response.

With respect to the effects of preferred and nonpreferred rates on movement control characteristics in the Sparrow et al. (in press) study, we also found that, as measured by the duration and length of drive and recovery phases, subjects tended to row with shorter faster strokes in the +20% phase and with longer slower strokes in the -20% phase. Thus, a combination of stroke length and duration appeared here, as in other studies (Dawson 1998), to be the critical control or "scaling" variables influencing the choice of preferred mode.

In summary, the literature on preferred modes can be characterised as a motor control phenomenon. Actions appear to be controlled, or "parameterised" or "scaled," with respect to speed, amplitude, or other scaling variables, in such a way that at any given level of practice metabolic energy is minimised relative to nonpreferred modes. The only qualifier to this observation is that, in some cases, other imperatives may override the propensity to minimise metabolic cost and the organism may, at least in the short term, employ less than metabolically optimal control parameters.

Pacing

We now raise a question as to the relationship between the concept of preferred mode, specifically preferred rate, and the practice of pacing as used in sport or other activities. While there is link between the two concepts it is not clear whether, to date, these ideas have been integrated in a systematic way.

In describing pacing, the first important distinction is between self-paced, or internally paced, and externally paced activities. Most everyday activities are self-paced, such that individuals meet the task demands at their own pace unconstrained by an outside agent. While most people are expected to maintain an acceptable level of productivity, many everyday work tasks can be self-paced. In order to maximise performance it is usual for individuals to establish a pace that allows work to be continued largely uninterrupted, except for prescribed breaks, for the duration of the working day. Poole and Ross (1983), for example, showed that while experienced sheep shearers tallied more sheep in a working day than their inexperienced colleagues, both groups worked at the same rate of metabolic energy expenditure as measured by their oxygen consumption. As an aside, the experienced shearers were, therefore, more economical of metabolic energy expenditure per sheep and, by this criterion, more skilled in being capable of greater output at the same metabolic energy cost.

Some activities are externally paced by an outside agent such as an employer, a machine, competitors, or teammates, and these outside agents may force the performer to adopt a nonoptimal pace from the point of view of maximising work output relative to metabolic energy expenditure. While there has been much "conventional wisdom" in sport, and presumably other domains, concerning the pace that coaches, instructors, or employers should impose to maximise performance, as Foster et al. (1993) have indicated, the issue has received little research attention. DeVries and Housh (1994) have also commented on the pacing issue, making the observation that in largely aerobic activities, such as a two- mile (3.2-km) or more run, consistent pace is a common feature of the performance. In swimming 1500 meters where the 100-meter split times increase as the race progresses, the stroke rate is maintained even though less force is produced per stroke due to fatigue.

One hypothesis, raised by DeVries and Housh (1994), is that there is an additional metabolic cost associated with changing pace, and consistent pace is, therefore, conducive to conserving metabolic energy. In a recent study of pacing in cycling Foster et al. (1993) found that an even-paced strategy produced the fastest time for a two-km ride, but there were no significant differences in metabolic measures, such as oxygen consumption, across the slow starting-pace to fast starting-pace strategies. In contrast, Ariyoshi, Yamaji, and Shepard (1979) had eight middle-distance runners perform three four-minute runs at three different paces, fast-slow, slow-fast, and steady pace. They found that the oxygen cost of the fast-slow pace was lower than for the other two paces, although the difference was not statistically significant. Heart rates were higher for the first minute of the fast-slow condition, but after this there was no difference in heart rates. Recovery proceeded faster with the fast-slow strategy; after four minutes of recovery, heart rate had fallen to 88 beats per minute; whereas in the slow-fast and steady-paced strategies heart rates remained in the mid 90s. The physiological advantage of the fast-slow pacing schedule, while only associated with 3.7% less oxygen consumption, may, however, be considered important given the narrow margins for success in many sports.

Having discussed the locus of the pacing strategy, either internal or external, it is also important to make an observation on the "time dependency" of the pacing strategy. Most of the laboratory-based research to date has considered pacing effects using protocols in which within a trial the work rate or other preferred mode such as preferred bicycle seat height, does not change over time and is, therefore, time independent. In real-world situations the pacing strategy is often time dependent, in that, over the time course of the task, the rate or pace that the performer adopts (internal pacing), or is constrained to adopt (external pacing), changes at least once during the time sample, trial, or event. Thus, time-dependent pacing is not characterised by a single value, but rather is reflected in a rate/time function, in which the cycle rate varies over time. At present little is known about the rate/time characteristics of everyday repetitive skills.

Some of our recent work has indicated that preferred work rate is not constant throughout an experimental trial. As can be seen from our data in the top panel of figure 4.4, the four participants' preferred rates while

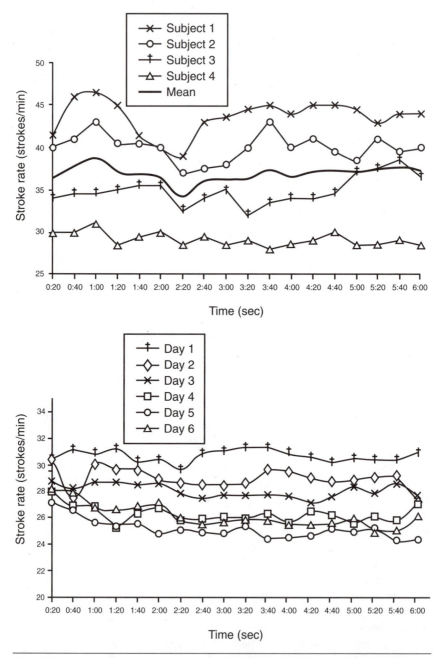

Figure 4.4 Top panel: preferred rate/time function for four individuals performing a six-minute rowing ergometer trial at fixed power output (100 Watts). The mean rate/time function for the group is indicated. Bottom panel: change in preferred rate/time function over days of practice for one subject.

rowing an ergometer show characteristic rate/time functions within the six-minute trial. The individual rate/time functions show, therefore, how these individuals satisfied the same task constraints of a fixed external power output for the same trial duration, but each had a characteristically different rate/time curve.

We have also drawn a curve in the top panel of figure 4.4 that is the mean of the preferred rates at each of the 20-second time intervals. We have added this curve to illustrate an externally paced rate/time function that is different from any of the internally paced (preferred) functions. In some tasks individuals might be compelled to "keep up" with others such that the group members work at an externally imposed pace that will be more or less close to their individual preferred pace. Presumably a less economical performance would be predicted dependent on the degree of difference between the individual's preferred pace and the externally imposed function. There is also likely to be an externally imposed function, such as the mean curve drawn in figure 4.4, that minimises the extent to which the group as a whole is working at a nonoptimal (with respect to metabolic energy cost) pace/time function. An interesting general question for future research is the effects or "consequences," with respect to maximising performance, of an external pacing regime that forces individuals away from a preferred internally paced rate/time function. We assume that disrupting the internal pacing is detrimental to performance and in sports measures are taken to drive competitors away from a preferred mode using strategies to "set," or "break," the pace. In some activities, such as rowing, an entire team effort is oriented at externally pacing competitors according to a preferred strategy.

In many sporting competitions success is determined by an athlete's ability to cover a specified distance in the shortest time. This may be achieved in two different competitive arrangements. First, the competition may be organised such that the athletes compete "head-to-head" such as in track running; in this situation pacing is influenced by the competitors' tactics. There are also a variety of competitions that require competition "against the clock," where the activity is entirely internally paced. In these sports such as Nordic skiing and some cycling events, success is determined by the athlete's ability to produce a fast time using some self-selected pacing strategy. In both of these competitive situations pacing is, presumably, an important determinant of success. It has been shown, for example, that individuals at different levels of performance have different preferred rates (Faria 1984; Hoffman 1992; Marsh and Martin 1993; Smith and Spinks 1995). In general, the data show that more advanced performers adopt rates that are closer to optimal with respect to oxygen consumed. Understanding how preferred and nonpreferred rates influence energy metabolism and movement economy may enable athletes to design more specific training programs and more effective competition strategies. In addition the ability of athletes to increase their preferred or most economical rate may increase their level of performance.

Transitions in Coordination

One question that has received considerable research attention in recent years concerns the reasons why, under certain conditions, humans and other animals shift, or make a transition, from one coordination pattern to another. In some situations such transitions have been suggested to be energy-saving mechanisms, such that when the transition is made it is more economical to adopt a new movement pattern than to continue in the same coordination mode. Considerable theoretical impetus for explaining transitions has been from a "dynamical systems" perspective because stability in coordination and energy minimisation are key characteristics of dynamical systems (Schmidt and Fitzpatrick 1996). Diedrich and Warren (1995) summarised the issue nicely in pointing out that motor behaviour in humans and animals exhibits two notable features: the presence of stable patterns of coordination and the sudden reorganisation that occurs when switching between them. One fundamental question, however, is whether such transitions in coordination are precipitated in order to conserve metabolic energy. If the economy-based hypothesis were to be supported the transition to another preferred coordination mode would be made precisely when the new coordination pattern is less demanding of metabolic energy.

Numerous studies of gait patterns—walking and running in humans; and walk, trot, gallop, and other patterns in quadrupeds—have provided data on which to draw in order to address the "stimulus-for-transition" hypothesis. Walking, running, and other gaits (such as creeping or hopping) utilise the massive muscle groups of the lower limbs and torso and, therefore, fundamental changes in coordination (such as switching from a walk to a run) and control (locomoting faster or slower) are reflected in measurable changes in metabolic cost. Most other tasks that have been used to examine stability and transition issues in coordination have been relatively undemanding of metabolic energy and make considerably less impact on metabolic energy demand.

One popular view of gait transitions in humans and other animals was that the expedient to conserve metabolic energy precipitated the transitions in coordination associated with the different gait modes. In other words, from this view, transitions are essentially an energy-conservation mechanism. An alternative hypothesis to the energy minimisation proposal is that transitions in coordination are made when the organism becomes unstable. Loss of stability may be associated, however, with a greater expenditure of metabolic energy and it has generally been concluded that the more stable the movement pattern, the more efficient the motion (Brisswalter and Mottet 1996; Holt, Hamill, and Andres 1991; Holt et al. 1995). In support of this observation, in walking at preferred rates metabolic cost is at a minimum, and there is maximal stability of the head and joint actions (Holt et al. 1995). Holt et al. (1995) also reported that the subjects commented on their feelings of being "unstable " or " unbalanced" when walking at nonoptimal rates. A possible explanation for the feeling of instability is that the longer and slower strides resulted in the subjects losing their dynamic equilibrium.

Mechanisms Underlying the Selection of Preferred Modes

In this section of the chapter we focus attention on the mechanisms underlying the selection of preferred modes. While most researchers have speculated as to the processes associated with preferred mode selection, there has not previously been a systematic review of these processes. Here, we present a review of some of the mechanisms that might be associated with preferred mode selection across a range of motor tasks. We have characterised these "mechanisms" as various categories of constraint consistent with a "constraints-based" framework of coordination and control proposed by Sparrow and Newell (1998).

Physiological Constraints

Physiological constraints associated with the rate of muscle contraction and muscle fibre type are two constraints on the organism that influence the selection of preferred modes. Early studies by Hill (1922) indicated that the efficiency of force production by human muscle was dependent on the rate of contraction. Thus, as suggested before (Sparrow 1983), it is reasonable to assume that when preferred modes are rate dependent economy will be influenced by the timing of muscular contraction with respect to the duration of the contraction and when the contraction takes place relative to the activation of other muscles. In more recent work Chapman and Sanderson (1990) have suggested that the power-velocity relationship of a muscle may influence the preferred rate during cyclical activities such as walking, running, and cycling. The power-velocity relationship in Chapman and Sanderson's (1990) experiment displayed an inverted U-pattern, representing a velocity that maximised power output and therefore determined the rate of movement.

Another factor that may influence preferred rate is the morphological makeup of the performer with respect to the percentage of fast- and slow-twitch fiber type and the cross-sectional area of the fibres. Coyle et al. (1992) observed that while cycling economy varied considerably within a group of well-trained cyclists, their biomechanical data indicated that the differences in economy were not due to cycling technique, as the percentage of force applied to the pedal did not correlate with cycling economy. Cycling economy was, however, related to the percentage of type I muscle fibers in the vastus lateralis suggesting that the greater oxidative capacity of type I muscle fibres contributed to certain individuals having greater mechanical efficiency. In the same study muscle fibre type was observed to positively correlate with economy during two-legged knee extension, supporting the hypothesis that type I muscle fibres are more efficient than type II fibers.

As suggested above, economy at optimum rates (such as pedal rates in cycling) may be related to the selective recruitment of muscle fibres, either type I or type II. Many studies have indicated that muscular efficiency occurs at approximately one-third of the maximal shortening velocity in both type I and type II muscle fibers. The maximal shortening velocity of type II muscle fibers is, however, three to five times greater than that of type I muscle fibers (Goldspink 1978; Kushmerick 1983; Fitts, Costill, and Gardetto 1989). Thus, a considerably faster pace or rate would be associated with optimising energy expenditure in actions dominated by type II fibers. One of the important applied science issues emerging from this section is, therefore, that there are likely to be individual differences in preferred rate that are influenced by muscle fiber type composition. For example, in activities in which a team of individuals is constrained to work at a fixed externally imposed cycle rate, such as in rowing or pursuit cycling, some members of the team may, at different times, be working at pace that is nonoptimal. Optimising performance, in such circumstances, might, in part, be assisted by selecting a collective pace-time function for the event that minimises the discrepancy or "distance" between individual preferred pace-time functions and those imposed by the coach.

Coupling or "Entrainment"

In recent years a body of research has developed that we have here subsumed under the heading of coupling or "entrainment." The entrainment phenomenon and its contribution to the literature on movement economy has already been identified in general terms (Sparrow and Newell 1998), but in this chapter we will discuss the entrainment issue with specific reference to preferred modes. The coupling, or entrainment, of the cardiorespiratory cycle to the timing of limb motion has been described in human and nonhuman subjects in various repetitive, rhythmic motor activities. Most of the activities studied in relation to coupling have been locomotor actions such as cycling or running, but performance at other tasks, such as lifting, also appears to be facilitated by entrainment of the movement cycle with respiration or other internal processes.

One possibility is that preferred rates are established to produce an economical coupling of the respiratory or cardiac cycle to the phasing of limb motion. It is thought that the coupling of breathing pattern and movement cycles provides favorable conditions for accomplishment of the motor task, such as the application of force (Garlando et al. 1985). In rowing, for example, the entrainment of breathing to the rowing cycle may be necessary to produce optimal power in the drive phase of the rowing stroke (Mahler et al. 1991). Coordination between respiratory muscles, which act to displace the thorax and abdomen, and the upper extremity muscles involved in the rowing stroke might be the mechanism associated with reduced oxygen consumption with entrainment (Maclennan et al. 1994). Consistent with the entrainment hypothesis, it has been suggested that breathing patterns selected by elite rowers may serve to either minimise the work of breathing or reduce the sense of respiratory effort, or both (Mahler et al. 1991).

Despite the weight of evidence to support the entrainment phenomenon, there is a question as to the type of motor action chosen for investigation. In some actions, such as running, particularly at high power outputs, the increased metabolic demand may cause the locomotor cycle and the breathing cycle to work out of phase (not entrained). In an action such as running there is, presumably, considerably less mechanical constraint on respiration than there would be in rowing or swimming. As an anecdotal observation, swimming seems to be an action in which it is very difficult not to entrain breathing with the stroke cycle.

There is, therefore, a general issue as to the extent to which breathing patterns are determined mainly by respiratory needs rather than mechanical influences. Kay, Petersen, and Vejby-Christensen (1975), for example, concluded that the selection of breathing pattern seems to be unrelated to the nature of the stimulus but closely geared to the metabolic needs of the body. They go on to explain that when subjects are asked to stride or cycle in time to an outside stimulus, for example, a metronome or flashing light, they are conscious of the rhythm and are more likely to entrain their breathing. This is then an experimenter-imposed locomotor coupling, and it has been argued that true coupling can only be established with years of training. Kohl, Koller, and Jäger (1981) provide support for this view in showing that the coordination between pedaling and breathing rhythm increase with pedaling training.

Kohl, Koller, and Jäger (1981) also found that locomotor-respiratory coupling reduced oxygen consumption at a moderate intensity of cycling and thereby enhanced exercise economy. In addition, at the same intensity of cycling, subjects who showed entrainment breathing (without feedback) had a lower oxygen cost compared with random breathing. Others have also noted that periods of uncoordination between breathing and cycling are frequently accompanied by an increase in oxygen consumption (Garlando et al. 1985). When subjects were constrained to control their breathing (with the aid of an acoustic signal), increased oxygen consumption was found in comparison with oxygen consumption during runs with a spontaneous preferred breathing rhythm. Although ratings of perceived exertion were not measured, subjects reported that the controlled breathing produced discomfort (Garlando et al. 1985).

Preferred rates (Cavanagh and Kram 1985; Sparrow et al. in press) elicit lower heart rates and oxygen consumption than nonpreferred rates at a fixed power output. It is an interesting question as to whether self-selected modes more likely to elicit entrainment of breathing and movement than are experimenter-imposed rates. Kohl, Koller, and Jäger (1981) experimented with free pedaling rates or preferred rates while a constant workload was maintained. They found that with the majority of participants (both cyclists and noncyclists) the pedaling and breathing rhythms were coordinated at preferred rates, which led to a decrease in oxygen consumption.

Preferred rate and level of training contribute to increases in performance, with lower metabolic data and more efficient biomechanical data at a fixed power output than lesser trained counterparts. Locomotor coupling in well-trained athletes rather than untrained counterparts would follow this trend. This minimisation of work leads to a reserve of energy, which can be utilised to improve performance. Overall, the theoretical advantage of entrainment of breathing is thought to be to enhance biomechanical efficiency and/or performance.

Anthropometric Constraints

Anthropometric constraints of the performer may influence the preferred rate of movement. As mentioned earlier, changes in stride rate away from the preferred rate in running decreases metabolic economy. Bergh et al. (1991) established that a higher body mass contributes to a lower aerobic demand per kilogram of body weight, and Williams and Cavanagh (1987) also observed inverse relationships between body mass and submaximal oxygen consumption for elite male and female runners.

Rowland (1989) and Unnithan and Eston (1990) showed that boys displayed shorter stride lengths and higher stride rates than men; the oxygen cost per stride was, however, similar for both groups. Differences in leg length do not, therefore, appear to influence running economy, a hypothesis supported by Pate et al. (1992) who found no significant correlation between leg length and running economy. These findings are in contrast to those by Williams and Cavanagh (1987) who observed that anthropometric variables associated with linear dimensions of the body such as leg length, foot length, and pelvic width had correlations ranging from -0.55 to -0.68 with economy in elite male runners.

Similarly, Burke and Brush (1979) also suggested a positive association between anthropometric variables and running economy. They found that successful female distance runners had smaller bone diameter and shorter upper leg length in proportion to lower leg length than other female runners. A biomechanical constraint that may have offered an advantage was the proximity of the centre of gravity of the whole leg to the hip. Increased proximity would reduce the limb's inertia during recovery, and there may have been an associated reduction in the metabolic cost moving the leg.

Other anthropometric factors such as foot length and trunk angle have been observed to influence running economy. Increasing the mass of the feet reduces running economy to a greater extent than does increasing the mass of other body parts (Claremont and Hall 1988; Martin, Heise, and Morgan 1993), and foot length has been observed to negatively correlate with running economy in elite marathon runners (Williams and Cavanagh 1986). Trunk angle has also been observed to influence running economy, as more economical runners possess a mean trunk angle of 5.9° relative to vertical while less economical runners have been observed to have mean trunk angles as low as 2.4° (Williams and Cavanagh 1987). It is believed that a trunk angle closer to vertical increases the mobility of the lumbar spine-pelvic tilt unit and in so doing less effort is required to maintain postural equilibrium (James and Brubaker 1973).

Sensory Information for Regulating Movement Economy

Economical movements are seen when individuals freely select a most economical mode and when refinements to the movement take place with practice. In this section we address the question of the informational support for movement economy and suggest the nature of the sensory information on the basis of which movements are coordinated and controlled in a metabolically economical fashion.

By way of introduction to our discussion of sensory information we reiterate one of Sparrow and Newell's (1998) major themes that ". . . although never explicitly denied a role in motor behavior, sensory information about metabolic energy expenditure has not previously been considered important for regulating movement" (p.191). Such sensory information is, in part, central or "interoceptive," information. Central information from the internal organs has not usually been considered central to understanding the sensory processes of movement coordination and control. A part of the chapter is, therefore, devoted to the use of Ratings of Perceived Exertion, which provide a measure of an individual's sensitivity to the sensory information concerning the energy expenditure or "effort" associated with performing a motor task.

Ratings of perceived exertion might provide an insight into the mechanism or process underlying the establishment of preferred rate. While there is strong evidence that individuals spontaneously adopt a locomotor pattern leading to the lowest energy cost (Brisswalter and Mottet 1996), it has also been suggested that other criteria might also influence the selection of preferred action modes. One proposal, for example, is that animals spontaneously adopt the mode of locomotion that minimises the peak musculoskeletal stress (e.g., Farley and Taylor 1991; Hreljac 1993). Such stresses are, presumably, related to the peripheral perception of effort and, in some cases, such peripheral sensations may override the expedient to perform with lower metabolic cost. It is an interesting question as to whether central and peripheral perceptions of perceived exertion, as measured using standardised scales, could be used to quantify, operationally, central sensory information, more closely related to central perceived exertion, and perceptions of a peripheral kind associated with musculoskeletal stress.

Not only does a shift away from a preferred mode decrease economy, but also, in the case of running, it has been reported that small deviations from either a freely chosen stride length (under- and overstriding) or stride rate influence ratings of perceived exertion (Cavanagh and Williams 1982). Messier, Franke, and Rejeski (1986) (cited in Bailey and Messier 1991) revealed that both local (legs) and general ratings of perceived exertion were significantly greater during runs in which the stride length of experienced runners was 14% longer than their freely chosen stride length. Local perceived exertion ratings increased significantly where these same subjects were asked to overstride by 7% or understride by 14%. The association of preferred modes and perceived exertion has also been reported by our group Sparrow et al. (in press) for rowing ergometry where increases or decreases in stroke rate, 20% faster and 20% slower than preferred, elicited statistically reliable differences in perceived exertion. Perceived exertion both central and peripheral may, therefore, guide our search for the optimum movement pattern to minimise energy expenditure. As Noble and Robertson (1996) observed ". . . the intensity of our perception provides the major intrinsic input for making decisions about our energy output" (p. 3). Sensations that we perceive as too intense for toleration require a decision to adjust the coordination and control characteristics of the action and thus, conserve energy.

In selecting freely chosen rate and in reducing metabolic energy expenditure with practice, metabolically optimal coordination and control parameters are adopted based on sensitivity to sensory stimulation from central sources and peripheral sensory information from receptors in the muscles, tendons, and joints. It is this discriminability of effort that guides the movement pattern to one that is more economical. Morgan (1994), for example, reported that 90% of experimental test subjects were able to accurately discern differences in power outputs of 25 watts in cycle ergometry. Sensitivity to peripheral stress may not only serve as a mechanism for guiding the performer toward an energetically optimal coordination and control function, but may also serve a protective function. Potential injury to the organism has been studied with regard to peak force stress on the limbs (Farley and Taylor 1991). As observed earlier, it has also been suggested that cyclists minimise peripheral muscle fatigue by pedaling at a rate that produces a higher than optimal oxygen cost, but that lowers crank forces (Patterson and Moreno 1990; Marsh and Martin 1993). The general conclusion from these observations is that peripheral sensations of stress, associated with joint forces or muscle fatigue may, in some cases, provide a more powerful stimulus for modifications to coordination and control than central, metabolic-energy-related sensory information.

Summary and Conclusion

This chapter has provided the opportunity to present our ideas concerning movement economy in, at times, a speculative manner. It is hoped, nevertheless, that we may have achieved some success if but a few of our speculations provide a stimulus to the reader's ideas on either these or related issues. At times we have had our own reservations concerning the weight of evidence for the "metabolic energy minimisation" hypothesis but have been sustained by the intuitive sense that humans and other animals are compelled to reduce the energy cost of everyday activities. To reinforce the intuition that we are pursuing scientifically important issues is the increasing body of evidence, only a small part of which we have presented here, that implicates metabolic energy considerations in the learning and control of a variety of motor tasks.

One aim we hope to have achieved here is to have framed a single hypothesis that unifies an extensive body of literature concerning the coordination and control of action. The hypothesis is that motor coordination and control parameters emerge as a consequence of the organism's propensity to minimise the metabolic energy expended in achieving the task goal. Metabolic energy cost may determine the pattern of muscle activation either in the control of action, when establishing a preferred mode, or in the learning of action, in which coordination and control parameters are modified with practice. We reviewed evidence to test this hypothesis and, in our view, the hypothesis fared well. One consideration, however, is that under some circumstances other imperatives might override the propensity to conserve metabolic energy. For example, peripheral sensations of effort associated with excessive forces that threaten the organism's integrity, or time constraints might, quite reasonably, justify more metabolically costly actions.

A further contribution is that we have outlined, in a systematic manner, various topics or subdomains related to metabolic energy expenditure and motor control. Our organisation of the literature into practice considerations and motor learning, and control issues and pacing, and our identifying the parameters by which the literature on entrainment can be identified, have been a useful exercise in organising our thinking about metabolic energy issues in particular and motor learning and control issues in general. Similarly, we have benefited from considering carefully the extent to which reading the literature presented here and undertaking our own experiments has been consistent with our everyday experience of learning complex, repetitive, high-energy-demanding skills. Our everyday experience has assisted in framing our research hypotheses, and our laboratory findings have been put to test on the track and in the pool. This, for us, has provided much of the motivation for our continuing interest in metabolic energy expenditure and motor learning and control.

References

Ariyoshi, M., K. Yamaji, and R.J. Shepard. 1979. Influence of running pace upon performance: effects upon treadmill endurance time and oxygen cost. *European Journal of Applied Physiology* 41: 83-91.

Bailey, S. P., and S.P. Messier. 1991. Variations in stride length and running economy in male novice runners subsequent to a seven-week training program. *International Journal of Sports Medicine.* 12: 299-304.

Bergh, U., B. Sjodin, A. Forsberg, and J. Svenenhag. 1991. The relationship between body mass and oxygen uptake during running in humans. *Medicine Science Sports and Exercise* 23: 205-211.

Brisswalter, J., and D. Mottet. 1996. Energy cost and stride duration variability at preferred transition gait speed between walking and running. *Canadian Journal of Applied Physiology* 21: 471-480.

Burke, E.J., and F.C. Brush. 1979. Physiological and anthropometric assessment of successful teenage female distance runners. *Research Quarterly* 50: 180-186.

Cavanagh, P.R., and R. Kram. 1985. Mechanical and muscular factors affecting the efficiency of human movement. *Medicine and Science in Sports and Exercise* 17: 326-331.

Cavanagh, P.R., and K.R. Williams. 1982. The effect of stride length variation on oxygen uptake during distance running. *Medicine and Science in Sports and Exercise* 14: 30-35.

Chapman, A.E., and D.J. Sanderson. 1990. Muscular coordination in sporting skills. In *Multiple Muscle Systems: Biomechanics and Movement Organization,* eds. J.M. Winters and S.L.Y. Woo, 608-620. New York: Springer-Verlag.

Claremont, A.D., and S.J. Hall. 1988. Effects of extremity loading upon energy expenditure and running mechanics. *Medicine and Science in Sports and Exercise* 20: 167-171.

Corlett, E.N., and K. Mahaveda. 1970. A relationship between freely chosen working pace and energy consumption curves. *Ergonomics* 14: 703-711.

Costill, D.L., E.W. Maglischo, and A.B. Richardson. 1992. *Swimming.* Oxford: Blackwell Scientific Publications.

Coyle, E., L. Sidossis, J. Horowitz, and J. Beltz. 1992. Cycling efficiency is related to the percentage of Type I muscle fibres. *Medicine Science Sports and Exercise* 24: 7825-7788.

Dawson, R.G., R.J. Lockwood, J.D. Wilson, and G. Freeman. 1998. The rowing cycle: sources of variance and invariance in ergometer and on-the-water performance. *Journal of Motor Behavior* 30: 33-43.

DeVries, H.A., and T.J. Housh. 1994. *Physiology of Exercise for Physical Education, Athletics and Exercise Science.* Dubuque, IA: Brown & Benchmark.

Diedrich, F. J., and W.H. Warren. 1995. Why change gaits? Dynamics of the walk-run transition. *Journal of Experimental Psychology* 21: 183-202.

Faria, I.E. 1984. Applied Physiology of Cycling. *Sports Medicine* 1: 187-204.

Farley, C.T., and C.R. Taylor. 1991. A mechanical trigger for the trot-gallop transition in horses. *Science* 253: 306-308.

Fitts, R.H., D.L. Costill, D.L., and P.R. Gardetto. 1989. Effect of swim exercise training on human muscle fiber function. *Journal of Applied Physiology* 66: 465-475.

Foster, C., A.C. Snyder, N.N. Thompson, M.A. Green, M. Foley, and M. Schrager. 1993. Effect of pacing strategy on cycle time trial performance. *Medicine and Science in Sports and Exercise* 25: 383-388.

Garlando, F., J. Kohl, E.A. Koller, and P. Pietsch. 1985. Effect of coupling the breathing and cycling rhythms on oxygen uptake during bicycle ergometry. *European Journal of Applied Physiology* 54: 497-501.

Goldspink, G. 1978. Energy turnover during contraction of different types of muscle. In *Biomechanics VI-A,* eds. E. Asumusses and K. Jorgensen, 27-39. Baltimore: University Park Press.

Gotshall, R.W., T.A. Bauer, and S.L. Fahmer. 1996. Cycling cadence alters exercise haemodynamics. *International Journal of Sports Medicine* 17: 17-21.

Hill, A.V. 1922. The maximum work and mechanical efficiency of human muscles and their most economical speed. *Journal of Physiology* 56: 19-41.

Heinert, L.D., R.C. Serfass, and G.A. Stull. 1988. Effect of stride length variation on oxygen uptake during level and positive grade treadmill running. *Research Quarterly* 59: 127-150.

Hoffman, M.D. 1992. Physiological comparisons of cross-country skiing techniques. *Medicine and Science in Sports and Exercise* 24: 1023-1032.

Högberg, P. 1952. How do stride length and stride frequency influence energy output in running. *Arbeitsphysiologie* 14: 437-441.

Holt, K.G., J. Hamill, and R.O. Andres. 1991. Predicting the minimal energy costs of human walking. *Medicine Science Sports and Exercise* 23: 491-498.

Holt, K.G., S.F. Jeng, R. Ratcliffe, and J. Hamill. 1995. Energetic cost and stability during human walking at the preferred stride frequency. *Journal of Motor Behavior* 27: 164-178.

Hreljac, A. 1993. Preferred and energetically optimal gait transition speeds in human locomotion. *Medicine Science Sports and Exercise* 25: 1158-1162.

James, S.L., and C.E. Brubaker. 1973. Biomechanical and neuromuscular aspects of running. *Exercise Sport Science Reviews* 3: 193-218.

Joyner, M.J. 1991. Modeling: optimal marathon performance on the basis of physiological factors. *Journal of Applied Physiology* 10: 683-687.

Kay, J.D.S., E.S. Petersen, and H. Vejby-Christensen. 1975. Breathing in man during steady state exercise on the bicycle at two pedalling frequencies and during treadmill walking. *Journal of Physiology* (London) 251: 645-656.

Kohl, J., E.A. Koller, and M. Jäger. 1981. Relation between pedalling- and breathing rhythm. *European Journal of Applied Physiology* 47: 223-237.

Kushmerick, M. J. 1983. Energetics of muscular contraction. In *Handbook of physiology, section 10: skeletal muscle,* eds. L.E. Peachey, R.H. Adrian, and S.R. Geiger, 189-236. Bethesda, MD: American Physiological Society.

Maclennan, S.E., G.A. Silvestri, J. Ward, and D.A. Mahler. 1994. Does entrained breathing improve the economy of rowing. *Medicine and Science in Sports and Exercise* 26: 610-614.

Mahler, D.A., C.R. Shuhart, E. Brew, and T.A. Stukel. 1991. Ventilatory responses and entrainment of breathing during rowing. *Medicine and Science in Sports and Exercise* 23: 186-192.

Marsh, A. P., and P.E. Martin. 1993. The association between cycling experience and preferred and most economical cadences. *Medicine and Science in Sports and Exercise* 25: 1269-1274.

Martin, P.E., G.D. Heise, and D.W. Morgan. 1993. Interrelationships between mechanical power, energy transfers, and walking and running economy. *Medicine and Science in Sports and Exercise* 25: 508-515.

Martin, P.E., and D.W. Morgan. 1992. Biomechanical considerations for economical walking and running. *Medicine and Science in Sports and Exercise* 24: 467-474.

Messier, S. P., W.D. Franke, and W.J. Rejeski. 1986. Effects of altered stride lengths on ratings of perceived exertion during running. *Research Quarterly for Exercise and Sport* 57: 273-279.

Morgan, W. P. 1994. Psychological components of effort sense. *Medicine and Science in Sports and Exercise* 26: 1071-1077.

Noble, B.J., and R.J. Robertson 1996. *Perceived exertion.* Champaign, IL: Human Kinetics.

Nordeen-Snyder, K.S . 1977. The effect of bicycle seat height variation upon oxygen consumption and lower limb kinematics. *Medicine Science Sports and Exercise* 9: 113-117.

Pate, R.R., C.A. Macera, S.P. Bailey, W.P. Bartoli, and K.E. Powell. 1992. Physiological, anthropometric, and training correlates of running economy. *Medicine and Science in Sports and Exercise* 24: 1128-1133.

Patterson, R.P., and M.I. Moreno. 1990. Bicycle pedalling forces as a function of pedalling rate and power output. *Medicine and Science in Sports and Exercise* 22: 512-516.

Poole, P.M., and B. Ross. 1983. The energy cost of sheep shearing. *Search* 14: 103-104.

Redfield, R., and M.L. Hull. 1984. Joint movements and pedalling rates in bicycling. In *Sports Biomechanics: Proceedings of the International Symposium of Biomechanics of Sports,* eds. J. Terauds et al., 247-258. California: Research Center for Sports.

Rowland, T.W. 1989. Oxygen uptake and endurance fitness in children: a developmental perspective. *Pediatric Exercise Science* 1: 313-328.

Salvendy, G. 1972. Physiological and psychological aspects of paced and unpaced performance. *Acta Physiologica Academiae Scientiarum Hungaricae* 42: 267-275.

Salvendy, G., and J. Piltisis. 1971. Psychophysical aspects of paced and unpaced performance as influenced by age. *Ergonomics* 14: 703-711.

Schmidt, R.C., and P. Fitzpatrick. 1996. Dynamical perspective on motor learning. In *Advances in Motor Learning and Control,* ed. H.N. Zelaznik, 195-223. Champaign, IL: Human Kinetics.

Smith, R.M., and W.L. Spinks. 1995. Discriminant analysis of biomechanical differences between novice, good and elite rowers. *Journal of Sports Sciences* 13: 377-385.

Sparrow, W.A. 1983. The efficiency of skilled performance. *Journal of Motor Behavior* 15: 237-261.

Sparrow, W.A., K.M. Hughes, A.P. Russell, and P.F. Le Rossignol. Under review. Effects of practice and preferred rate on perceived exertion, metabolic variables, and movement control. *Human Movement Science.*

Sparrow, W.A., and K.M. Newell. 1998. Metabolic energy expenditure and the regulation of movement economy. *Psychonomic Bulletin and Review* 5: 173-196.

Takaishi, T.T., Y. Yasuda, T. Ono, and T. Moritani. 1996. Optimal pedaling rate estimated from neuromuscular fatigue for cyclists. *Medicine Science Sports and Exercise* 28: 1492-1497.

Unnithan, V.B., and R.G. Eston. 1990. Stride frequency and submaximal treadmill running economy in adults and children. *Pediatric Exercise Science* 2: 149-155.

Williams, K.R., and P.R. Cavanagh. 1986. Biomechanical correlates with running economy in elite distance runners. In *Proceedings of the North American Congress on Biomechanics,* combined with the Tenth Annual Conference of The American Society of Biomechanics (ASB) and the Fourth Biannual Conference of the Canadian Society for Biomechanics, ed. P. Allard and M. Gagnon., 287-288. Montreal: Organizing Committee.

Williams, K.R., and P.R. Cavanagh. 1987. Relationship between distance running mechanics, running economy, and performance. *Journal of Applied Physiology* 63: 1236-1246.

Vanlandewijck, Y.C., A.J. Spaepen, and R.J. Lysens. 1994. Wheelchair propulsion efficiency: movement pattern adaptations to speed changes. *Medicine and Science in Sports and Exercise* 26: 1373-1381.

5

Triggers for the Transition Between Human Walking and Running

Alastair Hanna

Queensland Academy of Sport and School of Human Movement Studies,
University of Queensland, Australia

Bruce Abernethy

School of Human Movement Studies, University of Queensland,
Australia, and School of Physical Education, National Institute of Education,
Nanyang Technological University, Singapore

Robert J. Neal and Robin Burgess-Limerick

School of Human Movement Studies, University of Queensland, Australia

$\mathbf{P}$erhaps the primary motivation for gross physical movement across all species is the requirement to locomote from place to place. The mode of locomotion used depends inter alia upon the animal's environment (e.g., whether it is terrestrial or aquatic), its physical attributes (e.g., its number and relative length and strength of limbs), its developmental stage, and its desired speed of travel. Both across the developmental lifespan and during daily living, a number of important transitions occur in human gait. These transitions are characterised by discrete, relatively abrupt changes in movement pattern or coordination mode. At critical developmental ages characteristic infant patterns, such as crawling, are replaced (quickly, in lifespan terms) by primitive, but recognisable, forms of the bipedal adult gait modes of walking and running (Thelen and Ulrich 1989). With practice and maturation these adult patterns of coordination are refined; the same movement patterns are utilised, but with progressively more skilful execution (Clark 1995; Jeng, Liao, and Hou 1997).

Sparrow (1983) has suggested that one of the hallmarks of skilful movement is the minimisation of metabolic energy expenditure, and recent research has demonstrated that the transition from infant to adult gait patterns in humans is indeed closely linked to the minimisation of energy expenditure (Jeng et al. 1997). In this chapter we examine whether the major recurrent transition in mature human gait, that between the modes of walking and running[1], can also be explained on the basis of the optimisation (where minimisation is optimal) of physiological cost. We examine this as one of a number of possible triggers of transition between the walking and running gaits.

Adult humans walk at slow speeds of the total locomotion range and accelerate by increasing both stride rate and length. Over a wide range of walking speeds, a direct linear relationship exists between stride length and stride frequency (Grieve 1968; Inman, Ralston, and Todd 1981), although at fast walking speeds the upper limit to stride length is achieved first (Wollacott and Jensen 1996). As walking speed continues to increase, a critical speed is reached whereupon an apparently spontaneous change in movement pattern occurs and running results. In contrast to the voluminous research independently studying the biomechanics of the running and walking gaits (Vaughan, Murphy, and du Toit 1987; Williams 1985), it is only relatively recently that the transition between the two gait modes has attracted sustained research attention. The changes in movement pattern/ preferred coordination between gait modes are significant and interesting features of human gait, especially with respect to their control mechanisms, yet to date the mechanisms that drive these changes are not entirely clear. The relative dearth of research on human walk-run transitions appears to be a critical oversight given the growing use of spontaneous pattern transitions as a means of gaining an insight into underlying control mechanisms in a range of different motor and perceptual systems (e.g., Kelso 1986, 1995; Jeka and Kelso 1988, 1989). This chapter, organized into four major sections, details some of the ongoing work within our laboratories and those of others that explore proposed triggers for the transition between human walking and running. The chapter is organised into four major sections.

The first section examines what is known about the phenomenology of transitions between walking and running by providing an overview of past research that has attempted to describe the parameters of this predominant human gait transition. The merits and the constraints of the experimental designs used in the existing research are discussed, especially with respect to the means by which the required gait speed is manipulated; and an experiment that examines the reliability/replicability, as well as the hysteresis component, of the transitions between walking and running is described.

The second section introduces synergetics (the science of pattern formation and change) as a potential theoretical structure from within which to examine transitional phenomena. In this section we examine evidence that suggests that the transition between gait modes in human locomotion conforms to generic characteristics found in phase transitions in a host of other complex systems, including nonbiological ones.

In the third section of the chapter we explore the role of key anthropometric dimensions in determining individual differences in the speed of locomotion at which people prefer to change from a walking to a running gait. Within this section we discuss past research on biological scaling involving quadrupedal mammals, existing anthropometric studies on human gait, and the predictions of different mathematical models of human gait, in addition to presenting new experimental data from our own investigations. The exploration of possible links between individual differences in anthropometry and individual differences in preferred speed at transitions between walking and running is presented within the context of a more general search for a mechanical trigger for transitions.

In the final section of the chapter we turn our attention to the role of metabolic energy expenditure, or more specifically its minimisation, in determining the characteristics (stride rate and amplitude) of a specific gait mode at a particular speed. We present experimental data to extend the examination of within-gait mode energy expenditure to determine whether these same physiological parameters can be used to explain and/or predict the preferred speed at which transition occurs between walking and running.

The Phenomenology of Transitions Between Walking and Running

To commence an examination of transitions between walking and running it is necessary to first define the critical parameters of interest. This involves, minimally, a clear differentiation of the different modes of coordination (in this case the walking and running gaits) and a clear consideration of the means by which the changes in coordination mode can be induced (in this case by changes in the required speed of locomotion). In synergetic terms, as discussed in the second section of this chapter, these considerations relate, respectively, to the measurement of the *order* parameter and the manipulation of the *control* parameter.

Differentiation of Walking and Running as Modes of Coordination

The walking and running gaits are formally differentiated on the basis of the duty factor, which is the fraction of the stride duration for which each foot is grounded. When the duty factor is greater than 0.5, a person is considered to be walking, whereas if the duty factor is less than 0.5, resulting in the existence of a flight phase (i.e., a phase where neither foot is on the ground), then running is evidenced (Alexander 1992). In the walking gait, acceleration is achieved by increasing both stride frequency and stride length (Grieve and Gear 1966; Murray et al. 1966; Winter 1979) until a speed of approximately 2.0 m·s^{-1} is reached, whereupon a spontaneous switch in movement organisation occurs and the running pattern results. The reorganisation from walking to running (via the introduction of a flight phase) is brought about by an increase in the propulsive force applied in the stance phase. The identification of 2.0 m·s^{-1} as the approximate speed at which the walk-run transition in human gait occurs has been consistent across a number of studies (e.g., Beuter and Lalonde 1989; Durand et al. 1994; Hreljac 1993a, 1993b, 1995a, 1995b; Mercier et al. 1994).

Methodological Issues in the Manipulation of the Speed of Locomotion

A number of elements in the protocols used to manipulate gait speed have the potential to influence the point at which the preferred transition between walking and running gait occurs. Key methodological considerations include whether the required speed of locomotion is manipulated in a continuous or discrete fashion, the direction in which the speed is manipulated (i.e., increased or decreased), and whether the manipulation occurs using natural overground locomotion or the more conventional treadmill locomotion customarily used for laboratory studies.

Ramped Versus Stepped Protocols

A ramped protocol is one in which the speed of locomotion is continually increased or decreased while a stepped protocol, as the name suggests, involves the manipulation of speed in discrete steps, with the period spent at each step kept constant. We have previously reported data demonstrating a more consistent response, in terms of a more reliable, reproducible speed at transition between walking and running, when a stepped protocol (with 0.3 km·h^{-1} increments) is used rather than a ramped one (Abernethy et al. 1995). However, due to the limitations of the treadmill employed in our earlier investigation (with respect to the sensitive incrementing of speed), we were unable to control precisely the rate at which the belt changed between adjacent speed conditions. The belt would accelerate much more quickly between velocities at higher speeds (as opposed to low speeds) and during ascending trials (as opposed to descending trials). These belt characteristics are not unique to the particular motor-driven treadmill we used in our investigation (Abernethy et al. 1995), but are common to the majority of conventional laboratory treadmills. This constraint may become a particular concern during ramped trials where the rate of change in speed (i.e., belt acceleration) may be an important stimulus for transition. It is important to be aware of this issue as variability in the rate of change of required gait speed might confound simple comparison of the efficacy of different speed manipulation protocols.

Direction of Speed Manipulation

While it is usual to examine transitions between walking and running by simply commencing with the walking mode at a low speed of travel and then progressively incrementing required speed of travel until the change to the running mode occurs, it is equally important to also examine the converse situation where the starting coordination mode is running and the required locomotor speed is progressively decreased until the walking mode is preferred. The reason that it is critical that participants in gait transition studies experience both ascending and descending acceleration trials is that the walk-run transition and the run-walk transition may be phenomenologically different, i.e., the transitions may demonstrate *hysteresis*.

Hysteresis is one of the characteristics defining phase transitions in nonbiological systems. A hysteresis phenomenon is evident when the magnitude of the control parameter (e.g., speed of locomotion) at the point of transition in the order parameter (e.g., gait mode) varies depending upon the direction in which the control parameter is changed. Previous research has suggested that hysteresis may exist in human gait (e.g., Abernethy et al. 1995; Beuter and Lalonde 1989; Getchell and Whitall 1997; Thorstensson and Roberthson 1987), although its observation may be dependent on the type of speed manipulation protocol that is used and its magnitude upon whether or not the person is carrying a load (Beuter and Lalonde 1989). A continuous stepped protocol may provide a more natural picture of the presence of hysteresis in human gait transition than some of the quite artificial regimes that have previously been used to examine hysteresis. For example, Hreljac (1993a) examined hysteresis by using a stepped protocol but stopped the treadmill and had the participants in the experiment dismount and then remount between the different speed conditions.

Overground Versus Treadmill Locomotion

There is ongoing debate amongst researchers investigating human gait as to the differences, if any, between overground and treadmill locomotion. Much of the evidence suggests that treadmill running does not change the energy requirements of locomotion from that in overground running nor systematically change the gait kinematics (Bassett et al. 1985; Pink et al. 1994), although variability may be slightly lower on the treadmill (van Ingen Schenau 1980). Nevertheless, the evidence is far from unequivocal. At higher speeds of running, differences in energy uptake, stride length, and certain temporal gait parameters are evident (Elliott and Blanksby 1976; Nelson et al. 1972; Pugh 1970). For example, Frishberg

(1983) demonstrated substantial differences in energy uptake between overground and treadmill sprinting. However, these differences may occur because sprinting involves a much more active motion of the support leg (this is facilitated by the treadmill belt) than less intensive forms of running, such as jogging, which exist near the transition point.

The failure of some studies to show complete similarity between overground and treadmill running may also be due to differences between the two gait conditions existing for some but not, systematically, for all individuals (Nigg, De Boer, and Fisher 1995). As past research has tended to use statistical tests designed to determine if differences exist between treadmill and overground locomoting groups, these individual variations are largely ignored, and it is not possible to determine whether, for most people, the constraints imposed by the two conditions are the same. The most important issue with respect to examining the phenomena of gait transitions is not so much whether the same critical speed of locomotion defines the walk-run (or run-walk) transition in treadmill locomotion compared to overground locomotion, but rather whether the same characteristics typify the transition within each setting. Answering this question requires, in part, consideration of the replicability of the transitions between walking and running.

Experiment 1:
Replicability of Transitional Characteristics

In describing any phenomenon it is essential to not only understand the conditions under which the phenomenon occurs but to also determine the reliability or reproducibility of the phenomenon. Repeatable speed-specific stride frequency and amplitude combinations have been observed in previous research examining one or both gait modes (e.g., Inman, Ralston, and Todd 1981; Winter 1984), but little research has specifically addressed the reliability/replicability of the transitional phenomena. Our initial investigations of the transitions between walking and running were therefore concerned with determining the precise speed of locomotion at which the walk-run transition and the run-walk transition occur and then examining whether this speed was consistent and reproducible for each individual.

Methods

Forty-two participants (17 male and 25 female undergraduate Human Movement Studies students aged 18-25) were required to locomote on a motor-driven treadmill (Austredex) on four separate occasions. The first, second, and third sessions were each separated by two days and the final session took place one week after the third session. The first session was used to provide familiarisation on the treadmill and the subsequent sessions used for data collection.

Participants were instructed to keep pace with the treadmill as it was first accelerated, in 0.083 m·s⁻¹ (0.3 km·h⁻¹) increments every 20 s, from approximately 1.11 m·s⁻¹ (4 km·h⁻¹) (a slow walk) to approximately 2.78 m·s⁻¹ (10 km·h⁻¹) (a moderate running pace) and then decelerated in the same stepped fashion. The initial, final, and peak velocities experienced by the participants were randomly allocated to each trial to eliminate the possibility of participants changing gait mode in response to a certain number of steps rather than a critical speed of travel. A stepped protocol was used because of it being more favourable to the reproducibility of the phenomenon (Abernethy et al. 1995) and ascending and descending series were included to permit examination of hysteresis and the possible impact of direction of speed manipulation upon the reproducibility of transitional characteristics. Participants experienced five complete ascending and descending treadmill series during each testing session. Each trial took approximately 10 minutes to complete, and participants were given a minimum of five minutes recovery between trials.

Pressure-sensitive switches placed on the heel and toe of each foot illuminated LEDs positioned in the field of view of a high-speed (200 Hz) video camera (NAC). This information was used in determining the time at which the transition between the gait modes occurred. The transition speed for the walk-run transition was defined as the speed at which, during the ascending series, the last instance of double support phase was recorded and the transition speed for the run-walk transition was defined as the speed at which, during the descending series, the last flight phase was recorded.

Results

The participants demonstrated a mean speed of preferred transition between the gait modes of 2.16 m·s⁻¹ (SD = 0.2 m·s⁻¹), which closely approximated those from earlier research (Beuter and Lalonde 1989; Durand et al. 1994; Hreljac 1993a, 1993b, 1995a, 1995b; Mercier et al. 1994), although two studies that used ramped as opposed to stepped protocol for speed manipulation (Noble et al. 1973; Thorstensson and Roberthson 1987) have reported slightly lower transitional velocities (1.89 m·s⁻¹ and 1.88 m·s⁻¹ respectively).

Previous research has demonstrated that, for a given speed of locomotion, adult humans will consistently select the same stride frequency and amplitude combinations. The data from this experiment, presented in terms of Pearson product-moment correlations and intraclass correlation coefficients, suggest that the transition between the gait modes is also very consistent. (Correlations between days 1 and 2, 1 and 3, and 2 and 3 were respectively 0.924, 0.881, and 0.922 with an intraclass coefficient of 0.745.) We found no significant difference in mean transitional velocities among the three testing sessions (day 1 = 2.15 m·s⁻¹, day 2 = 2.15 m·s⁻¹, day 3 = 2.18 m·s⁻¹) (F (2,88) = 4.117, p > 0.01) and no significant interaction between the day of testing and the transition direction ($\underline{F}$ (2,88) = 1.371, $\underline{p}$ > 0.01). The walk-run and run-walk transitions in adults appear to be consistent, repeatable phenomena occurring at around 2.2 m·s^{-1} but with some evidence of individual variability in the precise transition speed (range = 0.78 m·s^{-1}, [1.82 m·s^{-1} - 2.6 m·s^{-1}]; SD = 0.17 m·s^{-1}; also see figures 5.1-5.4 to see group spread).

An interesting result from this particular experiment was the observation of a hysteresis effect, indicated by a significant mean difference (0.109 m·s^{-1}) between the preferred speed at the walk-run transition and the preferred speed at the run-walk ($\underline{F}$ (1,44) = 110.632, $\underline{p}$ < 0.01). This observation is consistent with those made in our previous work (Abernethy et al. 1995), which showed a walk-run to run-walk difference of 0.105 m·s^{-1}, and with observations reported by other researchers (Beuter and Lalonde 1989; Durand et al. 1994; Thorstensson and Roberthson 1987). The difference between the velocities observed at the preferred walk-run and run-walk transitions represented 131% of the "step" gap of 0.083 m·s^{-1}. As was concluded in our previous study (Abernethy et al. 1995) a clearer picture of hysteresis in human gait transition may be possible if a finer graded step protocol could be presented; however, this will require a treadmill with precision of speed control beyond that typically available. The implementation of a ramped protocol in which speed was linearly increased as a function of time may also produce useful information providing, as we noted earlier, that the rate of change of speed (acceleration) can be kept uniformly constant.

The apparent presence of hysteresis in transitions between the walking and running gaits suggests that the characteristics of gait transitional phenomena may parallel those existing for phase transitions in a range of other systems, including purely physical, nonbiological systems (Kugler and Turvey 1987).

Synergetics and Transitions Between Walking and Running

In this section we expand on the theme discussed above and attempt to understand transition through employing theoretical structures provided by synergetics and dynamical systems theory.

Open Complex Systems and Nonlinear Dynamics

One way of understanding transitions between different modes of gait is to view the human as an open complex system, as a physical system that is open to a flow of energy and has many internal degrees of freedom. The body is composed of a number of subsystems (e.g., neural, circulatory, digestive, skeletal, and muscular) which, in general, behave and interact in a nonlinear fashion. The consequence of an energy flow through a complex nonlinear system is the spontaneous generation of internal constraints (Bingham 1988; Iberall 1978; Kugler and Turvey 1987). Coherent self-organised behaviour results as the energy flow is converted into work cycles.

In the open complex human system only a few of the many possible combinations of posture and limb movement are stable. Which of these patterns of coordination are stable, and the relative stability of different patterns, is determined by the interaction of nonlinear components within the human system (Beek and Bingham 1991; Warren 1988a, 1988b). The many degrees of freedom of the human body can be coordinated by using those stable combinations of posture and movement that achieve task goals.

Goal-directed actions such as human gait are achieved by exploiting the system's dynamics harnessed, by intention, to perceptual information. That is, the goals of movement are achieved within the environmental constraints by the human being sensitive, via perception, to the system's stabilities and instabilities, the boundaries and transition points between them, and switching between appropriate stable patterns of coordination (Beek and Bingham 1991; Schmidt and Turvey 1989; Warren 1988a, 1988b).

Synergetics

Synergetics is a theory of pattern formation in nonlinear open systems developed by Haken (1983, 1990) that has proven particularly useful in understanding phase transitions in physical systems (e.g., lasers, chemical reactions) as well as in biological ones. The tools of synergetics have been used to describe and predict characteristics of transitions between coordination modes, or phase transitions, in human coordination during a number of repetitive movements analogous to locomotion (e.g., Kelso and Schöner 1988; Jeka and Kelso 1988, 1989). In all cases the description is based around the relationship between two key parameters—an *order parameter,* which uniquely characterises and distinguishes the spatial organisation of each pattern or coordination mode, and a *control parameter,* the continuous manipulation of which causes switching, at discrete values, between the different patterns of organisation.

The first example of phase transition in repetitive human movement to be systematically examined from this perspective was bimanual finger tapping (Kelso 1981, 1984; Mackenzie and Patla 1983; Yaminishi, Kawato, and Suzuki 1980). If a person is asked to tap both index fingers at a common frequency, but 180° out of phase (i.e., one finger reaches maximum flexion at the moment the other reaches maximum extension), this mode of coordination is stable and can be maintained accurately, at least at low tapping frequencies. If the frequency of finger tapping (a control parameter) is gradually increased, the 180° mode can be maintained for some time. However, at a critical value of the tapping frequency the coordination of the fingers suddenly (within one cycle) and spontaneously (unintentionally) changes so that flexion and extension of the two fingers occurs synchronously. In-phase coordination is now the only stable mode and this mode of coordination remains stable if the tapping frequency continues to increase (Kelso 1984, 1990).

This phenomenon has been examined in some detail primarily using finger tapping tasks (Kelso and de Guzman 1988; Kelso, Scholz, and Schöner 1986; Schöner and Kelso 1988a, 1988b). If tapping frequency is decreased after the transition, the system remains in the in-phase mode and no second transition occurs (i.e., the system exhibits hysteresis). If the system starts at low frequency in the in-phase mode, and then frequency is increased, no spontaneous transition occurs. Only the in-phase and out-of-phase modes are stable in that no other modes are spontaneously adopted and the in-phase mode is less variable than the out-of-phase mode. Intentional production of intermediate relative phase modes is difficult and the resulting coordination is much more variable than the in-phase or out-of-phase modes (Haken, Kelso, and Bunz 1985; Kelso et al. 1987; Schöner and Kelso 1988a).

In the bimanual finger tapping system relative phase is the order parameter as it succinctly describes the two different coordination modes or patterns (in-phase and out-of-phase) that can be exhibited; the control parameter is cycling frequency. This particular system displays a number of the characteristics (order parameter-control parameter relationships) that are typical of phase transitions in a host of different systems. These characteristics include the order parameter having more than one distinct value (the *modality* property), spatial organisations other than the preferred one being unstable and difficult to maintain (the *inaccessibility* property), small changes in the control parameter at some critical values inducing major changes in the order parameter (the *sudden jumps* property) and the magnitude of the control parameter at transition depending on the direction in which the control parameter is being manipulated (the *hysteresis* property) (Haken et al. 1985; Turvey 1990).

A synergetic framework also supports a number of other testable predictions for transitions in gait and other tasks. These include *critical fluctuations* (i.e., enhanced random fluctuations of the order parameter near the transition point), *critical slowing down* (i.e., the system takes longer to return to the stable mode after small perturbations when near the transition than when distant), and *intentional switching time* (i.e., intentional switching takes longer from more stable modes to less stable modes than the reverse) (Haken 1990; Kelso, Scholz, and Schöner 1988; Kelso and Schöner 1988; Scholz and Kelso 1989, 1990; Scholz, Kelso, and Schöner 1987). If these distinguishing characteristics of phase transitions can be found to hold not only in paired hand movements but also in gait, then the full array of synergetic tools (including sophisticated mathematical modeling) can be legitimately applied to extend understanding of not only transitions in human gait but the control of human gait in general. Theoretical treatments that consider bipedal (Taga, Yamaguchi, and Shimizu 1991), quadrupedal (Schöner, Jiang, and Kelso 1990), and hexapedal gait (Collins and Stewart 1993) as dynamical, synergetic systems with gait transitions viewed as nonequilibrium phase transitions accompanied by a loss of stability (Schöner, Jiang, and Kelso 1990) already exist. However experimental evidence on the dynamics of gait transitions from this perspective is still quite limited (but for an exception, see Diedrich and Warren 1995).

With speed of locomotion as a control parameter, the first step experimentally from a synergetic perspective must be to attempt to identify an order parameter for gait that has constant values within, but clearly distinct values between, the walking and running coordination modes, i.e., a parameter to describe gait mode succinctly in a manner analogous to relative phase for bimanual finger tapping. Diedrich and Warren (1995), following the empirical data of Nilsson, Thorstensson, and Halbertsma (1985), have suggested the relative phase of the segments within each leg as a potential order parameter and have demonstrated for it sudden jumps, critical fluctuations, and hysteresis. In an earlier paper (Abernethy et al. 1995) we suggested properties of the angular phase profile of the shank relative to the horizontal as a potential order parameter on the basis of perceptual studies requiring observers to discriminate the walking and running gaits (Cutting, Proffitt, and Kozlowski 1978; Hoenkamp 1978; Todd 1983). While there is still much evidence to accumulate to support fully a synergetic basis for the understanding and prediction of human gait control and transitions, the approach certainly appears promising. The similarity between gait transitions and transitions in nonbiological systems lacking any sort of nervous system suggests that an important starting point for the search for triggers for gait transitions may be not the brain and central nervous system, as has been the traditional focus of gait neurophysiologists, but rather the physical properties of the musculoskeletal system itself (Abernethy et al. 1995)

Anthropometry and Transitions Between Walking and Running

Anthropometry is the study of variability in the size, proportions, and composition of the human body. Our search to find a possible predictor of human gait transition started with an exploration of the possible correlates between the speed of locomotion at which the transition between the gait modes occurs and the anthropometric (body dimension) characteristics of an individual. Our justification for seeking out such a relationship was based upon studies on the walk-trot-gallop transitions of quadrupedal mammals, which implicate physical size parameters in transition determination; evidence that anthropometric variables dictate interlimb phase changes in human creeping; mathematical models based on anthropometric profiles that are capable of predicting many other parameters associated with human gait; and anecdotal evidence and experience from walking and running with long-legged colleagues. Given the apparent consistency of the walk-run transition speed for individuals, it may be reasonable to suggest that one or more physical parameters, linked to bodily dimensions such as limb length or mass, may be responsible for triggering the switch between walking and running. In this section we first review the existing evidence relevant to a possible linkage between human anthropometric variation and individual differences in speed at the transitional points between walking and running and then describe an experiment designed to search for such link(s).

Allometric Scaling and Quadrupedal Gait Transitions

A relationship between anthropometry and gait transition is suggested by studies demonstrating that, across a diverse range of quadrupedal mammals, a number of gait parameters (viz., speed of locomotion, stride frequency, and amplitude) scale allometrically with absolute body size (Heglund and Taylor 1988; Heglund, Taylor, and McMahon 1974). In fact, Alexander and Jayes (1983) have normalised gait mode transition velocities of different sized quadrupeds by normalising transport speed (v) in terms of limb length (L) to produce the dimensionless Froude number (F), which equals $v2/Lg$. The stability of this relationship implies that transitions within quadrupedal gait can be accurately predicted on the basis of physical dimensions.

Furthermore, across a wide variety of quadrupeds, the natural frequencies for the gait modes of walking, trotting, and cantering all scale commonly to body mass and leg length parameters (Hoyt and Taylor 1981; Kugler and Turvey 1987). The scaling exponents are precisely those predicted if the animal is modeled as a vibratory system of masses, springs, and levers (McMahon 1985) or, more elaborately, as a weighted pendulum system (Kugler and Turvey 1987; Turvey et al. 1988). In addition, the energetic cost of quadrupedal locomotion can be predicted reliably on the basis of the mass of the animal and the time for which the foot is in contact with the ground (Kram and Taylor 1990). Sparrow and Newell conducted an interesting investigation of quadrupedal gait using human subjects. After six weeks of training at creeping on a motor-driven treadmill participants were presented with a stepped ascending velocity trial. While the small number of participants (n = 3) limits generalisation, the study presented evidence supporting the hypothesis that movement patterns are dictated by the physical dimension of the system. Specifically, the two subjects with nearly identical anthropometry demonstrated an ipsilateral phase transition during exactly the same stride. Anthropometric variables apparently provide sufficient information to allow prediction of some gait parameters traditionally thought to be under higher level neural control.

Anthropometric Correlates of Bipedal Gait Transitions

Given their predictive value with respect to quadrupedal gait mode transitions, it is reasonable to expect that anthropometric characteristics may also serve as key variables in defining individual differences in the speed of locomotion at which changes are made between the bipedal gait modes of walking and running. This issue has attracted relatively little research attention to date and what has been undertaken has been largely equivocal. Hreljac (1995b) correlated the mean values of preferred transition speed obtained from 28 participants (13 males, 15 females) with a battery of standard anthropometric parameters (including mass, stature, lateral malleolus height, leg length, anterior iliac spine height, height, thigh length, thigh length/sitting height, and Froude number). Even after the removal of two "outlier" subjects (both male) only moderate correlations ($r = 0.57$) between the mean values of preferred transition speed and a number of highly intercorrelated length variables were demonstrated. Getchell and Whitall (1997) used stepwise multiple regression in an attempt to find physical parameters that might predict walk-run and run-walk transitions as well as transitions to galloping. Ten physical parameters were examined (standing and sitting height; weight; length of thigh, shank, and foot; range of motion of hip, knee, and ankle; and maximum quadriceps power) and the best correlations that could be obtained using a combination of parameters were 0.35 for the walk-to-run transition and 0.31 for the run-to-walk transition. The best single predictor variable was thigh length and the best combined predictor the thigh length to sitting height ratio.

These low to moderate correlations found by Hreljac (1995b) and Getchell and Whitall (1997) are inconsistent with predictions made on the basis of previous research involving mammalian quadrupeds (e.g., Heglund and Taylor 1988), where leg length and mass parameters were excellent predictors of gait mode changes. It should be noted that the chances of finding high anthropometric correlations with human gait are decreased relative to the quadrupedal cross-species studies because the latter featured considerable ranges in mass, limb length, height, and other physical parameters whereas the human variation studies are necessarily dealing with a within-species data set of smaller range. In addition, however, it is possible that Hreljac (1995b) and Getchell and Whitall (1997) may not have examined all of the potentially critical anthropometric characteristics that might influence gait transition speed. In this regard it is particularly noteworthy that inertial characteristics of the lower limb were not considered in either of these studies. Some insight into why this might be a critical oversight can be gained through examination of some contemporary mathematical and biomechanical models of bipedal locomotion.

Mathematical Models of Human Gait

A number of mathematical models have been developed for bipedal locomotion (e.g., Alexander 1980, 1989, 1992; Alexander and Maloiy 1984; Blickhan 1989; McGreer 1990a, 1990b; McMahon and Cheng 1990; Mochon and McMahon 1980). Walking is typically modeled as an inverted pendulum system with highly conservative kinetic-potential energy exchanges. Within the walking coordination mode, the whole body centre of mass cycles between exchanging kinetic energy for potential energy (the centre of mass loses speed as it gains height) and the reverse process. Running is typically modeled as a 'bouncing ball' system (in contrast to the 'rolling egg' of walking; Cavagna, Saibene, and Margaria 1963) featuring high kinetic energy-elastic energy exchanges. These exchanges are made possible by the elastic energy storage capacity of the tendons and muscles of the limb in contact with the ground. These models have proven quite accurate in predicting stride frequency and amplitude, duty factors and vertical ground reaction force patterns for both the walking and running gait modes.

A major shortcoming of these models is their failure to predict accurately the speed of locomotion at the point of transition between the gait modes (e.g., Alexander 1980, 1984, 1992). These models predict that the transition between the gait modes will occur at the mechanical limit of the physical system. Models based on inverted pendulum systems (e.g., the "rimless wheel" model of McGreer [1990a], as described in Alexander 1991) assume that the centre of mass of the body describes an arc around a rigid leg (radius = L). The tangential acceleration of the centre of mass towards the foot is equal to velocity^2/L. In order for the foot to remain in contact with ground during the swing phase of the contralateral limb (the definition of walking) this value of tangential acceleration cannot exceed the acceleration due to gravity. Hence, the transition between walking and running is predicted to occur at the point where the acceleration of the body's centre of gravity towards the ground exceeds the acceleration due to gravity. That is, transition occurs when

$$\text{velocity} > (\text{gravity} \times \text{leg length})^{0.5} \qquad (5.1)$$

When this speed of travel is reached the foot cannot remain in contact with the ground, a flight phase must result, and the running mode eventuates. As Diedrich and Warren (1995) point out, however, this method of predicting preferred transition velocities is inadequate. When substituting mean leg length values of 0.8 m to 0.9 m a preferred transition speed of approximately 3 m.s^{-1} is calculated and this figure is well in excess of those found experimentally.

A difficulty with the traditional modeling approach of treating walking and running as completely discrete systems with respect to energy conservation (walking energy being conserved through pendulum-like actions and running energy through spring-like actions) is that both coordination modes contain elements of both energy conservation methods (Holt 1998). As a consequence hybrid models that contain both pendular and spring (inertial and elastic) components may offer greater potential to capture the full biomechanical characteristics of each gait mode and the transitions between them. Holt and colleagues (chapter 9; Holt, Hamill, and Andres 1990, 1991; Holt et al. 1995; Holt, Jeng, and Fetters 1991) have developed one such hybrid model in which the inertial component is determined by gravitational acceleration and the mass and distance of the centre of mass of the whole body or limb segment of interest from its rotational axis and in which the spring component is given by soft tissue stiffness. This hybrid mass-spring pendulum model contains two conservative forces (those due to the body's inertia under gravity and to the spring energy return from muscular and connective tissues) and requires a periodic forcing function from the muscles to offset the energy transfer losses and viscous damping by soft tissue that occurs during each gait cycle.

This particular model appears to account well for a number of key gait phenomena, especially those that relate to walking. The natural resonant frequency of the model (the frequency at which a given force produces maximal amplitude or a minimal force produces a target amplitude) corresponds to preferred stride frequency for walking in children (Holt et al. 1990) and in adults (Holt, Jeng, and Fetters 1991) and manipulating inertial load, by adding weights to the ankle, changes preferred stride frequency in a manner consistent with that predicted by the model. Moreover, metabolic cost appears to be minimised at the resonant frequency of walking and forcing walking speed either below or above that which is self-selected and preferred is associated with an increased metabolic cost (Holt et al. 1995).

The hybrid model offers prospects for a more general model of gait control plus the potential to provide a foundation for linking dynamical models to the empirical data on metabolic energy minimisation (see the final section) by considering the metabolic costs associated with the muscular forcing function and the control of stiffness. Moreover, it also appears to offer a means of examining and understanding some of the variations in gait that accompany movement pathologies as well as the 'normative' range of individual differences (Holt 1998). However, while the model appears to provide an improvement on earlier models of gait, it is less clear whether an improved understanding of preferred coordination frequencies within the walking and running gaits will necessarily translate into an improved understanding of transitions between the two. An adiabatic transformability hypothesis for locomotion proposed by Turvey and associates (1996), in its early stages of development, attempts to address the transitional issue explicitly. The basic proposition of this hypothesis is that the ratio of conservative kinetic energy to nonconservative metabolic energy losses (the Q factor) is a critical variable, with transition between the walking and running gait occurring when $Q = 1$.

Experiment 2:
Individual Differences in Length, Mass, and Inertial Properties as Predictors of Transitional Velocities

Given the extent to which other gait parameters can be reliably predicted on the basis of anthropometric variables and the strength of the relationship between anthropometric variables and cross-species gait transitions in quadrupeds, it is not unreasonable to postulate that a link could exist between anthropometric variables and the speed of locomotion at which the transitions between the gait modes of walking and running occur in adult humans. It is possible that these links have not been apparent in previous studies because some of the possible critical parameters (e.g., inertial characteristics) have not been examined in the context of natural anthropometric variables. With this postulation in mind, we sought to examine the relationship between individual differences in anthropometry and individual differences in the speed of locomotion at which the mean preferred transition between gait modes occurs. It was anticipated that the use of a large sample with widely varying anthropometric characteristics and the inclusion of the inertial and strength characteristics of the lower limb in the analysis would allow a clearer picture of the relationship, if any, between anthropometry and bipedal gait transitions to be obtained.

Methods

Anthropometric data were collected from each of the 42 individuals who had participated in Experiment 1 and for whom preferred transition velocities between the walking and running and running and walking gait modes were already known. The task of selecting which anthropometric variables to include for measurement and subsequent correlation with preferred transition speed was a difficult one given the range of possibilities outlined in the previous section. In an attempt to maintain statistical power it was necessary to limit our study to those parameters that past research and present theory suggested would be most likely linked to transition. We chose anthropometric variables that could be used to broadly differentiate between different somatotypes (Carter 1995). In addition, we obtained strength measures of the lower limb, given that differences in these parameters might, in some way, determine individual differences in responding to the demands of different speeds of locomotion. Finally, we calculated some inertial values of the limbs, because these parameters are central to a number of current mathematical models of human gait.

Total body mass (m), standing height (SH), sitting height (ST), shank length (lateral malleolus to axis of knee) (SL), thigh length (TL), and total leg length (greater trochanter to lateral malleolus) (LL) were recorded for each participant. In addition, knee flexion and extension strengths were assessed using the Cybex 340 isokinetic dynamometer at angular velocities of $60°·s^{-1}$ and $240°·s^{-1}$. Leg length data were substituted into formula (5.1) to give predicted transition velocities (PRT). Following standard procedures (Winter 1979), the anthropometric data were used to calculate body mass index (BMI), leg length to shank length ratio (LL/SL), and the moment of inertia of the leg in a fully extended position.

Pearson product-moment correlation coefficients were computed to determine whether mean preferred transition speed was linearly related to any of the anthropometric variables. Those parameters that were shown to be most strongly correlated with mean preferred transition speed were then submitted to a multiple regression in an attempt to produce a robust prediction equation. Given the large number of comparisons made, a working alpha of 0.01 was adopted throughout the analysis.

Results

Few of the anthropometric variables had correlation coefficients with preferred transition speed that differed significantly from zero and, even for those which did, the variance in preferred transition speed explained by the anthropometric variables was small. For example, while a significant correlation between the mean transition speed and height was found for the combined sample, height accounted for only 20% of the variance between individuals in transition speed (figure 5.1). Similarly weak relationships were found between preferred transition speed and transition speed as predicted from standard inverted pendulum models (figure 5.2), shank length (figure 5.3), and leg length (figure 5.4). Multiple regression analysis combining the most highly correlated variables within the combined sample was unable to produce an equation capable of producing predictions of preferred transition speed that were superior to those gained from single variables. The most highly correlated variables for

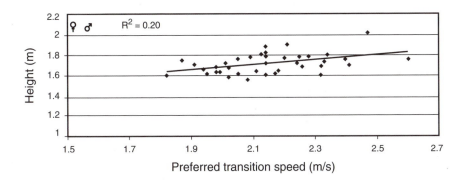

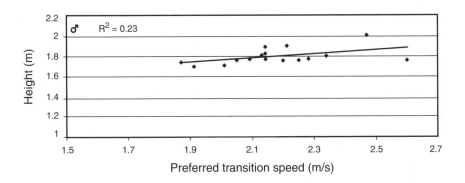

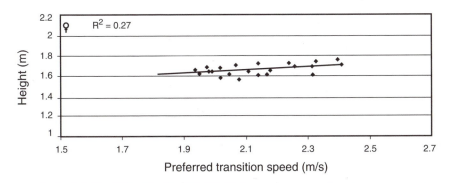

Figure 5.1 The relationship between preferred transition speed (PTS) and height for (top) the combined groups, (middle) the male group, and (bottom) the female group.

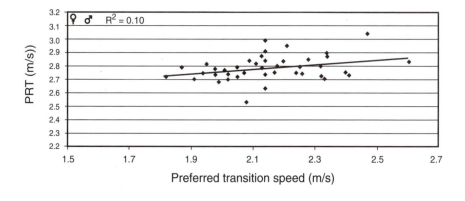

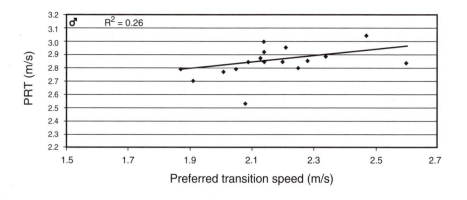

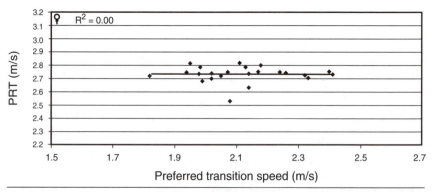

Figure 5.2 The relationship between preferred transition speed (PTS) and transition speed as predicted from equation 5.1 (PRT) for (top) the combined groups, (middle) the male group, and (bottom) the female group.

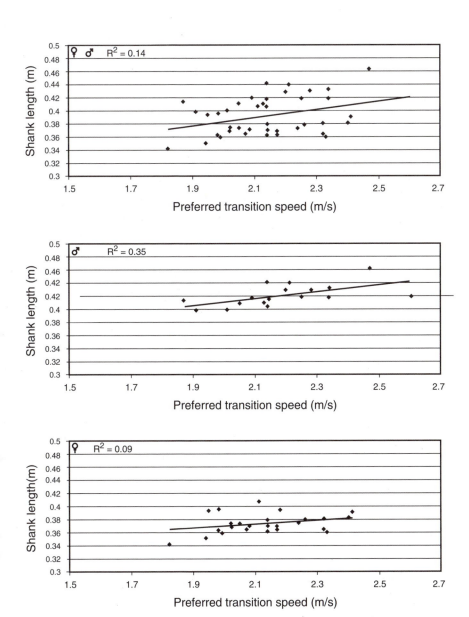

Figure 5.3 The relationship between preferred transition speed (PTS) and shank length for (top) the combined groups, (middle) the male group, and (bottom) the female group.

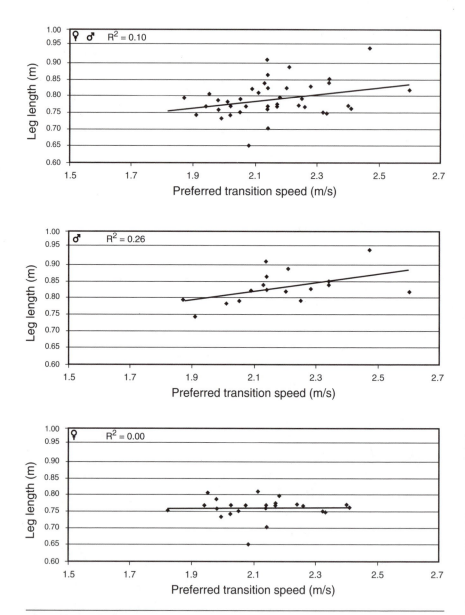

Figure 5.4 The relationship between preferred transition speed (PTS) and leg length for (top) the combined groups, (middle) the male group, and (bottom) the female group.

the female sub-sample were total body height and shank length; and for the male sub-sample total body height, shank length, and leg length. The most highly correlated variables for the combined sample were standing height, shank length, leg length, and total body weight.

The failure to reveal any strong relationships between individual differences in body dimensions, masses, moments of inertia, and strength, and individual differences in the point of preferred transition between human gait modes is consistent with the work of Hreljac (1995b). The results of Hreljac's study are very similar to ours, with the exception of the thigh length to standing height ratios, where Hreljac found much higher correlations with preferred transition speed than we did. Hreljac reports data obtained from Thorstensson and Roberthson (1987) of a correlation between leg length and preferred transition speed of 0.3, which is also in close agreement with the results of our work.

Some Conclusions Regarding Anthropometric Correlates of Gait Transitions

The existing studies on humans appear consistent with the view that individual differences in bodily dimensions and other anthropometric variables are only weak, or at the very best moderate, correlates of individual differences in preferred transitional speed. While it is possible that the failure to reveal a strong relationship may be due to methodological constraints (e.g., linear regression models may be insensitive to anthropometric variables related nonlinearly to preferred transitional speed), this cannot account for the capability of comparable approaches to reveal significant predictions of gait transitions from anthropometric variables in quadrupeds. The contradictory results of studies examining the relationship between anthropometry and preferred transition speed in humans and those examining comparable relationships in quadrupeds has a number of possible explanations. First, those studies that have demonstrated such strong positive relationships have involved a range of species spanning a considerable diversity of body sizes and shapes. Heglund, Taylor, and associates, for example, involved species ranging in mass from 0.029 kg (white mouse) through 1.15 kg (banded mongoose) and 3.5 kg (suni) to 680 kg (horse) (Taylor, Heglund, and Maloiy 1982; Heglund and Taylor 1988). This range of body sizes and preferred transition speed values adds power to the analysis, making possible the high correlations evident in this animal research. Many statistical texts note that homogeneity results in reduced correlations (Wright 1976). Given the small range of variability in our human sample (e.g., compare our mass range of 50.5 - 90.12 kg and the range of 49.5 - 86.9 kg reported in Hreljac (1995b) with the animal studies cited previously), it is not surprising that the correlation coefficients from studies on humans are much smaller than those on a range of animals. Further evidence of the effect of homogeneity on correlational data can be found in consideration of gender differences in the relationships between anthropometry and the mean preferred transition speed. In this study and that of Hreljac the male participants demonstrated slightly greater variability (SD) and range of values on both the anthropometric measures and the mean preferred transition speed scores. This contributed to the male sub-sample showing higher correlations with preferred transition speed than the female sub-sample on the majority of the variables examined.

A second explanation for the discrepancy between the strength of relationships between anthropometry and mean preferred transition speed found in the study of humans and those found in quadrupeds involves the gait modes involved. Comparisons of the walk-run transition in humans with the trot-gallop transition in quadrupedal mammals may be inappropriate if the mechanisms underlying these phenomena are different. An arguably more valid comparison would be between the walk-run transition in humans and the walk-trot transition in quadrupeds (or an investigation of human quadrupedal gait such as in Sparrow and Newell 1992); however, to date, walk-trot transition data are not available from the animal literature.

The presence of only weak-to-moderate correlations between physical (length, mass, and inertia) parameters and transitional velocities could mean one of at least two things. The first possibility, grounded in the animal literature and the biomechanical models of the walking and running gaits, is that anthropometric parameters are, in fact, important determinants of the walk-run and run-walk transitional velocities in humans, but that this relationship can be overridden (or masked) by one or a number of other factors. In other human paired-limb systems, intentionality has been presented as a variable capable of modifying the physically determined intrinsic (or natural) dynamics of the system (Carson et al. 1994, 1996; Scholz and Kelso 1990; Wuyts et al. 1996). Bonnard and Paihous (1993) have demonstrated the capacity for intentionality to alter the frequency-amplitude relationship within steady-state walking; and Getchell and Whitall (1997) have recently extended this proposition to gait control as well, as a means of explaining the weak correlations they observed between anthropometric variables and a range of adult human gait transitions. If intentionality imposes an additional dynamic on the natural dynamics of gait (cf. Schöner, Zanone, and Kelso 1992; Zanone and Kelso 1994), and if this intentionality involves primarily conscious, cognitive activity, then it is plausible that the greater cognitive development of humans may account for the diminished role of physical parameters in determining preferred gait mode for humans compared to quadrupeds, especially those quadrupeds with only very limited cortical development. Experiments are ongoing in our laboratories, as well as in others (e.g., Temprado et al. in press) that use conventional dual-task measures (such as probe reaction time) to examine the extent to which preferred and nonpreferred coordination modes place demands on cognitive processing resources. Greater attentional demand to sustain nonpreferred coordination modes at given transitional velocities may be indicative of the involvement of cognitive control (intentionality) in the selection and sustenance of different coordination patterns.

A second interpretation of the absence of strong relationships between anthropometric variables and preferred transition speed in humans, which is not necessarily mutually exclusive from the first, is that anthropometric parameters are secondary in importance to other factors in determining and driving the transitions between walking and running gait modes, and this necessitates the continued search and examination of alternative (stronger) predictors of transition. Physiological cost is an obvious candidate.

The Energetics of Transitions Between Walking and Running

There has been a long history of debate in the motor control literature as to which variable(s) the motor system seeks to control and/or optimise (e.g., Stein 1982). Optimisation appears to occur as an attempt to minimise cost to the motor system, and the particular cost that is minimised is dependent on the task objectives and constraints. In simple limb movements, such as those which underpin reaching, grasping, and handwriting, it has been proposed that the motor system seeks to optimise efficiency by making movements that are as smooth as possible, and hence that eliminate, as much as is possible, extraneous demands on muscle metabolic energy. A number of models have been proposed to suggest how optimisation of efficiency might take place. Prominent among these have been models that suggest control through the minimisation of jerk (the third derivative of limb position) or its mean square (Hogan and Flash 1987; Wann, Nimmo-Smith, and Wing 1988), the minimisation of changes in muscle torque (Uno, Kawato, and Suzuki 1989), and the minimisation of muscle stiffness (Hasan 1986). (See Latash 1993 for a review). Similar logic for the efficiency of energy expenditure can be, and has been, applied to the control of gross human movements, such as those in gait. For example, Sparrow (1983) has suggested that "selection," or modification, of a movement pattern may be in response to an underlying goal to minimise the expenditure of metabolic energy.

There is a widely held but largely untested view that metabolic energy cost drives human gait transition (Alexander 1989; Cavanagh and Franzetti 1986; Grillner et al. 1979; Heglund and Taylor 1988; Hoyt and Taylor 1981; McMahon 1985). This hypothesis is based largely on arguments that contend that the logical (from the perspective of animal survival, for example) parameter to be optimised, and hence control the organisation of human gait, is energetic efficiency. This argument is supported by studies demonstrating that the selection of speed of travel within the walking gait, and the selection of stride rate and length in both walking and running, occurs on the basis of minimisation of metabolic energy expenditure. In this section of the chapter we first briefly review the mechanisms of energy saving in walking and running, and the rationale to support the idea of an energetic trigger for human gait transition. We then report the results of an experiment designed to investigate the energetics of the transitions between walking and running in humans.

Energy Minimisation in Walking

Energy is used by the body in locomotion when muscles are active, contracting concentrically (shortening), contracting eccentrically (lengthening), or contracting isometrically (same length). The amount of energy used by the muscle depends upon the force and rate of contraction and the number of contractions used during each phase of the locomotory cycle. An examination of the optimisation of these three factors provides an explanation of much of what is observed in human walking.

Human walking is characterised by a straight leg during the support phase and a comparatively straight leg during the swing phase. This straight position of the leg is important for two reasons, as demonstrated by McGreer's (1990a) "rimless wheel" model of walking (as described in Alexander 1991). In McGreer's model the centre of mass of the body, situated near the hip, is considered to move forward along a series of arcs described by the length of each of the legs. The straight position of the leg minimises any force required to create or counteract a moment occurring around the knee and allows an interchange between the kinetic and potential energy possessed by the body's centre of gravity. Both these mechanisms act to limit the amount of force that the muscles need to produce and hence minimise the metabolic energy used by the system. As the leg has to be straight during the support phase, it is sensible that it also be carried in a relatively straight position during the swing phase; this eliminates unnecessary muscular action that would be involved in bending and straightening (flexing and extending) the leg.

While a straight leg position is clearly advantageous at low and moderate walking velocities, a straight leg position does become more problematic at higher walking speeds where a great deal of energy is needed to overcome the increased amount of inertia a straight leg possesses. The increased inertia possessed by an extended limb as opposed to a flexed one could explain why there is an energetically optimal speed for walking in humans, as demonstrated by the minimum evident in the energy uptake curve (see figure 5.5). This minimum value occurs at a speed of approximately 5.5 km·hr^{-1} (1.3 m·s^{-1}) (Hoyt and Taylor 1981; Margaria et al. 1963) with energy expenditure at this point being of the order of

0.79 cal·kg⁻¹·m⁻¹. It is important to note that this is the mean speed preferentially selected by humans during walking (Bobbert 1960; Corcoran and
Bregelmann 1970; Margaria 1976; Molen, Rozendal, and Boon 1972; Ralston
1976; Zarrugh, Todd, and Ralston 1974). Research involving animals has
shown that they also self-select walking speeds that minimise the physiological cost of locomotion (Hoyt and Taylor 1981; Pennycuick 1975; Perry
et al. 1988).

The fact that energy expenditure during a period of walking is dependent upon both the number and the speed of muscular contractions suggests that there will be a particular combination of stride rate and length
that, if adopted, will be the most energetically efficient at a given speed
(Cavagna and Kaneko 1977). Molen, Rozendal, and Boon (1972) and
Zarrugh, Todd, and Ralston (1974) have both demonstrated that people

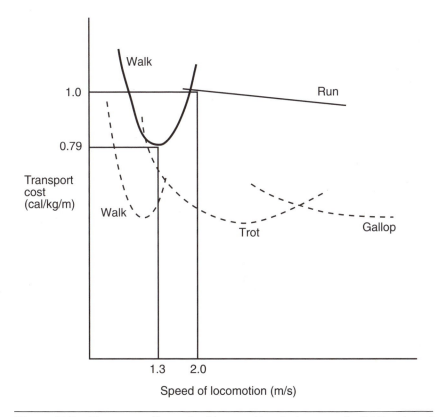

Figure 5.5 The energetic cost of locomotion in humans (solid lines) and
horses (dashed lines). The transport cost is minimised at a narrow range of
speeds for walking in humans and in walking, trotting, and galloping for horses.
Significantly, the transport cost is independent of running speed within the
human gait mode of running.

Based on Hoyt and Taylor 1981 and Margaria et al. 1963.

will preferentially self-select the optimal stride length to stride frequency ratio, which is approximately 1.61. Collectively, these observations provide compelling additional evidence for energy conservation as a determinant of the emergent patterns of coordination and control in human gait.

Energy Minimisation in Running

In contrast to the situation with walking, there is no optimal speed, in terms of metabolic energy expenditure, for running (see figure 5.5). Remarkably, the cost of running in terms of metabolic cost per unit of distance traveled remains virtually constant at 1.0 $cal \cdot kg^{-1} \cdot m^{-1}$ as speed of travel increases (Falls and Humphrey 1976; Kram and Taylor 1990; Margaria et al. 1963). Explanation of this requires consideration of the role of the Achilles tendon in the running gait. During running a large moment is created around the ankle joint at the time of foot contact, and this provides a tensile force to the Achilles tendon/gastrocnemius musculotendon unit. This action stores elastic energy within the musculotendon unit that can then be used subsequently during the propulsive phase of the movement. As the use of elastic energy requires no metabolic energy production, metabolic energy need not necessarily rise as the speed of running increases. Indeed it can be hypothesised that as speed of travel increases, greater and possibly also more efficient recruitment of the elastic component may occur, hence resulting in the metabolic cost-travel-speed relationship for running, as shown in figure 5.5. It is important to note that, despite the role played by the elastic energy component, the minimisation of metabolic efficiency nevertheless continues to play a role in the organisation of the running mechanics. During running, as in walking, the rate and amount of muscle recruitment dictates efficiency. If constrained to run at any speed within their normal running range, humans preferentially select the combination of stride frequency and amplitude that is optimal in terms of energy minimisation for that particular speed (Cavanagh and Williams 1982; Hogberg 1952; Knuttgen 1961).

Experiment 3:
An Energetic Trigger for Transitions Between Walking and Running?

Given the overwhelming evidence for the self organisation of kinematic parameters within each of the walking and running gait modes to minimise energy expenditure, it seems logical to believe that the transition between these different gait modes is also likely to be driven by energy constraints. Indeed, the primacy of the role of energetics in the transition between gait modes has been a common, but untested, assumption in the gait literature for decades. In 1991, however, Farley and Taylor presented evidence to suggest that the minimisation of energy expenditure may not necessarily be the driving stimulus for gait mode transitions. By measuring the physiological cost and velocities associated with the trot-gallop transitions in horses, Farley and Taylor demonstrated that these animals preferred to change between gait modes at speeds lower than those that were energetically optimal. Farley and Taylor suggested rather a mechanical trigger for the trot-gallop transition arguing that the transition is driven by the need to reduce mechanical stresses imposed by bone strain and peak muscle force. In support of this contention is experimental evidence that transitions to galloping reduce peak ground reaction forces (Biewener and Taylor 1986; Farley and Taylor 1991); that horses carrying loads make transitions at velocities significantly lower than those that are energetically optimal (Farley and Taylor 1991); and that, across a range of vertebrates, gait patterns are never preferentially adopted that cause the stresses on either joint or bone to exceed two-thirds of their breaking stress (Rubin and Lanyon 1984). However, major failings of a mechanical trigger hypothesis are that it cannot account for transitions in the reverse direction (from gallop to trot in the horse example) nor explain why critical ground reaction forces for transition are often exceeded at velocities where galloping is the preferred gait mode (Diedrich and Warren 1995). Moreover, the failure of individual differences in absolute mass to emerge in Experiment 2 as a correlate of preferred transition velocities also argues against a mechanical trigger based on critical ground reaction force values as a generic stimulus for gait transitions.

Following on the animal work of Farley and Taylor (1991), Hreljac (1993a) presented evidence that the walk-run transition in humans also occurs at nonenergetically optimal speeds. Consistent with the quadrupedal data, the walk-run transition for the individuals in Hreljac's study occurred at velocities slower than those that would be expected from a model based on the minimisation of energetic expenditure. Given this observation plus the observation that the participants in his study perceived walking as requiring more effort than running at the transitional speed even though less energy was actually being used, Hreljac concluded that the minimisation of energy expenditure was not the driving mechanism for the walk-run transition. A follow-up study (Hreljac 1993b), seeking a mechanical trigger for transition, in which five candidate kinetic variables were measured (maximum loading rate, braking, and propulsive impulse and force peak) concluded that kinetic factors are also not the trigger for human walk-run transitions.

More recently, and in contrast to Farley and Taylor (1991) and Hreljac (1993a), Mercier, Durand and others (Durand et al. 1994a, 1994b; Mercier et al. 1994) have concluded that the transition between gait modes is driven by the propensity to reduce physiological cost. Their evidence shows an extremely precise coincidence for each participant between the speed at which transition occurred and the point where the heart rates and oxygen consumption requirements for walking and running become equivalent. Our final experiment sought to examine this important and controversial facet of human gait control further.

Methods

A subgroup of 15 participants from Experiment 1, for whom the point and reliability of the preferred transition speed between walking and running were already known, participated in our investigation of the relationship between metabolic energy cost and transition speed. We compared the mean preferred transition speed obtained from the participants with a predicted value obtained from the intersection of metabolic curves derived from each of their walking and running trials. The participants all ran at a series of velocities above and below their point of preferred transition, and from these we generated curves for VO_2 ($ml \cdot kg^{-1} \cdot min^{-1}$) and transport cost ($ml \cdot kg^{-1} \cdot min^{-1} \cdot m^{-1}$) v speed (% of preferred transition speed). The same procedure was followed for walking, and then velocities of travel at the intersection of the walking and running trials were determined and compared with the mean preferred transition speed values previously obtained. A close coincidence of these points would be consistent with the notion that the transition between walking and running occurs in order to minimise energy cost (Hreljac 1993a). A discrepancy between these points would argue for factors other than energy minimisation underpinning gait transitions.

Participants walked and ran on a motor-driven treadmill at speeds equivalent to 70%, 80%, 90%, 100%, 110%, 120%, and 130% of the speed of preferred transition as determined by the speed elicited from all run-to-walk and walk-to-run trials undertaken in Experiment 1. Further habituation to the treadmill was deemed unnecessary given that the participants had already exceeded the 15-30 minutes of experience suggested by others as being necessary to accommodate to treadmill locomotion (Charteris and Taves 1978; Schieb 1986; Wall and Charteris 1980, 1981). Participants walked or ran for five minutes at each speed to ensure steady-state oxygen consumption was reached. During each trial the heart rate and oxygen consumption were continuously monitored using open circuit spirometry (Med Graphics CPX) and an electronic heart rate monitor (Polar Sportester Model No. 9000e), and mean steady-state values were determined for each speed/gait mode combination during the last minute. Transport costs were calculated by dividing the mass specific oxygen consumption by the speed of travel (following the procedures adopted by Farley and Taylor [1991]). To determine whether the participants' perceptions of effort paralleled their energetic output, all the participants were asked to indicate for each condition a Rating of Perceived Exertion (RPE), using the standard 15-point (6-21) scale of Borg (1962,

1973). The RPE data were to provide some insight into the likelihood that the conscious perception of energetic uptake might trigger, or at least influence the triggering of, the transition between gaits. Previous research has suggested a close link between RPE and energetic cost, regardless of the gait mode employed (Noble et al. 1973).

After values for oxygen uptake and transport cost were obtained for each individual at each speed, curves were fitted to each data set. Previous researchers have tended to use curvilinear models to fit the oxygen consumption data for walking (Hoyt and Taylor 1981; Margaria 1976; Margaria et al. 1963) and linear models for the data from running (Alexander 1989; Kram and Taylor 1990). Some have demonstrated better fits of their walking data sets using quadratic (Hreljac 1993a) and 2nd order polynomial (Minetti, Ardigo, and Saibene 1994) models. Using specifically designed software (Curvefit, Jandel Scientific, CA), we investigated the models that provided the most workable fitting for the oxygen cost and transport cost data sets. Consistent with traditional practice, the oxygen cost data were most accurately represented by a curvilinear model for walking and a linear model for running. For the transport cost data sets the lines for both walking and running were fitted using 4th order polynomial models.

Results

Of the 15 people selected to participate in this phase of our investigation, only nine were able to maintain a walking gait for the full data collection period at 130% of their normal walking gait. Figure 5.6 displays the group mean oxygen uptake curves for both the walking and running trials. As can be seen there was an extremely close coincidence between the intersection of the oxygen consumption curves for walking and running (the energetically optimal transition point) and the mean of the preferred transition points (grouped for the walk-run and run-walk conditions) collected in Experiment 1. In fact, the energetically optimal transition speed was 99.6 % of the preferred transition speed. These results provide, therefore, compelling evidence that the minimisation of energy expenditure plays a significant role in determining the speed at which the change between gait modes occurs in humans.

As was the case with the oxygen cost data, the energetically optimal transition speed as determined by the intersection of the walking and running transport cost curves coincided very closely with the mean preferred transition speed (grouped for the walk-run and run-walk conditions; figure 5.7). In this instance the energetically optimal transition speed was 100.5% of the preferred transition speed.

While walking was perceived to be more strenuous than running at speeds above the preferred transition point (RPEs walking were respectively rated 26%, 34%, and 32% higher than running at speeds 110%, 120%, and 130% of transition point), there was no meaningful difference in RPE

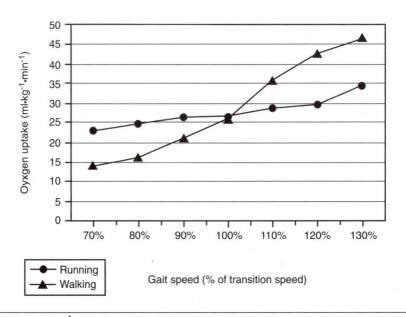

Figure 5.6 $\dot{V}O_2$ as a function of locomotion speed: a comparison of walking and running.

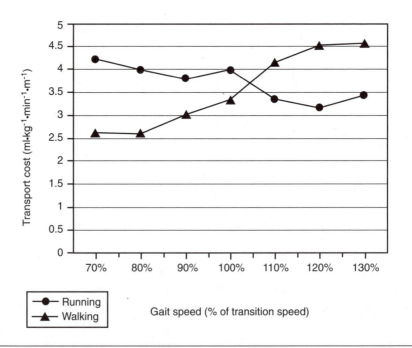

Figure 5.7 Transport cost as a function of locomotion speed for walking and running.

between the gait modes at or prior to the transition point (figure 5.8). The reasons why we were unable to replicate the findings of Hreljac (1993), who described a reduction of 26.2% in RPE at transition point, are unclear.

The RPE values under each of the experimental conditions did not provide clear evidence that the transition was made to reduce perceived effort. This would suggest that the reorganisation of movement pattern from walking to running, at least in this paradigm, is not a conscious decision, i.e., it is not a "decision" made at the same neural level as the scoring of a rating of perceived exertion value. Ratings of perceived exertion require conscious, deliberate judgement involving higher centres of the brain while gait transitions, at least as they occur in this particular paradigm, probably involve different (and lower) levels of the nervous system. Evidence from classical, spinalised animal studies (Shik and Orlosky 1976; Shik, Severin, and Orlosky 1966) demonstrate convincingly that gait transitions are possible using primarily subcortical and possibly only spinal structures. As indicated earlier, with respect to the issue

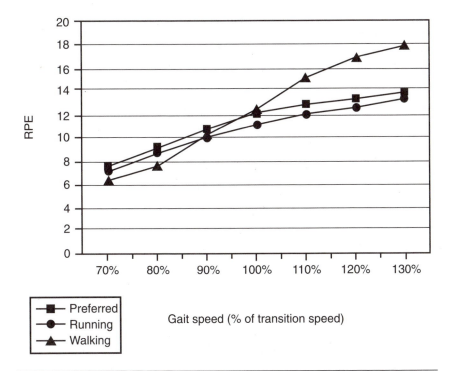

Figure 5.8 Rating of Perceived Exertion (RPE) as a function of locomotion speed and test condition. During the "preferred" condition participants were free to select their preferred gait mode while during the "walk" and "run" trials participants had to maintain the designated gait mode.

of intentionality, while cognitive involvement in human gait transition decisions is possible, this probably only occurs to a significant extent when a gait mode that is not the one naturally preferred has to be used.

Conclusions and Future Directions

Experiment 3 strongly suggests that the optimisation of energetic efficiency is central to the transition between gait modes in human locomotion. The questions remains, however, whether humans can "perceive" this increase in energetic uptake at all or quickly enough to trigger transition (given that physiological steady state is not reached for a number of minutes) (Thorstensson and Roberthson 1987). The role of metabolic energy uptake might best be understood when developed within a dynamical systems/synergetics perspective. As demonstrated by Holt et al. (1995) the optimisation of metabolic cost may simply be an a post-eriori consequence of the system optimising another parameter such as resonant frequency, postural stability, or musculoskeletal load; and the specific parameter that is to be optimised may vary with alterations in the specific task constraints. While physiological cost may not be the proximal cause of human gait transition, the total energy consumption may reflect the cost of driving the system away from its attractor states and into a new phase or coordination mode (Diedrich and Warren 1995).

We are currently investigating the mechanical energy production and transfers occurring within the human body during locomotion, as, among other things, these may allow an insight into the role played by the return of stored elastic energy through the loading of the Achilles tendon. If the action of the tendon can be implicated in transition initiation, it may be that stretch-sensitive structures within the musculotendon unit play a role in triggering the switch between the gait modes. The search for neural mechanisms underpinning the transitions that guarantee functional efficiency in the use of metabolic energy are important in the understanding of gait control systems as they are in the study of all types of coordinative systems of human movement.

Acknowledgments

We are grateful for the support of the Australian Research Council who provided funding for experiments presented within this chapter. The assistance of Annaliese Plooy and Megan Walters during the data collection and analysis phases of this project was invaluable and provided with the utmost proficiency. This chapter was completed while the second author was a Visiting Professor at the School of Physical Education, Nanyang Technological University, Singapore.

Note

[1]Children and adults are capable of consciously producing asymmetrical galloping gaits (Caldwell and Whitall 1995; Whitall 1989; Whitall and Caldwell 1992), but these are far less prevalent than walking and running and also apparently less stable as modes of coordination (Peck and Turvey 1997).

References

Abernethy, B., R.J. Burgess-Limerick, C. Engstrom, A. Hanna, and R.J. Neal. 1995. Temporal coordination of human gait. In *Motor control and sensory-motor integration: issues and direction,* eds. D.J. Glencross, and J.P. Piek, 171-198. Amsterdam: North-Holland Elsevier.

Alexander, R.McN. 1980. Optimum walking techniques for quadrupeds and bipeds. *Journal of Zoology* (London) 192: 97-117.

Alexander, R.McN. 1984. Walking and running. *American Scientist* 72: 348-354.

Alexander, R. McN. 1989. Optimisation and gaits in the locomotion of vertebrates. *Physiological Review* 69: 1199-1227.

Alexander, R.McN. 1991. Energy saving mechanisms in walking and running. *Journal of Experimental Biology* 160:55-69.

Alexander, R.McN. 1992. A model of bipedal locomotion on compliant legs. *Philosophical transactions of the Royal Society of London* 338(B): 189-198.

Alexander, R.McN., and A.S. Jayes. 1983. A dynamic similarity hypothesis for the gaits of quadrupedal mammals. *Journal of Zoology* (London) 201: 135-152.

Alexander, R.McN., and G.M.O. Maloiy. 1984. Stride lengths and stride frequencies of primates. *Journal of Zoology (London)* 202: 577-582.

Bassett, D.R., M.D. Giese, F.J. Nagle, A. Ward, D.M. Raab, and B. Balke. 1985. Aerobic requirements of overground versus treadmill running. *Medicine and Science in Sports and Exercise* 17: 477-481.

Beek, P. J., and G.P. Bingham. 1991. Task specific dynamics and the study of perception and action: a reaction to von Hofsten. 1989. *Ecological Psychology* 3: 35-54.

Beuter, A., and F. Lalonde. 1989. Analysis of a phase transition in human locomotion using singularity theory. *Neuroscience Research Communications* 3: 127-132.

Biewener, A.A., and C.R. Tayor. 1986. Bone strain: a determinant of gait and speed? *Journal of Experimental Biology* 123: 383-400.

Bingham, G. P. 1988. Task-specific devices and the perceptual bottleneck. *Human Movement Science* 7: 225-264.

Blickhan, R. 1989. The spring-mass model for running and hopping. *Journal of Biomechanics* 22: 1217-1227.

Bobbert, A.C. 1960. Energy expenditure in level and grade walking. *Journal of Applied Physiology* 15: 1015-1021.

Bonnard, M., and J. Paihous. 1993. Intentionality in human gait control: modifying the frequency-to-amplitude relationship. *Journal of Experimental Psychology: Human Perception and Performance* 19: 429-443.

Borg, G.A.V. 1962. *Physical performance and perceived exertion.* Lund: Gleerup.

Borg, G.A.V. 1973. Perceived exertion: a note on "history" and methods. *Medicine and Science in Sports* 5: 90-93.

Caldwell, G.E., and J. Whitall. 1995. An energetic comparison of symmetrical and non-symmetrical gait. *Journal of Motor Behavior* 27: 139-154.

Carson, R.G., W.D. Byblow, B. Abernethy, and J.J. Summers. 1996. The contribution of inherent and incidental constraints to intentional switching between patterns of bimanual coordination. *Human Movement Science* 15: 565-589.

Carson, R.G., D. Goodman, J.A.S. Kelso, and D. Elliott. 1994. Intentional switching between patterns of interlimb coordination. *Journal of Human Movement Studies* 27: 201-218.

Carter, L. 1995. Somatotyping. In *Anthropometrica*, eds. K. Norton, and T. Olds, 147-170. Sydney: UNSW Press.

Cavangna, G.A., and P. Franzetti. 1986. The determinants of step frequency in walking in humans. *Journal of Physiology* (London) 373: 235-242.

Cavangna, G.A., and M. Kaneko. 1977. Mechanical work and efficiency in level walking and running. *Journal of Physiology* 268: 467-481.

Cavagna, G.A., F.P. Saibene, and R. Margaria. 1963. External work in walking. *Journal of Applied Physiology* 18: 1-19.

Cavanagh, P.R., and K.R. Williams. 1982. The effect of stride length variation on oxygen uptake during distance running. *Medicine and Science in Sport and Exercise* 14: 30-35.

Charteris, J., and C. Taves. 1978. The process of habituation to treadmill walking. *Perceptual and Motor Skills* 47: 659-666.

Clark, J.E. 1995. On becoming skillful: patterns and constraints. *Research Quarterly for Exercise and Sport* 66: 173-183.

Collins, J.J., and I. Stewart. 1993. Hexapodal gaits and coupled nonlinear oscillator models. *Biological Cybernetics* 68: 287-298.

Corcoran, P.J., and G.L. Brengelmann. 1970. Oxygen uptake in normal and handicapped subjects, in relation to speed of walking beside a velocity-controlled cart. *Archives of Physical Medicine* 51: 78-87.

Cutting, J.E., D.R. Proffitt, and L.T. Kozlowski. 1978. A biomechanical invariant for gait perception. *Journal of Experimental Psychology: Human Perception and Performance* 4: 356-372.

Diedrich, F.J., and W.H. Warren, Jr. 1995. Why change gaits? Dynamics of the walk run transition. *Journal of Experimental Psychology* 21: 183-202.

Durand, M., C. Goudal, J. Mercier, D. Le Gallais, and J.P. Micallef. 1994a. Energy correlate of gait change according to locomotion speed. *Journal of Human Studies* 26: 187-203.

Durand, M., C. Goudal, J. Mercier, D. Le Gallais, and J.P. Micallef. 1994b. From walking to running: study of energy correlates. In *Movement and sport. Psychological foundations and effects. Vol 2: motor control and motor learning*, eds. J.R. Nitsch, and R. Seiler, 36-41. Germany: Academia Verlag.

Elliott, B.C., and B.A. Blanksby. 1976. A cinematographic analysis of overground and treadmill running by males and females. *Medicine and Science in Sports and Exercise* 8: 84-87.

Falls, H.B., and L.D. Humphrey. 1976. Energy cost of running and walking in young women. *Medicine and Science in Sport* 8: 9-13.

Farley, C.T., and C.R. Taylor. 1991. A mechanical trigger for the trot-gallop transition in horses. *Science* 253: 306-308.

Frishberg, B.A. 1983. An analysis of overground and treadmill sprinting. *Medicine and Science in Sports and Exercise* 15: 478-485.

Getchell, N., and J. Whitall. 1997. Transitions in gait as a function of physical parameters (abstract). *Journal of Sport and Exercise Psychology* 19: S55.

Grieve, D.W. 1968. Gait patterns and the speed of walking. *Biomedical Engineering* 3: 119-122.

Grieve, D.W., and R.J. Gear. 1966. The relationships between length of stride, frequency, time of swing and speed of walking for children and adults. *Ergonomics* 5: 379-399.

Grillner, S., J. Halbertsma, J. Nilsson, and A. Thorstensson. 1979. The adaptation to speed in human locomotion. *Brain Research* 165 : 177-182.

Haken, H. 1983. *Synergetics: an introduction*. 3rd ed. Berlin: Springer Verlag.

Haken, H. 1990. Synergetics as a tool for the conceptualization and mathematization of cognition and behaviour—How far can we go? In *Synergetics of cognition*, eds. H. Haken, and M. Stadler, 2-31. Berlin: Springer Verlag.

Haken, H., J.A.S. Kelso, and H. Bunz. 1985. A theoretical model of phase transitions in human hand movement. *Biological Cybernetics* 51: 347-356.

Hasan, Z. 1986. Optimized movement trajectories and joint stiffness in unperturbed, inertially loaded movements. *Biological Cybernetics* 53: 373-382.

Heglund, N.C., and C.R. Taylor. 1988. Speed, stride frequency and energy cost per stride: how do they change with body size and gait? *Journal of Experimental Biology* 138: 301-318.

Heglund, N.C., C.R. Taylor, and T.A. McMahon. 1974. Scaling stride frequency and gait to animal size: mice to horses. *Science* 186: 1112-1113.

Hoenkamp, E. 1978. Perceptual cues that determine the labelling of human gait. *Journal of Human Movement Studies* 4: 59-69.

Hogan, N., and T. Flash. 1987. Moving gracefully: quantitative theories of motor coordination. *Trends in the Neurosciences* 10: 170-174.

Hogberg, P. 1952. How do stride lengths and stride frequency influence the energy output during running? *Internationale Zeitschrift für Angewandte Physiologie Einschlesslich Arbeitsphysiologie* 14: 437-441.

Holt, K.G. 1998. Constraints in the emergence of preferred locomotory patterns. In *Timing of Behavior: Neural, computational and psychological perspectives*, eds. D.A. Rosenbaum, and C.E. Collyer. Cambridge, MA.: MIT Press.

Holt, K.G., J. Hamill, and R.O. Andres. 1990. The force-driven harmonic oscillator as a model for human locomotion. *Human Movement Science* 9: 55-68.

Holt, K.G., J. Hamill, and R.O. Andres. 1991. Predicting the minimal energy costs of human walking. *Medicine and Science in Sports and Exercise* 23: 491-498.

Holt, K.G., S.F. Jeng, R. Ratcliffe, and J. Hamill. 1995. Energetic cost and stability in preferred human walking. *Journal of Motor Behavior* 27: 164-179.

Holt, K.G., S.F. Jeng, and L. Fetters. 1991. Walking cadence of 9-year olds is predictable as the resonant frequency of a force-driven harmonic oscillator. *Pediatric Exercise Science* 3: 121-128.

Hoyt, D.F., and C.R. Taylor. 1981. Gait and the energetics of locomotion in horses. *Nature* 292: 239-240.

Hreljac, A. 1993a. Preferred and energetically optimal gait transition speeds in human locomotion. *Medicine and Science in Sports and Exercise* 25: 1158-1162.

Hreljac, A. 1993b. Determinants of the gait transition speed during human locomotion: kinetic factors. *Gait and Posture* 1: 217-223.

Hreljac, A. 1995a. Determinants of the gait transition speed during human locomotion: kinematic factors. *Journal of Biomechanics* 28: 669-677.

Hreljac, A. 1995b. Effects of physical characteristics on the gait transition speed during human locomotion. *Human Movement Science* 14: 205-216.

Iberall, A.S. 1978. A field and circuit thermodynamics for integrative physiology. III. Keeping the books—a general experimental method. *American Journal of Physiology* 234: R85-R97.

Inman, V.T., H.J. Ralston, and F. Todd. 1981. *Human walking.* Baltimore: Williams and Wilkins.

Jeka, J.J., and J.A.S. Kelso. 1988. Dynamic patterns of multi-limb coordination. In *Dynamic patterns in complex systems,* eds. J.A.S. Kelso, A.J. Mandell, and M. F. Shlesinger, 403. Singapore: World Scientific.

Jeka, J.J., and J.A.S. Kelso. 1989. The dynamic pattern approach to coordinated behavior: a tutorial review. In *Perspectives on the coordination of movement,* ed. S.A. Wallace, 3-43. Amsterdam: Elsevier.

Jeng, S., H. Liao, J. Lai, and W. Hou. 1997. Optimisation of walking in children. *Medicine and Science in Sports and Exercise* 29: 370-376.

Kelso, J.A.S. 1981. Contrasting perspectives on order and regulation in movement. In *Attention and performance IX,* eds. J. Long and A. Baddeley, 437-457. Hillsdale, NJ: Erlbaum.

Kelso, J.A.S. 1984. Phase transitions and critical behavior in human bimanual coordination. *American Journal of Physiology* 246: R1000-R1004.

Kelso, J.A.S. 1986. Pattern formation in multi-degree of freedom speech and limb movements. *Experimental Brain Research Supplement* 15: 105-128.

Kelso, J.A.S. 1990. Phase transitions: foundations of behavior. In *Synergetics of cognition,* eds. H. Haken, and M. Stadler, 249-268. Berlin: Springer-Verlag.

Kelso, J.A.S. 1995. *Dynamic patterns.* Cambridge, MA: MIT Press.

Kelso, J.A.S., and G.C. de Guzman. 1988. Order in time: how the cooperation between the hands informs the design of the mind. In *Neural and synergetic computers,* ed. H. Haken, 180-196. Berlin: Springer Verlag.

Kelso, J.A.S., J.P. Scholz, and G. Schöner. 1986. Nonequilibrium phase transitions in coordinated biological motion: Critical fluctuations. *Physics Letters A* 118: 279-284.

Kelso, J.A.S., J.P. Scholz, and G. Schöner. 1988. Dynamics governs switching among patterns of coordination in biological movement. *Physics Letters A* 134: 8-12.

Kelso, J.A.S., and G. Schöner. 1988. Self-organization of coordinative movement patterns. *Human Movement Science* 7: 27-46.

Kelso, J.A.S., G. Schöner, J.P. Scholz, and H. Haken. 1987. Phase-locked modes, phase transitions and component oscillators in biological motion. *Physica Scripta* 35: 79-87.

Knuttgen, M.G. 1961. Oxygen uptake and pulse rate while running with undetermined and determined stride length at different speeds. *Acta Physiologica Scandinavia* 52: 366-371.

Kram, R., and C.R. Taylor. 1990. Energetics of running: a new perspective. *Nature* 346: 265-267.

Kugler, P.N., and M.T. Turvey. 1987. *Information, natural law and the self assembly of rhythmic movement: theoretical and experimental investigations.* Hillsdale NJ: Erlbaum.

Latash, M.L. 1993. *Control of human movement.* Champaign, IL: Human Kinetics.

Mackenzie, C.L., and A.E. Patla. 1983. Breakdown in rapid bimanual finger tapping as a function of orientation and phasing. *Society for Neuroscience Abstracts* 9: 1033.

Margaria, R. 1976. *Biomechanics and energetics of muscular exercise.* Oxford: Clarendon Press.

Margaria, R., P. Cerretelli, P. Aghemo, and G. Sassi. 1963. Energy cost of running. *Journal of Applied Physiology* 18: 367-370.

McGreer, T. 1990a. Passive dynamic walking. *International Journal of Robotics Research* 9: 62-82.

McGreer, T. 1990b. Passive dynamic running. *Proceedings of the Royal Society of London* 240(B): 107-134.

McMahon, T.A. 1985. The role of compliance in mammalian running gaits. *Journal of Experimental Biology* 115: 263-282.

McMahon, T.A., and G.C. Cheng. 1990. The mechanics of running: how does stiffness couple with speed? *Journal of Biomechanics* 23: 65-78.

Mercier, J., D. Le Gallais, M. Durand, C. Goudal, J.P. Micallef, and C. Préfaut. 1994. Energy expenditure and cardiorespiratory responses at the transition between walking and running. *European Journal of Applied Physiology* 69: 525-529.

Minetti, A.E., L.P. Ardigo, and F. Saibene. 1994. The transition between walking and running in humans: metabolic and mechanical aspects at different gradients. *Acta Physiologica Scandinavica* 150: 315-323.

Mochon, S., and T.A. McMahon. 1980. Ballistic walking. *Journal of Biomechanics* 13: 49-57.

Molen, N.H., R.H. Rozendal, and W. Boon. 1972. Graphic representation of the relationship between oxygen-consumption and characteristics of normal gait of the human male. *Proceedings Koninklijke Nederlandse Academie van Wetenschnappen*, C-75: 215-223.

Murray, M.P., R.C. Kery, B.H. Clarkson, and S.B. Sepic. 1966. Comparison of free and fast speed walking patterns of normal man. *American Journal of Physical Medicine* 45: 8-24.

Nelson, R.C., C.J. Dillman, P. Lagasse, and P. Bickett. 1972. Biomechanics of overground versus treadmill running. *Medicine and Science in Sports and Exercise* 4: 233-240.

Nigg, B.M., R.W. De Boer, and V. Fisher. 1995. A kinematic comparison of overground and treadmill running. *Medicine and Science in Sports and Exercise* 27: 98-105.

Nilsson, J., A. Thorstensson, and J. Halbertsma. 1985. Changes in leg movements and muscle activity with speed of locomotion and mode of progression in animals. *Acta Physiologica Scandinavica* 123: 457-475.

Noble, B., K. Metz, K.B. Pandolf, C.W. Bell, E. Cafarelli, and W.E. Sime. 1973. Perceived exertion during walking and running-II. *Medicine and Science in Exercise and Sport* 5: 116-120.

Peck, A.J., and M.T. Turvey. 1997. Coordination dynamics of the bipedal galloping pattern. *Journal of Motor Behavior* 4: 311-325.

Pennycuick, C.J. 1975. On the running of the gnu (*Connochaetes taurinus*) and other animals. *Journal of Experimental Biology* 63: 775-799.

Perry, A.K., R. Blickhan, A.A. Biewener, N.C. Heglund, and C.R. Taylor. 1988. Preferred speeds in terrestrial vertebrates: are they equivalent? *Journal of Experimental Biology* 137: 207-220.

Pink, M., J. Perry, P.A. Houglum, and D.J. Devine. 1994. Lower extremity range of motion in the recreational sport runner. *American Journal of Sports Medicine* 22: 541-549.

Pugh, L.G.C.E. 1970. Oxygen intake in track and treadmill running with observations on the effect of air resistance. *Journal of Physiology* 207: 823-835.

Ralston, H.J. 1976. Energetics of human walking. In *Neural control of locomotion,* eds. R.M. Herman et al., 77-98. New York: Plenum.

Rubin, C.T., and L.E. Lanyon. 1984. Dynamic strain similarity in vertebrates: an alternative to allometric limb bone scaling. *Journal of Theoretical Biology* 107: 321-327.

Schieb, D.A. 1986. Kinematic accommodation of novice treadmill runners. *Research Quarterly for Exercise and Sport* 57: 7.

Schmidt, R.C., and M.T. Turvey. 1989. Absolute coordination: an ecological perspective. In *Perspectives on the coordination of movement,* ed. S. A. Wallace, 123-156. Amsterdam: Elsevier.

Scholz, J.P., and J.A.S. Kelso. 1989. A quantitative approach to understanding the formation and change of coordinated movement patterns. *Journal of Motor Behavior* 21: 122-144.

Scholz, J.P., and J.A.S. Kelso. 1990. Intentional switching between patterns of bimanual coordination depends on the intrinsic dynamics of the patterns. *Journal of Motor Behavior* 22: 98-124.

Scholz, J.P., J.A.S. Kelso, and G. Schöner. 1987. Nonequilibrium phase transitions in coordinated biological motion: critical slowing down and switching time. *Physics Letters A* 123: 390-394.

Schöner, G., W.Y. Jiang, and J.A.S. Kelso. 1990. A synergetic theory of quadrupedal gait and gait transitions. *Journal of Theoretical Biology* 142: 359-391.

Schöner, G., and J.A.S. Kelso. 1988a. Dynamic patterns of biological coordination: theoretical strategy and new results. In *Dynamic patterns in complex systems,* eds. JJ.A.S. Kelso, A.J. Mandell, and M.F. Shlesinger, 77-102. Singapore: World Scientific.

Schöner, G., and J.A.S. Kelso. 1988b. A theory of learning and recall in biological coordination. In *Dynamic patterns in complex systems,* eds. J.A.S. Kelso, A.J. Mandell, and M.F. Shlesinger, 409. Singapore: World Scientific.

Schöner, G., P.G. Zanone, and J.A.S. Kelso. 1992. Learning as a change of coordination dynamics: theory and experiment. *Journal of Motor Behavior* 24: 29-48.

Shik, M.L., and G.N. Orlosky. 1976 Neurophysiology of locomotor automatism. *Physiological Reviews* 56: 465-501.

Shik, M.L., F.V. Severin, and G.N. Orlosky. 1966. Control of walking and running by means of electrical stimulation of the mid-brain. *Biophysics* 11: 756-765.

Sparrow, W.A. 1983. The efficiency of skilled performance. *Journal of Motor Behavior* 15: 237-261.

Stein, R.B. 1982. What muscle variables does the central nervous system control? *The Behavioral and Brain Sciences* 5: 535-577.

Taga, G., G.Yamaguchi, and H. Shimizu. 1991. Self-organized control of bipedal locomotion by neural oscillators in unpredictable environments. *Biological Cybernetics* 65: 147-159.

Taylor, C.R., N.C. Heglund, and G.M. Maloiy. 1982. Energetics and mechanics of terrestrial locomotion. 1. Metabolic energy consumption as a function of speed and body size in birds and mammals. *Journal of Experimental Biology* 97: 1-23.

Temprado, J.J., P.G. Zanone, A. Monno, and M. Laurent. In press. Intentional stabilization of bimanual coordination: a study through attentional local measure. *Journal of Experimental Psychology: Human Perception and Performance.*

Thelen, E., and B.D. Ulrich. 1989. Self-organisation in development processes: can systems approaches work? In *Systems and development. The Minnesota symposia on child psychology, Vol. 22*, eds. M.R. Gunnar, and E. Thelen. Hillsdale, NJ: Erlbaum.

Thorstensson, A., and H. Roberthson. 1987. Adaptations to changing speed in human locomotion: speed of transition between walking and running. *Acta Physiologica Scandinavica* 131: 211-214.

Todd, J. 1983. Perception of gait. *Journal of Experimental Psychology: Human Perception and Performance* 9: 31-42.

Turvey, M.T. 1990. Coordination. *American Psychologist* 45: 938-953.

Turvey, M.T., K.G. Holt, J.P. Obusek, A. Salo, and P.N. Kugler. 1996. Adiabatic transformability hypothesis of human locomotion. *Biological Cybernetics* 74: 107-115.

Turvey, M.T., R.C. Schmidt, L.D. Rosenblum, and P.N. Kugler. 1988. On the time allometry of co-ordinated rhythmic movements. *Journal of Theoretical Biology* 130: 285-325.

Uno, Y., M. Kawato, and R. Suzuki. 1989. Formation and control of optimal trajectory in human multijoint arm movement: minimum torque-change model. *Biological Cybernetics* 61: 89-101.

van Ingen Schenau, G.J. 1980. Some fundamental aspects of the biomechanics of overground vs. treadmill locomotion. *Medicine and Science in Sport and Exercise* 12: 257-261.

Vaughan, C.L., G.N. Murphy., and L.L. du Toit. 1897. *Biomechanics of human gait: an annotated bibliography.* 2d ed. Champaign, IL: Human Kinetics.

Wall, J.C., and J. Charteris. 1980. The process of habituation to treadmill walking at different velocities. *Ergonomics* 23: 425-435.

Wall, J.C., and J. Charteris. 1981. A kinematic study of long-term habituation to treadmill walking. *Ergonomics* 24: 531-542.

Wann, J.P., I. Nimmo-Smith, and A. Wing. 1988. Relation between velocity and curvature in movement: equivalence and divergence between a power law and minimum-jerk model. *Journal of Experimental Psychology: Human Perception and Performance* 14: 622-637.

Warren W.H. Jr. 1988a. Action modes and laws of control for the visual guidance of action. In *Complex movement behaviour: the 'motor-action' controversy*, eds. O.G. Meijer, and K. Roth, 339-380. Amsterdam: Elsevier.

Warren W.H. Jr., 1988b. Critical behavior in perception-action systems. In *Dynamic patterns in complex systems*, eds. J.A.S. Kelso, A.J. Mandell, and M.F. Shlesinger, 370-387. Singapore: World Scientific.

Whitall, J. 1989. A developmental study of the interlimb coordination in running and galloping. *Journal of Motor Behavior* 21: 409-428.

Whitall, J., and G.E. Caldwell. 1992. Coordination of symmetrical and asymmetrical human gait: kinematic patterns. *Journal of Motor Behavior* 24: 339-353.

Williams, K.R. 1985. Biomechanics of running. *Exercise and Sport Science Reviews* 13: 389-441.

Winter, D.A. 1979. *Biomechanics of human movement*. New Jersey: Wiley.

Winter, D.A. 1984. Kinematic and kinetic patterns in human gait: variability and compensating effects. *Human Movement Science* 3: 51-76.

Wollacott, M.H., and J.L. Jensen. 1996. Posture and locomotion. In *Handbook of perception and action. Vol. 2: motor skills*, eds. H. Heuer, and S.W. Keele, 333-403. London: Academic Press.

Wright, R.L.D. 1976. *Understanding statistics: an informal introduction for the behavioral sciences*. New York: Harcourt Brace Jovanovich.

Wuyts, I.J., J.J. Summers, R.G. Carson, W.D. Byblow, and A. Semjen. 1996. Attention as a mediating variable in the dynamics of bimanual coordination. *Human Movement Science* 15: 877-897.

Yaminishi, J., M. Kawato, and R. Suzuki. 1980. Two coupled oscillators as a model for the coordinated finger tapping by both hands. *Biological Cybernetics* 37: 219-225.

Zanone, P.G., and J.A.S. Kelso. 1994. The coordination dynamics of learning. In *Interlimb coordination: neural, dynamical, and cognitive constraints*, eds. S. Swinnen et al. 462-490. San Diego: Academic Press.

Zarrugh, M.Y., F.N. Todd, and H.J. Ralston. 1974. Optimisation of energy expenditure during level walking. *European Journal of Applied Physiology* 33: 293-306.

6

Learned Changes in Behavioral Efficiency: The Effects of Concurrent and Terminal Exteroceptive Feedback of Response Success

Jasper Brener and Scott Carnicom

Department of Psychology, State University of New York at Stony Brook, United States

The Role of Heredity and Environment in Determining Behavioral Efficiency

It is generally accepted that behavior tends to maximal efficiency. Numerous studies have demonstrated that when organisms are able to earn equal amounts of reinforcement (SR) via alternative responses, the less burdensome alternative is usually selected (DeCamp 1920; Kuo 1922; Gengerilli 1928; Solomon 1948; Tolman,1932; Tsai 1932). DeCamp showed that rats learned to travel down the shorter of two paths in order to earn reinforcement, while Gengerelli found that rats tended to follow the path that led to food in the shortest time. Tsai required rats to open differentially weighted doors for food reward and found that they usually selected the lightest door. These phenomena are described by the principle of least effort, which contends that organisms respond, "... in such a manner as to expend the least amount of physical energy in the achievement of a goal object," (McCulloch 1934, p. 85).

The principle of least effort has been incorporated into theories of optimal foraging by behavioral ecologists (Krebs 1978; Kamil and Roitblat 1985; Stephens and Krebs 1986). In order to survive, organisms must balance the energy cost of foraging for food and the energy earned from ingesting the food. The most favorable survival strategy, which is also the most efficient, involves minimizing the costs and maximizing the benefits of food capture, thereby achieving the greatest cost-benefit ratio. On this basis, optimal foraging theory argues that organisms have evolved to maximize their net energy gain. By the processes of natural selection, organisms with natural tendencies towards the least effortful behavioral routes to prey capture and ingestion survived to pass these traits on to their progeny.

Several studies with a variety of species have shown that in situations other than foraging, organisms will select the most energetically efficient behavior for meeting the demands of that situation (Baz 1979; Hoyt and Taylor 1981; Ketelaars and Tolkamp 1996; Sparrow 1983). For example, Hoyt and Taylor trained horses to progress at different speeds on a treadmill with three different gait patterns (walking, trotting, and galloping). During each of the gait patterns, energy efficiency was significantly greater at speeds freely selected by the horses than at speeds imposed by the experimenters. Similarly, Ketelaars and Tolkamp showed that the intensity of foraging behaviors in ruminants is also self-selected at a level that maximizes net energy gain. This automatic selection of a preferred intensity of behavior that is also maximally efficient has been called a "comfort mode" (Sparrow 1983). Furthermore, since the same rates of pedaling a cycle ergometer are the most comfortable and most energetically efficient for both novice and experienced cyclists (Stegemann 1981), it would seem that the preference is hard wired and relatively immune to experiential influence (Brener 1986a). Thus, when behavioral options are unconstrained, inexperienced individuals will automatically select the least costly behaviors that satisfy the reinforcement criteria. These behaviors, as products of evolution, are already performed at, or close to, the biomechanical optimum that is maximally efficient. This suggests that organisms are genetically predisposed to maximize behavioral efficiency.

A predisposition towards maximal behavioral efficiency is also implicit in nearly all learning theories (Killeen 1974). Hull (1943) stated, "if two or more behavior sequences, each involving a different amount of energy consumption or work (W), have been equally well reinforced an equal number of times, the organism will gradually learn to choose the less laborious behavior sequence leading to the attainment of the reinforcing state of affairs," (p.294). In other words, increases in behavioral efficiency provide both the motivation and the reward for learning. The importance of learning in the optimization of foraging strategies has been recognized by behavioral ecologists (e.g. Hughes 1979; Kamil and Roitblat 1985). Improvements in energy efficiency result in survival advantages because the time and energy spared by efficient performance releases resources for other survival functions. Furthermore, learning provides a means of adjusting survival strategies to the changing demands of the environment. Staddon and Simmelhag (1971), for example, have recognized that the process by which learning selectively strengthens effective behaviors is similar to natural selection. Within the lifetime of a single organism, the processes of learning and reinforcement work to protect effective behavioral variants from extinction.

Several studies have demonstrated that behavioral efficiency in foraging and nonforaging situations gradually increases with practice. The total energy cost of working for reinforcement is generated by task-relevant behaviors, task-irrelevant behaviors, and basal metabolic rate (Brener 1987). Since basal metabolic rate remains relatively constant, only variations in task-relevant and task-irrelevant behaviors can explain changes in energy efficiency. The striate muscles, through which movement is expressed, are the major source of variations in overall energy expenditure, and therefore alterations in the control of these effectors is a major determinant of the changes in energy expenditure seen during learning (Brener 1986a). One illustration of how refined striate muscle control may result in energy economies comes from a continuous reaction time task in which humans were required to press one of four signaled beams with appropriate force (Brener 1987). Across four experimental sessions, EMG activity diminished while performance improved, indicating that with practice, redundant muscular activity decreased and motor activity came to approximate the minimal response for satisfying task requirements. Thus, task-irrelevant behaviors diminished while successful response variants were made more efficient.

Sparrow and Irizarry-Lopez (1987) required human subjects to walk on their hands and feet (creeping) on a motor-driven treadmill and demonstrated systematic decreases in oxygen consumption per unit distance traveled. These gradual increases in efficiency were associated with changes in interlimb timing and intralimb coordination. Sparrow and Newell (1994) also provide data that suggest that with practice, task-irrelevant behaviors diminish and task-relevant behaviors become more efficient. With practice on the same creeping exercise, subjects exhibited subtle alterations in their gait (viz., decreased limb swing duration and increased stride length) that led to increases in the efficiency of their locomotion.

Similar increases in efficiency have been demonstrated in operant conditioning paradigms. Sherwood, Brener, and Moncur (1983) demonstrated that rats trained to run in a running wheel to avoid electric shocks significantly reduced the volume of oxygen consumed per shock avoided across trials. This effect was attributable partly to reductions in overall oxygen consumption achieved through reduction of redundant or unnecessary responses. However, it was mainly due to increases in the effectiveness of their avoidance behavior. Thus, in addition to redundant behaviors dropping out, effective behavior was refined to increase efficiency. These investigators also found that subjects presented with stimuli that reduced temporal uncertainty about impending electric shocks achieved higher levels of efficiency than subjects not presented with this information. Provision of this information resulted in the synchronization of motor output with the demands of the shock-avoidance schedule.

Brener and Mitchell (1989) also showed that rats significantly decreased oxygen consumed per reinforcement across 16 days of training when required to produce criterion isometric response forces to earn liquid food. In the initial stages of training, the proportion of responses meeting the force criterion gradually increased as a reflection of increases in the average response force. These increases in response force were associated with increases in the energy cost of responding, which, in the case of isometric responses, has been shown by Jobsis and Duffield (1967) to be directly related to the area under the force-time trajectory. Brener and Mitchell found that the rate of task-related work was increased by responses becoming larger and the interval between successive responses declining. Since, in parallel, rates of oxygen consumption declined, it could be concluded that behaviors unrelated to the reinforcement contingencies extinguished.

Once the proportion of successful responses reached a plateau, changes in the temporal and kinetic characteristics of individual responses occurred; this led to further increases in behavioral efficiency. As predicted by Notterman and Mintz (1965), peak force levels eventually regressed to the criterion and remained stable. However, response duration systematically decreased across the 16 days, reducing the area under the force-time trajectory and therefore the work being performed on each response. Thus, with continued exposure to the contingencies, the form of individual responses changed systematically so as to preserve criterion peak forces while at the same time decreasing the energy consumed by the press (refer to figure 6.2 on page 174). Since less work was being performed per response and a higher proportion of responses were meeting the force requirement, work per reinforcement decreased further with practice. Thus, not only do unnecessary behaviors extinguish, but successful behaviors are refined in such a way as to lead to greater efficiency within a response.

Mitchell and Brener (1991) observed a similar pattern of energy expenditure and response dynamics in rats as they adjusted their motor output to meet progressively increasing force requirements. Within each successive higher force condition, the amount of work performed per response increased linearly. However, overall energy expenditure (oxygen consumption per minute) fell across successive force conditions, being significantly higher in the lowest force condition, which was encountered first, than in the highest force condition, which was encountered last. This pattern of results with increasing task work and decreasing oxygen consumption indicates that nontask work diminished. Within each augmented force condition, the amount of work performed per response increased as a linear function of practice. Nevertheless, work per reinforcement decreased across the six days within each condition. This was again accomplished by a greater proportion of responses meeting the prevailing force requirement: The additional costs of generating larger responses was less than the costs incurred by making sub-criterion responses that did not contribute to food acquisition.

Within each of the successive higher force conditions, response force reliably increased to maintain a stable reinforcement rate. The duration of individual responses initially lengthened, leading to transitory increases in work per response. However, once the proportion of correct responses plateaued, the force-time trajectories of individual responses were reorganized in such a way as to decrease the work per press. The increase in force came at a higher cost initially, but response form was then refined to maintain reinforcement while maximizing net energy gain. The development of more efficient performance with learning appears to follow a systematic course. When faced with novel environmental demands, organisms demonstrate greater variability in their behavior associated with higher levels of energy expenditure (Brener 1987). Since the behavior necessary for meeting the demands of novel situations is uncertain, heightened behavioral variability increases the probability of generating an adaptive act. By protecting effective responses from extinction, reinforcement acts to counteract the effects of habituation. Working together, these two processes whittle away irrelevant behaviors until the class of behavior exhibited in the situation contains an acceptable proportion of successful responses. However, even after a stable rate of reward comes to be generated under a particular set of contingencies, the class of effective responses continues to be successively refined so that in the final analysis it converges on the minimally effective (or most efficient) response. Hull (1943), among others, inferred that the processes responsible for selecting the most efficient forms of the successful response are like intrinsic forms of reinforcement generated by the fatigue-like consequences of responding.

In summary then, the course of force learning in rats suggests that there exist distinct orderly steps by which behavioral efficiency is maximized. First, a class of effective responses is identified. Second, task-irrelevant behavior is eliminated. Third, task-relevant behavior comes to meet the reinforcement requirements with minimal redundancy.

The Role of Feedback and Reinforcement in Determining Behavioral Efficiency

Feedback refers to stimulation that is caused by an organism's own activities. Most movements generate feedback in the visual, auditory, kinesthetic, and proprioceptive modalities (Bilodeau 1969; Holding 1965; Schmidt 1988). In addition to these intrinsic forms of feedback, experimenters may add extrinsic feedback to augment information about particular aspects of the movement (Bilodeau 1969). Operant reinforcement is an example of such extrinsic feedback. Response-contingent feedback is clearly of primary importance in both operant conditioning and motor skill acquisition. Two behavioral functions of operant reinforcers that may be distinguished are an incentive or motivational function, and a feedback or informational function. In operant conditioning, reinforcer delivery serves both these functions, whereas in motor learning experiments, feedback is frequently manipulated independently of the factors that motivate performance (Powers 1973). It is highly probable that feedback as a source of information plays a decisive role in determining the systematic improvement of behavioral efficiency seen during operant learning.

In their important book, *Dynamics of Response*, Notterman and Mintz (1965) reinforced subjects for, among other things, achieving criterion response forces. However, in those experiments, they did not adopt the usual practice of presenting the reinforcing stimulus as soon as a response met the reinforcement criterion (concurrent feedback); but rather they delayed reinforcer delivery until the ends of criterion responses (terminal feedback). Their reason for this unusual practice was to prevent subjects from using reinforcer delivery during response execution to regulate such response characteristics as response force, for example, by increasing force until reinforcer delivery was detected. They assumed that their method of delaying reinforcer delivery until response termination forced subjects to rely on internal (kinesthetic) cues to regulate the criterion dimension of their responses. It was reasoned that under delayed reinforcement conditions, but not under immediate reinforcement conditions, subjects would have had to learn criterion response forces and encode them into memory.

Until recently, the assumption that subjects will use immediate reinforcer delivery as feedback to regulate response characteristics during response execution had gone largely unquestioned. An indirect test was reported by Skinner (1938), who found that approximately one out of three responses failed to meet the force criterion even when reinforcers were presented as soon as response force met the criterion (concurrent feedback). Response failures should not occur if subjects are using reinforcer delivery as a signal for response termination. Skinner's results therefore suggest that at least the failed responses were generated independently of the feedback provided by reinforcer delivery, or in a "feedforward" mode. This implies that provision of concurrent external feedback does not guarantee that it will be used during response execution to regulate the criterion response dimension.

Nevertheless, a recent direct comparison of concurrent and terminal feedback of response success by Slifkin and Brener (1998) suggests that concurrent feedback is used in this way and that it generates more efficient performance than does terminal feedback. In that experiment a concurrent feedback group of rats were presented with a brief auditory stimulus as soon as they met an 18 g force criterion and a terminal feedback group were presented with the auditory stimulus immediately following the end of each criterion response. Although both feedback groups achieved similar average response forces, subjects in the concurrent feedback group made significantly fewer noncriterion responses than did subjects in the terminal feedback group. As implied by this result, response forces were less variable under conditions of concurrent feedback than terminal feedback. Since noncriterion presses entail useless expenditures of energy and time, concurrent feedback may be deemed to have permitted more efficient performance.

It is unclear whether the more efficient performance of Slifkin and Brener's (1998) concurrent feedback group was due to their having learned the motor skill to a higher level of proficiency than the terminal feedback group or to their use of the concurrent feedback to regulate response force during response execution. Like Skinner's (1938) rats, the concurrent feedback subjects in this experiment met the force criterion on only about two thirds of their presses, indicating that at least some of their responses were generated in a feedforward mode. Perhaps, as suggested by the literature on "automatization" of skills (Brener 1986b; Schmidt 1988), external concurrent feedback is used during the early stages of motor learning, but once an effective response has been acquired, behavior is driven in a largely feedforward manner. However, since subjects provided with terminal feedback are able to learn new skills (e.g., Notterman and Mintz 1965), it must be concluded that concurrent feedback is not essential for learning. Indeed Bilodeau (1969) noted that while concurrent feedback was more effective than terminal feedback in the performance of a positioning task, when feedback was removed, terminal feedback subjects maintained higher levels of performance than concurrent feedback subjects. These results corroborate Notterman and Mintz's (1965) rationale for adopting terminal feedback in that they support the idea that when provided with concurrent feedback, subjects use the feedback during response execution to guide the response to the target rather than learning to achieve target position on the basis of internal cues.

Despite these results, a case can also be made that the availability of concurrent feedback should enable more rapid and precise calibration of criterion responses than will terminal or delayed feedback (Brener 1986b). By virtue of its direct and immediate association with the effective response dimension, concurrent feedback carries more information about the reinforcement criterion than do stimuli that occur after a delay and when the effective response dimension is no longer at the criterion value. This prediction is supported, amongst others, by Smith and Sussman (1969), who found that delays in feedback (as is the case with terminal feedback) lead to more variability in performance and decreased accuracy.

Experimental Studies of the Effects of Concurrent and Terminal Feedback on Behavioral Efficiency

The two experiments to be reported here were undertaken to examine the effects of concurrent and terminal feedback of response success on the development of behavioral efficiency. The first experiment replicated Slifkin and Brener's (1998) procedure. Rats could earn liquid food by pressing a beam with criterion forces that considerably exceeded their default response force (it has been shown in previous studies that rats produce forces between 5 and 8 centi-Newtons (cN) even when no explicit force requirement is in effect). One group of subjects received concurrent feedback, which was initiated in the same millisecond that response force first exceeded the reinforcement criterion. Another group received terminal feedback, which was initiated immediately following presses on which a criterion force had been achieved. The second experiment was undertaken to examine the effects of concurrent and terminal feedback when a force criterion was not employed, but rather, when animals were required to perform a certain amount of work for each reinforcement. This way of defining the costs of reinforcement does not constrain the way in which the animal must perform its work. Hence, subjects had more degrees of freedom in packaging their work, which presumably they would package in such a way as to minimize reinforcement costs.

Data were collected using a modified operant chamber (figure 6.1), built to the specifications of Notterman and Mintz (1965). The front wall of the chamber housed three force-sensitive beams above each of which was a signal lamp and below each of which was a food tray. In this experiment, rats were rewarded with a fixed amount of sugar water (32 g/ 100 ml water), delivered to the central food tray on each occasion that they pressed the central beam with a criterion force. More detailed descriptions of the apparatus have appeared in several previous papers (Brener and Mitchell 1989; Mitchell and Brener 1991; Slifkin, Brener, and Mitchell 1995; Liu, Strecker, and Brener 1996). Feedback stimuli were delivered by a piezo-oscillator that was situated directly behind the panel that housed the response beams and food trays.

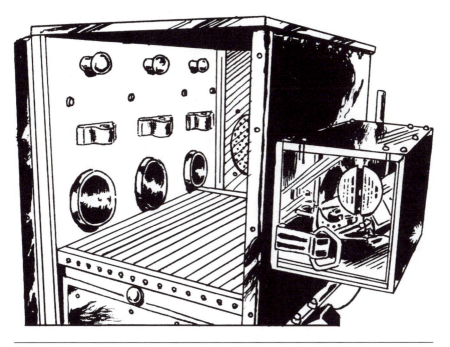

Figure 6.1   Modified operant chamber with three force-sensitive beams, three signal lights, and three food trays.

Animals were maintained at between 85% and 90% of their preexperimental body weights by supplemental feeding with standard lab chow. Throughout the experimental lifetimes of each subject, detailed recordings were made of all beam presses and visits to the food trays. The force-time trajectory of each beam press was recorded in its entirety with a temporal resolution of 1 ms and a force resolution of approximately 0.1 cN (1 cN = .01 N = 1 g force). This high resolution recording allowed for a detailed examination of the dynamics of operant motor responding. Figure 6.2 illustrates the force-time trajectory of idealized beam presses along with the principal kinetic, temporal, and energetic measures made on each response and illustrations of different strategies for increasing peak response force.

Response-shaping procedures were not employed since they lead to a different training experience for each subject (Notterman and Mintz 1965). Instead, rats were simply introduced to the experimental chamber and reinforced for presses on the central beam that met or exceeded a 1 cN force requirement. Each day the subjects participated in one experimental session that terminated after 200 reinforcements had been earned, or failing this, after 60 minutes. The rats were said to have learned the beam pressing response once they earned 200 reinforcements in under 60 minutes. Midway through the session following response acquisition, i.e.,

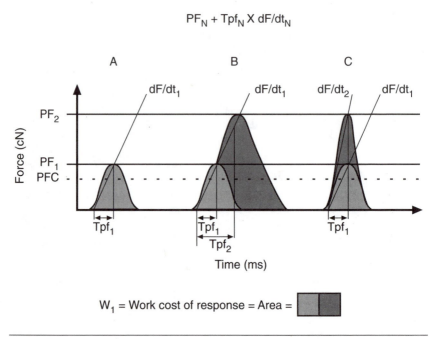

$$PF_N + Tpf_N \times dF/dt_N$$

W_1 = Work cost of response = Area =

Figure 6.2   *(A)* An idealized force-time trajectory depicting peak force criterion (PFC: cN), peak force (PF: cN), time to peak force (Tpf: milliseconds), and rate of rise of force (dF/dt: cN/s). Peak force is the product of Tpf and dF/dt. Therefore, PF can be doubled either by doubling Tpf while holding dF/dt constant *(B)*, or by doubling dF/dt while holding Tpf constant *(C)*. The shaded area under the force-time trajectory represents the Work per response (W_R: cN·s). Note that the strategy used to double PF in *(C)* results in a smaller area under the curve for PF_2 and therefore less W_R than does the strategy shown in *(B)*.

as soon as the subject had earned 100 reinforcements, the force requirement was increased to 20 cN for the remaining 100 reinforcements of that session. The force criterion was maintained at this higher value for the following 25 sessions on each of which subjects earned 200 reinforcements. A 20 cN force criterion was chosen because it is above the default response force of rats (5-8 cN) in our apparatus and therefore requires a force adjustment.

Six subjects received concurrent feedback in the form of a brief (30 ms) auditory stimulus that was delivered as soon as response force met the reinforcement criterion. Another group of six subjects received terminal feedback in which the auditory stimulus was presented immediately following termination of a criterion response (see figure 6.3).

Data were tested using ANOVA with feedback (concurrent/terminal) as a between-subjects factor and repeated measures on sessions (25). All results reported below were significant at the $p < 0.05$ level or be-

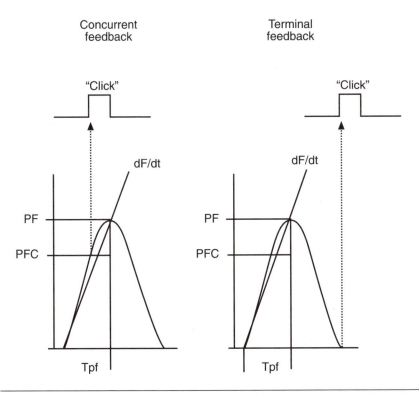

Figure 6.3 The placement of concurrent and terminal exteroceptive auditory feedback stimuli (30 ms "clicks").

yond. As illustrated in figure 6.4, three measures of behavioral efficiency, Responses per Reinforcer (R/SR), Time per Reinforcer (T/SR), and Work per Reinforcer (W/SR), improved significantly over the 25 days that the 20 cN reinforcement criterion was in effect. It will also been seen from these figures that the concurrent feedback group exhibited more rapid improvements in efficiency than did the terminal feedback group. As reflected by significant Groups by Days interactions, these effects were statistically reliable for W/SR and R/SR. A main effects for R/SR was also found, reflecting that concurrent feedback subjects made fewer responses for each food reward than terminal feedback subjects throughout the experiment. Note that temporal efficiency (T/SR) was not responsive to our feedback manipulation under these reinforcement contingencies.

The greater W/SR efficiency exhibited by the concurrent feedback group may be attributed to the R/SR result. Because a higher proportion of presses in the terminal feedback group did not meet the reinforcement criterion, subjects in this group generated more wasted work. Interestingly however, the average kinetic characteristics of beam presses did not differ significantly between the two groups. As shown in figure 6.5,

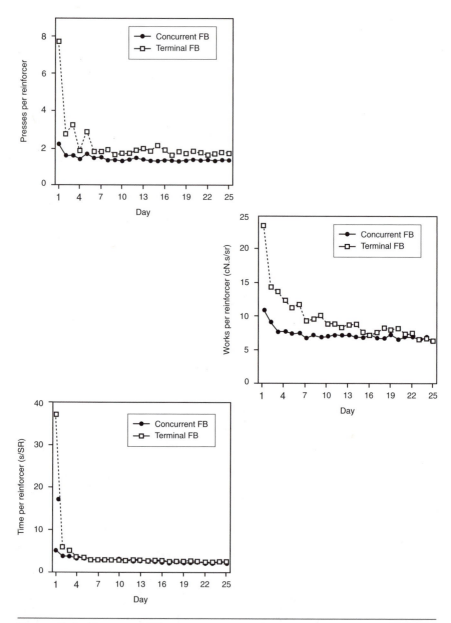

Figure 6.4 Top panel: The mean number of responses made per reinforcer earned (R/SR) as a function of number days within the experiment for the concurrent and terminal feedback groups. Middle panel: The mean amount of work (cN·s) performed per reinforcer (W/SR) earned as a function of number days within the experiment for the concurrent and terminal feedback groups. Bottom panel: The mean amount of time (s) spent working for each reinforcer (T/SR) as a function of number days within the experiment for the concurrent and terminal feedback groups.

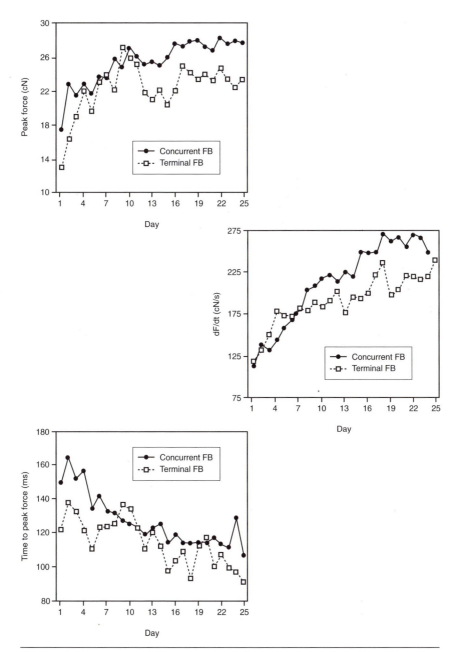

Figure 6.5 Top panel: The mean peak force (cN) as a function of number days within the experiment for the concurrent and terminal feedback groups. Middle panel: The mean dF/dt (cN/s) as a function of number days within the experiment for the concurrent and terminal feedback groups. Bottom panel: The mean time to peak force (ms) as a function of number days within the experiment for the concurrent and terminal feedback groups.

peak force and its major determinants, dF/dt (the rate of rise of force) and Tpf (time to peak force) exhibited similar statistically reliable changes over the 25 days of the experiment. Peak force rose to achieve similar asymptotes in the concurrent and terminal feedback groups and these changes were accompanied by increases in dF/dt and decreases in Tpf.

Recently we have found that these changes in the form of beam presses reflect a simplification of the force-time trajectory suggestive of increased feedforward and decreased feedback control (Brener and Carnicom 1998). The processes involved are illustrated in figure 6.6. Lengthening of Tpf reflects an underlying correction process in which force is increased during response execution to reduce the disparity between the current response force and the force required for reinforcement. The associated lengthening of the response results in a decrease in the average rate of rise of force (dF/dt) and an increase in the area under the force-time trajectory, and hence the energy burned during response execution. The converse process occurs as the required response is more precisely formulated and the need for corrections in the force-time trajectory recede. The more precise encoding of the required response, which is associated with reductions in response variability, permits presses to be generated in a feedforward fashion with fewer corrections during response execution. This results in a shortening of Tpf, increases in dF/dt, and reductions in the area under the force-time trajectory. Thus, the transi-

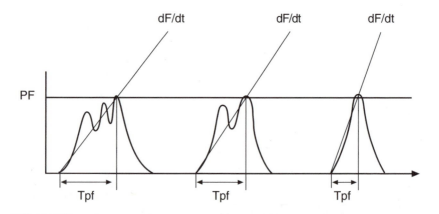

Figure 6.6 Iterative feedback force control model: The number of corrective sub-movements generated during a response decreases as the force produced during the initial ballistic phase of the response comes to approximate the PF target. Decreasing numbers of sub-movements leads to a shortening Tpf, an increase in dF/dt, and a decrease in the amount of work per response (area under the curve). This change from multiphasic to monophasic response form as a function of learning may be associated with the change from feedback to feedforward control of response force.

tion from feedback to feedforward control of force that occurs during learning and that is marked by systematic alterations in the temporal and kinetic parameters of the response, is also associated with more efficient performance.

The R/SR result shows that although the groups did not differ in their mean kinetic performances, the response forces generated by the concurrent feedback group were distributed so as to meet the force criterion on a significantly higher proportion of presses than in the terminal feedback group. Further evidence of the effects of the feedback on behavioral variability came from analyses of the Coefficients of Variation (SD/mean), which are illustrated in figure 6.7. Peak force and dF/dt were significantly less variable in the concurrent feedback than the terminal feedback group. Furthermore, peak force variability achieved its lower asymptote more rapidly in the concurrent feedback group than in the terminal feedback group.

Two explanations for the greater efficiency of the concurrent feedback group and the lower variability of their motor performance were introduced earlier. The first is that subjects in this group used the extrinsic feedback during response execution to regulate their forces, whereas subjects in the terminal feedback group were not afforded this opportunity. Slifkin and Brener (1998) attributed the greater efficiency observed in the concurrent feedback group to this source. However, in that experiment, concurrent feedback subjects exhibited significantly longer Tpf than did subjects in the terminal feedback group. This result, which is consistent with subjects processing the external feedback during response execution, was not found in the current study (see figure 6.5, bottom panel).

The other explanation of the superiority of concurrent feedback is that this form of feedback facilitates learning. Concurrent feedback is presented at the exact moment that the subject's motor output meets the criterion for reinforcement and may therefore aid in encoding the concurrent effective motor state of the subject. This encoded state may then be used as a template to generate future successful operant responses (Brener 1986b). While terminal feedback also identifies successful responses, this information is presented at a time that is relatively remote from achievement of the reinforcement criterion. Terminal feedback is not simultaneous with the criterial features of the response and therefore cannot identify these features with the same precision as concurrent feedback. Thus, it is to be expected that a broader class of response characteristics will be encoded by terminal feedback than by concurrent feedback. This prediction, which was born out by the Coefficient of Variation data presented above in figure 6.7, is also supported by the data presented in figure 6.8, which illustrates peak force distributions of the concurrent and terminal feedback groups at different stages of training. It will be seen here that the peak force distributions of subjects with

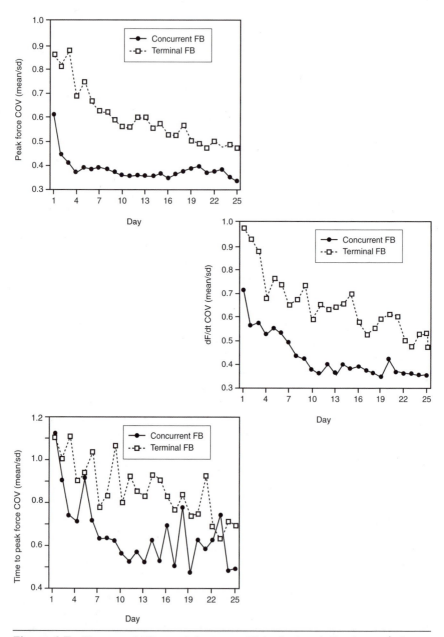

Figure 6.7 Top panel: The peak force coefficient of variation(mean/sd) as a function of number days within the experiment for the concurrent and terminal feedback groups. Middle panel: The dF/dt coefficient of variation (mean/sd) as a function of number days within the experiment for the concurrent and terminal feedback groups. Bottom panel: The time to peak force coefficient of variation (mean/sd) as a function of number days within the experiment for the concurrent and terminal feedback groups.

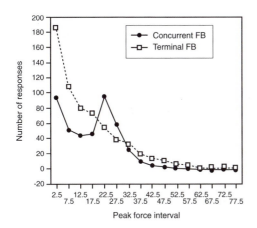

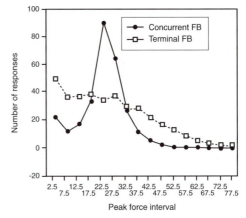

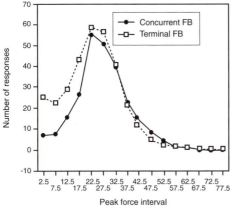

Figure 6.8 Top panel: Frequency distributions of peak forces for concurrent and terminal subjects during first full day of the 20-cN peak force criterion (PFC) (top panel), sixth full day of 20-cN PFC (middle panel), and last full day of 20-cN PFC (bottom panel).

concurrent feedback generates a clear mode at the force required for reinforcement, whereas the distribution of subjects with terminal feedback does not. Thus concurrent feedback enables subjects to tailor their behavior more precisely to the requirements of the situation, and this results in more efficient performance.

The available data do not provide definite evidence of the involvement of either the "online" or "learning" explanations of the observed higher efficiency of the concurrent feedback group, although the absence of longer Tpf in the concurrent feedback group does not favor the "online" explanation.

It has been mentioned that the peak force requirement in this study (20 cN) exceeds, by a considerable margin, the default response force exhibited by rats in our apparatus (5-8 cN). Therefore, in meeting the force requirement subjects had to exceed their "freely chosen" force. As pointed out in the introduction to this chapter, deviations from freely chosen behavior patterns generally result in lower behavioral efficiency. While it is unclear whether this applies also to deviations from freely chosen response forces, the results do show that concurrent feedback aided subjects in achieving a more efficient accommodation to the elevated force criterion. The next experiment to be reported investigated whether this advantage of concurrent feedback was specific to meeting a peak force requirement or whether the availability of feedback during response execution confers a more general advantage that is realized by more efficient motor performance regardless of the specific contingencies.

The results of the first experiment showed that different measures of behavioral efficiency varied in their response to the concurrent/terminal feedback manipulation. While R/SR, W/SR, and T/SR all showed improvements over the 25-day course of the experiment, only R/SR and W/SR exhibited greater efficiency under concurrent than under terminal feedback. In the second experiment, an additional and more global measure of efficiency was introduced: O_2/SR served to index the average total energy (oxygen) burned for each unit of food that was earned. This measure, which is directly related to net energy gain, has considerable face validity as an index of behavioral efficiency in foraging situations. We were interested in whether the provision of concurrent feedback of response success would result in greater efficiency expressed by the O_2/SR metric and if so, how it produced this effect.

The reinforcement contingencies that define the behavioral requirements for reward constrain the degrees of freedom that may be controlled in generating efficient motor performance. If, for example, a criterion response force is required for reinforcement, then in calculating a maximally efficient motor adaptation, force itself is not free to vary. So as not to limit the potential behavioral solutions to the problem of minimizing O_2/SR, reinforcement contingencies were employed that did not impose such a constraint on the form of beam presses. Rather, rats were permitted to earn liquid food rewards by performing a criterion amount of work on the beams. It has been mentioned that the "work" associated with each beam press is directly related to the area under its force-time trajectory (Jobsis and Duffield 1967). The work contingency in the current experiment permitted subjects to meet the work requirements for food delivery by accumulating work over successive beam presses. The contingencies did not impose any constraints on the temporal or kinetic characteristics of individual beam presses and thus subjects could "choose" to perform all the work in one press or to spread it over several presses.

One implication of these contingencies was that in the first experiment, concurrent feedback always occurred when the force currently being generated by the subject was equal to the force criterion. However, in the second experiment, concurrent feedback could coincide with different attributes of the current response depending on the amount of work needed from the current response to satisfy the work requirement. In this sense, it could be said that concurrent feedback carried less information about current motor performance in the second than in the first experiment.

The experiment was run in the same apparatus as that employed in the force contingency experiment described above and using the same general protocols for food deprivation and animal maintenance. In addition to the measures described for the first experiment, oxygen consumption was monitored continuously throughout each session using a dual-channel paramagnetic oxygen analyzer as described by Brener and Mitchell (1989).

In this experiment, each of the daily experimental sessions lasted for 100 reinforcers or 60 minutes, whichever came first. Rats were said to have acquired the beam-pressing response when they earned 100 rewards in less than 60 minutes. Following achievement of this acquisition criterion, all subjects received 30 days of training using a work requirement of .5 cN·s, which approximates the mean default work produced by responses that have not been augmented through training. This 30-day period was chosen to habituate the animals to the experimental environment since our previous research had shown that rats exhibit elevated rates of oxygen consumption for a considerable period after first encountering a new situation (Brener 1987). After 30 days, the workload was increased to 1 cN·s, which is somewhat above the mean default work per response and after 20 days at that work requirement, to 4 cN·s, 8 cN·s, and finally to 16 cN·s after spending 12 sessions at each of these higher work requirements. In order to assess the effects of feedback on stable performance under each of the work requirements, the statistical analyses on which the results reported below are based were restricted to the last five days under the 1-, 4-, 8-, and 16-cN work requirements.

It has been mentioned that the work requirements investigated (1, 4, 8, and 16 cN) all exceed the mean default work per response. Under these work requirements, subjects could "choose" to make multiple default responses, they could reprogram their beam presses to meet higher work requirements in a single press, or they could choose some intermediate strategy. The strategy of making multiple default responses carries the costs of lower probabilities of reward (R/SR) and longer times to acquire each reward (longer T/SR), but avoids the costs of reprogramming the beam press and may minimize W/SR since smaller overshoots of the work requirement are to be anticipated with smaller responses. However, in order to maintain R/SR and T/SR constant in the face of increasing work requirements, subjects would have to reprogram beam presses so as to increase the area under the force-time trajectory. This could be achieved by increasing the peak force of the press and/or the press duration (see figure 6.2).

A concurrent feedback group of 10 rats was presented with an auditory feedback stimulus (30 ms "click") as soon the work requirement was completed, whereas a terminal feedback group of 10 rats received the feedback stimulus immediately following the response on which the work requirement was completed. The computation of work over responses and the feedback arrangements are illustrated in figure 6.9. Following response acquisition and habituation to the apparatus, all subjects were run for 56 consecutive daily sessions on each of which they earned 100 reinforcers and over the course of which they experienced the four consecutive work requirements. As in the previous experiment, results were analyzed using ANOVA with feedback (concurrent/terminal) as a between-subjects factor and repeated measures on work requirement (four levels) and sessions (five). All effects reported below were significant at the $p < 0.05$ level or beyond.

Figure 6.10 illustrates oxygen consumed per reinforcer (O_2/SR) and its two determinants, oxygen consumed per minute (O_2/min) and time per reinforcer (T/SR). It is immediately clear from these figures that feedback-associated variations in O_2/SR across the four work requirements are largely due to the influence of the feedback variable on T/SR. O_2/min remained relatively constant over the four work requirements in the terminal feedback group and exhibited a small but significant decline in the concurrent feedback group. However, as the work requirements increased from 4 cN·s to 8 cN·s, and then to 16 cN·s, terminal feedback subjects exhibited substantial increases in the time taken to earn each reinforcer, whereas the time costs of reinforcement remained relatively constant in the concurrent feedback group. The question of how concurrent feedback generates a lower energy cost for each reinforcer (O_2/SR) than terminal feedback therefore resolves to the question of how concurrent feedback generates lower time costs for reinforcement (T/SR) than terminal feedback.

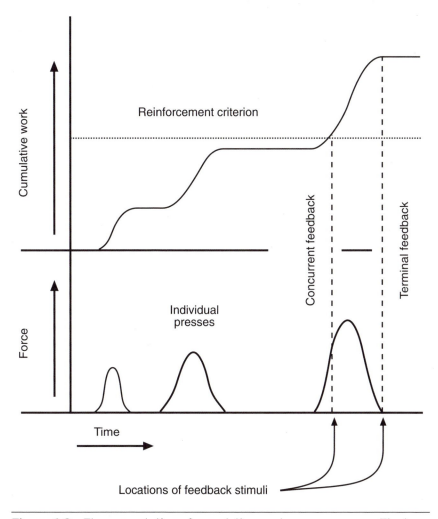

Figure 6.9   The computation of cumulative work over responses. The locations of concurrent and terminal feedback are shown.

There are two possible routes through which concurrent feedback could generate this outcome: by producing a higher rate of response (shorter interpress time) or by decreasing the number of presses required to produce each reinforcer (R/SR). Figure 6.11 indicates that interpress time remains constant over the different work requirements and is uninfluenced by the feedback contingencies, suggesting that rate of response is determined by biomechanical constraints inherent in the structure of the implicated effectors and their interactions with the experimental environment. In distinction to this variable, presses per reinforcer (R/SR) shows a clear effect of the feedback contingency. Subjects in the

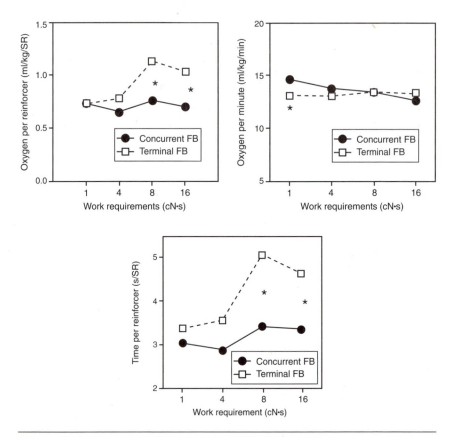

Figure 6.10   Top panel: The mean amount of oxygen consumed (ml/kg) per reinforcer (O_2/SR) as a function of the work required for reinforcement (cN·s) for the concurrent and terminal feedback groups. Middle panel: The mean amount of oxygen consumed (ml/kg) per minute (O_2/min) as a function of the work required for reinforcement (cN·s) for the concurrent and terminal feedback groups. Bottom panel: The mean amount of time spent (s) per reinforcer (T/SR) as a function of the work required for reinforcement (cN·s) for the concurrent and terminal feedback groups. Asterisks (*) indicate significant ($p < 0.05$) differences between the concurrent and terminal feedback groups as assessed by Tukey's H.S.D. test.

concurrent feedback group sustained approximately 1.8 presses per reinforcer until the work requirement was raised to 16 cN·s when they increased R/SR to 2.3 presses per reinforcer. On the other hand, terminal feedback subjects exhibit a systematic increase in presses per reinforcer as a function of the work requirement.

In order to sustain lower numbers of presses per reinforcer, subjects must generate larger presses. The lower right panel of this figure shows that at all work requirements greater than 1 cN·s, concurrent feedback subjects generated more work per press than terminal feedback sub-

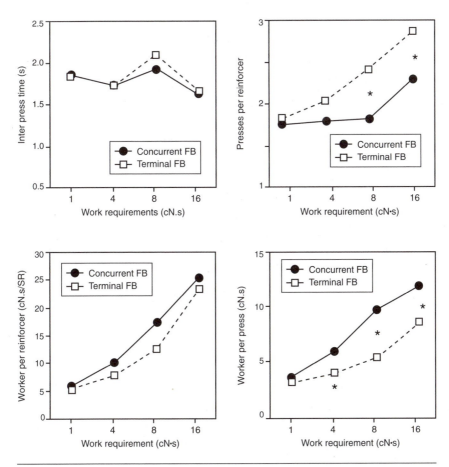

Figure 6.11 Top left panel: The mean amount of time (s) between beam presses as a function of the work required for reinforcement (cN·s) for the concurrent and terminal feedback groups. Top right panel: The mean number of beam presses per reinforcer (R/SR) as a function of the work required for reinforcement (cN·s) for the concurrent and terminal feedback groups. Bottom left panel: The mean amount of work (cN·s) performed per reinforcer (W/SR) as a function of the work required for reinforcement (cN·s) for the concurrent and terminal feedback groups. Bottom right panel: The mean amount of work (cN·s) performed per beam press (W_R) as a function of the work required for reinforcement (cN·s) for the concurrent and terminal feedback groups. Asterisks (*) indicate significant ($p < 0.05$) differences between the concurrent and terminal feedback groups as assessed by Tukey's H.S.D. test.

jects. Furthermore, until the work requirement was raised to 16 cN·s, subjects in the concurrent feedback group fulfilled the requirements for reinforcement with the work performed by an average press. Because the concurrent feedback group made larger presses, they also made fewer presses per reinforcer and therefore as shown in the left bottom panel of figure 6.11, they did not perform significantly more work per reinforcer than subjects in the terminal feedback group.

Since the work performed by each press is measured by the area under the force-time trajectory, concurrent feedback could have augmented work per press either by extending the duration of each press or by increasing its peak force. The bottom panel of figure 6.12 shows that while response duration and Tpf were both systematically influenced by the work requirement, neither variable was affected by the concurrent/terminal feedback distinction. Since the higher peak force observed in the concurrent feedback group, which was responsible for the greater energy efficiency of their behavior in this situation, cannot be attributed to lengthening of Tpf, it must have been due to an increase in dF/dt as illustrated in the middle panel of figure 6.12. Thus, providing subjects with immediate feedback on reaching the work criterion resulted in their exhibiting more energy-efficient behavior, and this was mediated by the effects of the feedback on the rate of rise of force.

Figure 6.13 illustrates the decomposition of O_2/SR into more basic variables and traces the effects of concurrent feedback on behavioral efficiency. It is not immediately clear why concurrent feedback should have influenced dF/dt rather than time to peak force. As illustrated in figure 6.2, increments in peak force due to lengthening of Tpf result in greater augmentations in work per response than do increases in dF/dt that produce the same increments in peak force. Furthermore, Slifkin and Brener (1998) found that concurrent feedback tended to increase peak force through lengthening of Tpf, an effect that he attributed to the strategy of increasing force on the beam at a constant rate (i.e., dF/dt remaining constant) until the external feedback stimulus occurred, and then releasing the beam. However, as indicated by the results of the first experiment reported here, this feature of Slifkin and Brener's results was not replicated. Differences in Tpf between concurrent and terminal feedback were not significant in Experiment 2 either. While we have been unable to localize the source of this disparity, there were several apparently minor procedural differences between the two studies including the strains of rats employed (Slifkin and Brener used Long-Evans rats, whereas Sprague-Dawley rats were used in the study reported here).

While force control via Tpf has been viewed as an indicator of online feedback regulation of motor output, good arguments can be adduced for interpreting force control via the rate of rise of force (dF/dt) as an expression of preprogrammed feedforward control (Gordon and Ghez 1987). Acceptance of this interpretation implies that in Experiment 2, concurrent feedback was implicated in reprogramming beam presses rather than serving an online guidance function. If so, perhaps this was because the implicated muscles were always active when concurrent feedback occurred and never when terminal feedback occurred.

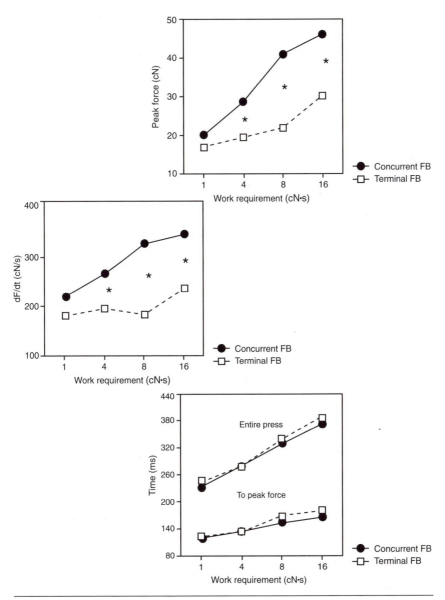

Figure 6.12 Top panel: The mean peak force (cN) as a function of the work required for reinforcement (cN·s) for the concurrent and terminal feedback groups. Middle panel: The mean dF/dt (cN/s) as a function of the work required for reinforcement (cN·s) for the concurrent and terminal feedback groups. Bottom panel: The mean time of the entire press (ms) and the mean time to peak force (ms) as a function of the work required for reinforcement (cN·s) for the concurrent and terminal feedback groups. Asterisks (*) indicate significant (p < 0.05) differences between the concurrent and terminal feedback groups as assessed by Tukey's H.S.D. test.

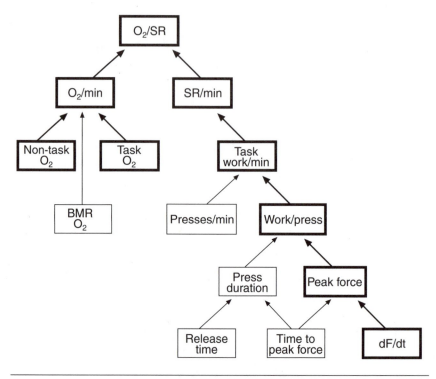

Figure 6.13 Sources of variation in overall behavioral efficiency (O_2/SR). The variables that are outlined with heavy lines illustrate the route through which concurrent feedback produced greater efficiency than terminal feedback. Oxygen consumed per reinforcement (O_2/SR) is a product of the overall rate of oxygen consumption (O_2/min) and the rate of reinforcement (SR/min). The sum of three variables determine the rate of oxygen consumption (O_2/min): basal metabolic rate (BMR), oxygen consumed for task irrelevant behavior (nontask O_2), and oxygen consumed for task relevant behavior (task O_2). Task O_2 is determined by the rate of task relevant (task work/min). Task work/min, which also determines SR/min, is itself a product of the rate of beam pressing (presses/min) and the amount of work performed on each press (work/press). Work/press is determined by the press duration and peak force. Press duration is the sum of time to peak force and beam release time, whereas peak force is the product of time to peak force and the rate of rise of force (dF/dt). Concurrent feedback appears to influence O_2/SR through its effects on dF/dt.

General Discussion

The first experiment reported in this chapter provides good evidence of improvements in behavioral efficiency with practice. On successive exposures to reinforcement contingencies that provided reward for generating criterion response forces, rats decreased the number of presses, the amount of work, and the period of time required to earn each food reward. These improvements in behavioral efficiency were accomplished by alterations to the force-time trajectories of beam presses and by reductions in behavioral variability. Superimposed on these general improvements in behavioral efficiency were variations in efficiency that could be attributed to the type of external feedback provided for successful responses.

In both the first and second experiments, rats that received concurrent feedback performed fewer presses for each reinforcer (R/SR) than did subjects that received terminal feedback. In Experiment 1, which employed a peak force contingency, this result could be attributed to concurrent feedback having generated a distribution of peak forces that was more precisely tuned to the reinforcement criterion. Under conditions of concurrent feedback, subjects exhibited lower asymptotic levels of variability in motor performance and they approached these asymptotes more rapidly than terminal feedback subjects. The superior R/SR ratio exhibited by the concurrent feedback group in this experiment resulted in their performing less work per reinforcer (W/SR) than the terminal feedback group, but did not influence the time costs of each reinforcer (T/SR).

In Experiment 2, which employed a work criterion for reinforcement, concurrent feedback subjects again earned each reinforcer with fewer presses than did terminal feedback subjects. Unlike the first experiment, in this experiment the lower R/SR of the concurrent feedback group did not result in less work being performed for each reinforcer (W/SR), but did generate significantly lower time costs (T/SR) at the higher work requirements. Since overall rates of oxygen consumption were not influenced by the feedback variable or, indeed, by the work requirement, the more rapid reinforcement rate in the concurrent feedback group resulted in their burning less oxygen per reinforcement (O_2/SR). The higher net energy gain achieved by subjects in the concurrent feedback condition can be traced to their generating more work on each press. By so doing, the number of presses required to earn each reinforcer was reduced. Furthermore, since pressing rate was uninfluenced either by the feedback variable or the work requirement, concurrent feedback subjects spent less time earning each reinforcer (T/SR).

The contingencies governing reinforcement procurement were substantially different in the two experiments and not surprisingly, they resulted in different motor adaptations. Comparisons of the results are also limited due to other procedural differences. For example, subjects in Experiment 1 were submitted to a single reinforcement criterion, whereas subjects in Experiment 2 were submitted to progressively more taxing criteria. Nevertheless, in both experiments, subjects receiving concurrent feedback earned reinforcers in significantly fewer presses (R/SR) than subjects receiving terminal feedback. The observation of this common outcome in the two experiments suggests that the minimization of R/SR (maximization of probability of reinforcement) may be a specific product of providing concurrent feedback.

Two explanations of how concurrent feedback may generate this outcome have been considered: The first is that concurrent feedback provides information that can be used during response execution to control the criterion response dimension; the second is that concurrent feedback facilitates learning and encoding of the criterion response. These possibilities could be tested easily by withdrawing the feedback stimuli following training. Maintenance of performance would imply that the feedback had served a learning function, whereas immediate increases in behavioral variability and decreases in efficiency would imply that the external feedback was serving an online control function.

Acknowledgments

We are most grateful to Suzanne Mitchell, Andy Slifkin, and David Echevarria for their invaluable collaboration in the experiments and to Bill Guethlein, Glenn Hudson, Ralph Molaro, and Bob Chorley for their expert technical assistance.

References

Baz, A. 1979. Optimization of man's energy during underwater paddle propulsion. *Ergonomics* 22: 1105-1114.

Bilodeau, I.M. 1969. Information feedback. In *Principles of skill acquisition*, eds. E.A. Bilodeau, and I. McD. Bilodeau, 255-285. New York: Academic Press.

Brener, J. 1986a. Behavioural efficiency: a biological link between informational and energetic processes. In *Energetics and human information processing*, eds. G.R.J. Hockey, A.W.K Gaillard, and M.G.H. Coles, 113-122. Dordrecht, the Netherlands: Martinus Nijhoff.

Brener, J. 1986b. Operant reinforcement, feedback and the efficiency of learned motor control. In *Psychophysiology: systems, processes and applications*, eds. M.G.H. Coles, E. Donchin, and S.W. Porges, 309-327. New York: The Guilford Press.

Brener, J. 1987. Behavioural energetics: some effects of uncertainty on the mobilization and distribution of energy. *Psychophysiology* 24: 499-512.

Brener, J., and S. Carnicom. 1998. High resolution analysis of force learning and memory in rats. *Cahier de Psychologie Cognitive* 17: 699-724.

Brener, J., and S. Mitchell. 1989. Changes in energy expenditure and work during response acquisition in rats. *Journal of Experimental Psychology: Animal Behavior Processes* 15: 166-175.

DeCamp, J.E. 1920. Relative distance as a factor in the white rat's selection of a path. *Psychobiology* 2: 245-253.

Gengerilli, J.A. 1928. Preliminary experiments on the causal factors in animal learning. *Journal of Comparative Psychology* 8: 435-457.

Gordon, J., and C. Ghez. 1987. Trajectory control of targeted force impulses: II. pulse height control. *Experimental Brain Research* 67: 241-252.

Holding, K.H. 1965. *Principles of training.* New York: Macmillan (Pergamon).

Hoyt, D.F., and C.R. Taylor. 1981. Gait and the energetics of locomotion in horses. *Nature* 292: 239-240.

Hughes, R.N. 1979. Optimal diets under the energy maximization premise: The effects of recognition time and learning. *American Naturalist* 113: 209-221.

Hull, C.L. 1943. *Principles of behavior.* New York: Appleton-Century.

Jobsis, F.F., and J.C. Duffield. 1967. Force, shortening, and work in muscular contraction: relative contributions to overall energy expenditure. *Science* 156: 1388-1392.

Kamil, A.C., and H.L. Roitblat. 1985. The ecology of foraging behavior: implications for animal learning and memory. *Annual Review of Psychology* 36: 141-169.

Ketelaars, J.J.M.H., and B.J. Tolkamp. 1996. Oxygen efficiency and the control of energy flow in animals and humans. *Journal of Animal Science* 74: 3036-3051.

Killeen, P. 1974. Psychophysical distance functions of hooded rats. *Psychological Record* 24: 229-235.

Krebs, J.R. 1978. Optimal foraging: decision rules for predators. In *Behavioral ecology: an evolutionary approach,* eds. N.B. Davies, and J.R. Krebs, 23-63. Oxford: Blackwell Scientific.

Kuo, Z.Y. 1922. The nature of unsuccessful acts and their order of elimination in animal learning. *Journal of Comparative Psychology* 2: 1-27.

Liu, X., R.E. Strecker, and J.M. Brener. 1996. Low doses of apomorphine suppress operant motor performance in rats. *Pharmacology, Biochemistry & Behavior* 53: 335-340.

McCulloch, T.L. 1934. Performance preferentials of the white rat in force resisting and spatial dimensions. *Journal of Comparative Psychology* 18: 85-111.

Mitchell, S.H., and J. Brener. 1991. Energetic and motor responses to increasing force requirements. *Journal of Experimental Psychology: Animal Behavior Processes* 17: 174-185.

Mitchell, S.H., and J. Brener. 1997. The work costs of earning food as a determinant of patch leaving. *Journal of Experimental Psychology: Animal Behavior Processes* 23: 136-144.

Norberg, R.A. 1977. An ecological theory on foraging time and energetics and choice of optimal food searching method. *Journal of Animal Ecology* 46: 511-529.

Notterman, J.M., and D.E. Mintz. 1965. *Dynamics of response.* New York: Wiley.

Powers, W.T. 1973. *Behavior: the Control of Perception.* Chicago: Aldine Publishing.

Schmidt, R.A. 1988. *Motor control and learning : a behavioral emphasis.* Champaign, IL: Human Kinetics.

Sherwood, A., J. Brener, and D. Moncur. 1983. Information and states of motor readiness: their effects on the covariation of heart rate and energy expenditure. *Psychophysiology* 20: 513-529.

Skinner, B.F. 1938. *The behavior of organisms.* New York: Appleton-Century.

Slifkin, A.B., and J. Brener. 1998. Control of operant response force. *Journal of Experimental Psychology: Animal Behavior Processes* 24: 1-8

Slifkin, A.B., J. Brener, and S.H. Mitchell. 1995. Variation of isometric response force in the rat. *Journal of Motor Behavior* 27: 375-381.

Smith, K.U., and H. Sussman. 1969. Cybernetic theory and analysis of motor learning and memory. In *Principles of skill acquisition*, eds. E.A. Bilodeau, and I. McD. Bilodeau, 103-139. New York: Academic Press.

Solomon, R.L. 1948. The influence of work on behavior. *Psychological Bulletin* 45: 1-40.

Sparrow, W.A. 1983. The efficiency of skilled performance. *Journal of Motor Behavior* 15: 237-261.

Sparrow, W.A., and V.M. Irizarry-Lopez. 1987. Mechanical efficiency and metabolic cost as measures of learning a novel gross motor task. *Journal of Motor Behavior* 19: 240-264.

Sparrow, W.A., and K.M. Newell. 1994. Energy expenditure and motor performance relationships in humans learning a motor task. *Psychophysiology* 31: 338-346.

Staddon, J.E.R., and V.L. Simmelhag. 1971. The "superstitious" experiment: a re-examination of its implications for the principles of adaptive behavior. *Psychological Review* 78: 3-43.

Stegemann, J. 1981. *Exercise physiology.* Stuttgart: Thieme.

Stephens, D.W., and J.R. Krebs. 1986. *Foraging theory.* Princeton, NJ: Princeton University Press.

Tolman, E.C. 1932. *Purposive behavior in animals and men.* New York: Century.

Tsai, L.S. 1932. *The laws of minimum effort and maximum satisfaction in animal behavior.* Monograph of the National Institute of Psychology (Peiping, China), 1, 1932. (From *Psychological Abstracts*, 1932, 6, Abstract No. 4329.)

Mechanical Power and Work in Human Movement

Vladimir M. Zatsiorsky

Biomechanics Laboratory, Department of Kinesiology,
The Pennsylvania State University, United States

Robert J. Gregor

Department of Health and Performance Sciences,
Georgia Institute of Technology, United States

Consider a slow horizontal arm extension with a load in the hand. The mass of the body parts, as well as the work to change the kinetic energy of the load, is neglected in the example shown in figure 7.1. During the movement represented by the broken line, the muscles of the shoulder joint perform positive (concentric) work: They generate an abduction moment and elevate the arm. The elbow joint extends while producing a flexion moment. Therefore, the flexors of the elbow produce negative (eccentric) work. The work of the force exerted by the hand on the load is zero. The direction of the gravity force is at a right angle to the direction of the load displacement and, as a result, the potential energy of the load does not change. The question is: What is the total amount of work *performed by the subject*?

Though the first estimation of mechanical work in human movement was done as early as 1836 (Weber and Weber 1836), the determination of mechanical power and work in human movement still remains a challenging task for biomechanists. In the scientific community, frequent misunderstanding and the lack of unified terminology complicate the solution of the problem of defining mechanical work. To preclude any future uncertainty, a clear-cut discussion of the problem is essential. The goal of this chapter is to discuss the basic aspects of the problem. To do that, we analyze several mechanical models.

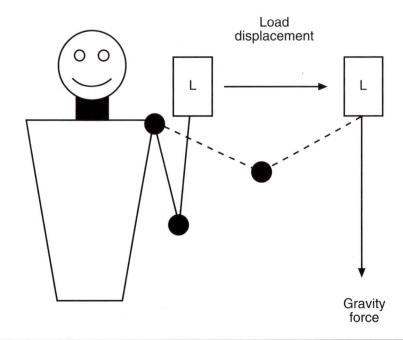

Figure 7.1   Horizontal arm extension. The load L is moving strictly horizontally and its potential energy does not change. The arm mass is neglected. The movement is performed in a slow manner and the change in the kinetic energy of the load is disregarded. The work at the shoulder joint is positive (concentric) and the work at the elbow joint is negative (eccentric). The work of the force exerted by the hand on the load is zero and depends neither on the load magnitude nor on the number of repetitions. The question to ponder: What is the mechanical work performed by the subject?

In all the mechanical models under discussion, the links are rigid and the joints are frictionless hinges. The examples and formulas are limited to planar movements. For three-dimensional models, mathematical description would be much more complicated without changes in conclusions.

The chapter is divided into six sections. In section 1, the topic of discussion is outlined and the notion of apparent power and work is introduced. Section 2 illustrates the main controversies of the problem and describes why a discussion is necessary. Section 3 is a short refresher of some basic mechanical concepts. Sections 4 and 5 are the core sections of the chapter. In section 4, the basic concepts are introduced. They include the concepts of produced (developed) and used (net) power and work, as well as a notion of mechanical energy expenditure (subsection 4.1) and the concept of energy compensation (subsection 4.2). In section 5, the previously introduced concepts are employed to discuss the main methods used to calculate apparent power and work. Section 6 addresses some additional issues of the problem.

1. The Topic of Discussion—
Apparent Power and Work

Mechanical energy from the contractile elements of individual muscles is the primary source of human movement. Due to inevitable losses, the power output of a whole muscle-tendon unit is less than the power production from contractile elements. Because of elastic and viscous qualities of the complex, a time lag may exist between the power (force, velocity) input from contractile elements and the power (force, velocity) output registered on the tendon. A more detailed discussion of the power transport from the contractile elements to the tendon is, however, beyond the scope of this chapter. The terms "internal" and "external" muscle power are sometimes used to distinguish the two types of power mentioned, but we will not follow this practice. The power/work generated by muscle-tendon complexes is called mechanical muscle power (work) or *muscle power/work* for short.

If we were able to directly register forces and velocities of shortening (lengthening) of all skeletal muscle-tendon complexes in a body, the problem of determining mechanical power in human and animal movements would be straightforward. At this time, however, one cannot do that except for several selected muscles and under unique conditions (for review, see Gregor and Abelew 1994). Mechanical power in human movements is, therefore, *estimated* by registering the external forces acting on the body and the movement performed. Following these methods, however, it is impossible to determine muscle power precisely because this approach does not take into account the power expended

1. to overcome antagonistic activity of muscles,
2. against friction and other passive forces in the body ("nonconservative power" in the terminology of van Ingen Shenau and Cavanagh [1990]),
3. against elastic internal forces, e.g., for ligament extension ("conservative power"),
4. for displacement of muscles relative to the skeleton and internal organs with respect to the trunk, and
5. for breathing; the mechanical work used for breathing during strenuous muscular activity can be very high (for review see Zatsiorsky et al. 1982).

Energy expenditures to activate muscles (registered as 'heat of activation') and to maintain isometric force are not included in the list above.

The power expended to overcome internal resistance in the musculoskeletal system (fractions 1-4) can be called *hidden power*. Given that measurement of mechanical power based on the movements performed and the external forces does not reflect in full the muscle power, a special term was introduced, *apparent power and work.*

Definition 1—Apparent power is the fraction of the muscle power liberated in joints and expended to overcome external resistance and to change the mechanical energy of body segments.

The fraction of apparent power dissipated against external forces, with the exception of gravity force, can be called *external power;* and the power expended to move the body links (to change their total mechanical energy) can be designated *internal power.* Note that by definition the power expended against gravity is included in *internal,* not *external,* power because work against gravity increases the body's potential energy. If the suggested definitions are accepted it will mean, for instance, that power (and work) of the force applied to pedals in cycling should be referred as *external power,* and power to move the legs themselves as *internal power.* The power to lift body parts is defined as a fraction of *internal power.* In routine functional testing with a bicycle ergometer, when the mechanical power is determined as a product of the moment of force applied to the pedals by the angular velocity of the pedaling, the external power is registered, while in treadmill tests internal power is measured. The suggested terminology is presented in figure 7.2.

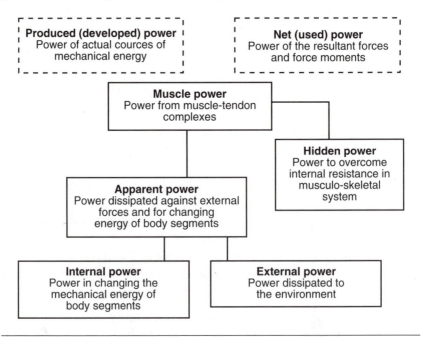

Figure 7.2 The flow of mechanical power in human movement. The concepts of the produced (developed) and used (net) power are explained later in the text in section 4.1.

The proposed definitions resemble formulations given by other authors (Winter 1978, 1979, 1990; van Ingen Shenau and Cavanagh 1990; van Ingen Shenau et al. 1990). However, the definitions of *external* and *internal* power and work differ from the meaning of these terms in early publications (Fenn 1930; Cavagna et al. 1963, 1964; Aleshinsky 1986b; Thys et al. 1996a,o.) where these expressions were used to designate the work expended in changing the motion of (a) the general center of mass and (b) the body links relative to the general center of mass.

The determination of external power in itself, if one does not bother about power/work at the joints, is not complicated with conceptual problems. For example, as it was mentioned previously, the external power in cycling can be easily calculated by multiplying the force applied to the pedals by the velocity of the pedals. This chapter deals only with internal power and work. Hence, the topic of the discussion is the fraction of the muscle power liberated in joints and expended to change mechanical energy of body segments. In the following section, the main controversies in determining apparent power and work in human movement are briefly summarized.

2. Main Controversies

In the literature, conflicting techniques are used to compute mechanical work and power in human movement. In this section, three main controversies are highlighted: (1) fraction vs. source approach, (2) calculating total power/work of several sources, and (3) calculating work of a source over time.

(1) The two main methods employed to measure mechanical power and work in human movements give inconsistent results. The first method of measuring mechanical work, developed by Fenn (1930) and coined the 'fraction approach' (Aleshinsky 1986a; Zatsiorsky 1986), is based on the determination of the changes in total mechanical energy of human body segments. The terms *Fenn's method* and *fraction approach* will be considered synonymous. In the framework of the fraction approach, the total mechanical energy (TME) of a body segment is represented as the sum of three 'fractions': potential energy (PE), kinetic translational energy (KTE), and kinetic rotational energy (KRE):

$$\text{TME} = \text{PE} + \text{KTE} + \text{KRE} = mhg + \frac{mv^2}{2} + \frac{I\omega^2}{2}, \qquad (7.1)$$

where m stands for mass, h is vertical location of the segment's center of mass, I is moment of inertia, v and ω are correspondingly linear and angular velocity of the body segment, and g is acceleration due to gravity. The TME values are measured over discrete sampling intervals and the difference in the calculated values from one data calculation point to another provides an estimation of the mechanical work done and, if calculated per unit time, the mechanical power.

The second method, first suggested by Elftman (1939), is based on the determination of power and work of joint moments. The method can be considered an example of the 'source approach' as defined by Aleshinsky (1986a) and Zatsiorsky (1986). By definition, the source of energy is any force and force moment acting on the system, which develops or absorbs mechanical energy during its motion. Joint power is computed as the product of joint angular velocity and the so-called joint moment:

$$P_j = M_j \, (\dot{\theta}_1 - \dot{\theta}_2) = M_j \omega_j \qquad (7.2)$$

where Mj is the joint moment (the notion of the joint moments will be addressed more precisely later.), $\dot{\theta}_1$ are $\dot{\theta}_2$ are angular velocities of the adjacent segments forming the joint, and ω_j is the joint angular velocity, i.e., the relative angular velocity of the adjacent segments with respect to one another. Note that when M_j and ω_j are of different sign (one value is positive and the second is negative), P_j is negative. The terms *Elftman's method, source approach,* and *joint power/work method* will be used to designate this approach.

While the two methods seem to be based on straightforward mechanical principles, they have resulted in ambiguous findings to the extent that the discrepancies between the methods may be as high as nine-fold (Pierrynowski et al. 1980; Williams and Cavanagh 1983; Prilutsky and Zatsiorsky 1992).

(2) To calculate the total mechanical power/work generated in several joints, two approaches are advocated. Some authors (for instance, van Ingen Shenau and Cavanagh 1990) recommended a formula:

$$P_{tot} = \sum_j P_j \qquad (7.3)$$

where $P_j = M_j \omega_j$ is the power generated by joint moment M_j at the angular velocity ω_j in joint j, P_{tot} is the total power produced in all the joints under consideration, and Σ is the summation across the joints.

In contrast, other authors (for instance, Aleshinsky 1986 a-e; Blickhan and Full 1992) are in favor of the summation of absolute rather than real values of joint power

$$P_{tot} = \sum_j |P_j| \qquad (7.4)$$

It is easy to provide arguments both for and against both of these methods. For instance, the second method has been criticized because summation of the absolute values of power is not defined and is not used in classical mechanics. Imagine these two approaches applied to the following movement. A human with left arm raised lifts the right arm and simultaneously lowers the left one. In this case, the joint power values at all joints of the right arm are positive, and the joint power values at all joints of the left arm are negative. In addition, the joint power values for the right and left arm are equal in magnitude, $|P_{left}| = |-P_{right}|$ (we will call such movements *antisymmetrical*). For antisymmetrical movements, the value of total power equals zero if the first approach is used and equals 2P when the second approach is applied. Intuitively, since movement takes place, the first approach does not look appealing as a method for quantifying the total mechanical power of raising and lowering the arms.

(3) When mechanical work rather than power is the object of interest, the problem arises as to how to sum positive and negative values. Again, two methods are most popular. In the first, the real (signed) values of work (W) are summed, while in the second, the absolute values are added.

$$W_{tot} = \Sigma W \qquad (7.5)$$

or

$$W_{tot} = \Sigma |W|, \qquad (7.6)$$

where W values are calculated separately for the positive and negative work. If one is lifting and lowering a load, W equals the potential energy of the lifted body at the top of the lift. The first approach gives zero total work; in biological literature, this is often called the *zero-work paradox*. With the second approach, $W_{tot} = 2W$, the magnitude of the total work is twice the maximal value of the potential energy of the body measured at the highest point of the trajectory. Some authors have found this result unacceptable (de Köning and van Ingen Schenau 1994) because in their opinion these values should be equal, $W = PE_{max}$.

We intend to discuss the source of the mentioned controversies and to suggest some concepts that may help to clarify the problem of determining mechanical work and power in human movement. However, prior to that, we would like to recollect several concepts and theorems of classical mechanics.

3. Mechanical Work and Power

(A) Strictly speaking, concepts such as work and power do not exist in classical mechanics. Instead, the notion of the *work of a force (power of a force)* is defined. The difference is of paramount importance because the magnitude of the mechanical work cannot be found until the force under consideration is specified. For example, the expression 'mechanical work in walking' is uninterpretable if the forces of interest are not identified. Before discussing (determining) mechanical work, the forces under consideration must be explicitly defined. It is common knowledge that the elementary work done by a force F is defined as the product $W = F \cdot \cos\alpha \cdot ds$, where ds is an elementary displacement and α is the angle between the direction of the force and the direction of the displacement.

(B) All of the external forces and force couples acting on a (solid) body can be replaced by an equivalent system of forces. This replacement may be done in many ways. The most simple is to replace all of the external forces by one resultant force applied to the body's center of mass and one couple. As a result of this operation, the movement of the body is not changed.

(C) The total work done by several forces, ΣW_i, equals the work of their resultant, W_{res}. The proposition is valid for any system of forces, including forces acting in opposite directions; it is also valid for power, which is the time rate of doing work.

(D) According to the so-called *work-energy principle for a rigid body,* the work done by all of the (nonconservative) external forces and couples acting on the body is equal to the change in the body's total mechanical energy.

$$W = TME_{fi} - TME_{in} = \left(mgh_{fi} + \frac{m^2_{fi}}{2} + \frac{I\omega^2_{fi}}{2}\right) - \left(mgh_{in} + \frac{mv^2_{in} + I\omega^2_{in}}{2}\right) \quad (7.7)$$

where subscripts "fi" and "in" stand for final and initial values correspondingly. Hence, from the change in the total body's mechanical energy, the work of the resultant force and couple, but not the work done by individual forces, can be determined.

The main 'take home message' of this section is that to calculate the power and/or work, the force under consideration must be explicitly defined.

4. Basic Concepts

In this section, the basic concepts of analysis of mechanical work and power in human movement are introduced.

4.1 Produced (Developed) and Used (Net) Power and Work

The goal of this subsection is to introduce a concept of produced (developed) and used (net) power and work.

Consider the case when forces are acting in opposite directions and their action is, in part, canceled. In a simple example, which resembles a tug of war, two forces, F_1 and F_2, act collinearly in opposite directions ($|F_1| > |F_2|$), figure 7.3.

The work of three forces can be considered F_1, F_2, and their vector: sum F_{res}. Assume that $F_1 = 10{,}001$ N, $F_2 = -10{,}000$ N, $F_{res} = 1$ N, and displacement d is 1 m. Correspondingly, the magnitudes of the work are $W_1 = 10{,}001$ Nm, $W_2 = -10{,}000$ Nm, and $W_{res} = 1$ Nm. The work W_{res}, as compared with W_1 and W_2, is negligibly small because the positive mechanical work W_1 was almost canceled by the negative work W_2.

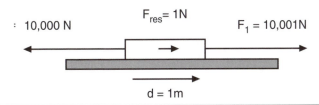

Figure 7.3 A 'tug-of-war' example to illustrate the difference between the produced (developed) and used (net) power and work.

At this point in the discussion, a dilemma is faced: If one is interested in a general measure of power and/or work, should the power/work of the resultant force, W_{res}, be determined or something else? Nothing can prevent the calculation of power and/or work of the resultant force (and couple, if it exists) or changes in the total mechanical energy of the body. It will be done in strict accordance with classical mechanics. The result of this calculation will be justly called the power or work (of all the forces acting on the body, of the resultant force and couple, total power/work, the power/work done on the body, net power/work, etc.). Note that textbooks in mechanics and physics deal mostly with net power. The reason is evident. Net force, net moment, net power, net work determine the movement, its result, so to speak. For instance, they determine how the mechanical energy of the body is changed. Without any research, it is evident that for antisymmetrical movements, the mechanical power calculated in such a way is zero (and this is absolutely correct, because the total mechanical energy of the human body is constant during such maneuvers) and that for all of the movements beginning and ending at rest at the same vertical location the mechanical work is also zero. This finding is also legitimate because after activity (horizontal arm extension with the load analysed in figure 7.1, marathon run, mountaineering on Everest, etc.), the mechanical energy of the body is not changed. Hence, there is nothing paradoxical in the *zero-work paradox* that is an immediate consequence of how the very notion of 'work' has been defined. However, while W_{res} is still an appropriate measure of the work *done on the body*, it can hardly be used to measure the total amount of mechanical energy *supplied by the forces* F_1 and F_2.

The question as to which power and work calculation (P_{res}/W_{res}, P_1/W_1, or P_2/W_2) is correct is senseless. All the three are correct, but they represent power and work of different forces. P_1 and P_2 measure power of actual forces F_1 and F_2. Net power P_{res} is the power of the fictitious (resultant) force. If this force were applied to the body its movement would be the same as under the common action of the actual forces. However, the power and work of the resultant force may differ from the power and work of the actual forces. In particular, the power of actual forces may exceed many times the net power, as in the tug-of-war example. It is up to the researchers to decide whether they are interested in the net power/

work or in the power/work generated by the actual forces. Sometimes in biomechanics, net power/work is the issue of interest. Much more often biomechanists are, however, interested in the power of actual forces acting on the body, and the object of interest is usually the power and work 'produced by the teams' rather than the power/work 'done on the rope.' In the tug-of-war example the mechanical work values W_1 and W_2 were produced by two independent sources of energy. Consequently, if an integral measure (a total power or work) is of interest, it seems reasonable to add the values of power and/or work produced by the two teams, rather than subtract them from each other.

The total work of several forces equals the sum of the work done by each of the forces, $W_{tot} = \Sigma W_f$ and because an integral of a sum equals the sum of integral,

$$W_{tot} = \int_{t_1}^{t_2} \left(\sum_f P_f \right) dt \qquad (7.8)$$

When, however, the forces act in opposite directions and a calculation of the total **produced** work (not **net** work!) is desired, summing the absolute rather than real values of the work of participating forces is appealing. This measure, $W_{tot} = \Sigma |W_f|$, the merit of which will be discussed later, can hardly be called 'work,' however, because it does not conform to the classical definition of work accepted in mechanics. Above, the term 'produced work' was used without a strict definition. Aleshinsky (1986) and Zatsiorsky (1986) suggested the term 'mechanical energy expenditure' (MEE) to describe the amount mechanical energy spent to perform a given movement. Formally, MEE may be defined via integration of the absolute values of the developed power. Thus by definition,

$$MEE = \int_{t_1}^{t_2} \left(\sum_f |P_f| \right) dt \qquad (7.9)$$

Equation 7.9 is valid for noncompensated sources of energy (see below). If the sources are intercompensated or compensated over time, the equation should be changed. To make future discussion easy, let us introduce formal definitions:

Definition 2—Produced (or developed) power is the power of the sources of mechanical energy.

Definition 3—Used (or net) power is the power of resultant forces and moments (the power of an equivalent system for the actual force system).

Definition 4—Mechanical energy expenditure equals an integral over time of the absolute values of power produced by the sources of energy.

Hence, replacement of an actual force system by an equivalent system can change the estimation of power and work of involved forces. To clarify the distinction between the power of actual forces and equivalent ones, the concepts of produced and net power were introduced, and the mechanical energy expenditure was defined as an integral over time of the absolute values of produced power.

4.2 Energy compensation

In this subsection two concepts are introduced, intercompensation of sources and compensation of sources during time (recuperation).

4.2.1 Introductory Examples

Consider a three-link kinematic chain with two frictionless joints, as shown in figure 7.4. Links 1 and 2 are rotating in the same direction with equal angular velocities ($\omega_1 = \omega_2$). The corresponding force moments are M_1 and M_2 ($M_1 = |-M_2|$) and the powers P_1 and P_2 ($P_1 = |-P_2|$). Note that the total mechanical energy of the system does not change; therefore, the *net* power equals zero. What is the magnitude of the total *developed* power? There is no definite answer to this question, although several answers are possible depending on the assumptions of the model employed.

1. Two one-joint muscles serve the joints; production of negative power requires energy. Since the power is generated by two different sources, the real values of P_1 and P_2 cannot be summed here. The total power P_{tot} equals $2P_1$.

$$P_{tot} = |P_1| + |-P_2| = 2P_1 \qquad (7.10)$$

Equation 7.10 characterizes summed (total) mechanical power expended by two single-joint muscles. Similarly, equation 7.11 is valid for a multijoint system with independent sources of energy in joints:

$$P_{tot} = \sum_j P_j^{pos} + \sum_j |-P_j^{neg}| = \sum_j |P_j| \qquad (7.11)$$

2. One two-joint muscle serves both joints. As a result, total produced power equals zero

$$P_{tot} = P_1 + (-P_2) = 0 \qquad (7.12)$$

Negative power from decelerating link 2, with decreasing mechanical energy, is used to increase the mechanical energy of accelerating link 1. This is due to the so-called 'tendon action' of the two-joint muscle (Elftman 1939; Wells 1988; van Ingen Schenau 1989; Prilutsky and Zatsiorsky 1994). In the example under consideration, the length of the muscle is kept constant and the muscle does not produce mechanical power.

In general, the used power equals the developed power only when one common source of power exists for all joints. If equation 7.12 were applied to the system served by one-joint muscles, it would give

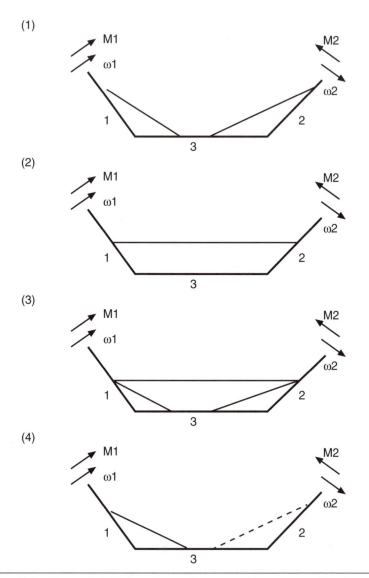

Figure 7.4   Three-link kinematic chains served by one- and/or two-joint muscles.

the correct estimation of the net power and it would provide the wrong estimation of the expended joint power. Summed joint power is equal to the net power, that is, to the rate of change of total mechanical energy of the system (plus the power which flows to the environment), but not to the developed power. The comprehensive formula is

$$\frac{dE}{dt} = \Sigma P_j + \Sigma P_e v_e + \Sigma M_e \omega_e = \Sigma P_j + \Sigma P_e \qquad (7.13)$$

where P_e is the power produced by external forces, F_e, and force moments, M_e. Equation 7.13 was proven by Aleshinsky (1986b).

3. Total power is equal to P_1. Two one-joint muscles and one two-joint muscle serve two joints under consideration and, by assumption, all of the three muscles develop power in joints 1 and 2 of the same magnitude. The power in each joint (P_j, $j=1,2$) can be presented as a sum of powers produced by a one-joint muscle ($P_j^{(1)}$) and a two-joint muscle ($P_j^{(2)}$). Similar to case 2, the total power from the two-joint muscle that is developed in two joints under consideration equals zero:

$$P^{(2)} = P_1^{(2)} + (-P_2^{(2)}) = 0 \tag{7.14}$$

Since $P_1^{(1)} = P_1/2$, $P_2^{(1)} = P_2/2$ and $|P_1| = |-P_2|$ the total power from the two one-joint muscles, similar to case 1, equals

$$\left|P_1^{(1)}\right| + \left|-P_2^{(1)}\right| = \left|P_1/2\right| + \left|P_2/2\right| = P_1 \tag{7.15}$$

4. Also, the total power for two joints equals P_1, when the negative power does not cost energy from the system.

$$P_{tot} = P_1 + (-P_2) = P_1 + 0 = P_1 \tag{7.16}$$

This calculation has been used, for instance, by Alexander (1980).

5. Consider positive and negative power as two separate entities that cannot be added. In this case, two individual parameters should be analyzed. This approach was suggested by B. Prilutsky (1994, a personal communication).

If the objective is to calculate the *net* power, which is equal to the sum of the rate of the energy content of all segments of the system, it can be done without conceptual problems. Equation 7.13 suits this purpose. However, if one wants to estimate the generated joint power, preference must be given to one of several models, some of which are presented in table 7.1. Note that activity of the antagonists is disregarded in all of the models.

In the examples from table 7.1, the total joint (apparent) power represents the total muscle power with the exception of the hidden power, i.e., the losses for overcoming activity of antagonists and internal resistance in the musculoskeletal system. Note that the knowledge of muscle geometry (force moment arm, muscle length) is not required to make such an estimation.

When a kinematic chain is served by two-joint muscles, the total power from various joints does not represent the developed muscle power even though all the hidden power is disregarded. Consider as an example a four-segment, three-joint kinematic chain served by two biarticular muscles $m_{1,2}$ and $m_{2,3}$, figure 7.5.

Table 7.1   Models to Calculate Total Generated Joint Power

	Formula	Model	
		Muscles	**Cost of negative joint power**
1a	$P_{tot} = \sum_j |P_j|$	One-joint muscles only.	Same as for positive power.
1b	$P_{tot} = \sum_j P_j^{pos}$, where P_j^{pos} is positive joint power.	One-joint muscles only.	Zero.
1c	$P_{tot} = \sum_j P_j^{pos} + k \sum_j |P_j^{neg}|$ where P_j^{neg} is negative joint power and $0<k<1$.	One-joint muscles only.	Less than for positive power.
2	$P_{tot} = \sum_j P_j$	One multijoint muscle serves all the joints. (This assumption can barely be considered realistic.)	Same as for positive power.

Muscle $m_{1,2}$ passes joint 1 and 2, muscle $m_{2,3}$ goes through joints 2 and 3. Joint 2 is served by two muscles, $m_{1,2}$ and $m_{2,3}$. Compare the power, P, produced by the muscles (columns) with the power liberated in joints (rows), table 7.2. The superscripts near P designate the muscles, and the subscripts indicate the joints. The total muscle power is

$$P_{tot}^m = |P^{m1,2}| + |P^{m2,3}| = |P_1^{m1,2} + P_2^{m1,2}| + |P_2^{m2,3} + P_3^{m2,3}| \qquad (7.17)$$

Consider the joint power. The power in joints 1 and 3 is from muscles $m_{1,2}$ or $m_{2,3}$, correspondingly. The power in joint 2 comes from two muscles under consideration, $P_2 = P_2^{m1,2} + P_2^{m2,3}$. The total joint power calculated

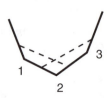

Figure 7.5   A four-link chain served by two biarticular muscles.

Table 7.2   Muscle Power Versus Joint Power of a Kinematic Chain Served by Two-Joint Muscles

	Muscle Power	
Joint power	$m_{1,2}$	$m_{2,3}$
$P_1 =$	$\|P_1^{m1,2}$	
$P_2 =$	$P_2^{m1,2}\| \quad +$	$\|P_2^{m2,3}$
		$+$
$P_3 =$		$P_3^{m2,3}\|$

with the assumption that one-joint muscles only are acting (case 1a, table 7.1) is

$$P_{tot} = \sum_j |P_j| = |P_1^{m1,2}| + |P_2^{m1,2} + P_2^{m2,3}| + |P_3^{m2,3}| \qquad (7.18a)$$

If one three-joint muscle is assumed

$$P_{tot} = \sum_j P_j = P_1^{m1,2} + P_2^{m1,2} + P_2^{m2,3} + P_3^{m2,3} \qquad (7.18b)$$

Equations 7.18a and 7.18b provide identical results only when the power values are all positive or all negative. Note that to arrive at the total power value, the power produced by particular two-joint muscles in individual joints must be known and to do that muscle geometry, specifically the points of muscle origin and insertion must be established.

We may conclude that knowledge of the power values generated in individual joints does not permit an unequivocal solution for the total power produced in all the joints. Additional information concerning the sources of energy is needed to arrive at the total power value.

4.2.2 Energy Intercompensation

The negative power from one-joint muscles cannot be used in another joint. In contrast, a two-joint muscle can produce negative power in one joint and positive power in the second. When two-joint muscles are active, the power from the joint may be used in the neighboring joint. This feature of the energy sources is called *intercompensation*. By definition (Aleshinsky 1986a; Zatsiorsky 1986), the sources are not intercompensated if the total power they produce equals the sum of absolute values of the power generated by them

$$P_{tot} = \sum_s |P_s| \qquad (7.19)$$

where P_s is the power of individual sources of energy (forces and/or moments). The sources are intercompensated if the total power they generated equals the absolute value of the algebraic sum of the powers developed by them.

$$P_{tot} = \left| \sum_s P_s \right| \tag{7.20}$$

Evidently, the joint moments that are generated by one-joint muscles are not intercompensated sources of mechanical energy while those that are due to two-joint muscles are intercompensated sources (cf. equations 7.19 and 7.20 with equations 7.11 and 7.12). When the total muscle power, rather than joint power, is the object of interest, individual two-joint muscles are regarded as nonintercompensated sources (cf. equation 7.17).

4.2.3 Energy Compensation Over Time (Recuperation)

When muscles develop force eccentrically (in the direction opposite to the motion), negative work is performed. During periods of eccentric muscle action, the mechanical energy is stored temporarily as elastic energy of muscle and tendon deformation; the elastic energy can recoil to the system later in time. This property is called *energy recuperation,* or *energy compensation over time.* For a source of energy compensated during time, the MEE equals the absolute value of the integral over the time of the power developed by the source (Aleshinsky 1986a; Zatsiorsky 1986)

$$MEE = \left| \int_{t1}^{t2} P_s dt \right| \tag{7.21}$$

For a nonrecuperative source

$$MEE = \int_{t1}^{t2} |P_s| dt \tag{7.22}$$

To conclude, the concepts of intercompensation and compensation over time (recuperation) were introduced in this subsection.

5. Models and Methods Employed to Calculate Work and Power

The goal of this section is to examine various models employed to study mechanical power and work in human movements. To do that we will use the concepts introduced in the previous sections.

5.1 Single-Mass Model

In the framework of the single-mass model, the human body is represented as a single particle with massless trunk, head, and extremities.

Hence, the movement of the general center of mass (GCM) only is considered and movement of all the body parts with respect to the GCM is disregarded. The great advantage of the model is its simplicity and the opportunity to compute the power and work in locomotion by measuring ground reaction forces. The calculations are based on the well-known proposition of classical mechanics: The sum of the external forces acting on a system equals the product of the system mass ($m = \Sigma m_i$, where m_i is the mass of an individual particle) times the acceleration of a single fictitious particle located at the CM of all the particles, a_{CM}

$$\Sigma F_e = ma_{CM} \tag{7.23}$$

In locomotion, when the air resistance and friction forces are disregarded, there exist only two external forces, ground reaction and gravity. In experimental research, the power values are determined in three steps (Cavagna, Saibene, and Margaria 1963, 1964; Cavagna 1975; Blickhan and Full 1992):

1. Acceleration of the GCM is calculated by dividing the ground reaction force (minus body weight for the vertical force component) by the subject's mass.

2. The instantaneous velocity values are determined by integration of the acceleration. The integration constants are obtained from the boundary conditions of the system, in particular from average horizontal velocity registered independently.

3. The instantaneous power values (P_{CM}) are calculated as the · products of the ground reaction force (F_{GR}) and the GCM velocity (v_{CM}).

$$P_{CM} = F_{GR} \cdot v_{CM} \tag{7.24}$$

With the model in equation 7.24, the power used to move a fictitious particle located at the GCM is determined. When the model is employed, all the forces acting on the human body are replaced by a single force acting at the GCM, as if a rope were fixed to the GCM; and then one determines the power and work expended to pull it. This power/work can be coined *locomotor power/work*. It is clear that the power/work determined in such a way does not represent in full the total power/work generated by joint moments. In addition, it does not represent a fixed proportion of the total joint power.

Consider, as an example, one special case, *comfortable walk*. When walking such that the GCM moves horizontally at a constant velocity, the gait pattern is called *comfortable* and is of a special interest for designing biped walking machines. Future pilots and passengers of such walking devices will not experience unpleasant accelerations during each step if the machine uses a comfortable walk. Since horizontal acceleration of the GCM is zero and the GCM is moving at the same height, the mechanical power/work of the resultant force applied at the GCM is equal to zero in this case. According to the calculations done by Beletsky (1984), the total work of joint moments is almost four times greater for the comfortable walk than for the habitual walk. As everywhere, we should pay for luxury and comfort.

The relationship between the locomotor power, the power used to change the mechanical energy of a fictitious point located at the body's CM, and the total joint power in human movement is poorly understood and, with one exception (Aleshinsky 1986b), has not been subjected to rigorous mechanical analysis. It is a common knowledge that the total kinetic energy of a moving system equals the sum of the kinetic energy of the GCM and the summed kinetic energy of the links that move relative to the GCM. The first term is usually called *external* energy and the second *internal* energy. At first glance, it seems attractive to represent in a similar way the two additive fractions of the total joint work expended for motion. In the framework of this approach, the total work is considered the sum of two independent fractions: first, the work expended in changing the motion of the GCM ("external work"; we prefer the term *locomotor work*) and, second, the work expended in changing the body segment motions relative to the GCM ("internal work"). Note that the terms "external work" and "internal work" when defined in such ways differ from the definitions made above; see figure 7.2.

Aleshinsky (1986b) proved, however, that the total MEE is not equal to the sum of the "external" (locomotor) work and "internal" work, the work expended in changing the body segment motions relative to the GCM. To illustrate the main idea, we have simplified the Aleshinsky equations omitting details. First, Aleshinsky evolved the system's total energy balance equation in the following form

$$\frac{d}{dt}E_{CM} + \frac{d}{dt}E_{REL} = \sum_e P_{e/CM} + \sum_e P_{e/REL} + \sum_j P_j \qquad (7.25)$$

where E_{CM} is the energy of the center of mass, E_{REL} is the energy of the links that move relative to the general center of mass, $P_{e/CM}$ is the power of external forces acting on the human body and changing the CM's energy, $P_{e/REL}$ is the power of external forces and moments changing the energy of the links, and P_j is joint power. Then, Aleshinsky (1986b) derived the equation for the total work/power of the system as the sum of the two fractions. The equation is rewritten below for a particular case of single support without slip and air resistance with no external moments applied.

$$P_{tot} = P_{CM} + P_{REL} = |\mathbf{F}_{GR} \cdot \mathbf{v}_{CM}| + |-(\mathbf{F}_{GR} \cdot \mathbf{v}_{CM}) + \sum_j P_j| \qquad (7.26)$$

The absolute rather than real values are added because the sources of the 'external' and 'internal' power are considered not intercompensated. Equation 7.26 describes the procedures that are employed when the total work/power is represented as the sum of the two fractions.

There are two critical comments to make regarding the method represented in equation 7.26. First, the real joint power values are summed algebraically, thus, their complete intercompensation is implicitly assumed. From table 7.1, item 2, it follows that this summation would be valid for all of the movements only if all of the joints were served by one multijoint muscle. This supposition is, of course, not correct. When a subject produces negative power in the knee joint and an equal amount of positive power in the elbow joint, it does not mean that he or she develops no mechanical power.

The second point to make is that there is an external force, $\mathbf{F}_{GR}$, inside the expression for P_{REL}. Hence, P_{REL} depends upon external forces and the two fractions, P_{CM} and P_{REL}, are not independent. The dot product $\mathbf{F}_{GR} \cdot \mathbf{v}_{CM}$ representing the power expended in moving the GCM is included with different signs in the expressions for P_{CM} and P_{REL}. It means that these powers cancel each other. However, in the method, because the sources for the P_{CM} and P_{REL} are treated as independent, the absolute values of the power are added, and as a result the method prevents canceling out these powers. It ends in calculating these powers twice. For instance if a subject 'freezes' all joints (power in all joints is zero and consequently $\Sigma P_i = 0$) and moves on a support as an inverted pendulum, equation 7.26 yields nonzero power values, which is clearly an incorrect result. Thus, the representation of total developed power as the sum of the two fractions, $P_{CM} + P_{REL}$, is ambiguous.

In spite of limitations in calculating the power/work *expended* for motion, the single-mass model is a useful tool in studying of how the expended energy was *used*. It helps to understand mechanisms of human ambulation. The well-known inverted-pendulum model of human walking and spring-mass model of running (Cavagna, Saibene, and Margaria 1963, 1964) may serve as an example of the helpful application of the single-mass model of the human body.

The main conclusion from subsection 5.1 is that the power or work used to move a fictitious particle located at the GCM does not represent the power/work performed by the joint moments.

5.2 Multisegment Model (Fraction Approach)

The multisegment model is based on the work-energy principle for a rigid body described above: The work done by all the external nonconservative forces and couples acting on a rigid body is equal to the changes in the body's total mechanical energy (see equation 7.7). In experiments, the total mechanical energy of the individual human body segments, regarded as rigid, is determined (equation 7.1) and then its changes are calculated. As the work done by all the external forces and couples acting on the rigid body equals the work of the resultant force and couple applied at the body's CM, the fraction model estimates the power/work of fictitious sources of energy (forces and couples) acting at the CMs of individual body segments. The calculated power and work are the *net* power and *net* work rather than *produced power* and *mechanical energy expenditure*. To illustrate, imagine rods attached at the segment's CM similar to those used to manipulate puppets. The work of forces that the rods exert on the body segments would be equal to the changes of body's potential and kinetic translational energy. Precisely this work, plus the work done to rotate the body segments, is measured with the fraction approach. As stated above, the net power, i.e., the power of the resultant forces and couples, differs from the developed power (the power of actual forces), when some of the forces produce negative work. When this happens, the fraction method provides estimations of the net power and work that differ from the values of the produced power and work calculated with the source method.

An important delimitation of the fraction approach is the necessity to make additional assumptions about conditions of the energy transfer between body segments. The energy transfer between human body segments is actualized solely via the forces and moments acting at the joints. Unfortunately, the fraction model does not explicitly include these forces and moments. As a consequence, in the literature the assumptions are made not about the model itself, but about the energy transfer permitted; and the effects rather than the causes are postulated. The potential causes of the assumed effects (energy transfer) are summarized in table 7.3.

Some of the assumed variants of energy transfer are based on models that are difficult to accept. For instance, the ban on within-segment energy transfer means that potential energy of the body segment cannot be used to increase its kinetic energy, and vice versa. This assumption contravenes the law of conservation of energy and, as such, cannot hold. The fourth assumption implies that antisymmetric motion does not require energy supply, but this would be possible only if all the body segments were served by one muscle.

The strictures of the fraction approach do not mean that this method of estimation of mechanical power and work is not useful. With some exceptions, however, it is not an appropriate way for determining the power and work *produced* by the joint moments. At the same time, it is an invaluable method for determining the work *done* on the human body segments. When the net power/work is object of the interest, the fraction approach is indispensable. Here is one example of its application. There is a century-long discussion about the role of pendular-like leg motion in minimizing energy expenditure for walking. It has been postulated, that during the swing phase, the leg is moving as a free pendulum at the expense of its potential energy. Zatsiorsky and Iakumin (1980) showed, however, that during the walking cycle, maximal potential energy of the human leg (48 J) is much smaller that its peak kinetic energy (261 J). Hence, the leg movement during gait cannot be considered free

Table 7.3 Potential Causes of the Assumed Energy Transfers

	Assumed effects Permitted energy transfer	Potenial causes	Comments
1	Not permitted both within and between body segments.	The law of conservation of energy is not valid.	Barely realistic assumption.
2	Permitted within but not between body segments.	All body segments are disconnected. There are no forces and/or moments in joints.	The model provides an estimation of what would happen if the body segments were disconnected.
3	Permitted between the segments of the same extremity.	All the segments of the same extremity are served by one conjoint muscle.	As compared with the other conditions, this is the most realistic model, although still too simple to be valid.
4	Permitted between all the body segments.	All the body parts are served by one conjoint muscle.	Barely realistic assumption.

oscillation, and other explanations should be sought to explain the high economy of human walking.

In summary, the fraction method attempts to determine the work *done* on the human body segments. It is not usually an appropriate technique for determining the power and work *produced* by the joint moments.

5.3 Joint Power Models (Source Approach)

The source approach is based on summation of the power values produced in individual joints. The joint power is determined as the product of the joint angular velocity and the joint moment; see equation 7.2.

5.3.1 What Does a 'Joint Moment' Mean?

In classical mechanics, the notion of 'joint moment' or 'joint torque" is not defined and is not used. In the biomechanics literature (e.g., Zajac 1993), the term collectively refers to two moments, equal in magnitude and opposite in direction, acting on adjacent segments that form the joint. In this approach, all the forces acting on a human body segment are replaced by (a) gravity force, (b) two resultant forces acting at joints, and (c) two force couples exerting moments about the joint rotation centers, as shown in figure 7.6.

Rotation of the link around its center of gravity is determined by the combined action of two joint moments and two joint forces:

$$I\dot{\omega} = M_{res} = M_1 + M_2 + M(F_1) + M(F_2) \, d \qquad (7.27)$$

where I is the moment of inertia, $\dot{\omega}$ is angular acceleration, M_{res} is the resultant force moment acting on the link, M_1 and M_2 are the joint moments, and $M(F_1)$ and $M(F_2)$ are the moments generated by the joint forces ($M(F) = F \cdot d$, where d is the moment arm taken with respect to the center of gravity). Note that the joint forces elicit not only translatory motion of the body segment, but also, if they do not pass through the segments' center of gravity, its rotation.

In the joints served only by uniarticular muscles, the existence of two equal and opposite moments acting about the common joint axis upon the adjacent segments is a straightforward consequence of the Newton's third law. When a two- or multijoint muscle spans the joint, the problem becomes more complex because biarticular muscles do not exert force, and consequently moment about the joint, on an intermediate body segment to which they have no attachments. As a result, force moments acting on adjacent segments of a joint served by a biarticular muscle may be different in magnitude (for the proof and detailed discussion, see Zatsiorsky and Latash 1993). For that reason, they cannot be collectively referred to as "joint moment/torque." In current literature, however, the specificity of biarticular muscles is commonly disregarded and "joint moments" are being computed. To do that, a real force system is replaced by an equivalent system. This procedure does not change the movement of the body, but it does affect the calculation of the total joint power.

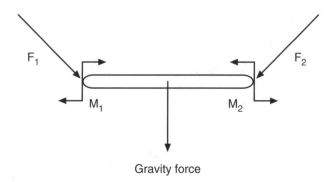

Gravity force

Figure 7.6   Forces and couples acting on a body segment.

For the 'actual' joint moments, developed by only uniarticular muscle, the total developed power should be calculated as a sum of absolute values of joint power (equation 7.4). This is true because energy dissipated in one joint (negative power) cannot be compensated by an increased energy production (positive power) in another joint. Hence, the 'actual' joint moments are not intercompensated sources of energy. In contrast, the total power of two joints served by a biarticular muscle (the power of "fictitious" joint moments) can be summed as in equations 12 and 20. Thus, 'fictitious' joint moments, calculated for the system served by only two-joint muscles, are intercompensated sources of mechanical energy.

5.3.2 Aleshinsky's Model: Source Versus Fraction Approach

The various joint-moment models are different with regard to the permitted intercompensation, compensation over time, and the energy cost of negative work. At this time, only one such model has been subjected to rigorous analysis based on classical mechanics (Aleshinsky 1986a-e). In Aleshinsky's model, the following assumptions are made:

1. Motion control is performed by the joint moments acting relative to the hinge axes.
2. The sources of energy are not intercompensated; in other words, only one-joint muscles are permitted.
3. The sources of energy are not recuperative. When the total mechanical energy of body segments is lost the energy cannot be returned to the system later in time; in other words, storage and recoil of elastic deformation energy is not permitted into the model.
4. The costs of the positive and negative power/work are equal, and therefore,
   a. the total power of several joint moments equals the sum of the absolute values of power developed by them (equation 7.19); and
   b. the mechanical energy expenditure equals the integral over time of the absolute value of the developed power (equation 7.22).

In Aleshinsky's model total joint power is determined as the sum of absolute values of power developed in individual joints (equation 7.4) and mechanical energy expenditure as an integral over time of the absolute values of the developed joint power (equation 7.22). Aleshinsky studied the 'energy balance equations,' i.e., the relationships between the power of the sources (source approach) and the time rate of the links' total mechanical energy (fraction approach), and arrived at the following conclusions:

1. The net power/work equals the produced power/MEE only when (a) all the sources develop power of the same sign (there is no 'tug-of-war'

situation), or (b) all the sources are intercompensated (the human body is served by only one muscle) and recuperative (the muscle is an ideal spring able to recoil one hundred percent of the stored elastic energy).

The second assumption is unrealistic, and the first was confirmed experimentally by Prilutsky (1990) and de Looze et al. (1992), who showed that during landing and lifting weights, when all the joint powers are of the same sign, both approaches yield similar results.

2. The joint force action cannot change the system's total energy, but it can redistribute the energy between the links and the links' fractions.

3. Total MEE is not equal to the sum of the work 'to move GCM' and the work 'to move body links relative to the GCM'.

4. Replacing the actual force and moment system by a resultant force system changes the estimates of the MEE (in 2.2 it has been shown for power and work).

5. The methods of calculating mechanical work that are based on various assumptions about energy transfer within and between body links (see table 7.3) cannot lead to correct results (except for the movements where the transfer is absent).

Aleshinsky's study is the only in which the problem of mechanical work and power in human movement was subjected to a scrupulous examination based on classical mechanics. The analysis rested on the definition of work as an integral of the product of force/force moment and velocity/angular velocity over time. The Aleshinsky model has obvious limitations in that one-joint muscles only are permitted, elastic forces are disregarded, and the summation of the absolute values of positive and negative joint power remains a debatable operation. The strength of the Aleshinsy's model is that when joint moments but not muscle forces are known, this is the only model that allows estimating mechanical energy expenditure for motion in a non-controversial way. The model should be regarded as a necessary intermediary step rather than the final solution of the problem of determining mechanical power and work in human movement.

5.4 Muscle-Power Models. Prilutsky's Model

The aim of these models is calculating total muscle power rather than joint power. The model, developed primarily by Prilutsky (Prilutsky and Zatsiorsky 1994), may serve as an example of models of this sort. In Prilutsky's model, both one- and two-joint muscles are included and muscle forces, rather than joint moments, are considered the sources of mechanical energy. The expenditure of mechanical energy is calculated as

$$\text{MEE} = \int_{t_1}^{t_2} [\sum_{1,(j,j+1)} |P(t)_{j,j+1}^{m_k^{(2)}}| + \sum_{1,j} |P_j^{m_1^{(1)}}|] dt \tag{7.28}$$

where $P(t)_{j,j+1}^{m_k(2)}$ is the power developed in joints j and j+1 by the kth two-joint muscle $m_k^{(2)}$, and $P_j^{m_l(1)}$ is the power generated in joint j by the lth one-joint muscle $m_l^{(1)}$. The summation is done across all of the muscles. To calculate the total MEE, the power developed by individual muscles is estimated based on the assumption that none of the one-joint antagonists are active. From this assumption it follows that the model provides the lowest estimate of the real values of the muscle power and work. Force $F_{i,j}$ of the ith muscle (i = k,l) serving the jth joint was obtained from the expression

$$F_{i,j}(t) = A_{i,j}[M_j(t) - \sum_k M_j^{m_k(2)}(t)]/\sum_{q=1}^{n_j} d_{q,j}(t)A_{q,j} \qquad (7.29)$$

where $M_j(t)$ is the moment at the jth joint; $\sum_k$ is the sum of the moments induced by the action of two-joint muscles serving two joints, including the given one, and determined by calculations for the preceding joint; n_j is the number of agonists serving the jth joint and located on the proximal link; $A_{q,j}$ is the physiological cross-sectional area of the qth agonist serving the jth joint and located on the proximal link; and $d_{q,j}(t)$ is the moment arm of the qth agonist serving the jth joint and located on the proximal link. Since only approximate estimates of the required parameters (cross-sectional areas, moment arms, etc.) are available, the model is not presumed to be very accurate; nevertheless it allows for comparison of the total muscle power (Prilutsky's model) with the apparent joint power (Aleshinsky's model). Since both models are based on the same principles except one (power intercompensation for two-joint muscles) the energy economy due to activity of these muscles can be studied. It has been reported that the saving of MEE by a two-joint muscle is possible when the following three conditions are satisfied: (1) The muscle produces the positive power in one joint and the negative in another, (2) the moments developed by the muscle in each of the joints coincide in direction with the control moments in these joints, and (3) the one-joint antagonists are inactive. The model also allows for computation of the energy transfer between joints (see below). The transfer due to the two-joint muscles can be large. For instance in a squat vertical jump, the energy generated by the hip extensors is used in approximately equal amounts for extension at the hip joint and for extension at the knee and ankle joints (Prilutsky and Zatsiorsky 1994).

In summary to this section, the source approach is the only method that is rested on the classical definition of work as an integral of the product of force/force moment and velocity/angular velocity over time. However, to apply the method, additional information on the sources of energy, and their intercompensation and compensation over time (recuperation) is needed.

6. Mechanical Power and Work in Human Movement: Some Issues

The aim of this section is to discuss some issues pertinent to mechanical energy production, absorption, transformation, and transfer in human motion.

6.1 Eccentric Muscle Action (Negative Work)

All of the models of mechanical work and power in human movement discussed above, and also models that will be developed in the future, differ from each other with respect to the forces under consideration, the cost of the negative work, and permitted energy intercompensation and recuperation. The last two issues concern how negative work should be handled; if there is no negative work performed in a given activity the determination of the mechanical power and work is straightforward. In contrast, there are many problems associated with negative muscle work. Some of them have been solved or can be easily solved, while others will require elaborate experimental research and revision of the main concepts involved.

1. **Energy turnover and metabolic cost of negative muscle work.** When a muscle is forcibly stretched there are two flows of energy, to and from the muscle:

a. The external force does the work on the muscle, and the energy goes to the muscle. The energy is partly stored as potential energy of elastic deformation, partly dissipated as heat and, according to a hypothesis suggested by Abbott, Aubert, and Hill (1951), partly used in unknown biochemical reactions.

b. The (active) muscle spends energy to provide resistance against the external force.

One example to illustrate the energy turnover is cycling downhill. In this case gravity force produces work on the cyclist-bicycle system, and the cyclist spends energy for braking. When the bicycle stops at the bottom of the hill, the potential energy loss that formally equals the negative work performed can be higher than the athlete's energy spent to decelerate the system. As a result, efficiency (the mechanical work to energy expenditure ratio) is higher than 100%. For uphill/downhill cycling, the ratio of the consumed oxygen values $+\dot{V}O_2/-\dot{V}O_2$ as high as 125 has been reported (Asmussen 1953), and the efficiency equals 3,485% in this case. This finding contradicts the law of conservation of energy and, as such, cannot be accepted. Evidently, something is fundamentally wrong in the calculation of efficiency for negative work, but there is nothing specifically biological in these observations. It is well known that some technical devices, e.g., electromagnets, require energy to develop force. For the negative work of such a force, 'efficiency' can be greater than 100%. At this time, there is no established physical theory to deal with such phenomena and it is, therefore, typically suggested that we distinguish between the forces that are developed with or without energy expenditure (electromagnet vs. gravity, elasticity, or friction) and to exercise caution.

Negative work in human movement still remains an underinvestigated and badly understood phenomenon.

2. **Intercompensation.** Incorporating two-joint muscles into the models allows for the solution of this problem, but the force moments generated by these muscles should be known.

3. **Recuperation.** The time course of the storage and recoil of the elastic deformation energy during various activities should be known. In principle, it can be determined experimentally.

4. **Negative change of the body's mechanical energy vs. the negative work.** According to the work-energy principle, the work of joint moments equals the change in the body's total mechanical energy (see equations 7 and 13). This principle is based on the assumption that the human body segments do not deform, but the real body segments are not completely rigid. The work-energy principle for human movement holds only when the deformation of body parts is negligible. In some situations the principle cannot be applied. For instance, when someone sustains a fall in walking, the potential energy of the body decreases without any work produced by the joint moments. In general, when the mechanical energy of the body decreases, a portion of the energy is dissipated without negative work of joint moments via 'passive' forces that are developed without energy spending by the joint moment sources. Hence, the negative change of the body's mechanical energy is usually larger than the negative work of joint moments. To calculate the proportion of negative work done on the body by the joint moments, the ratio (negative work of joint moments/reduction of total mechanical energy), called the *index of softness of landing* (Zatsiorsky and Prilutsky 1987), was suggested.

6.2 Energy Transformation and Energy Transfer

The term 'energy transformation' will be used to designate the conversion of mechanical energy from translational kinetic into rotational kinetic form and back, and from kinetic into potential form and back (cf. Aleshinsky 1986a). This term is recommended instead of the expression 'transfer of energy within a body segment' because the word 'transfer' means to carry from one place to another, and if energy conversion occurs at the same place, the term 'transformation' is more appropriate. The term 'energy transfer' will be used to designate the energy flow between body segments and/or joints.

6.2.1 Energy Transformation

Energy transformation in human body movement is realized in two forms, as a 'whip' motion and as a 'pendulum' motion. Whip motion is seen, for instance, in walking, where during swing phase the knee linear velocity decreases, inducing an increase of angular shank velocity. The kinetic energy of the lower leg translation is transformed into the kinetic energy of rotation. This phenomenon is seen in above-knee amputees and, thus, knee joint movement during the swing phase can be performed without the knee joint muscles (Bernstein 1935). The whip-like energy transformation has also been reported in throwing activities.

Pendular motion of body segments has attracted the curiosity of researchers for over a century (Weber and Weber 1836), and its presence in human movement is very often taken for granted. However, in each individual case, the existence of pendular motion must be determined and proved biomechanically. For any free ideal pendulum (a) the total mechanical energy (the sum of the kinetic and potential energy) is constant over an oscillation cycle; (b) the kinetic and potential energy of the body change is exactly out of phase; and (c) the motion is performed at the expense of the transformation of the potential energy into kinetic energy, and vice versa. If these three conditions are not satisfied, the movement, even though it looks like a free pendulum, is not of a pendular type. Leg movements during the swing phases of walking, for example, resemble the movements of a compound pendulum in that the legs are periodically raised and lowered under the influence of gravity. Therefore, the idea of pendulum-like leg movements during walking seems quite reassurable. However, the peak values of leg kinetic energy during the swing phase greatly exceed the peak values of its potential energy. In addition, the total mechanical energy of the leg during a stride is not constant, especially for the foot. During the support period, when the foot is on the ground, both its potential and kinetic energy fractions are at a minimum; the foot assumes the lowest possible position and does not translate. Thus, the leg during walking can barely be considered a free pendulum; in other words, it is not a conservative system. The issue of which body segments move in a pendulum-like fashion during walking is a matter of contention among researchers. At least three theories have been developed according to which the involved body parts are: (a) the legs; (b) the body as a whole, specifically its general center of mass (CM) and head-arms-trunk segment; and (c) the CM and extremities (for an extensive review, see Zatsiorsky, Werner, and Kaimin 1994).

6.2.2 Energy Transfer

The term 'energy transfer' has been used rather loosely in the biomechanics literature and, as a result, controversy has arisen due to the lack of a unified terminology. For instance, van Ingen Schenau (1989) reported that during vertical jumps the transfer of energy takes place from proximal to distal joints. When the leg approaches full extension, the gastroc-nemius is acting as an energy transmitter transporting the energy of the thigh rotation to the ankle joint. As a result, the thigh's rotational energy decreases and the power and work registered in the ankle joint increases. In contrast, Pandy and Zajac (1991) have shown that during takeoff the energy transfer is directed from the distal to proximal links and the work done in the ankle joint increased the energy of the proximal body segments. The contradictory inferences concerning the energy transfer during takeoffs are consequence of different interpretation of the expression 'transfer of mechanical energy.'

In our view, not including the possible flow of energy from a link to the muscles, four kinds of energy transfer can be discerned, as follows.

1. **Joint to link.** The power/work produced in a joint is used to change mechanical energy of remote links. For instance, during arm abduction with the elbow joint and wrist joint locked, the energy generated by the shoulder joint muscles is transferred to the hand. Ankle plantar flexion with the resulting toe-rising changes energy content of all the body segments. During a vertical jump, this transfer of energy takes place from the distal joint (ankle) to the proximal links.

2. **Link to joint.** For example, when during takeoff, the knee approaches full extension, the thigh rotational energy is transmitted to the ankle joint through two-joint muscles (for review see van Ingen Schenau et al. 1990). The energy of the thigh that was lost at deceleration appears as mechanical work at the ankle. The transfer of energy occurs from the proximal link (the thigh) to the distal joint (the ankle).

3. **Joint to joint.** Consider a movement in which the hip joint extensors produce positive work. If the two-joint rectus femoris muscle acts isometrically it does not produce mechanical work itself. It may, however, transport the energy from the hip joint to the knee joint and, as a result, the fraction of the work developed by the hip extensors appears as mechanical work at the knee joint. The difference between the link-to-joint and joint-to-joint transfer is where the energy comes from. In the link-to-joint case, the energy of the moving body part is used, whereas in the joint-to-joint transfer the muscle work is the immediate source of the transported energy. In both cases, the energy comes to the joint through two-joint muscles.

The rate at which the energy is transferred to or from a given joint of the leg by two-joint muscles is given by the following equation (Prilutsky and Zatsiorsky 1994):

$$P_j^{tr}(t) = P_j(t) - \Sigma_j P^m(t), \, j = 1,2,3 \qquad (7.30)$$

where subscript j is the number of the leg joint, t is the time, $P_j(t)$ is the power developed by the joint moment in the jth joint, and $\Sigma_j P^m(t)$ is the arbitrary designation of the sum of the powers developed by all the muscles serving the j*th* joint. If the total power of muscles serving a given joint, $\Sigma_j P^m(t)$, and the power of moment at the joint, $P_j(t)$, have the same sign, and the difference, $P_j(t)$, is positive, an extra amount of mechanical energy comes to the joint.

4. **Link to link.** When two body segments interconnected by a muscle are rotating in the same direction and the muscle is active, energy exchange takes place. For one of the links the directions of the muscle force and the link velocity are opposite to each other; hence, the link gives off energy. This energy is acquired, in part, by the second link, and is partially absorbed by the muscles. This type of energy transfer was studied first by Pierrynowski, Winter, and Norman (1980).

In natural movements, complex circular energy exchange occurs. In a vertical jump, for example, the energy generated by the knee extensors is used to accelerate the thigh and the upper part of the body, the joint-to-link transfer in the from-distal-to-proximal direction. When the gastrocnemius is active, the thigh and upper part of the body give off energy that appears as mechanical work in the ankle joint (the link-to-joint transfer from the proximal links to the distal joint), which causes the ankle plantar flexion (the link-to-link energy transfer). If the knee extensors still develop mechanical work, this work is manifested partly as the work at the ankle joint (the joint-to-joint transfer). Finally, the work produced at the ankle joint is used to lift the whole body (the joint-to-link transfer from the distal joint to proximal links).

7. Concluding Remarks

There are three fundamental methods of determining power and work in human movement; the methods determine:

1. the power and work of an imaginable force applied to a fictitious point located at the body's CM (single-mass model); or
2. the net power and work done by the resultant forces and force couples applied to the body segment CMs (the fraction method), or
3. the apparent power and MEE of joint moments (the source model, specifically Aleshinsky's model).

None of these methods represents a fixed proportion of the muscle work, and the first two methods do not represent a fixed proportion of the power and work of the joint moments. In addition, as nobody knows how to handle negative muscle work, the arbitrary assumptions are made about (a) energy intercompensation, (b) energy recuperation, and (c) cost of negative work. Thus, at first sight, the situation looks rather discouraging. However, in spite all of the delimitations of the power/work calculations, these calculations are still a powerful tool of research and gaining new knowledge about human movement. The methods provide estimations that are useful for making comparisons among various subjects, experimental conditions, and movements.

Acknowledgments

The discussions with Dr. S. Aleshinsky, Dr. R. Nelson, and Dr. B. Nigg are gratefully acknowledged. We are indebted to Dr. B.I. Prilutsky whose comments have been incorporated into this chapter. Special thanks are extended to Andrew Hardyk and Tony Sparrow for their assistance in editing the manuscript.

References

Abbott, B.G., X.M. Aubert, and A.V. Hill. 1951. The absorption of work by a muscle stretched during a single twitch or a short tetanus. *Proceedings of the Royal Society of London, Series B* 139: 86-104.

Aleshinsky, S.Yu. 1986. An energy 'sources' and 'fraction' approach to the mechanical energy expenditure problem. 1. Basic concepts, description of the model, analysis of a one-link system movement. *Journal of Biomechanics* 19: 287-293.

Aleshinsky, S.Yu. 1986b. An energy 'sources' and 'fraction' approach to the mechanical energy expenditure problem. 2. Movement of the multi-link chain model. *Journal of Biomechanics* 19: 295-300.

Aleshinsky, S.Yu. 1986c. An energy 'sources' and 'fraction' approach to the mechanical energy expenditure problem. 3. Mechanical energy expenditure reduction during one link motion. *Journal of Biomechanics* 19: 301-306.

Aleshinsky, S.Yu. 1986d. An energy 'sources' and 'fraction' approach to the mechanical energy expenditure problem. 1Y. Criticism of the concept of 'energy transfers within and between links.' *Journal of Biomechanics* 19: 307-309.

Aleshinsky, S.Yu. 1986e. An energy 'sources' and 'fraction' approach to the mechanical energy expenditure problem. Y. The mechanical energy expenditure reduction during motion of the multi-link system. *Journal of Biomechanics* 19: 311-315.

Alexander, R.McN. 1980. The mechanics of walking. In *Aspects of animal movement,* eds. H.Y. Elder, and E.R. Trueman, 221-234. Cambridge: Cambridge University Press.

Asmussen, E. 1953. Positive and negative muscular work. *Acta Physiologica Scandinavica* 28: 364-382.

Beletsky, V.V. 1984. *Biped walking.* Moscow: Nauka Publishers (in Russian).

Bernstein, N.A. 1935. *Study of biodynamics of locomotion.* Moscow: VIEM (in Russian).

Blickhan, R., and R.J. Full. 1992. Mechanical work in terrestrial locomotion. In *Biomechanics—Structures and Systems: a practical approach,* ed. A.A. Biewener, 75-95. New York: IRL Press.

Cavagna, G.A. 1975. Force platforms as ergometers. *Journal of Applied Physiology* 39: 174-179.

Cavagna, G.A., F.P. Saibene, and R. Margaria. 1963. External work in walking. *Journal of Applied Physiology* 18: 1-9.

Cavagna, G.A., F.P. Saibene, and R. Margaria. 1964. Mechanical work in running. *Journal of Applied Physiology* 19: 249-256.

deKoning, J., and G.J. van Ingen Schenau. 1994. On the estimation of mechanical power in endurance sports. *Sport Science Review* 3: 34-54.

deLooze, M.P., J.B.J. Bussmann, I. Kingma, and H.M. Toussaint. 1992. Different methods to estimate total power and its components during lifting. *Journal of Biomechanics* 25: 1089-1095.

Elftman, H. 1939. Forces and energy changes in the leg during walking. *American Journal of Physiology* 125: 339- 356.

Fenn, W.O. 1930. Work against gravity and work due to velocity changes in running. *American Journal of Physiology* 93: 433-462.

Gregor, R.J., and T.A. Abelew. 1994. Tendon force measurements in musculoskeletal biomechanics. *Sport Science Review* 3: 8-33.

Komi, P.V. 1990. Relevance of in vivo force measurements to human biomechanics. *Journal of Biomechanics,* 23 (Suppl.1): 23-34.

Pandy, M.G., and F.E. Zajac. 1991. Optimal muscular coordination strategies for jumping. *Journal of Biomechanics* 24: 1-10.

Pierrynowski, M., D. Winter, and R. Norman. 1980. Transfer of mechanical energy within the total body and mechanical efficiency during treadmill walking. *Ergonomics* 23: 147-156.

Prilutsky, B.I. 1990. *Eccentric muscle activity in human locomotion.* Ph.D. diss., Latvian Research Institute of Traumatology and Orthopaedics, Riga (in Russian).

Prilutsky (Prilutskii), B.I., and V.M. Zatsiorsky (Zatsiorskii). 1992. Quantitative estimation of the "tendon action" of two-joint muscles. *Biophysics* 36: 154-156.

Prilutsky (Prilutskii), B.I., V.M. Zatsiorsky (Zatsiorskii), and L.N. Petrova. 1991. Mechanical energy expenditure on the movement of man and the anthropomorphic mechanism. *Biophysics* 37: 1001-1005.

Prilutsky, B.I., and V.M. Zatsiorsky. 1992. Mechanical energy expenditure and efficiency of walking and running. *Human Physiology* 18: 118-127.

Prilutsky, B.I., and V.M. Zatsiorsky. 1994. Tendon action of two-joint muscle: transfer of mechanical energy between joints during jumping, landing, and running. *Journal of Biomechanics* 27: 25-34.

Thys, H., P.A. Willems, and P. Saels. 1996. Energy cost, mechanical work and muscular efficiency in swing-through gait with elbow crutches. *Journal of Biomechanics* 29: 1473-1482.

vanIngen Shenau, G.J., 1989. From rotation to translation: constraints on multijoint movements and the unique action of biarticular muscles. *Human Movement Science* 8: 301-337.

vanIngen Shenau, G.J., and P.R. Cavanagh. 1990. Power equations in endurance sports. *Journal of Biomechanics* 23: 865-881.

vanIngen Shenau, G.J., W.W.L.M. van Woensel, P.J.M. Boots, R.W. Snackers, and G. de Groot. 1990. Determination and interpretation of mechanical power in human movement: application to ergometer cycling. *European Journal of Applied Physiology* 61: 11-19.

Weber E., and W. Weber. 1836. *Mechanik der Mensclichen Gehwerkzeuge: Eine anatomisch physiologische Untersuchung.* Gottingen.

Wells, R.P. 1988. Mechanical energy costs of human movement: an approach to evaluating the transfer possibilities of two-joint muscles. *Journal of Biomechanics* 21: 955-964.

Whiting, W.C., R.J. Gregor, R.R. Roy, and V.R. Edgerton. 1984. A technique for estimating mechanical work of individual muscles in the cat during treadmill locomotion. *Journal of Biomechanics* 17: 685-694.

Williams, K.R., and P.R. Cavanagh. 1983. A model for the calculation of mechanical power during distance running. *Journal of Biomechanics* 16: 115-128

Winter, D.A. 1978. Calculation and interpretation of mechanical energy of movement. *Exercise Sport Science Reviews* 6: 183-201.

Winter, D.A. 1979. A new definition of mechanical work done in human movement. *Journal of Applied Physiology* 46: 79-83.

Winter, D.A. 1990. *Biomechanics and motor control of human movement.* 2d ed. New York: Wiley.

Zajac, F.E. 1993. Muscle coordination of movement: a perspective. *Journal of Biomechanics* 26 (Suppl.): 109-124.

Zatsiorsky, V.M. 1986. Mechanical work and energy expenditure in human motion. In *Contemporary problems of biomechanics 3: optimization of biomechanical movements*, ed. I.V. Knets, 14-32. Riga: Zinatne Publishing House. (in Russian).

Zatsiorsky, V.M., and N.A. Iakunin. 1980. Mechanical work and energy during locomotion. *Human Physiology* 6: 579-596 (in Russian).

Zatsiorsky, V.M., S.Yu. Aleshinsky, and N.A. Iakunin. 1982. *Biomechanical basis of endurance.* Moscow. (In Russian, published also in German, 1986).

Zatsiorsky, V.M.and B.I. Prilutsky. 1987. Soft and stiff landing. In Johnson B.(Ed.) *Biomechanics X-B,* ed. B. Johnson, 739-744. Champaign, IL: Human Kinetics.

Zatsiorsky, V.M., and M.A. Latash. 1993. What is a 'joint torque' for joints spanned by multi-articular muscles? *Journal of Applied Biomechanics* 9: 333-336.

Zatsiorsky, V.M., S. Werner, and M.A. Kaimin. 1994. Basic kinematics of walking: step length and step frequency: a review. *Journal of Sports Medicine and Physical Fitness* 34: 109-134.

8

Optimisation in the Learning of Cyclical Actions

Bjørn Almåsbakk

Department of Sport Sciences, NTNU, Trondheim, Norway

H.T.A. Whiting

Department of Sport Sciences, NTNU, Trondheim, Norway and Department of Psychology, University of York, England

Roland van den Tillaar

Department of Sport Sciences, NTNU, Trondheim, Norway

The term "optimisation" appears frequently in the literature on motor behavior, although its definition is seldom made explicit, making the extent of its usage difficult to determine. Some authors, for example, use the related terms "optimal" and "optimum," terms that also lend themselves to differing interpretations. If there is communality across authors, it is the link, either explicit or implicit, that is often made to the concept of adaptation which, in turn, is viewed from a number of different perspectives. One is struck, for example, by the frequent reference to efficiency of energy utilisation as a possible principle underlying the optimisation/adaptation process, although the generality of this position requires considerable qualification. As efficiency, in the context of the learning of cyclical actions, will be the major focus of attention in the latter part of this chapter, it is worth spending some time on the conceptual problems associated with the term "optimisation" before addressing that issue.

Recourse to the English language dictionary is a useful, albeit vague, starting point. To optimise, we are told, is to make optimum! Optimum, usually equated with optimal, refers to the best compromise between opposing tendencies, a recognition that organisms are integrated systems and, as Gould (1980) reminds us, adaptive change in one subsystem can lead to nonadaptive changes in another. Thus, while the functioning of the system as a whole may be optimal, subsystem functioning may well be suboptimal. This standpoint is reflected in dynamical systems approaches to human behavior as operationalized in Levine and Leven's (1995) statement that

> If one's thoughts, feelings, beliefs, concepts, memories, decisions and so on, are viewed as a dynamical system, no two subsystems, even if strongly connected, are likely to have identical states at all times. (p. 206)

These conceptual systems impose constraints on human action, that is, they limit the degrees of freedom. Constraints come in a number of guises—physical, organismic, informational, social, neural, etc. Intentions are not only shaped by such constraints, but the relationship between intention and action is modulated by the priorities assigned to one or other of these categories of constraint at a particular point in time.

Adaptation and Optimisation

Although adaptation, viewed as the evolution of structures to deliver a better performance, has implications for optimisation, the terms should not be looked upon as equivalent. Coveney and Highfield (1995) express this view in the following definition: "Although adaptation produces organisations and interactions that are highly refined, they are invariably still improvable and not truly optimal" (p. 119). Thus, adaptations bring about some of the necessary structural/functional changes that foster the striving towards higher levels of optimisation. In a motor learning context, for example, adaptations indexed by changes to the intrinsic dynamics of the system enable the instantiation of novel movement coordination patterns which, in turn, might lead to more efficient task completion.

The term "intrinsic dynamics" is used by Kelso (1995) to refer to relatively autonomous coordination tendencies that exist before learning something new, i.e., as a descriptor of already existing capacities. Such movement coordination tendencies, when instantiated, can be described in terms of their order parameter(s), i.e., the dimension(s) along which movement pattern changes can be shown to occur. When animals are allowed to move relatively unconstrained (i.e., the system is in control of its own control parameter; see below) their limbs have been shown to adopt particular phase relations to one another. The nature of these phase relations is determined by the speed at which the animal is moving. In this way, a number of different regimes of the gait pattern have been isolated. At an everyday level, if the horse is taken as a paradigm example, these are subjectively perceived as the walk, trot, canter, and gallop actions. In dynamical systems terms, these different regimes of gait are demarcated by different values of the order parameter(s), limb phase relation(s). These values have been shown to change, in a nonlinear fashion when the horse is required to change pace (Hoyt and Taylor 1981). Such temporary switches between different regimes are brought about by the scaling of a control parameter (in this case, change in pace) leading the system through the variety of possible regimes (patterns or states), but does not prescribe or contain the code for the emerging pattern (Kelso 1995). In the case of locomotion, the argument goes that when the animal is required to locomote at speeds beyond those preferred, it becomes more metabolically expensive to maintain the same gait pattern. The animal, in consequence, is forced to change to another regime that is more economical for the newly required speed of locomotion. What is unclear is the extent to which such movement coordination pattern regimes in animals in their natural habitat are genetically determined and what adaptations take place as a consequence of learning. What *is* clear, however, to remain with the example, is that horses in captivity can be trained to exhibit gait patterns that are 'unnatural' (e.g., for competition purposes); that is, adaptations to the intrinsic dynamics can be achieved, but have to be worked for—often over extended periods of time. This may require the imposition of a variety of (physical) constraints on the horse which, at least initially, might lead to economy of energy expenditure being assigned a lower priority by the system. How such priorities might change with extensive practice of the newly acquired coordination pattern is a subject that has received little empirical investigation. There would, presumably, be a shift over time in optimisation priorities with economy of energy competing more strongly for position. This is an issue that the present authors are addressing in the context of the learning of cyclical actions by humans, an issue that will be returned to in the latter part of the chapter.

Action and Reaction

Neither the successive instances of adaptation nor the striving towards optimisation should, necessarily, be seen to be the consequence of reactive processes, an impression sometimes given in the evolutionary concept of adaptation. With respect to human movement it is clear that individuals not only interact with their environment, but also take the initiative to act upon it with all the means at their disposal and, in so doing, they do not necessarily maximise a particular utility function. This synergy was nicely captured in Warburton's (1969) division of Cattell's fourth order (superordinate) personality factor, integration, into the third order factors, adaptation, and thrust. Warburton saw these as contrasting tendencies to conform to environmental demands or to attempt to change them. While the high loading of the second order factor, conservatism, on adaptation might suggest a reactive phenomenon directed towards maintaining the status quo, it has to be recognised that the life process is not only a coming into balance with the environment but also its conquestæan advance towards fulfilment of the developmental and self-preservation program of the genus (Bernstein 1967). This distinction can be exemplified in the field of motor skill acquisition. Either deliberate (thrust) or fortuitous (adaptation) processes, to use Warburton's terms, might bring about changes to extant intrinsic dynamics.

In the first place, it is not uncommon for people to deliberately set about acquiring the capacity to instantiate a particular movement coordination patternædefined by the task constraint conformity to a prescribed sequence of movements. Paradigm examples might be the dancer required to learn a choreographed routine or the high-jumper wishing to learn a novel technique like, for example, the Fosbury Flop. Those presented with such a task can attest to the active involvement and commitment of the learner, often over an extended period of time. The initial priority assigned by the system would, necessarily, be conformity to that task constraint or, in Bernstein's (1967) words to achieve as determinate a formulation and as rapid a stabilisation of the motor structure as possible—a process that is ongoing rather than static:

> ... practice, when properly undertaken, does not consist in repeating the means of solution of a motor problem time after time, but in the process of solving this problem again and again by techniques which are changed and perfected from repetition to repetition ... practice is a particular type of repetition without repetition. (p. 134)

Thus, moving towards an optimal solution is an active, convergent process, a process of *becoming*, which may extend over a considerable period of time. Crossman (1959), for example, in his observations of cigar making showed how, if minimum cycle time is taken as the optimum to be striven for, workers are still showing improvement after three million trials spread over two years of practice.

In the second place it has to be appreciated that modifications to intrinsic dynamics do not necessarily have to be specifically catered for, particularly in the case of young children where discovery learning, a process that is function rather than movement oriented, tends to be the predominant mode. There is likely to be less concern with how an action is carried out than whether it achieves its purposeæto intercept the moving object, to convey food to the mouth, to move the body from A to B, and so on. Nevertheless, in so doing, changes to the child's intrinsic dynamics, as indexed by new movement coordination possibilities, quickly become apparent. Just how rapidly such changes come about is apparent from the observation of babies over the first year of life without, it should be noted, verbal language mediation. It is a form of latent or implicit learning.

The point about both these examples (and the earlier example of the horse being required to learn novel gait patterns) is that while the focus is on the task constraint other constraints may, temporarily, be subordinated. At a later stage these other constraints may well compete for attention. A dancer, for example, required to learn a complex choreographed sequence of actions might initially assign the highest priority to acquiring the procedural skill (i.e., what follows what) and low priority to aesthetic presentation or energy expenditure per se. Once this procedure has been acquired, artistic presentation and/or efficiency in movement production might well be assigned higher priorities and the system expected to adopt appropriate strategies towards that end.

Adaptation and Attunement

This dual perspective on adaptation—active and reactive—indexed by changes to intrinsic dynamics should be kept in mind when distinguishing between adaptation and attunement (Whiting 1984). From a dynamical systems perspective, adaptation would be considered to have taken place when the intrinsic dynamics of the acting subject have been changed. Indices of such changes would be the emergence of a new regime, for example, the 90 degrees in-phase between the fingers (where this was not already within the repertoire of the system) in the coupling of finger oscillators' experiment of Zanone and Kelso (1992). The ability to move the body as a 'buckling' rather than a 'hanging' pendulum in the ski apparatus experiments of Vereijken (1991) is another example.

It is important to stress that such modifications to the intrinsic dynamics not only make it possible to produce the novel coordination pattern towards which training procedures may have been directed, but its effects would be expected to generalise, as any learning theory would predict, to other related patterns. It is the system that is changed and this, in turn, makes possible new solutions to particular classes of motor problem. For years movement scientists have been engaged, with little success, in the enterprise of determining optimal movement patterns for particular classes of event. Given the ubiquity of motor equivalence this has proved to be a difficult venture. There are so many qualifications that would have to be put on such an ideal pattern when consideration is taken of the many constraints that play a role in performance.

Adaptations are, thus, future directed because they are concerned with changes in potential for environmental encounters yet to come. This is particularly well illustrated in the field of rehabilitation. It has been suggested, for example (Latash and Anson 1996), that the often bizarre movement coordination patterns seen in impaired populations should not be considered as abnormal but as adaptive changes brought about by a rearrangement of CNS priorities. They consider such movement patterns, in many cases, to be optimal (presumably in the sense of being the best compromise for that particular individual at that point in time) and that, in terms of intervention, it might be better to adopt a 'hands-off' policy. While there would seem to be considerable merit in the statement, such an interpretation has to be viewed with caution because, as Biryukova et al. (1996) point out, in recovery from CNS lesions (for example, a hemiplegic stroke) the CNS, because of cortical plasticity, is probably permanently evolving. For this reason it makes more sense to talk about the ongoing process of optimisation rather than of achieving the optimum (result).

In contrast, attunement has to do with the here and now, with control rather than coordination. In providing a solution to a motor problem, it implies the online mapping of the physical degrees of freedom of the body onto perceptual degrees of freedom in the external environment. In catching a ball, for example, one is constrained not only by one's intrinsic dynamics, that is, the capacity to instantiate an appropriate catching action, but also by the informational constraints of position, velocity, acceleration, and direction of the approaching ball. The hand has to be in the right place at the right time if a successful outcome is to be brought about. It should be noted that, whatever other constraints may be operating, most of our actions in the real world are constrained by perceptual information of this kind.

Activities of Daily Life

It is perhaps an appreciation of the extent of these adaptation and attunement requirements when new complex skills of this kind are to be acquired that force the researcher, and often the teacher, to focus on one at the expense of the other, for example, to explore the phenomenon of adaptation of intrinsic dynamics in situations in which the attunement requirements are minimised (i.e., the skill is taken out of context). Unfortunately, in activities of daily life such adaptations are required to function in context! It is perhaps not surprising; therefore, that those concerned with influencing human movement at the shop-floor level should express pessimism about the relevance of motor learning and motor control theory for practice. Perhaps this, in itself, accounts for the fact that daily practice often appears to have no clear-cut relationship to theory.

The dilemma alluded to above has recently been expanded upon by the psychologist Gilgen (1995) in examining the way in which scientists deal with complexity. He points out that except when they construct theories or are engaged in explicitly integrative research, scientists generally deal with complexity by restricting the options of subjects and taking out of play things that cannot be controlled via experimental designs. Descriptive statistics are usually preferred because they reduce the inherent complexities of group data via means, standard deviations, or other summarising values and inferential statistics because they provide information about the likelihood that the variables singled out for study had the predicted effect. In summary, complexity is handled by neutralising aspects of it. Unfortunately, for the practitioner, these are aspects that often play a determining role in activities of daily life in the sense that they are assigned higher priorities than the variables on which the researcher chooses to focus attention.

In this respect, it has to be appreciated that motor skills common to everyday life are of a telescoped nature (Whiting 1990). Any skilled performance is part of a larger whole, the event, culture, and society at large. To take an example from the world of sport, the skill of controlling an ice-hockey puck in a game has to be seen in relation to the particular competition, the ice-hockey culture in general and, if it happens to be within the Olympic Games, society at large. Any of these wider contexts may be a constraint on decision making and performance. Or, to take a clinical example, walking is an individual skill that can be defined in terms of biomechanical gait parameters. But it is used as a method of moving around in the environment, often in cluttered environments, in situations where there are cultural norms for such behavior, often under the influence of medication and cognisant of the burden that is being imposed on family and other caretakers. Is it therefore surprising that what the patient chooses to optimise in such situations is different from what the theorist or therapist would like him to optimise? The practitioner is left with the difficult task of determining which constraints in everyday life situations exert a major controlling influence. This is not, of course, a new consideration, it was recognised, and lip service was paid in the earliest days of the development of information-processing approaches to motor learning and control. Welford (1968), as one of the pioneering exponents of an information processing approach to human skill learning and performance (particularly in the context of aging), pointed out as long ago as 1958 the importance of looking not only at overall achievement in a task but also at the manner in which it was attained. Compensatory shifts in the method and manner of performance under adverse conditions or in states of impairment serve to optimise the performance as a whole and to make the best use of capacities and conditions available at the time. In short, Welford is reiterating the point that optimisation criteria change from occasion to occasion.

What is central to these kinds of arguments is that motor behavior in the real world is subject to a wide variety of constraints. If, in developing our theories, or in carrying out research, we artificially control or remove some of these constraints in order to reduce the problem to manageable proportions, we should not be surprised that the information and theories we develop may be more appropriate to the body considered as a biomechanical system rather than as a social organ constrained by other parameters. From the former perspective, optimisation might well focus on minimal energy expenditure as a guiding principle. The potential limitations in this respect, when it comes to ecologically valid situations have, however, to be taken into account. The physical therapist Scholz (1996) recently reminds us for example, that a patient with altered movement patterns may well be able to play the game but does so inefficiently, i.e., using excessive energy. What criteria, one might ask, would determine that in such a case one should try to bring about optimisation in terms of minimal energy usage? What must be optimised in motor learning?

The operational difference made between adaptation and attunement has much in common with Boden's (1984) distinction between the fine tuning of an already adapted system and changing the constraints of the system itself. It is clear that the answer to the question of what must be optimised in motor learning has to be pursued in relation to both concepts. They may or may not be highly correlated and this, in turn, may be determined by the stage of learning reached. Acquiring the capacity to perform a Fosbury Flop, for example, might be seen as an end in itself, where that end is defined in terms of conformity to a prescribed sequence of movements. Continued reproduction of such a movement pattern would lead to its optimisation as indexed by degree of conformity to a prescribed movement pattern and/or efficiency of energy expenditure. On the other hand, the purpose of learning a Fosbury Flop is, generally speaking, to enable greater heights to be jumped. Optimisation in these terms might then be indexed by the successive increases in heights jumped. Eventually, at the peak of performance, it might be expected that there would be a high correlation between an efficient movement pattern defined in terms of smoothness (absence of jerk) and outcome defined in terms of height jumped, but this has yet to be shown.

If we stay with the efficiency question and move from a description of economy to an explanation as to how economy is brought about, the problem becomes more difficult. This difficulty arises because it is not known with any degree of certainty as to what is being controlled by the CNS. The position today would appear to be little further advanced than it was in 1982 when Partridge pointed to the variety of (mechanical) motor control variables that had been postulated over the years. This would appear to be particularly true, as Ito (1982) reminded us, when it comes to questions about how the system is organised towards a superordinate goal above the level of the various parameters each of which may be related only partially to the goal.

Given this state of affairs, it is perhaps not so surprising that opinions about what is being optimised would also be speculative. How does the CNS as a self-organising system determine the 'optimal' solution among the many configurations of possible muscular activation? The difficulty in this respect is apparent if cognisance is taken of Bernstein's (1967) principle of nonunequivocality. This principle originated in his observations of the striking actions of blacksmiths such that only the trajectory of the tip of the hammer remained relatively invariant from occasion to occasion (Latash 1996), while joint trajectories and patterns of muscle activation were poorly reproduced. Bernstein was led to conclude that the motor effect of a central impulse cannot be decided at the centre, but is decided entirely at the periphery. Requin, Semjen, and Bonnet (1984) on the basis of this and other evidence, argued that the concept of optimisation would only make sense if it were possible to specify the variable in relation to which the optimum is to be located. The logical step from there is to propose, as they did, that there is no 'optimal' solution to the control of action, but rather a set of solutions, probably 'equivalent' because of the multiplicity of points of view from which their 'advantages' and 'disadvantages' may be evaluated. More recently, Biryukova et al. (1996) made a similar point. While one might question their adoption of a 'levels' (of control) argument, the implications of adopting such a departure point would be to accept that the neural structures at different levels would be involved in optimisation procedures of their own, directed towards the attainment of a common goal. As examples they suggest attaining equilibrium, reaching an object, avoiding pain, and satisfying a social relation and so on. This leads them to propose two types of adaptation, corresponding to two optimisation processes in two different neural populations. The first would imply acquiring a different motor strategy, the adaptation being understood as the acquisition of an alternative motor plan, while the second would require maintaining the same motor plan while executing the movement with a different coordination pattern.

While there is general agreement in the field of therapy with their standpoint that therapeutic techniques should be directed more to the goal of the action in a functionally related task, such a standpoint begs many questions. In the first place, who defines the goal? Is it the subject or some external agent? Would there, necessarily be agreement between the two? Even if the goal is defined, who sets the priorities that lead to goal attainment, i.e., who determines what is to be optimised? Is there a choice in this respect or is the outcome a dynamic play-off between what Holt (1996) terms task constraints (successfully completing the task), personal constraints (an individual's perception-action capabilities) and optimality constraints (least cost to the system)? In these terms, optimality may be only one of the constraints operating and this may well be overruled if other constraints take preference.

Thus, while biological modes of operation may well be self-organising and evolutionary, there is another side to the coin. Beside its biological nature, in which ergonomic man can be described as a 'skilled animal,' Jones (1967) reminds us that the human being is capable of conscious thought. A human has a personality and may possess other nonmaterial qualities that characterise performance, which defy description in system terms and which are usually left out of calculations. It is this kind of multiperspective that makes one appreciate the difficulties likely to be encountered if one were to attempt to explore the whole gamut of constraints that might affect performance. It is perhaps for this reason that

Zanone and Kelso (1992), in this context, consider learning to be indexed by a relatively permanent change in behavior in the direction of a to-be-learned movement coordination pattern specified by the environment. Learning is conceived as adaptation that, in turn, implies modifications to intrinsic dynamics.

The to-be-learned pattern, as an expression of environmental or task requirements, is defined in terms of extrinsic dynamics or what Zanone and Kelso (1992) refer to as behavioral information (which, they claim, may be environmentally specified or arise from memory), which becomes the attractor for the new coordination behavior. Interesting as this elaboration may be, the limitations in this respect have been signaled by Michaels and Beek (1994). They point out that the concept of behavioral information has no relationship to the informational variables that may be picked up from the various flow fields. In consequence, the resulting models have no bearing on issues of perception and perceptual learning—issues that, it should be noted, are central to the attunement of coordination patterns to task demands.

Rather than being overcritical of the limitations inherent in this approach to learning, it might be seen as a step towards achieving a paradigm shift in explanations of at least some aspect of motor behavior without the need to invoke abstract notions of representation. It might well be that an approach to optimisation from a dynamical systems point of view would be to treat the person as a biomechanical system; after all, their theoretical paradigm derives from concepts rooted in natural physics. Adopting such a perspective would only be detrimental if, in so doing, there was a failure to appreciate fully that only limited explanations of everyday behavior are, by this means, possible (Ingvaldsen and Whiting, 1997). Many other categories of constraint need to be taken into consideration if, ultimately, it should prove possible to explain what Bernstein (1967) referred to as the structural and completeness of motor tasks.

In summary, approaches to optimisation in the context of motor skills, as will be illustrated in what follows, would generally be seen to have been concerned with *adaptation* rather than *attunement,* particularly when the focus has been on efficiency of energy expenditure. Exceptions, which are few and far between, are those that involve learning rather than performance and particularly where such learning requires both adaptation and attunement simultaneously, as in the novel experiments to be described and taking place in the authors' laboratory.

The Concept of Efficiency in Motor Learning

Here the concept of efficiency is examined in the context of adaptation, where adaptation is operationalised as modifications to intrinsic dynamics. Thus, we endorse the statement of Wade and Guan (1996) that performance should be viewed in a physical context and looked at from the point of view of efficiency. This led Wade and Guan to align with Sparrow and Irrizary-Lopez's (1987) work on skill learning, which focused on the evaluation of optimal efficiency in terms of energy usage. This perspective led Sparrow (1996) more recently, in his discussion of cost and effort in relation to motor control and learning, to suggest that it is not unreasonable to propose that movements are modified on the basis of sensory information concerning energy expenditure. This departure point is fine providing that it is recognised, as discussed in detail above, that this is not the only constraint responsible for modification to intrinsic dynamics. While efficiency of energy expenditure might well be reflected in technical merit, it is unlikely that this in itself can determine whether a piano player will become a concert pianist.

Optimisation of Energy Expenditure

Efficiency can be defined as minimal expenditure of time and effort in carrying out a task. Hämäläinen (1978) in his work on optimisation concepts in models of biomechanical systems added the criteria of maximum efficiency and output, minimum effort, time, mechanical work rate and energy expenditure, stability, and combinations of criteria or multiple criteria. On these criteria an optimisation problem or a solution to a problem can be built. Although not suitable for all tasks, oxygen consumption in carrying out a task has been shown to be a reliable measure of total energy expenditure. It takes into account that changes in efficiency depend upon the exploitation of the reactive forces (e.g., muscular tension) within a system, an advanced stage in skill acquisition (Bernstein 1967). Research into optimisation using energy expenditure as a criterion, has focused on two major levels, discussed in the following paragraphs.

Energy Expenditure and Movement Patterning

Research that takes energy expenditure and movement patterning as its dependent variables focuses on the nature of the movement pattern developed when energy expenditure is minimised. Much of the research using these variables has used walking as a paradigm example (Zarrugh, Todd and Ralston, 1974; Minetti and Saibene 1992). Zarrugh et al. (1974) and Minetti et al (1991), for example, showed that, for a given walking speed, humans choose the stride frequency that minimises their oxygen consumption. Warren (1984) also found this to be the case in stair climbing. Their results showed the riser height requiring minimum energy expenditure to be over one quarter of the length of the leg for both short and tall climbers. This finding was taken as evidence of an optimal point in the climber-stair synergy. Unlike simple grade walking, the stairway's dimensions determined stride, so that an optimal gait cannot be freely adopted. Thus, to a great extent, the metabolic efficiency of stair climbing was determined by the fit between the dimensions of stairway and climber. They concluded that an optimal riser height is a consequence of two factors: First, as risers become lower, more step cycles are required to ascend a given distance; hence, total muscle activity and energy expenditure increase. On the other hand, as riser height increases relative to leg length, energy expenditure also increases due to greater flexion at the knee and hip. Consequently, there is greater initial muscle length (Hill 1930; Morrison 1970), greater cocontraction for joint stabilisation (Joseph and Watson 1967; Morrison 1969; Townsend et al. 1978), and higher raising of the lower limbs during the swing phase (Cappozzo and Leo 1974). The combination of these factors yields an optimal ratio riser height/leg length with minimum energy expenditure. In practical terms this means that each and every one of us will experience the energy cost of walking up stairs relative to step height and our leg length.

Energy Expenditure and Coordination Patterning

Here the focus will be on the coordination pattern, and hence, the neuromuscular strategy when energy expenditure is minimised. Broadly, it can be said that changes to the intrinsic dynamics are brought about by adaptive changes to the contractile characteristics of muscles and/or as adaptations within the nervous system, altering the recruitment pattern. The result of a particular coordination pattern can be shown to be a specific kind of movement pattern. In other words, by training, a specific firing sequence of the different nerves (coordination pattern) may be developed; this will manifest itself in a specific movement pattern, for example walking, where the energy expenditure has been minimised. Sparrow and Irrizary-Lopez (1987) and Sparrow and Newell (1994) both came to the conclusion that the preferred coordination pattern was that which minimised energy expenditure. Sparrow and Irrizary-Lopez further concluded that minimisation of energy expenditure, as a principle of organisation governing the coordination and control of normal gait, might be considered a natural consequence of evolutionary adaptation. The problem with this approach is that the coordination patterns talked about were not measured but assumed, and as Zajac and Levine (1979) pointed out, it is not clear what in fact the central nervous system (CNS) is trying to accomplish during locomotion. Their suggestion, however, was that the function of command signals from the CNS may be ". . . to steadily propel an animal while minimising energy consumption and, at the other extreme, to propel an animal as fast as possible while assuming that only a finite energy supply exists" (Zajac and Levine 1979, p. 260).

They concluded that energy consumption could be a variable controlled by specific CNS command signals.

Winters and Seif-Naraghi (1991) tried to explain coordination patterns by using computer simulation of EMG measurements. They assumed that control strategies for a given movement task, especially once practised, would tend towards an optimised (nearly optimal) neural strategy where energy expenditure was minimal. In each case, given certain assumptions about the neuro-input structure that had to be optimised, predictions were made that could then be compared with experimental data. They found optimised neurocontrol strategies in a practised movement task and concluded that if subjects were not satisfied with their performance, they could change their approach to the task at hand (e.g., by changing the relative weights between performance subcriteria), which in turn, via the goal-directed dynamic optimisation process, resulted in a new neuromotor strategy evolving. These better solutions require years of practice, and even then 'perfection' remains elusive, e.g., most professional basketball players still miss about 25% of their free throws despite many thousands of practice attempts—a well-controlled task, and a large margin for error (see any year player performance statistic from the U.S. National Basketball Association).

Minimal Effort

A number of studies have shown that in motor skill acquisition force application patterns become smoother, such that there is less force necessary for the same movement with changes taking place in the intensity and duration of the muscular demand (Hatze 1976; Hobart and Vorro 1974; Kamon and Gormley 1968; Durand et al. 1994). The full scale of energy is not used, meaning that reserve capacity is available to compensate for disturbance. Much of Brener's work has been directed towards providing behavioral data test predictions arising from the principle of least effort (e.g., Brener and Mitchell 1989; Brener, Philips, and Sherwood 1983). This principle, elucidated in a number of papers published in the 1920s and 1930s, is that organisms will tend to expend the least amount of physical energy in the achievement of a goal object (McCulloch 1934). The rider was later added that organisms will choose the least energy demanding of a number of alternative means of attaining a goal. Minimum effort control may also be motivated because it avoids stress or structural damage caused by 'overload' situations (Hämäläinen 1978). This is clearly seen in wildlife, where prey (e.g., antelopes) may jump high into the air when predators are near, thereby avoiding the stress of running from the predator.

Work Rate

It is sometimes possible to choose the operational work rate and environmental conditions of a system so that performance efficiency is maximised. Due to the technical difficulties of measuring free, unconstrained activity, it is often only in the experimental laboratory that such optimum work rates can be found in physiological systems. A typical example is the dependence of the gas exchange efficiency of haemoglobin on blood pH and pCO_2. These optima can then be used as reference information for other control systems so that their performance criteria give operation points that do not make the basic system deviate from its optimum (Margaria 1963). Another example was provided earlier by Hill (1922). He examined the speed of muscular contraction of the biceps and brachialis anterior in male and female subjects and related the duration of contraction to mechanical efficiency in terms of an optimum contraction rate. Sparrow (1983) has referred to this contraction rate as one possible mechanism underlying preferred tempo maintaining that, for a variety of tasks, this tempo is the most efficient in that particular physiological characteristics of muscles become, in this way, optimally organised. The optimal dynamic relation between muscles and muscle groups is likely to be disturbed by changes in tempo around the preferred tempo.

The performance of many physiological systems can be measured by integration of total force and velocity, thus making minimum work rates a valid performance criterion. Otis, Fenn, and Rahn (1950), for example, pointed out that breathing frequencies are chosen according to the criterion of mechanical work minimisation. They demonstrated that, for a given alveolar ventilation, the elastic work tends to be higher at low frequencies due to high tidal volumes while viscous work increases with frequency due to high airflow. Thus, the total mechanical work (the sum of the previous two) shows a minimum at a certain frequency. In normal running, there is also an optimal stride length found at which mechanical power output is minimised (Lin 1980; Wirta and Golbranson 1990). There exist, however, a number of situations where mechanical work rate does not have significance. For example, static muscular work sometimes requires a large effort, although no mechanical work is done. It can clearly be seen in many activities how we strive to avoid inefficient coordination situations. Solutions that come to mind are the use of backpacks or the balancing of a water container on the top of the head.

Minimum Time

If a goal can be defined that can be reached within a minimum time and without bounded controls, one could, according to Hämäläinen (1978), adopt a minimum time criterion. When the goal is changing, as in a learning situation, such a criterion becomes ill-defined (Hämäläinen 1978). An example of research using this criterion is the minimum jerk model proposed by Hogan (1984) and Flash and Hogan (1985). Hoff (1992) has extended this model by allowing the duration of the movement to be a free parameter, because longer movements can always be made smoother than shorter movements. Hoff created a trade-off between duration and smoothness by penalising duration. In optimisation terms this will mean that during optimisation, jerk will be less and the time to perform a task will decrease. The procedure has been to minimise or maximise certain cost functions based on movement kinematics, movement dynamics, energy, or functions related to such notions as 'comfort' and 'effort.' Models such as the minimum jerk model of Flash and Hogan (1985); and Gutman, Gottlieb, and Corcos's (1992) kinematic model have demonstrated an impressive correspondence between the actual movement kinematics and those predicted. This does not mean that the CNS is minimising the function of jerk (but rather that the CNS does not violate the minimum-jerk principle too much) or calculating an exponential function based on a nonlinear 'internal time'; once again, therefore, the actual CNS priorities remain unknown.

Optimal Stability

Stabilisation of performance is evident in all motor learning experiments. When a desired performance has been reached the individual's goal is to stay at that level, even when conditions change. Optimal stability is maintained by minimising deviation of the actual variable values from the path they should follow. With nonmechanical systems this is very difficult, because the reaction is not to one condition but to many. Speed skating is a good example. In high-pressure weather, performance is generally not as good as when barometer pressure is low (van Ingen Schenau 1982). It is difficult, therefore, to talk about stable performance, i.e., optimal stability is very difficult to define because it is dependent on conditions. A stable performance, for example, stride length, is a generally accepted strategy to economise movement in terms of energy cost. In speed skating this is often apparent over longer distances, where athletes strive to keep a steady pace. As weather conditions seldom remain stable, every race represents a new search for the most efficient pace, with the consequence that the level of performance is changed.

Combined Optimisation Criteria

Combinations of the above mentioned criteria often have to be included in describing biomechanical systems whose performance is directed towards maximising efficiency at minimal cost. Which one of these two factors dominates the solution depends on the parameter values. If time was the most important efficiency criterion, maximal efficiency would dominate. Some researchers have used a combination of the minimum energy expenditure criterion with one or two of the other optimisation criteria like maximal efficiency, minimum work rate, and minimal effort. This is not unreasonable because they are closely related. For example, maximum efficiency can be calculated as the ratio of total mechanical work rate divided by net energy expenditure at different step frequencies in running on a motor-driven pacemaker (Kaneko Matsumtoto, and Fuchimoto 1987). Sparrow (1983) noticed that a range of "cyclical" tasks must be considered in order to demonstrate that an individual has an optimum rate of performance maximising efficiency in relation to the amount of work done and energy expended. In biomechanics, work rate and energy expenditure has the same SI unit, as shown in the definition of power: Power is the rate at which work is done or energy is expended (Watt). The only difference between the two is that work rate is calculated from the integral of force by velocity and energy expenditure from oxygen uptake over time (van Ingen Schenau and Touissaint 1994). In a physiological sense energy expenditure is defined as the caloric cost of an activity derived from indices such as oxygen consumption, heart rate, or respiratory rate, whereas "efficiency" refers to the relative energy required to perform a given amount of mechanical work (Sparrow 1983).

Other research has held the work rate constant, or limited, while determining the efficiency, thereby allowing the performer to use the energy supply optimally. As Sparrow (1983) indicated in his early review of efficiency and skill, competitive cyclists keep their pedal rate fairly constant by changing gear in order to accommodate changes in the gradient of the terrain (Sloane 1980). Sparrow's review also cited a study by Baz (1979), who compared the efficiency of swim fins to an "underwater bicycle," and demonstrated that the greater mechanical efficiency of the underwater bicycle allows the scuba diver to travel further with the same oxygen supply. Brener and Mitchell (1989) found support for the principle of least effort in operant training work with rats. Their results showed that metabolic energy expenditure and mechanical work per reinforcement in a learning study declined over trials. Overall, the research cited here collectively points to the fact that energy expenditure, efficiency, work rate, and minimal effort are concepts that are closely related to each other. These concepts will be explored in the context of the learning of cyclical actions.

The Learning of Cyclical Actions

Dynamical systems approaches to motor behavior focus on repetitive (cyclical) phenomena and the use of statistics in the time-serial domain.

In order to demonstrate that behavior is guided by a control parameter one has to observe individual behavior under conditions that allow the demonstration of changes between regimes of a particular coordination pattern when driven by an appropriate control parameter. While locomotor tasks have been an obvious choice for demonstrating this phenomenon, in effect, any cyclical action requiring the coupling of oscillators would serve the same purpose. In our own laboratories, for example, the focus has been on the development of coordination using weight lifting and slalom-ski type cyclical actions as paradigm examples.

In the learning of actions of this kind it is accepted, with some qualification, that in the course of movement skill acquisition the amount of energy expended decreases and/or the mechanical output increases. This observation implies that with practice not only may the dynamics of the system be exploited (in energy usage terms), but unless the task constraints are kept constant (Sparrow and Irrizary-Lopez 1987) increasing demands are made on the output, such as the amount of force that needs to be applied. The efficiency of the learner would not then be characterised by decreasing energy expenditure *per se* but by a more efficient use of the extra energy demanded.

The ongoing work on slalom-ski-type cyclical actions, using a laboratory ski training apparatus, continues the paradigm originally developed by den Brinker and van Hekken and elaborated upon by Vereijken and co-workers (for an overview, see Vereijken 1991). In the context of optimisation a recent learning experiment (Almåsbakk et al. 1998a) explored the development of movement coordination from the point of view of the hypothesis of a parallel reduction in overall energy expenditure, relative to the increase in energy expenditure demanded by the inevitable improvements in work output. Durand et al. (1994) had previously tackled this question, but there were a number of methodological problems with their study that needed to be controlled. The problems that presented themselves were difficulties in measuring the actual work done and their use of oxygen uptake as a measurement of energy expenditure when subjects were making movements with maximum effort. Under such conditions oxygen uptake may not be a precise indicator of the demand for energetic resources, because of the obvious risk that subjects are working above their anaerobic threshold. Finally, their use of an index—the ratio of oxygen uptake to the product of the amplitude and frequency—to quantify efficiency is at the best questionable, because they did not know either the amount of work done or whether they had, in fact, measured the total energy expenditure.

The task employed in the Durand et al. study (1994) as well as in the experiments carried out in our own laboratory involved learning to make cyclical, slalom-like, ski movements on a ski apparatus as shown in figure 8.1. A novel development for the purposes of our own study was the

Figure 8.1   The ski apparatus.

mounting of the ski apparatus on a force platform, which allowed online direct measurement of force thereby negating the problems of the measurement of actual work done. Development of coordination was indexed by changes in the timing of forcing (phase lag between the position of the subjects centre of mass and the position of the platform, vis-à-vis the centre of the apparatus). This can be looked upon as a measure of the extent to which the two systems (the operator and the apparatus) become attuned, while online measurement of oxygen consumption was used as an index of energy expenditure and, by inference, changes to the intrinsic dynamics of the operator. Six female volunteers served as subjects, two being experienced alpine skiers. The training period was 14 days, during which the subjects took part in nine training sessions, measurements being taken on sessions 1, 3, 5, 7, 9 and the post-test. This experiment not only addressed the concept of increased efficiency in a given task, but also addressed it while allowing the subjects to increase their work output, a natural consequence of improved skill. This was made possible by exploiting the fact that during exercise carried out aerobically there is a close linear relationship between the work done and the oxygen uptake. The best-fitting straight line for each stage in the skill development could then be found by using the method of least squares, and the oxygen uptake could then be estimated from any given workload within the measured range. By then implementing a standard workload, it was possible to examine how the efficiency of energy expenditure developed across sessions. Results indicated that the oxygen cost of movement decreased as exemplified in figure 8.2, which provides data for, in this case, the 250W-workload condition.

It is important to note that efficiency was still improving at the stage at which the experiment terminated. This finding provides experimental support for Sparrow's (1983) hypothesis that energy expenditure will continue to improve even after performance reaches a plateau. Performance was measured, in this case, by the amplitude and the frequency of platform movement. This increased efficiency was paralleled by

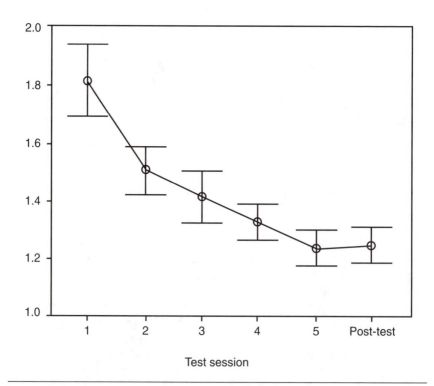

Figure 8.2   The development of energy expenditure at a workload of 250W. Values are mean +SE (N=6).

changes in phase lag between the position of the operating subject's centre of mass and the position of the platform vis-à-vis the centre of the apparatus, i.e., in the attunement of the subject to the subject-apparatus system. This phase lag, an order parameter, was deemed by Vereijken, Whiting, and Beek (1992) to reflect the timing of forcing of the platform. It is clear, however, that while the phase lag had reached a performance plateau, efficiency was still improving. This interesting finding was followed up in another study (Almåsbakk, Whiting, and van den Tillaar 1998) where the same methods were applied, but the number of sessions was increased to 19. Preliminary results, as can be seen in figure 8.3, show that even in a prolonged period of training, where the subjects by all apparent performance criteria have become experts, efficiency continues to improve while performance levels are maintained.

Further support for this phenomenon is provided in the study by Almåsbakk et al. (1998) in which two of the subjects (subjects 1 and 3) were highly skilled alpine skiers. The skilled skiers showed similar improvements in efficiency to the unskilled subjects. But over the period of training only relatively small changes in their phase lag variable were

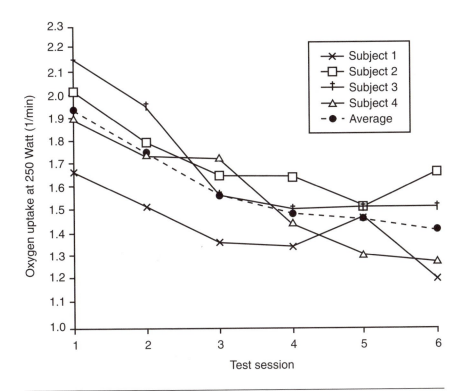

Figure 8.3   The development of energy expenditure at a workload of 250W, for a prolonged study (preliminary data). Values are mean +SE (N=6).

found, making it apparent that some transfer in terms of efficiency of energy expenditure can be made from previous training of a related, but different, skill (see figure 8.4). The possibility that this transfer is more in terms of attunement than adaptation or that there might be a positive effect of the one upon the other is currently being pursued in the context of a more precisely structured transfer paradigm.

The above improvements in efficiency shown during the experimental trials might, from a dynamical systems perspective, reflect changes to the intrinsic dynamics manifested in new movement coordination patterns. Vereijken (1991), for example, suggested three regimes in a pendulum model of the movements of the subject when operating this apparatus; an inverted pendulum, a hanging pendulum, and a buckling pendulum (figure 8.5). While she was able to identify all three regimes at various stages of learning on the apparatus, she was not able to demonstrate (as a dynamical systems interpretation might predict) nonlinear shifts between these regimes by the same subject when a suitable control parameter is scaled. Thus, attempts to operationalise changes to subject intrinsic dynamics in terms of changes in behavior patterning remain speculative.

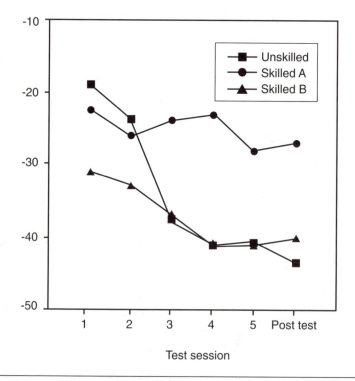

Figure 8.4   The development of phase lag. Skilled alpine skiers compared to the average values of the other subjects.

Figure 8.5   The pendulum model.

In one of our ongoing experiments (Almåsbakk et al. 1998) subjects have, however, shown marked individual differences in the way in which the phase lag changed with practice. Given that these changes in phase lag reflect the way in which subjects exploit the dynamics of the system (Vereijken Whiting, and Beck 1992) it is clear that this can be done with a number of different movement coordination patterns. Figure 8.6 presents various combinations of rotational and translatory forces that reflect subtle forms of the buckling pendulum model. It is by an elaboration of analyses of this kind that we hope, in the future, to be more explicit about changes to intrinsic dynamics in the context of optimisation of energy expenditure and how this relates to progress in attunement to task demands.

Conclusion

In conclusion it can be said that economy of energy expenditure seems to stand out from the host of optimisation concepts applicable to a biomechanical system. Not only is it directly measurable, but there is a consensus among researchers that it is a prime optimisation candidate in the establishment of motor coordination patterns. While it is possible to restrict the term motor learning to adaptation so defined, the Fosbury Flop technique was presented earlier as a paradigm example; such patterns can also be learned in the context of motor problems to which they provide a solution. In the case of the Fosbury Flop the motor problem was to jump over a prescribed height. In such cases the learner, to be successful, is confronted, simultaneously, with considerable adaptation and attunement requirements. The extent to which one acts as a constraint on the other (in either a positive or negative way) is an interesting question with which teachers of motor skills have always been confronted. A variety of pragmatic solutions to this problem have been presented.

The ski apparatus with which the second part of this chapter has been very much concerned is particularly interesting in this respect, as the adaptation and attunement requirements are difficult to separate. It seems likely that the attunement requirements (the changing phase relation

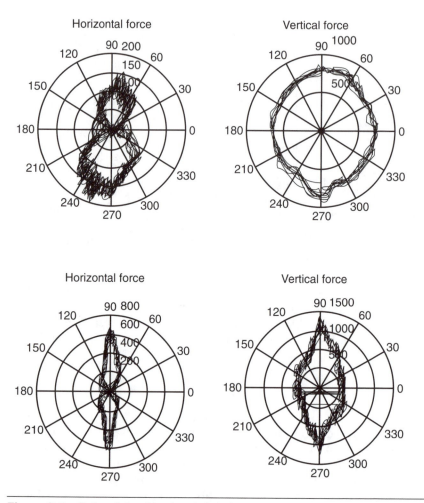

Figure 8.6 Polar plots of horizontal and vertical force at the beginning (top) and at the end (bottom) of the learning period.

between subject and apparatus) demand and drive changes to the intrinsic dynamics, which allow the necessary modified coordination patterns to be instantiated. Such changes are indexed by the horizontal and vertical force phase plane portraits presented and the efficiency of energy expenditure measures, although the direction of any causal relation between the two remains speculative.

References

Almåsbakk B., H.T.A. Whiting, and J. Helgerud. 1998a. The efficient learner. *Under Review*

Almåsbakk, B., Whiting, H.T.A. and R. van den Tillaar 1998b. The improving expert (work title). *In Preparation*

Baz, A. 1979. Optimisation of man's energy during underwater paddle propulsion. *Ergonomics* 22: 1105-1114.

Bernstein, N.A. 1967. *The coordination and regulation of movements.* Oxford: Pergamon.

Biryukova, E.V., A.A. Frolov, Y. Burnod, and A. Roby-Brami. 1996. Evaluation of central commands: toward a theoretical basis for rehabilitation. *Behavioral and Brain Sciences* 19: 69-71.

Boden, M.A. 1984. Failure is not the spur. In *Adaptive control in ill-defined system*, eds. O.G. Selfridge, E.L. Rissland, and M.A. Arbib. New York: Plenum.

Brener, J., and S. Mitchell. 1989. Changes in energy expenditure and work during response acquisition in rats. *Journal of Experimental Psychology: Animal Behavior Processes* 15: 166-175.

Brener, J., K. Philips, and A. Sherwood. 1983. Energy expenditure during response-dependent and response-independent food delivery in rats. *Psycholophysiology* 20: 384-392.

Cappozzo, A., and T. Leo, eds. 1974. *Biomechanics of walking up stairs. On theory and practice of robots and manipulators. Proceeding of the first CISM-IFToMM symposium.* Vol. I. New York: Udine/Springer-Verlag.

Coveney, P., and R. Highfield. 1995. *Frontiers of complexity: the search for order in a chaotic world.* New York: Faber and Faber.

Crossman, E.R.F.W. 1959. A theory of the acquisition of speed-skill. *Ergonomics* 2: 153-166.

Durand, M., V. Geoffroi, A. Varray, and C. Prefaut. 1994. Study of the energy correlated in the learning of a complex self-paced cyclical skill. *Human Movement Science* 13: 785-799.

Flash, T., and N. Hogan. 1985. The coordination of arm movements: an experimentally confirmed mathematical model. *Journal of Neuorscience* 5: 1688-1703.

Gilgen, A.R. 1995. Prefatory comments. In *Chaos theory in Psychology*, eds, F.D. Abraham and A.R. Gilgen. London: Praeger

Gould, S.J. 1980. *The panda's thumb.* New York: Norton.

Gutman, S.R., G.L. Gottlieb, and D.M. Corcos. 1992. Exponential model of a reaching movement trajectory with non-linear time. *Comments in Theoretical Biology* 2: 357-384.

Hämäläinen, R.P. 1978. Optimisation concepts in models of physiological systems. *Progress in Cybernetics & Systems Research* 3: 539-553.

Hatze, H. 1976. Biomechanical aspects of a successful motion optimisation. In *Biomechanics V-B*, ed. P.V. Komi, 5-12. Baltimore: Universtity Park Press.

Hill, A.V. 1922. The maximum work and mechanical efficiency of human muscles and their most economical speed. *Journal of Physiology* 56: 19-41.

Hill, A.V. 1930. The heat production in isometric and isotonic twitches. *Proceedings of the Royal Society of London. Series B* 107: 115-131.

Hobart, D.J., and J.R. Vorro. 1974. Electromyographic analysis of intermittent modifications during the acquisition of a novel throwing task. In *Biomechanics IV*, eds. R.C. Nelson and C.M. Morehouse, 559-566. Baltimore: University Park Press.

Hoff, B.R. 1992. A computational description of the organization of human reaching and prehension (Computer Science Tech. Rep. No. USC-CS-92-523). Los Angeles: University of Southern California.

Hogan, N. 1984. An organising principle for a class of voluntary movements. *Journal of Neuroscience* 4: 2745-2754.

Holt, K.G. 1996. "Constraint" versus "choice" in preferred movement patterns. *Behavioral and Brain Sciences* 19: 76-77

Hoyt, D.T. and C.R. Taylor. 1981. Gait and the energetics of locomotion in horses. *Nature* 292: 239-240.

Ingvaldsen, R.P., and H.T.A. Whiting. 1997. Modern views on motor skill learning are not 'representative'! *Human Movement Science* 1: 705-732.

Ito, M. 1982. The CNS as a multivariable control system. *Behavioral and Brain Sciences* 5: 552-553.

Jones, J.C. 1967. The designing of man-machine systems. In *The human operator in complex systems,* eds. W.D. Singleton, R.S. Easterby, and D.C. Whitfield. London: Taylor and Francis.

Joseph, J., and R. Watson. 1967. Telemetering electromyography of muscles used in walking up and down stairs. *Journal of Joint and Bone Surgery* 49B: 774-780.

Kamon, E., and J. Gormley. 1968. Muscular activity pattern for skilled performance and during learning of a horizontal bar exercise. *Ergonomics* 11: 345-357.

Kaneko, M., M. Matsumtoto, A. Ito, and T. Fuchimoto. 1987. Optimum step frequency in constant speed running. In *Biomechanics X-B*, ed. B. Johnson, 803-807. Champaign, IL: Human Kinetics.

Kelso, J.A. 1995. *Dynamic patterns: the self-organisation of brain and behavior.* London: MIT Press.

Latash, M.L. 1996. *The Berstein problem: how does the central nervous system make its choices?* Mahwah, New Jersey: Lawrence Erlbaum.

Latash, M.L., and J.G. Anson. 1996. Movements in atypical populations. *Behavioral and Brain Sciences* 19: 5-68.

Levine, D.S., and S.J. Leven. 1995. Of mice and networks: connectionist dynamics of intention versus action. In *Chaos theory in psychology*, eds. F.D. Abraham and A.R. Gilgen. London: Praeger.

Lin, D.C. 1980. *Optimal movement patterns of the lower extremity in running.* Ph.D. diss., University of Illinois at Urbana-Champaign.

Margaria, R.A. 1963. Mathematical treatment of the blood dissociation curve for oxygen. *Clinical Chemistry* 9: 745-762.

McCulloch, T.L. 1934. Performance preferentials of the white rat in force-resisting and spatial dimensions. *Journal of Comparative Psychology* 18: 85-111.

Michaels, C., and P. Beek. 1994. *The state of ecological psychology.* Third European Workshop on Ecological Psychology. Marseille.

Minetti, A.E., and F. Saibene. 1992. Mechanical work rate minimization and freely chosen stride frequency of human walking: a mathematical model. *Journal of Experimental Biology* 170: 19-34.

Morrison, J.B. 1969. Function of the knee joint in various activities. *Biomedical Engineering* 4: 573-580.

Morrison, J.B. 1970. The mechanics of muscle function in locomotion. *Journal of Biomechanics* 3: 431-451.

Otis, A.B., W.O. Fenn, and H. Rahn. 1950. Mechanics of breathing in man. *Journal of Applied Physiology* 2: 592-607.

Partridge, L.D. 1982. How was movement controlled before Newton? *Behavioral and Brain Sciences* 19: 85-86.

Requin, J., A. Semjen, and M. Bonnet. 1984. Bernstein's purposeful brain. In *Human motor actions: Bernstein reassessed,* ed. H.T.A. Whiting. Amsterdam: North-Holland.

Scholz, J.P. 1996. How functional are atypical motor patterns? *Behavioral and Brain Sciences* 19: 85-86.

Sloane, E.A. 1980. *The all new complete book of bicycling*. New York: Simon and Shuster.

Sparrow, W.A. 1983. The efficiency of a skilled performance. *Journal of Motor Behavior* 15: 237-261.

Sparrow, W.A. 1996. What is the appropriate criterion for therapeutic intervention in the motor domain? *Behavioral and Brain Sciences,* 19: 86.

Sparrow, W.A., and V.M. Irrizary-Lopez. 1987. Mechanical efficiency and metabolic cost as measures of learning a novel gross motor task. *Journal of Motor Behavior* 19: 240-264.

Sparrow, W.A., and K.M. Newell. 1994. Energy expenditure and motor performance relationships in human learning a motor task. *Psychophysiology* 31: 338-346.

Townsend, M.A., S.P. Lainhart, R. Shaivi, and J. Caylor. 1978. Variability and biomechanics of synergy patterns of some lower-limb muscles during ascending and descending stairs and level walking. *Medical and Biological Engineering and Computing* 16: 681-688.

van Ingen Schenau, G.J. 1982. The influence of air friction in speed skating. *Journal of Biomechanics* 15: 449-458.

van Ingen Schenau, G.J. and H. Touissaint. 1994. *Klassieke mechanica toegepast op het bewegen van de mens.* Amsterdam: Vrije Universiteit (in Dutch).

Vereijken, B. 1991. *The dynamics of skill acquisition*. Ph.D. diss., Free University, Amsterdam.

Vereijken, B., H.T.A. Whiting, and W.J. Beek. 1992. Phase lag as an order para meter in the learning of a complex skill. *Quarterly Journal of Experimental Psychology* 45A: 323-344.

Wade, M.G., and J. Guan. 1996. Anthropomorphizing the CNS: is it what or who you know? *Behavioral and Brain Sciences* 19: 90-91.

Warburton, F.W. 1969. The structure of personality factors. Unpublished paper. Department of Education, University of Manchester.

Warren, W.H., Jr. 1984. Perceiving affordances: visual guidance of stair climbing. *Journal of Experimental Psychology: Human Perception and Performance* 10: 683-703.

Welford, A.T. 1968. *Fundamentals of skill*. London: Methuen.

Whiting, H.T.A. 1984. The concepts of adaptation and attunement in skill learning. In *Adaptive control in ill-defined system*, eds. O.G. Selfridge, E.L. Rissland, and M.A. Arbib. New York: Plenum.

Whiting, H.T.A. 1990. Decision-making in sport. In *Sport Psychology*, eds. F.C. Bakker, H.T.A. Whiting, and H. van der Brug. Alphen aan den Rijn: Samson.

Winters, J.M., and A.H. Seif-Naraghi. 1991. Strategies for goal-directed fast movements are by products of satisfying performance criteria. *Behavioral and Brain Sciences* 14: 357-359.

Wirta, R.W., and F.L. Golbranson. 1990. The effect of velocity and SF/FL ratio on external work and gait movement waveforms. *Journal of Rehabilitation Research and Development* 27: 221-228.

Zajac, F.E., and W.S. Levine. 1979. Novel experimental and theoretical approaches to study the neural control of locomotion and jumping. In *Posture and movement*, eds. R.E. Talbot, and D.R. Humphrey, 259-279. New York: Raven Press.

Zanone, P.G., and J.A.S. Kelso. 1992. The evolution of behavior attractors with learning: Nonequilibrium phase transitions. *Journal of Experimental Psychology: Human Perception and Performance* 18: 403-421.

Zarrugh, M. Y., F.N. Todd, and H.J. Ralston. 1974. Optimisation of energy expenditure during level walking. *European Journal of Applied Physiology* 33: 293-306.

Dynamic and Thermodynamic Constraints and the Metabolic Cost of Locomotion

Kenneth G. Holt

Applied Kinesiology Program, Sargent College of Allied Health Professions, Department of Physical Therapy, Boston University; and Center for the Ecological Study of Perception and Action, University of Connecticut, United States

Sergio T. Fonseca

Applied Kinesiology Program, Sargent College of Allied Health Professions, Department of Physical Therapy, Boston University; and Departamento de Fisioterapia e Terapia Ocupacional, Universidade Federal de Minas Gerais, Brazil

John P. Obusek

Army Medical Specialist Corps, U.S. Army

"The secret of coordination lies not in wasting superfluous force in extinguishing reactive phenomena but, on the contrary, in employing the latter in such a way as to employ active muscle forces only in the capacity of complementary forces. In this case the same movement (in the final analysis) demands less expenditure of active force." (Bernstein 1967, p. 109)

Human motor skills are often accompanied by the perception of ease that accompanies the action when performed well. The most powerful and accurate shots in tennis are not accompanied by a feeling of great effort as one might expect. A personal best marathon is often not so much indexed by a feeling of exhaustion as by one of exhilaration. The seeming paradox is potentially explained if the notion of optimality of performance is invoked (Wilke 1977). The hallmarks of skilled performance include minimal metabolic cost; the most effective use of muscular and reactive forces; or being pain free, or well balanced or, some combination resulting in efficient (or 'proficient'—see chapter 3 movement. We, among others, have argued that optimality criteria may drive the organization of the motor system insofar as they limit the number of observed coordinations of joints and segments to those that have lower 'costs' associated with them. From this point of view, skill learning is a matter of becoming sensitive to, and meeting, the relevant criteria for a particular skill (Holt, Hamill, and Andres, 1991; Holt et al. 1995).

While many well-learned actions demonstrate a number of optimality criteria, the actual mechanisms by which optimality is achieved is poorly understood. For example, walking at the preferred speed, cadence, and stride length is characterised by a minimal metabolic cost, maximal stability of the head, and least shock transfer from the foot to the head (Holt et al. 1995; Ratcliffe and Holt 1997). Furthermore, the preferred frequency of that gait pattern is predictable from an oscillatory model of the leg and soft tissues. One important question to ask is whether the optimality criteria drive the system's mechanical (oscillatory) behavior, or whether the laws that apply to oscillatory processes cause the emergence of optimal behaviors. It is difficult to differentiate cause and effect. Yet solutions are critical if one wishes to improve performance in an athlete or elicit the greatest function from an impaired individual. In this chapter, we seek to come to some resolutions to these issues using a dynamical systems perspective originated by Bernstein (1969) and developed in some detail in the early 1980s (Kugler, Kelso, and Turvey 1980; Kelso et al. 1981). In particular, insights from our research in the dynamics of locomotion will be used to argue that minimal metabolic cost, maximal stability, and maximal shock absorption are both causes for, and consequences of, the human operating under certain biomechanical, thermodynamical, and physical constraints. Furthermore, we wish to demonstrate that those constraints are due to the type of task, the action capabilities of the individual performing the task, the environment in which the task is performed, and the interrelationships between them.

The concept of constraints that are due to the rhythmical nature of human movements is central to the dynamical systems approach. The emphasis of much of the research in this domain has been to show that coordination arises from physical laws that cause the system to self-organize in very specific ways. The dynamical systems approach developed as an alternative account to computer metaphor "motor programming" accounts in which it is difficult to avoid the idea that control and organization of the motor system is due to a programmer (in generic terms, a homunculus) that oversees the control and coordination of movements (cf. Turvey et al. 1978). The dynamic approach also evolved as a way to account for the emergence of only certain preferred coordinations in the light of a multiplicity of potential solutions to a movement problem (the degrees of freedom problem) and to account for the influence of the interaction of the biological system with its environmental context (the context-conditioned variability problem).

Oscillatory dynamics, in particular, are at the core of the dynamical systems approach to understanding the control and coordination of movement pioneered by Turvey and his colleagues at the University of Connecticut, and Kelso and colleagues at Florida Atlantic University. The major experimental emphasis of their work in the last 10 years or so has been to try to understand the abstract mathematical nonlinear dynamic constraints governing the behavior of *coupled* oscillators (for reviews, see Kelso 1995; Amazeen Amazeen, and Turvey 1998). For example, when an individual is asked to swing two hand-held pendulums of different masses and lengths at the same frequency, one will tend to lag behind the other. The lag can be predicted using a term in the mathematical formula that accounts for differences in the natural frequencies of the two limb-pendulums. Further expansion of the terms in the formula can account for lags that are due to handedness, and when individuals are asked to swing their hands at different frequency multiples (2:1 for example). It is noteworthy that the expansion of the formula is a purely mathematical manipulation that does not depend on the physical properties of the objects or limbs being manipulated. The experimental approach similarly makes no attempt to include metabolic influences on movement patterns.

There are, however, two other aspects of the earlier work of Turvey's group that we have pursued in the Physical Therapy Department at Boston University. One deals with the types of real physical oscillators and oscillatory behavior that determine parameters of locomotion such as walking speed, frequency, and stride length; and their relationships to metabolic and other biomechanical parameters. By real oscillators we are referring to models of forced pendulums and springs that have instantiations in real properties of musculoskeletal tissues. Our research program has also included investigations of impaired populations, most often children with spastic cerebral palsy. This has given us some insights as to how constraints on the dynamic action capabilities of the individual influence the parameters of the oscillators, the extent to which optimality constraints are modified, and the emergent gait patterns. The other aspect of Kugler and Turvey's work that we have pursued is to extend the idea that humans are themodynamic engines, periodically drawing energy from a continuously available chemical/metabolic source for a mechanical purpose such as locomotion. Thermodynamic laws are used to understand the flows of energy from which movement patterns arise, and may give greater insights into lawful relationships between metabolic, mechanical parameters, and movement patterns. In this chapter we will pay particular attention to the relationships between the dynamical and the physiological constraints on movement control and coordination.

An Oscillatory Model of Locomotion

Observation of walking suggests a pendulum type of motion in which two types of pendulum are operative. During the swing phase, the legs look like ordinary pendulums, in which the mass of the leg oscillates around the hip axis of rotation. During stance, the body mass oscillates over the the fixed foot around the ankle axis suggesting an inverted pendulum. Energy is interconverted from kinetic to potential as the body or leg mass first picksup potential energy as the mass is raised. Potential energy is then lost and picked up as kinetic energy. On each cycle, the push-off leg serves a forcing function to help push the body mass over the ankle axis as the body loses energy to frictional losses within the body and ground contacts. Small amounts of energy may also be stored and released in the soft tissues due to their elastic capabilities. In running or hopping, there is still conservation of energy through pendular mechanisms, but more energy is interconverted between kinetic and elastic sources. For this reason the body is often described as a bouncing ball or spring (Cavagna 1997; Farley et al. 1991). As in walking, running requires a forcing function to overcome frictional losses. In both walking and running, therefore, energy is conserved through pendulum and elastic mechanisms, and forcing is required. Whereas walking is mostly pendular, running is mostly elastic. A simple model of locomotion is therefore hybrid in nature, whereby energy is conserved through both mechanisms; and lost energy is replaced through the forcing produced by concentric muscle actions.

The natural frequency of a hybrid pendulum and spring depends on the gravitational pull on the mass (of the leg in an ordinary pendulum, and the body mass in an inverted pendulum), and the global stiffness of the leg or body spring. The natural frequency refers to the frequency at which the pendulum will swing unless forced into some other frequency. The natural frequency proves to be an important determinant of preferred stride frequency in both human and animal gaits.

The natural frequency of the hybrid model of the swing leg is given by:

$$\tau = 2\pi \, (mL_e^2 / (mL_e g + kb^2))^{1/2} \qquad (9.1)$$

where, τ is the resonant period (1/frequency), mL_e^2 is the moment of inertia of the leg, $mL_e g$ is the restoring moment due to gravity, and kb^2 is the restoring moment due to stretch on soft tissues, in which k is the global stiffness of the system, and b is the perpendicular distance of the global spring from the axis of rotation (figure 9.1).

Since $mL_e g$ and kb^2 have a common dimensionality (ML^2T^{-2}), one can be expressed in terms of the other (Turvey et al. 1988). For example, an equality in the two conservative moments (Kugler and Turvey 1987)

$$kb^2 = mL_e g \qquad (9.2)$$

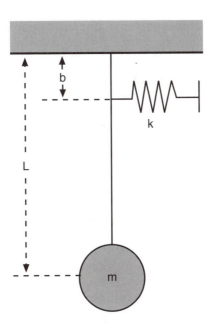

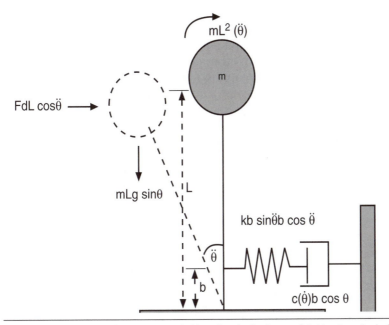

Figure 9.1 Schematic representation (top). Ordinary frictionless hybrid pendulum and spring model (bottom). Inverted damped pendulum and spring with escapement. See text for details.

allows for substitution so that equation 9.1 can be written as:

$$\tau = 2\,\pi\,(L_e / 2g)^{1/2} \qquad\qquad (9.3)$$

The natural period calculated from the simple pendulum equivalent of leg length, and the gravitational multiple successfully predicts the preferred periods at preferred walking speed of quadrupeds (Kugler and Turvey 1987), human adults (Holt, Hamill, and Andres 1990, 1991; Holt et al. 1995), and children (Holt, Jeng, and Fetters 1991). There is a simple organizing physical principle (resonance) that determines gait frequency regardless of taxa or the numbers of limbs.

Natural Frequency, Optimality, and the Oscillatory Model

If humans are cued to walk at different stride frequencies (SF), using a metronome and stride lengths (SL) for the same preferred speed, metabolic costs rise (figure 9.2). This is explained by the fact that when operating at its natural frequency a minimal driving force is required to maintain the amplitude, in this case, stride length of a hybrid system. Driving a system at its natural frequency is often referred to the resonant frequency. Since driving force is supplied by active muscle contractions which in turn have an associated metabolic demand, metabolic energy expenditure is minimized at resonance. The force produced by the muscles is similar to an escapement in a grandfather clock, in which force is supplied periodically by the spring, is dependent on the position of the pendulum, and does not influence the pendulum frequency. In the same way, in walking and running force is generated for a short period during the push-off phase of the gait cycle, is dependent on the phase of the limb, and does not move the pendulum from its natural frequency. In the Bernsteinian perspective (1967), the force would serve to replace only damping (frictional) losses, and would complement the natural frequency of the pendulum and spring. The finding that equation 9.3 predicts the preferred walking frequency of many species suggests that resonance is a common organizing principle and that minimization of metabolic energy expenditure is a (fortuitous) consequence.

As locomotor speed is increased from the preferred, stride frequency and stride length also increase, as does metabolic cost. At first glance these findings suggest that the individual is no longer operating at the natural frequency, since the resonance equation 9.3 can no longer predict the new frequency. For example, in order to predict preferred running frequency, the constant under the root becomes 5 (Holt, Slavin, and Hamill, 1990; Kugler and Turvey 1987):

$$\tau = 2\pi\,(L_e / 5g)^{1/2}$$

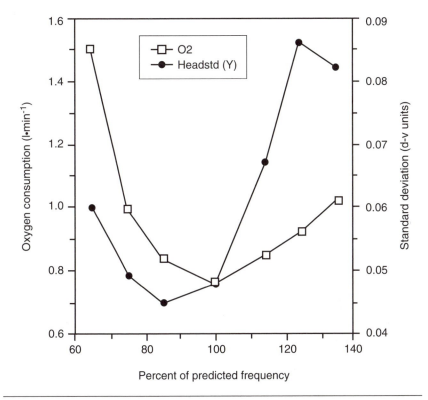

Figure 9.2   Metabolic cost and variability of head trajectory in adults as a function of the walking frequency at a fixed treadmill speed. Predicted frequency is calculated from equation 9.3 in text. Skewed curves suggest that the optimal frequency is constrained by both variables (Holt et al. 1995).

From *Journal of Motor Behavior* 27 (2): 164-178. Reprinted with Permission of the Helen Dwight Reid Educational Foundation. Published By Heldref Publications, 1319 18th St. N.W. Washington, D.C. 20036-1802. Copyright 1996.

However, as speed increases, there is still a minimal metabolic cost at the preferred stride frequency compared to other frequencies and stride lengths (Zarrugh and Radcliffe 1978; also see figure 9.3 for running). These findings suggest that if the modeling is correct, there may be multiple natural frequencies in locomotion constraining the preferred SF-SL combinations and providing a minimal cost for any particular speed. The question arises as to how natural frequency and hence resonance might be achieved as locomotor speed changes.

According to the model (equation 9.1), the resonant frequency is dependent on the inertial characteristics of the leg (mL_e^2), the gravitational effect $mL_e g$, and the tissue stiffness kb^2. In physical pendulums these values are time invariant and there can only be one natural frequency. However in a biological system, while inertial characteristics and gravitational effect are fixed, stiffness can potentially be varied to effect a

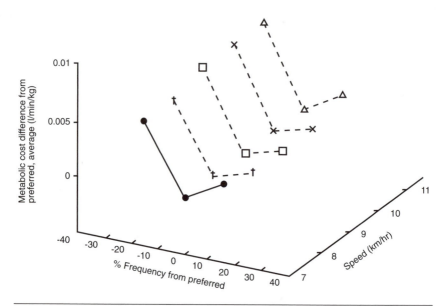

Figure 9.3   Metabolic cost ($\dot{V}O_2$) of running at different speeds under pre-ferred SF-SL conditions and at $\dot{+}25\%$ of preferred SF for each speed. Mini-mal cost is always in the preferred condition.

change in natural frequency. In walking, increased stiffness may be brought about voluntarily by co-contraction of antagonistic muscles, or by isometric contraction against gravity (for example, in foot strike). Several models and experimental results in the motor control literature suggest that the stiffness may be manipulated in upper extremity move-ments either by directly increasing muscle stiffness or by changing rest-ing lengths of antagonist muscle groups (for review see Latash 1993). In the biomechanics literature changes in running and hopping frequency are produced by changes in lower extremity stiffness (Farley et al. 1991; Farley, Glasheen, and McMahon, 1993). Our own data show a linear in-crease in stiffness (kb^2)as a function of loads added to a swinging limb (Obusek, Holt, and Rosenstein, 1995), and as walking speed is increased (figure 9.4). Thus, evidence suggests that stiffness may be manipulated in order to bring about increases in walking speed while maintaining a natural frequency. Figure 9.4 shows that individuals increase stiffness in a linear fashion with increases in speed. The fact that frequency increases linearly with increasing speed is predicted from the equations of motion for the hybrid model and, therefore, again provides a common organiz-ing principle for changes in frequency (and stride length) with increased speed founded in oscillatory dynamics (Obusek 1995).

In addition to minimizing metabolic energy expenditure at any speed, there are other advantages to operating at or close to the natural fre-

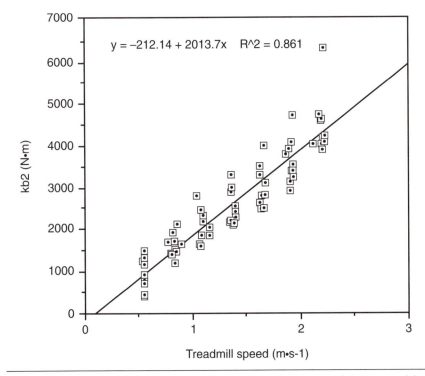

Figure 9.4 Regression of stiffness against walking speed (measured by treadmill speed) across all subjects. Regressions for group and individuals are all significant.

quency. In walking, energy is added twice per stride as the gastrocnemius-soleus concentrically contracts to plantar flex the foot and push the center of mass forward and over the support foot. Compare this to pushing a child on a playground swing. In order to push someone effectively with as little effort as possible, you must insert the push at the right time during the cycle. Specifically, the push occurs when the kinetic energy is at a minimum and in the direction that the swing will pick up velocity under gravitational effects. The push also has to occur at the same frequency as the person's mass and the length of the swing dictate. In other words, for the optimally timed push, force is in phase with the velocity, and the system is maintained at its natural frequency. To push at any other time would require a lot more force over a longer period, and require you to change the direction of the swing. In effect, this would not only be metabolically costly to you as the pusher, but the swing would become unstable and the directional change would cause abrupt changes in velocity. A system that is pushed at its natural frequency at the appropriate time in the cycle is more stable and is less subject to shock (figures 9.2 and 9.5).

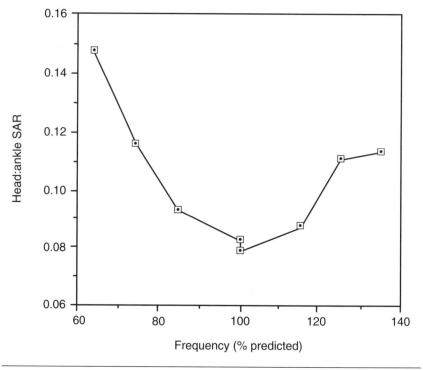

Figure 9.5   Shock absorption expressed as a function of the proportion of shock reaching the head relative to that experienced in the ankle (Shock Acceleration Ratio [SAR]). Smaller values indicate greater shock absorption.

The Problem With Resonance as the Overriding Constraint on SL-SF

So far data support the claim that maintaining a natural frequency is an important constraint on the adopted frequency and stride length for any speed. Unfortunately, the story becomes more complex. If stiffness is an adjustable parameter, it should hypothetically be possible to set up different natural frequencies not only for any speed, but also for any SL-SF condition within a speed. Our data suggest, and the escapement model requires, that the system is forced at its natural frequency not only in preferred conditions, but also in forced SL-SF conditions for any speed (figure 9.6). Essentially, as locomotors we are always at resonance regardless of speed, frequency, or stride length. In light of these findings, the argument that resonance constrains SL-SF and that minimal metabolic costs fall out as a fortuitous consequence is incorrect. However, the fact that there is a unique dynamic constraint that is common to

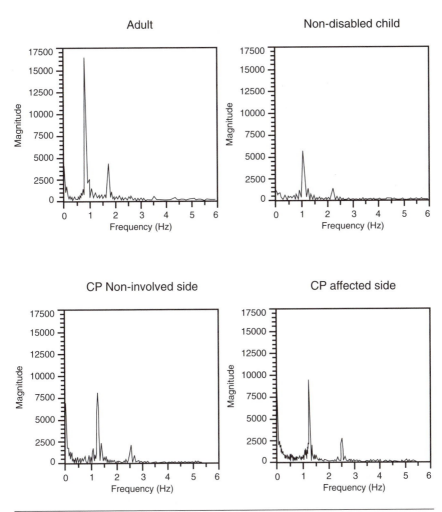

Figure 9.6 Power at the stride (large peak) and step frequencies (small peak). Combined stride and step power for the group accounted for approximately 95% of the total power.

individuals at their preferred and increasing speed still suggests that there is a common physical organizing principle in operation.

The predominence of the particular resonance (where $kb^2 = mLg$) adopted by nonimpaired animals and humans is further brought into question by two other findings. Suh Fang Jeng, a physical therapist and faculty member at National Taiwan University, has shown that some individuals suffering from upper motor neuron lesions do not walk at the frequency predicted by equation 9.3. The preferred overground walking frequency of children with spastic hemiplegic cerebral palsy is predicted by a mean constant of 2.43 under the root, as opposed to a constant of 2 for nonimpaired adults, children, and quadrupeds (Jeng et al. 1996). According to the model (equations 9.2 and 9.3) the unique 1:1 ratio of stiffness to gravitational torque is increased to 1.43:1, representing an almost 50% increase in stiffness. This suggests that the organizing principle $kb^2 = mLg$ for preferred walking only holds for individuals with normal tissue and musculoskeletal mechanics. We will return to the case of disordered locomotion in cerebral palsy later.

Another problem with resonance is its limited ability to predict preferred parameters of walking other than stride frequency. Preferred speed of walking is about 1.3 ms-1 (Turvey et al. 1996), but there is nothing within the equation of motion for the hybrid model (equation 9.1) that specifies from which any value for speed is derivable. However, a plot of metabolic cost per unit distance against speed shows a minimal cost at about 1.3 ms-1 (Turvey et al. 1996). Taken together these findings suggest that metabolic cost must be accounted for in preferred locomotor parameters.

An *Inverted* Hybrid (Pendulum and Spring) Model of Locomotion

If resonance does not drive the preferred stride length and frequency, does the requirement for maintaining a minimal metabolic cost constrain an individual to adopt a particular SL-SF pattern? One answer to the question may lie in recent research in which we have further developed the hybrid model with a number of modifications. The earlier model (figure 9.1a, equation 9.1) was a model of the swing leg and assumed that the leg swings without friction. We now expand the model to include the muscle forcing term and the frictional (damping) losses that forcing overcomes. We have also inverted the model, so that it represents the motion of the center of mass (rather than the swing leg) acting over the ankle-foot axis (figure 9.1b). The full equation of motion of the inverted pendulum and spring is

$$mL^2 \, (\theta \ddot{Y}) = F_d L\cos\theta + mL \, g \sin\theta + kb \sin\theta b \cos\theta + c \, (\theta \dot{Y})b\cos\theta \quad (9.4)$$

where $mL^2 \, (\theta \ddot{Y})$ is the net moment of the center of mass, $F_d L\cos\theta$ is the driving moment produced by active muscle contraction, $mL \, g \sin\theta$ is the moment produced by gravity on the center of mass, $kb\sin\theta b\cos\theta$ is the moment produced by stretch on soft tissues, and $c(\theta \dot{Y})b\cos\theta$ is the moment produced by viscous properties of soft tissues and energy absorption in the opposite limb during foot contact and weight acceptance (in which c represents a damping term). Since the model is one in which force is produced like the escapement in a clock, oscillations occur only at the natural frequency. In this oscillatory state muscle force overcomes damping and influences only the amplitude (as measured by stride length), and if damping is small the stiffness influences only frequency. By assuming that damping is a velocity-related constant, it is possible to tease out the proportional contribution of each of the factors (muscle force, stiffness, gravity) that contribute to the continued oscillations of the hybrid system. Analysis of this data with respect to the physiological cost of walking reveals that there is a unique SL-SF relationship that minimizes costs (figure 9.7). The data in figure 9.7 also show that forcing by changing stride length is metabolically more costly than stiffening. Two predictions can be made from the model with respect to metabolic cost. First, there will be a unique forcing-stiffness (SL-SF) relationship that produces a minimal metabolic cost. Not surprisingly, the preferred SL-SF at any speed is at the bottom of the metabolic potential well. Second, in the forced walking experiment, it would be predicted that driving the system in the long stride length, low-frequency conditions would be metabolically more costly than in the short stride length, high-frequency conditions for a particular speed. A skewed curve with higher metabolic values at the long SL-low SF is predicted and observed (Holt, Hamill, and Andres 1991; Holt et al. 1995, figure 9.2) such that metabolic cost

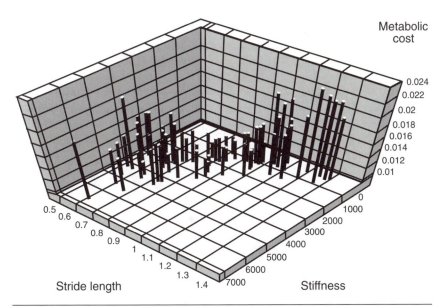

Figure 9.7 Three-dimensional graph of the relationship between metabolic cost per unit distance (ml·min⁻¹·kg⁻¹), stride length (m) given as amplitude and directly related to force, and stiffness (kb²) for all stride frequencies tested. Note that the global minimum in metabolic cost occurs at the preferred stride frequency and steeper rise in metabolic cost due to force versus stiffness (Obusek, 1995).

appears to drive the preferred stride length (muscle force) and stride frequency (soft-tissue stiffness) at any speed.

An important prediction of the model is that in order for the inverted hybrid pendulum to remain oscillating at resonance across changes in speed, the magnitude of the driving moment must be linealy related to the magnitude of stiffness. The experimental data confirm the prediction (figure 9.8) and further support the model. In effect, once a particular dynamic has been assembled, changes in stride length and frequency across changes in speed are lawfully constrained by the steady state requirements of the model.

To summarize so far, the equation of motion of the dynamic locomotor system (equation 9.4) can be satisfied in a number of ways. That is, oscillations of the center of mass can be maintained by many combinations of stiffness and forcing. In terms of the kinematics, there is no dynamic constraint on preferred SL-SF. Nevertheless, humans and animals do have

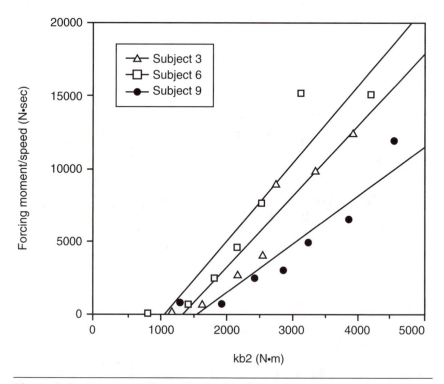

Figure 9.8 Representative sample of individual linear regressions of forcing moment normalized by speed as a function of the elastic component for subject 3 (*forcemoment / speed* = 4.9(kb^2) - 6635, $r^2(1,6)$= 0.92, p< .0006); subject 6 (*forcemoment / speed* = 5.3(kb^2) - 5772, $r^2(1,6)$= 0.89, p< .001); subject 9 (*forcemoment / speed* = 3.3(kb^2) - 5150, $r^2(1,6)$= 0.88, p< .002).

preferred patterns, and those patterns appear to be governed by a common dynamic principle that determines a particular ratio of forcing, stiffness, and the gravitational environment that remains constant between nonimpaired individuals across different speeds of walking. Our interpretation is that the dynamics that give a minimal metabolic cost are discovered in the process of learning, but that once that dynamic has been discovered it can be generalized to different speeds by simple linear scaling of the parameter values according to the constraints of the steady-state equation. Metabolic cost is a determinant of the way in which the dynamics are assembled. Once assembled, the dynamic constraints ensure that the metabolic cost is minimized across changes in task requirements. The finding that stiffness and forcing are not linearly related across speeds also implies a simplified form of control in that they need not be independently controlled.

Development and Disease

The proposed relationships between optimality criteria and oscillatory constraints is both supported by, and provides understanding for, development of gait and the types of gait patterns observed in pathological states. In some ways unimpaired adult gait is stereotypical, normally taking only two forms, walking and running, whose characteristics are similar between individuals. Adults do not walk in knees flexed position (except perhaps for the famous Groucho Marx), and the coordination of the joints is relatively invariant between individuals. Although other patterns are available (e.g., hopping, galloping), they are not usually observed. On the other hand, the gait patterns of children in the early stages of walking are marked by their variability. New walkers appear to explore the dynamics at many different levels. For example, they locomote by galloping, hopping, walking, and running (exploring the coordination or coupling dynamics). They also walk at different speeds and SL-SF relationships, and with different joint angles (exploring the parameters of their hybrid pendulum and spring). Explorations of this kind would lead to discoveries about which patterns are least metabolically costly (fatiguing), produce least shock (hurt less), and are most stable (lead to less falls). While a wide range of movement patterns (and dynamic resources) are available, only those that do not hurt, do not cause falls and/or are not so tiring will be repeated consistently. Repetition will lead to reinforcement of both the neuronal networks and adaptations of the musculoskeletal system that support the pattern (see Edelman 1987; Sporns and Edelman 1993, for similar developmental and evolutionary arguments). Eventually many of the less optimal patterns fall out of the movement repertoire (although they remain available) leaving a limited number of preferred adult patterns.

Intuitively, it seems reasonable to assume that because the genetic makeup that produces the musculoskeletal system of individuals is similar within a species, the optimal patterns that are discovered will be similar. According to the dynamic approach we are proposing, any differences in gait patterns between individuals should be based on some lawful understanding of the differences in dynamic parameters (of the model) that contribute to the gait cycle. Thus, we have shown that segment lengths and body mass parameters influence SL-SF relationships in ways that are predictable according to the laws governing the behaviors of a hybrid pendulum and spring. Length and mass parameters directly influence the gravitational effect in the model. The capability to forcefully contract and stiffen muscle respectively influence the forcing and elastic parameters in the model. These parameters in turn will influence the SL-SF relationships. Given this basic premise it should, in principle, be possible to understand gait patterns that arise by virtue of changes in the dynamic resources (ability to force and stiffen) available to an individual. Cerebral palsy is an excellent model of a pathology that illustrates the importance of dynamic resources as a constraint on the SL-SF relationships. The model also gives insights on adaptations that result in coordination patterns that make the gait look 'abnormal,' but are nevertheless optimal in terms of metabolic cost and stability.

The Case of Spastic Cerebral Palsy

Cerebral Palsy (CP) is an upper motor neuron lesion that results in significant changes in neuromuscular functioning, tissue morphology, and movement patterns. The overall dynamic effect of these changes is to increase soft tissue stiffness and to decrease the ability to produce sufficient muscle power and timing of muscle power production in a movement cycle. Increases in the mechanical stiffness of the muscle-tendon unit occur as a function of a hyperactive stretch reflex and connective tissue infiltration into muscle (Tardieu et al. 1982.; Dietz, Quintern, and Berger 1981; Katz and Rymer 1989). The latter causes a change in the mechanical properties of the muscle-tendon unit and as a result there is increased resistance to passive stretch on the muscle without an increase in electromyographical (EMG) activity (Dietz and Berger 1983). Stiffness is also increased by hypertonicity and co-contraction of muscle (Berbrayer and Ashby 1990; Brouwer and Ashby 1991; Myklebust 1990). It is interesting to note that increases in stiffness in the foot plantar flexors along with the plantar flexed foot (Berger, Quintern, and Dietz 1982) produce a potential spring and lever mechanism similar to that in the foot and ankle of animals, such as the kangaroo, that use elastic energy during the locomotory cycle. The decreased ability to produce concentric muscle power during the gait cycle (Olney, MacPhail, and Hedden 1990) results from atrophy of type I and II fibers and a reduced number of motor units.

There are also a number of kinematic effects of the upper motor neuron lesion on the gait pattern of children with cerebral palsy. While the mean preferred overground walking speed of 7- to 12-year-old children with mild spastic hemiplegia is the same (1.3 ms-1) as in their nonimpaired peers, they walk at a higher frequency and with a shorter stride length (Jeng et al. 1996). There is longer stance phase, decreased swing phase, increased vertical displacement of the body, and greater within subjects variability in these parameters (Strotzky 1983). The walking gait in cerebral palsy has also been likened to running. Cerebral palsy gait is characterized by a lack of energy exchanges between PE and KE (Olney, Costigan, and Hedden 1987), by in-phase flexion of the hip, knee, and ankle (Bruin et al. 1982; Gage 1990; Strotzky 1983; Leonard, Hirschfeld, and Fossberg 1991), and by increased vertical displacement of the center of mass (Strotzky 1983). These factors are indicative of a gait pattern that more characterizes running than walking.

Despite the differences in kinetic and kinematic profiles of children with spastic hemiplegic cerebral palsy during locomotion, the preferred gait patterns of CP result in a minimal metabolic cost, although two to three times higher than the nonimpaired peers (Jeng et al. 1996). Many also demonstrate greatest head stability and least interjoint variabilty in the preferred pattern. Nevertheless, as noted earlier, the predictive equation 9.3 underpredicts the preferred frequency of children with mild spastic hemiplegic CP. We hypothesized that the preferred locomotor pattern reflects the ways in which children with cerebral palsy can utilize the dynamic action capabilities that are available to them. Weakness and poor timing of muscle action in walking suggests that they may be unable to apply enough force at the right time during the gait cycle. In normal walking gait about two-thirds of the propulsive power is supplied by the gastrocnemius-soleus muscle group during the push-off phase. If the power is not available, but the child is still able to locomote, the question arises as to how this may be achieved. It is the case that a number of the other features of CP gait are potential adaptations that would lead to an increase in elastic energy storage and return. Increased co-contraction and isometric contraction against gravity (hypertonicity), a plantar flexed foot, mass-flexion patterns, and increases in elastic tissue in the muscle-tendon complex are all potential sources for increasing stiffness and allowing the child to use elastic energy return in order to maintain oscillations.

A number of predictions about the gait patterns of children with a greater contribution of elastic energy contribution and less muscle force can be made using equation 9.4. First, it would be expected that locomotion would show an increase in stride frequency (reflecting increased stiffness) and a decrease in stride length (reflecting decreased concentric muscle action). As noted earlier, this finding was supported in our data (Jeng et al. 1996). Increases in stiffness on the involved side of hemiplegic CP compared to the noninvolved side, and between CP and non-impaired peers would also be predicted if there was a greater contribution of elastic energy to loco-motion. This prediction was met using estimates of stiffness derived from the model (figure 9.9) and independent of the model using Hooke's Law to derive estimates of vertical stiffness (figure 9.10). The running-like gait pattern observed in CP gait is also indicative of a locomotory system that uses a greater elastic energy contribution.

The nonaffected side is marked by an increase in the angular displace-ment of the center of mass, accompanied by an increase stride length compared to the affected side, and to the nonimpaired peers (figure 9.11). Our preliminary interpretation of this data is that the children push the

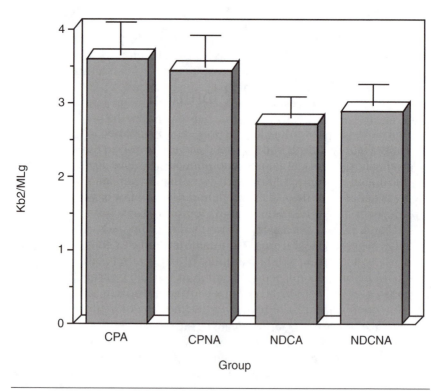

Figure 9.9 Stiffness to gravitational inertia during walking in children with CP and nonimpaired peers. CP shows greater ratios in both the affected and nonaffected legs (CPA, CPNA) compared to nonimpaired (nonimpaired, cor-responding to the affected leg of the matched child; NDCA, and correspond-ing to the nonaffected leg; NDCNA).

Vertical stiffness

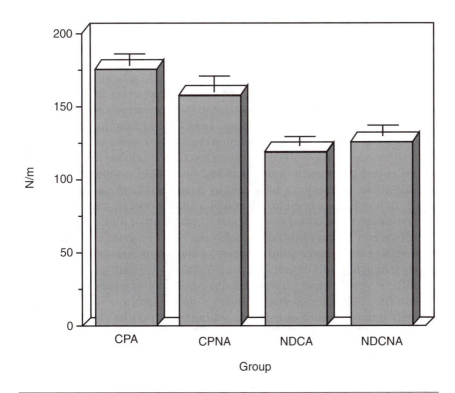

Figure 9.10 Vertical stiffness during weight acceptance during walking. The affected leg shows greater stiffness than the nonaffected leg in CP. The CP group is also stiffer in the nonaffected leg than the nondisabled group (see figure 9.9 for abbreviations).

center of mass (CM) forward with as much force as possible and drop it onto the stiff affected leg to 'load' the spring. The affected leg spring, in turn, generates elastic energy that is returned to the center of mass (figure 9.12). This interpretation is supported by the mechanical energy data that shows large forward kinetic energy of the nonaffected side, with only small transfers into potential energy on the affected side (figure 9.13), indicating that the energy is transferred into nonobservable energetic forms (i.e., elastic).

Thus, the asymmetric gait patterns observed in hemiplegic CP are reflections of adaptations that ensure the continued oscillations of the center of mass. Essentially, the force production is left to the nonaffected side, because the affected side, being unable to produce active force makes adaptations that allow it to store and return in elastic form the energy that is generated by the nonaffected side. In the case of diplegic

Angular displacement

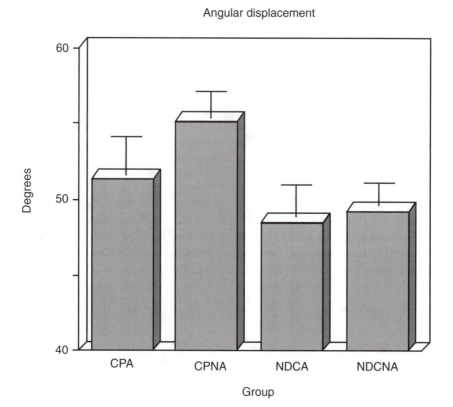

Figure 9.11   Angular displacement of the center of mass during walking. Nonaffected side shows greater angular displacement than the affected side (see figure 9.9 for abbreviations).

CP, it is reasonable to argue that the ability to generate and conserve enough energy to satisfy the equation of motion for the hybrid oscillator may be one boundary condition that determines whether or not bipedal gait is a viable prospect.

In terms of development, we suggest that children with CP are exploring the relationships between task, the environment in which they are required to operate, and their own dynamic action capabilities just as their nonimpaired counterparts. The differences in the gait pattern solutions that appear between the nonimpaired and the impaired are driven by differences in the underlying dynamic resources available. Nevertheless, the optimality constraints in the task of locomotion are the same regardless of the resources brought to the action, namely to minimize metabolic costs and maintain stability.

In summary, cerebral palsy gait illustrates how coordination patterns emerge from the individual performing in a metabolically optimal manner within the constraints imposed by his or her own dynamic action

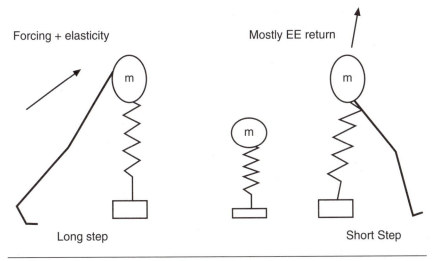

Forcing + elasticity

Mostly EE return

m

m

m

Long step

Short Step

Figure 9.12 Illustration of the gait pattern of child with CP. Left caption shows long step on nonaffected leg (nonspring leg) with energy generated through forcing and elastic functions. Middle caption shows elastic compression of affected leg. and return of mostly elastic energy for the next cycle (right caption).

capabilities. A deep understanding of these constraints can be gained by investigating the dynamic requirements of maintaining oscillations of a hybrid pendulum and spring model of the locomoting body.

Thermodynamics in the Control of Stride Frequency and Stride Length

The branch of dynamical systems theory that deals with the coupling of limbs (synergetics, dynamic pattern theory, coupling dynamics, coordination dynamics) does not incorporate the influence of minimization of metabolic cost or other optimality criteria on preferred action patterns, although reference to these criteria is present in that literature. For example, Kelso (1995), in arguing for a synergetics approach to gait transitions in horses, notes,"Normally horses avoid potentially unstable regions; they select only a discrete set of speeds from the broad range available. In fact, just the ones that minimize energy" (pp. 73-74). Unfortunately, there is no term in the abstract equations of motion for coupled limbs that describe the influence of such criteria. In effect, metabolic cost is left as an unanalyzed residual, and the horse is left to "select" a gait pattern that minimizes cost. Such an explanation invokes the idea of a little man (or horse!) sitting inside the head making choices about what gait patterns to use. One of the philosophical underpinnings

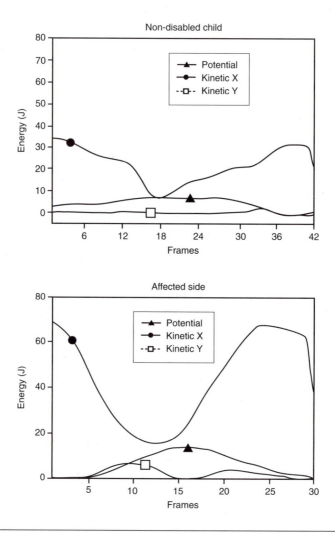

Figure 9.13   Energy profiles for nondisabled (top) and CP affected leg (bottom). Note large forward kinetic energy (kinetic X) at heel strike in CP with rapid energy loss that is not reflected in energy gain in vertical (kinetic Y) or potential energy.

of the dynamical systems approach is to avoid this reliance on an unexplained executive intelligence (Turvey, Fitch, and Tuller 1982).

To be consistent with dynamical systems philosophy, a movement pattern performed optimally must emerge from the *lawful* relationships between metabolic processes and the mechanical actions produced. The resonance approach that we have described is one attempt to understand these relationships. A second approach that we are currently exploring in gait analysis is thermodynamics, a branch of physics that explicitly addresses energy flows between thermal (metabolic) processes and mechanical actions (Turvey et al. 1996). Thermodynamic laws may hold the key to understanding the lawful relationships between these two frames of reference and the emergent coordinated movements.

To begin, let us return briefly to the forced hybrid pendulum and further refine the model. During the gait stride cycle, the gastrocnemius-soleus muscles inject force (energy) into the pendulum twice (once for each leg). The energy is injected during the push-off phase only, and in our modeling we have assumed it occurs only during plantar flexion of the foot while it is on the ground. The mechanism can be likened to pushing a person on a swing or like the phase-dependent release of energy from the spring of a grandfather clock into the pendulum swing. The energy in a clock comes from a wound spring. The energy in a locomoting animal comes from muscle contractions E_M (the mechanical motion of sliding protein filaments) that result from the conversion of chemical energy E_{chem} (metabolic breakdown of ATP) in the sarcomeres. However, not all of the muscle energy is converted into the mechanical work (kinetic energy) E_m of locomotion. Some is required to offset thermal losses in the energy conversion cycle $E_{t'}$. The energy is thus partitioned into two components, that which results in mechanical actions that can be observed in the experimental frame (conservative), and that which exists in the internal (chemical-thermal-mechanical) energy cycles (nonconservative). The first law of thermodynamics specifies that the energy bookkeeping is closed over the entire energy exchange $E_{chem} \rightarrow E_M = E_m + E_{t'}$. The second law of thermodynamics ensures that there are no free work cycles, $E_t > 0$. Human locomotion is in this sense open, dissipative, and thermodynamic. Furthermore, in the hybrid model (mechanical) reference frame, energy can be conserved through gravitational and elastic means. It is not surprising therefore that the escapement energy is not rigidly coupled to the mechanical energy measured in locomotion.

Now consider the original findings with respect to metabolic cost and frequency. It has been shown that there is a specific frequency that results in a minimal metabolic cost at any walking speed (Zarrugh and Radcliffe 1978). The problem is now restated in terms of the thermodynamic argument. It is to understand the above finding in light of the thermodynamic laws that govern the energy flows between the internal (metabolic) frame, and those in the external (mechanical) frame. For each new speed of walking the hybrid system has to be reassembled. Specifically, the questions are (1) whether thermodynamic law governs the frequency transformation per increases in speed, and (2) if thermodynamic law constrains the transformations in such a way as to keep metabolic cost to a minimum. To answer these questions we first draw on the concept of an *adiabatic transformation* derived from thermodynamic law. An adiabatic transformation is one in which an invariant ratio exists between two variable quantities as the quantities are increased or decreased. Of particular relevance is the Ehrenfest hypothesis that relates the kinetic energy (E_k) of a body to the frequency (f) with which it moves through an *adiabatic invariant* (H), such that

$$E_k/f = H$$

The Ehrenfest hypothesis was proposed for conservative systems in which changes occur very slowly. The hypothesis was extended by Kugler and Turvey (1987) to nonconservative, nonrate-limited systems. In the nonconservative case the dissipative losses are indexed by a negative intercept on the kinetic energy axis (figure 9.14a). An example of this type of transformation is in the pirouetting ice skater. As the arms are retracted the frequency at which he or she rotates increases linearly with the rotational kinetic energy. The sliding friction of the skates leading to energy loss through heat is dependent on the rate of rotation. Thus, energy losses are time (rate) independent. A critical test of the hypothesis for locomotion is that increases in speed should be accompanied by increases in frequency (f) that are linearly related through increases in kinetic energy (E_k) as indexed by the slope (H), and that there should be a negative intercept on the KE axis (E_i) to represent the losses. Our data on running (Turvey et al. 1996) shows highly significant linearity between changes in kinetic energy and frequency with a negative energy intercept as predicted (figure 9.14b). This finding suggests that frequency changes that accompany speed changes in running are governed by an adiabatic invariant trajectory. The story is not yet complete though. It remains to be shown how the adiabatic trajectory also produces a minimal metabolic cost for the system.

The parameters of a hybrid pendulum and spring are its mass, length, active muscle force, and stiffness of soft tissues. Mass and length are relatively fixed quantities for mature animals, while stiffness (or resting muscle lengths) and forcing can be manipulated. An adiabatic trajectory ensures that the energy losses are time invariant across these different parameterizations of force and stiffness needed for speed changes. It has been argued that the adiabatic trajectory serves a "vegetative" function in that it ensures that once the metabolic bookkeeping is complete (i.e., once the metabolic cost of a particular stride length and frequency has been established) the energetic cost is one of replacing heat losses (a so-called 'inward-looking stability,' Kugler and Turvey 1987). That cost is reflected in the dissipative term (E_i) in figure 9.14a that is constant across locomotor speed. The argument is supported by studies that have consistently shown that the energetic cost *per unit distance* (a function of speed and frequency) is constant across running speeds in humans (e.g., Falls and Humphrey 1976) and variations in animal morphology, physiology, size, and taxa (e.g., Full 1989). Simply put, when an animal (or human) follows an adiabatic trajectory across changes in speed it is ensuring a minimal metabolic cost for that speed.

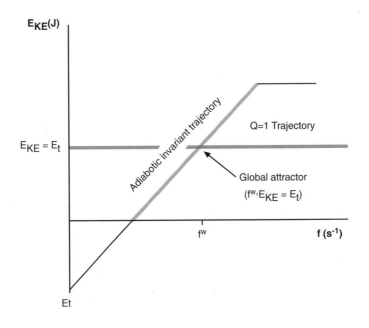

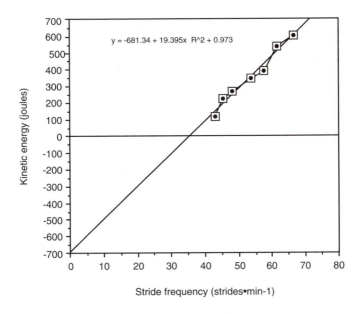

Figure 9.14 Top: Hypothesized relationship between kinetic energy changes (E_{KE}), and frequency of motion according to an adiabatic trajectory. Energy dissipation is denoted by E_t. Bottom: Data for running in healthy adult subjects showing strong adherence to the adiabatic trajectory with anticipated negative intercept.

Stability and Metabolic Cost Revisited

A second thermodynamic constraint is based on the concept of a Q, or quality factor that indexes the thermodynamic processes in a single oscillatory cycle (Kugler and Turvey 1987). The Q-factor is a dimensionless ratio of the mechanical energy produced to the energy lost as heat. In human locomotion this ratio is reflected in changes in kinetic energy at a constant speed divided by changes in the metabolic cost. When $Q > 1$ it implies that the kinetic energy observed is greater than the muscle energy supply to it. This can happen only if the movement takes advantage of the reactive forces available to it. That is, some of the kinetic energy has to be supplied through elastic energy return. In human locomotion, this is achieved by a running-type gait in which much of the energy is conserved through a spring or 'bouncing-ball' type of mechanism (Cavagna, Heglund, and Taylor 1977). This system is open to external perturbations, and is therefore inherently unstable. At the same time it is fundamentally efficient in that the metabolic cost is minimized with respect to speed. When $Q < 1$, less kinetic energy is observed than the muscular energy available for it. Since the energy for locomotion is generated mostly through internal muscular sources and does not need to rely on reactive forces, it is less susceptible to external perturbations. Nevertheless, the movement is inherently more metabolically costly relative to the mechanical actions produced. Such a mechanism would be a hallmark of a walking pattern of gait. At $Q = 1$, there is a balance between the two energy forms. In this case, ". . . energy bookkeeping for both the first and second laws of thermodynamics is closed at the completion of each and every cycle." (Kugler and Turvey, p. 351)

A number of hypotheses were derived from the two constraints, adiabatic invariance and the Q factor. It was shown that the preferred speed of transition from walking to running (about $2ms^{-1}$) can be predicted from the intercept of the adiabatic trajectory and $Q = 1$ at about 2.02 ms^{-1} (figure 9.15). Running occurred at values $Q > 1$, while walking was confined to Q1.

In summary, the thermodynamic approach shows promise as a principled way to relate changes in frequency with changes in speed, the associated minimization of metabolic cost, and the oscillatory dynamics of the body during gait and changes in gait.

Future Directions: Coordination Patterns

Most of the research in dynamical systems has concentrated on the dynamic coupling of limbs, an essential feature of coordination. The emphasis has been placed on mathematical models in which many of the terms of the equations are abstractions that do not have physical

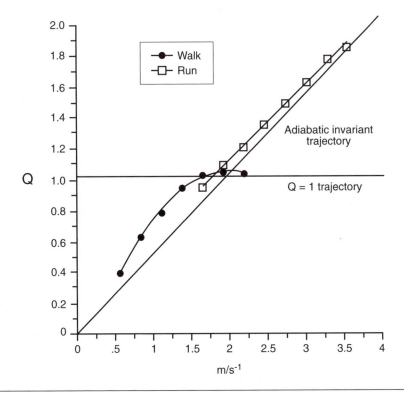

Figure 9.15 Data for adult walking and running showing adherence of the running gait to the adiabatic trajectory, and the tendency for walking to follow both the adiabatic trajectory and Q = 1.

Reprinted, by permission, from *Biological Cybernetics*, "Adiabatic transformability hypothesis of human locomotion," by M.T. Turvey, K.G. Holt, J.P. Obusek, A. Salo, and P.N. Kugler, vol. 74, page 107-115, 1996. Copyright Springer-Verlag.

instantiations. Furthermore, changes in coordination patterns are determined by control parameters that are kinematic rather than dynamic. An example lies in transitions between in- and out-of-phase coordination of the fingers that occur at critical frequencies (a kinematic control parameter).

So far our work has been directed to the emergence of locomotor *parameters* (stride frequency, stride length and speed) that are due to the *dynamic* constraints on the human body operating as a damped pendulum and spring that is driven by a thermodynamic engine. We have also touched briefly on the way in which different locomotor forms (walking and running) might emerge from thermodynamic constraints. In future research we wish to show how those dynamic constraints might result in changes in coordination patterns themselves. In locomotion, we define coordination patterns as those particular phasings of limbs and limb segments that are recognizable as running, or walking.

The hypothesis is that the coordination patterns that arise are determined by the specific values of force, pendular, and elastic energy (of the equation of motion) to the continued oscillations. For example (and as noted earlier), running is characterized by large contribution of elastic energy to the kinetic energy in helping to maintain the oscillations of the center of mass. It is often described as a mass-spring. In walking the action is more pendular depending on its conservation of energy for cycling on the transfer of potential to kinetic energy and vice versa (McMahon 1984). It would be expected that the coordinations that arise would be so assembled as to take full advantage of the two types of energy transfer. Mass-flexion of the foot, knee, and hip, followed by extension of the same would facilitate storage and return of elastic energy. In dynamical systems terms, the motions of the limb segments about a joint would move (closer to) in-phase. In contrast, time delays between the flexion and extension patterns of the joints would facilitate potential-kinetic transfers, and the limb segments would move in a more out-of-phase pattern.

In the more general case, the coordination patterns should correlate highly with the dynamic requirements of the task. An individual discovers the coordination pattern that best facilitates varying contributions from (1) the transfer of muscularly produced force to push the body mass, (2) energy transfers through pendular mechanisms, and (3) elastic energy return. The work on hemiplegic cerebral palsy gait supports these claims. Cerebral palsy gait in some subjects has been shown to have in-phase flexion patterns (Bruin et al. 1982; Gage 1990; Strotzky 1983; Leonard, Hirschfeld, and Forssberg 1991). Our own preliminary data shows that the coordination patterns between the hip, knee, and ankle are more in-phase on the affected side than on the nonaffected side. Along with our other data showing a greater elastic contribution on the affected side, our interpretation is that the asymmetries in coordination patterns between sides are a direct reflection of the differences in dynamic resource availability and use between the two. This approach aligns more appropriately with the original Bernsteinian (as the originator of the dynamical systems approach) thrust that emphasizes the importance of learning coordinations that take full advantage of reactive forces. Referring again to the quotation from Bernstein at the beginning of this chapter, the reactive phenomena to which Bernstein refers, and we interpret as energy conservation for oscillations, have clear repercussions for energetic costs. In taking full advantage of energy-saving mechanisms, metabolic requirements will be diminished. A significant future challenge for understanding the coordination of movement is to determine the optimal biomechanical configuration of the musculoskeletal system that leads to the best transfer of energy, be it through muscular forces, elastic energy return or pendular mechnanisms.

Summary

In this chapter we have emphasized the interdependency of dynamic task requirements, the individual's action capabilities, and the tendency or self-optimize behaviors in locomotion. The following conclusions can be tentatively made:

1. Locomotor parameters arise from constraints due to the dynamic requirements of the task, the individual's dynamic action capabilities, and the environment in which the task is performed.

2. Self-optimization of metabolic cost and stability is both a constraint on and a result of dynamic and thermodynamic laws.

3. Many gait patterns are available to an individual. Learning is the process of discovering the most effective use of the available dynamics to fulfill the task requirements at a minimal metabolic cost and in a most stable fashion.

4. Disordered gait patterns are adaptations that take advantage of the limited dynamic resources available to a functionally impaired individual.

5. It is hypothesized that preferred locomotor coordination patterns arise as solutions to the equations of motion for a force-driven hybrid pendulum and spring model of the human body oscillating in such a way as to take full advantage of available energy transfer mechanisms.

References

Amazeen, P.G., E.L. Amazeen, and M.T. Turvey. 1998. Dynamics of human intersegmental coordination: theory and research (Ch. 11). In *Timing of behavior: neural, psychological, and computational perspectives*, eds. D.A. Rosenbaum, and C.E. Collyer. Cambridge, MA.: MIT Press.

Berbrayer, D., and P. Ashby. 1990 Reciprocal inhibition in cerebral palsy. *Neurology* 40: 538-548.

Berger, W., J. Quintern, and V. Dietz. 1982. Pathophysiology of gait in children with cerebral palsy. *Electroencephalography and Clinical Neurology* 53: 538-548.

Brouwer, B., and P. Ashby. 1991. Altered corticospinal projections to lower limb motoneurons in subjects with cerebral palsy. *Brain* 114: 1395-1407.

Bruin, D.D., P. Eng, J. Russell, J.E. Latter, and J.T.S. Sadler. 1982. Angle-angle diagrams in monitoring and quantifications for children with cerebral palsy. *American Journal of Physical Medicine* 61: 176-192.

Cavagna G.A., N.C. Heglund, and C.R. Taylor. 1977. Mechanical work in terrestrial locomotion: two basic mechanisms for minimizing energy expenditure. *American Journal of Physiology* 233: R243-R261.

Diedrich, F.J., and W.H. Warren. 1995. Why change gaits? Dynamics of the walk-run transition. *Journal of Experimental Psychology: Human Performance and Perception* 21: 183-202.

Dietz, V., and W. Berger. 1983. Normal and impaired regulation of muscle stiffness in gait: a new hypothesis about muscle hypertonia. *Experimental Neurology* 79: 680-687.

Dietz, V., J. Quintern, and W. Berger. 1981. Electrophysiological studies of gait in spasticity and rigidity: evidence that altered mechanical properties of muscle contribute to hypertonia. *Brain* 104: 431-439.

Edelman, G.M. 1987. *Neural Darwinism*. New York: Basic Books.

Falls, H.B. and L.D. Humphrey. 1976. Energy cost of running and walking in young women. *Medicine and Science in Sports and Exercise* 8: 9-13

Farley, C.T., R. Blickhan, J. Saito, and C.R. Taylor. 1991. Hopping frequency in humans: a test of how springs set stride frequency in bouncing gaits. *Journal of Applied Physiology* 71: 2127-2132.

Farley, C.T., J. Glasheen, and T.A. McMahon. 1993. Running Springs: speed and animal size. *Journal of Experimental Biology* 185: 71-86.

Full, R.J. 1989. Mechanics and energetics of terrestrial locomotion: bipeds to polipeds. In *Energy transformations in cells and organisms,* eds. W. Weiser, and E. Gnaiger, 175-182. Theime, NY.

Gage, J. R., D. Fabian, R. Hicks, and S. Tashman. 1984. Pre- and postoperative gait analysis in patients with spastic diplegia: a preliminary report. *Journal of Pediatric Orthopedics* 4: 715-725.

Gage, J.R. 1990. Surgical treatment of knee dysfunction in cerebral palsy. *Clinical Orthopedic Research* 253: 45-54.

Holt, K.G., J. Hamill, and R.O. Andres. 1990. The force-driven harmonic oscillator as a model for human locomotion. *Human Movement Science* 9: 55-68.

Holt, K.G., J. Hamill, and R.O. Andres. 1991. Predicting the minimal energy costs of human walking. *Medicine and Science in Sports and Exercise* 23: 491-498.

Holt, K.G., M.M. Slavin, and J. Hamill. 1990. Running at resonance: is it a learned phenomenon? In *Proceedings of the Canadian Society for Biomechanics,* Quebec: Organizing Committee, CSB.

Holt, K.G., S.F. Jeng, R. Ratcliffe, and J. Hamill. 1995. Energetic cost and stability in preferred human walking. *Journal of Motor Behavior* 27: 164-179.

Holt, K.G., S.F. Jeng, and L. Fetters. 1991. Walking cadence of 9-year olds is predictable as the resonant frequency of a force-driven harmonic oscillator. *Pediatric Exercise Science* 3: 121-128.

Jeng, S.F., K.G. Holt, L. Fetters, and C. Certo. 1996. Self-optimization of walking in non-disabled children and children with spastic hemiplegic cerebral palsy. *Journal of Motor Behavior.* 28, 15-27.

Katz, R.T., and W.Z. Rymer. 1989. Spastic hypertonia: mechanisms and measurement. *Archives Journal of Physical Medicine and Rehabilitation* 70: 144-155.

Kelso, J.A.S., K.G. Holt, P. Rubin, and P.N. Kugler. 1981. Patterns of human interlimb coordination emerge from the properties of non-linear, limit cycle oscillatory processes: theory and data. *Journal of Motor Behavior* 13: 226-261.

Kelso, J.A.S. 1995. *Dynamic patterns: the self-organization of brain and behavior.* Cambridge, MA.: MIT Press.

Kelso, J.A.S., and G.S. Schöner. 1988. Self-organization of coordinative movement patterns. *Human Movement Science* 7: 27-46.

Kugler, P.N., J.A.S. Kelso, and M.T. Turvey. 1980. On the concept of coordinative structures as dissipative structures. 1. Theoretical lines of convergence. In *Tutorials in Motor Behavior*, eds. G. E. Stelmach and J. Requin, 3-47. Amsterdam: North Holland.

Kugler, P.N., and M.T. Turvey. 1987. *Information, natural law, and the self-assembly of rhythmic movement.* New Jersey: Erlbaum.

Latash, M.L. 1993. *Control of Human Movement.* Champaign, IL.: Human Kinetics.

Leonard, C.T., H. Hirschfeld, and H. Forssberg. 1991. The development of independent walking in children with cerebral palsy. *Developmental Medicine and Child Neurology* 33: 567-577.

McMahon, T.A. 1984. *Muscles, reflexes, and locomotion.* Princeton, NJ: Princeton University Press.

Myklebust, B.M. 1990. A review of myotatic reflexes and the development of motor control and gait in infants and children: a special communication. *Physical Therapy* 70: 188-203.

Obusek, J. 1995. *The force-driven hybrid oscillator model in the control of human walking speed and stride frequency.* Ph.D. diss., Boston University.

Obusek, J., K.G. Holt, and R. Rosenstein. 1995. The hybrid mass-spring pendulum model of leg swinging: stiffness in the control of cycle period. *Biological Cybernetics* 73: 139-147.

Olney, S.J., P.A. Costigan, and D.M. Hedden. 1987. Mechanical energy patterns in gait of cerebral palsied children with hemiplegia. *Physical Therapy* 67: 1348-1354.

Olney, S.J., H.A. MacPhail, and D.M. Hedden. 1990. Work and power in hemiplegic cerebral palsy. *Physical Therapy* 70: 431-438.

Ratcliffe, R., and K.G. Holt. 1997. Low frequency shock absorption in human walking. *Gait and Posture.* 5: 93-100.

Sporns, O., and G.M. Edelman. 1993. Solving Bernstein's problem: a proposal for the development of coordinated movement by selection. *Child Development* 64: 960-981.

Strotzky, K. 1983. Gait analysis in cerebral palsied and nonhandicapped children. *Archives of Physical Medicine and Rehabilitation* 64: 291-295.

Turvey, M.T., H.L. Fitch, and B. Tuller. 1982. The Bernstein Perspective: 1. The problems of degrees of freedom and context-conditioned variability. In *Human Motor Control*, J.A.S. Kelso, 239-252. Hillsdale, NJ: Erlbaum.

Turvey, M.T., K.G. Holt, J.P. Obusek, A. Salo, and P.N. Kugler. 1996. Adiabatic transformability hypothesis of human locomotion. *Biological Cybernetics* 74: 107-115.

Turvey, M.T., R.C. Schmidt, L.D. Rosenblum, and P.N. Kugler. 1988. On the time allometry of co-ordinated rhythmic movements. *Journal of Theoretical Biology* 130: 285-325.

Wilke, J.T. 1977. Ulradian biological periodicities in the integration of behavior. *International Journal of Neuroscience* 7:125-143.

Zarrugh, M.Y., and C.W. Radcliffe. 1978. Predicting metabolic cost of level walking. *European Journal of Applied Physiology* 38: 215-223.

Epilogue

In this book the contributing authors have presented their views on the principal thesis that motor learning and control is influenced by the propensity to reduce the metabolic energy cost of attaining the task goal. In some cases the authors illustrated their position with reference to specific tasks, such as human gait, but the chapters also review findings from a variety of other motor tasks that have used metabolic energy expenditure as a dependent variable.

Collectively the chapters provide, as far as I am aware, the first book with a specific focus on movement economy, and most of the contributions could be reasonably described as taking a contemporary movement science perspective. There is, therefore, evidence to suggest that economy is emerging as a clearly recognised topic within movement science. Humans and other animals use sensory information, either from internal or external sources, in order to interact adaptively with their environment. A unified focus on the fundamental question of how such adaptation is achieved is the type of enterprise that justifies the status of movement science or "kinesiology" as an independent scientific discipline. One of the interesting features of adaptation by optimisation of energy expenditure is that it is amenable to investigation from a variety of movement science subdisciplines, and the chapters in this book nicely reflect approaches based on biomechanics, physiology, and psychology-based motor learning.

This summary chapter provides a general commentary on the chapters and, in addition, makes some observations that emerged while the book was in preparation. The chapter is organised in subsections, each of which presents the "take-home messages" of one or more of the contributions.

Learning

This section summarises our observations on the energetics of learning motor tasks. My chapter with Hughes, Russell, and LeRossignol was designed to address the control of action, such that pacing and the selection of preferred modes is underpinned by sensations of effort or exertion associated with metabolic energy expenditure. While my colleagues and I did not, therefore, address changes in economy with practice, other contributors did address learning issues. Of particular interest to motor learning theorists is the recent work of Almåsbakk, Whiting, and van den

Tillaar, using the ski-simulator task, described at the end of their chapter. Some of the key findings concerning energy expenditure and learning are presented below.

Energy Conservation Is Fundamental to All Animal Learning

Brener and Carnicom illustrated that the principles of metabolic energy conservation that most of us have explored in human motor learning and control can also be applied to nonhuman subjects. As they pointed out in the first pages of their chapter, the history of minimum principles in learning dates back to studies with rats in the 1920s and 30s. Their chapter serves an important role in reminding us of our debt to the experimental psychologists of that time, with Edward Tolman the most prominent. Taking the Thordikian view that the same laws of learning can be applied to all mammals, the findings from animal research, using operant conditioning and studies of optimal foraging, provide compelling evidence that humans, as animals that have also evolved to be well-adapted to the natural environment, are similarly driven to conserve metabolic energy in the execution of everyday motor tasks. Compelling evidence of humans' propensity to conserve metabolic energy is the fact that a major public health issue in wealthy industrial societies is the "lifestyle diseases" associated with low physical activity. There is, therefore, a compelling case that coordination and control parameters that emerge with practice are highly constrained by the imperative to meet the task goal with minimum metabolic energy cost.

Sensory Information for Skill Learning

O'Dwyer and Neilson made an important contribution concerning the sensory signals available to the CNS that might be associated with the learning of metabolically optimal movements. If metabolic economy *is* a fundamental expedient in the learning and control of action, there must be associated sensory information underlying the selection of economical coordination and control parameters. O'Dwyer and Neilson gave a detailed account of the sensory signals associated with economical movements. In the first section of their chapter, they made the general point that the potentially relevant muscle-related signals available to the CNS are a reasonable focus for understanding the sensory underpinnings of economical movements. One interesting twist to the sensory information story, however, was the fact that O'Dwyer and Neilson also presented evidence that central *efferent* commands contribute significantly to the "sense of effort" associated with muscle contractions. If the central sense of effort reflects muscle activation, such sensations would also reflect the muscle's metabolic energy expenditure. Thus, the sensory information associated with muscle contraction levels and associated metabolic energy may, to some extent, be central in origin.

Muscle Activation and Learning

A second major contribution to learning issues made by O'Dwyer and his collaborators has been to revisit a very old topic in motor behavior, but one that has enjoyed very little experimental attention. This is the observation that there are changes to patterns of muscle activation with practice. Many readers will be familiar with Kamon and Gormley's (1968) paper on muscle activation patterns associated with learning the gymnastic skill of an upstart on the horizontal bar. This paper illustrated two phenomena associated with electromyographic (EMG) records of motor skill acquisition. The first is an overall reduction in muscle activation with practice, an outcome predicated on a "reduction hypothesis." A second general finding would be predicted by a "shift hypothesis," that is, a shift in muscle activation patterns from one muscle group to another. Recent findings from one of our studies of practice effects on EMG patterns and metabolic variables in learning to row an ergometer showed for all subjects an overall reduction in integrated EMG activity of the vastus lateralis (leg) and biceps brachii (arm). For one subject in our study, however, the EMG activation pattern showed a decrease in biceps brachii activation and an increase in vastus lateralis activity (Hughes, Lay, and Sparrow, 1999). Given that the participants also showed a significant decrease in metabolic energy expenditure with practice, we speculated that this shift in muscle activation from arms to legs might be associated with the greater metabolic economy of leg-powered ergometry. While our study provided only weak support for the shift hypothesis, it is interesting to speculate as to whether practice at a novel motor task is associated with reduced muscle activation *and* a shift to more metabolically efficient muscle groups.

The second major part of the O'Dwyer and Neilson chapter provides a systematic review of the effects of practice on muscle activation. One possible explanation for some of the inconsistencies in the research findings is that practice at some novel skills can be associated with increased speed, increased amplitude, or both. Such practice-related changes may be associated with increased mechanical power production. Almåsbakk, Whiting, and van den Tillaar emphasised this point in the opening comments of their section on the learning of cyclical actions. In learning cyclical actions such as the slalom ski task used in their laboratory, energy expenditure decreases and/or the mechanical work output increases. As a general principle, it is therefore important to ensure that hypothesised practice effects on muscle activation and associated metabolic energy expenditure are not confounded by an increase in work rate. Thus, two potential outcomes of improved economy with practice are that individuals can either take advantage of metabolic energy savings and perform the same task with less energy cost or, as suggested here, performers may invest the metabolic energy savings in increased power output. In the latter case EMG activity and metabolic cost may rise over practice trials.

Almåsbakk, Whiting, and van den Tillaar also made the link between EMG patterns as a measure of coordination changes with practice and optimisation of energy expenditure. They quoted a *Behavioural and Brain Sciences* commentary by Winters and Seif-Naraghi (1991) that is important in the context of our interest in muscle activation patterns because it addressed optimization in the context of *learning* goal-directed movements. The concluding paragraph to their article raised the possibility that "strategies" of motor control may emerge as a balance between ". . . on the one side, concepts such as 'effort', 'energy' or even 'pain,', and on the other side fairly crude global task kinematic measures such as movement distance, timing, or end-point accuracy" (p. 359). The main point, in summary, is that muscle activation patterns do not simply reflect the specific kinematic or kinetic demands of the response; they are also a reflection of the requirement to accommodate the "effort" or "energy" constraints that are intrinsic to motor learning and control.

Learning to Meet Task Demands

A recurring theme in these pages has been that learning in the motor domain can be characterised as a process of accommodating task demands, or "constraints." Learning to adapt motor coordination and control in the context of constraints imposed by the task and the environment provide a useful conceptual framework for understanding motor learning in general. An earlier paper by Newell (1986) put forward a constraints-based model of motor learning. Recently, Newell and I extended the model within the context of metabolic energy expenditure and the optimisation of motor behaviour (Sparrow and Newell, 1998). Caldwell's group also cited Newell's (1986) paper, and the constraints-to-action concept appears from time to time in other chapters. The constraints framework is a useful way of understanding the essential challenges faced by the human motor system in interacting adaptively with the environment via the execution of various motor tasks. This view of the essential challenge or "problem" faced by the motor system can be shared whether or not metabolic energy minimisation is seen as the primary goal of the organism's adaptation to task-environment constraints.

Energetics of Gait

For the majority of people the most energy demanding of everyday activities is locomotion. While there are some physically demanding jobs that are fairly static, most high energy-demanding occupations also have a major locomotor component. Humans locomote through the environment in various ways, but by far the most common mode is the walking gait. Three of the chapters focused primarily on human gait and collectively addressed the principal issues that are identified below.

Metabolic Cost as an Optimality Criterion for Human Gait

Patla and Sparrow's chapter began by emphasising the evolutionary forces that have shaped human bipedal locomotion and, based on Taylor and Rowntree's (1973) work, concluded that the evolution of bipedal gait may not have incurred a greater metabolic cost of transport than an habitual four-limbed gait. In sympathy with the position of Holt and his coauthors, Patla and Sparrow concluded that "multiple objectives" are optimised during locomotion. By inference, proposing metabolic energy minimisation as the only optimality criterion for human gait might be an oversimplification. Similarly, Hoyt and his colleagues wrote that " . . . many well-learned actions demonstrate a number of optimality criteria" (p. 2), and walking at preferred speed is not only characterised by minimum metabolic cost but also maximal head stability and minimum "shock transfer" from the foot to the head. Thus, it could be argued that, in the case of human gait, the metabolic energy minimisation hypothesis has only qualified support.

One of the most important contributions to the general issue of optimality in gait control was that by Holt and his group, showing how dynamical systems theory might be used to explain gait control in individuals with neuromuscular impairments, such as cerebral palsy. It is a truism that if one has a complete understanding of how a complex system works, it is possible to understand the conditions under which it does not. Holt and his colleagues have, therefore, shown how gait patterns observed in hemiplegic cerebral palsy are consistent with predictions based on the lower-limb dynamics. As an aside, it is also important to summarise their contribution by re-emphasising the fact that gait impairments are invariably associated with an increase in metabolic energy cost. Despite the "qualified support" for the energy minimisation hypothesis in the previous paragraph, it is interesting to consider whether it would be possible to make any modifications to the mechanics of normal gait that would not be reflected in increased metabolic energy expenditure.

The Walk-Run Transition

Human gait is of considerable interest to motor behaviour researchers for two reasons. First, the ability to move independently, while no longer absolutely essential for survival is, arguably, the most fundamental determinant of our quality of life. Impediments to independent locomotion are, therefore, of such importance that there is an impressive applied science enterprise devoted to maintaining individuals' capacity to walk. The second reason that gait is important, and more closed related to the chapters in this book, is that human gait is a fundamental human action that has provided valuable insights into motor learning and control of a more general or "basic science" nature. One question that has intrigued motor behaviour researchers for some time is the processes or mechanisms underlying fundamental changes in coordination or "transitions." The transition from walking to running in human gait is an interesting case in point and in recent years researchers have considered, to use the term in the title of the chapter by Hanna and his collaborators, the "trigger" for the transition from walking to running.

Hoyt and Taylor's (1981) paper on gait transitions in horses is becoming a classic reference in motor behaviour research because the authors addressed the transition question. In addition, and most important here, they proposed that in horses the trigger for the transition from walk to trot to gallop was the metabolic energy cost associated with each gait mode. When the energy cost of the three gait modes was measured on a motor-driven treadmill, it was shown to change in a curvilinear manner as shown in the figure reproduced in Patla and Sparrow's chapter. The conclusion was, to quote Hoyt and Taylor (1981), " . . . that horses, like humans, change gait and select a speed within a gait that minimises energy consumption" (p. 240). The reader might also be interested to note that within each of the gait modes the minimum energy cost to move one meter was constant at approximately 14 ml of oxygen consumed. The same phenomenon has also been observed in human running (Kram and Taylor, 1990). A later influential paper by Diedrich and Warren (1995) took a dynamical systems approach to the transition phenomenon. That paper concluded that the walk-run transition in humans is due to instability in the system dynamics. The mean transition speed for eight participants in Diedrich and Warren's (1995) first experiment (2.09 m/s) was, however, perfectly consistent with transition speeds found using metabolic methods. In this regard it is also important to note that Deidrich and Warren (1995) did not measure directly the metabolic cost of walking and running pre- and post-transition.

Hanna and his group also addressed the walk-run transition and their work in this chapter provides a clear, detailed, and extensive review of the proposed triggers for the abrupt shift in intralimb coordination associated with human gait. In addition to the empirical findings presented in the triggers-for-transition chapter the authors' detailed comments on the methodological issues in this work would be considered essential for a sound assessment of the empirical findings from transition studies. Most importantly, however, the experimental data presented in their chapter showed that the energetically optimal transition speed was 99.6%

of the preferred transition speed which, they concluded, " . . . strongly suggests that the optimisation of energetic efficiency is central to the transition between gait modes in human locomotion" (p. 37).

One final retrospective comment on the coordination shift in bipedal gaits is that unlike quadrupedal gait transitions there is no speed-related change in the interlimb coordination function. Except for hopping gaits, in which there is no phase difference in interlimb timing, bipedal footfall patterns remain half a cycle out-of-phase independent of speed. Newell and I conducted an experiment in which individuals adopted a four-limbed gait mode (creeping) on a motor-driven treadmill at progressively faster speeds (Sparrow and Newell, 1994). Our stride-by-stride analysis of the video record showed that the limbs of the same girdle, arms, and legs, always maintained a half-cycle phase difference up to a speed of approximately 2.0 m/s (7.2 km/h). The ipsilateral limbs (hand and foot on the same side) did, however, show an abrupt phase transition at approximately 50% of maximum speed. Unfortunately trial duration was too short to enable steady-state oxygen consumption to be collected in order to determine whether the ipsilateral phase shift (from approximately 0.25 to 0.45 of a cycle) was associated with a metabolic trigger.

An additional finding from our study, consistent with the interests of Hanna and his coauthors, was that the ipsilateral phase transition was observed on exactly the same stride (from the beginning of the trial) in two subjects of almost identical body mass and stature. The transition occurred earlier for a participant of relatively shorter stature. While the proposal that "dynamic constraints" are influential in triggering transitions would be supported by these data, for normal upright gait Hanna's data did not reveal strong relationships between anthropometric variables and the walk-run transition speed. The theory that the dynamics of limb action is an important determinant of the walk-run transition appears, therefore, to have only qualified support from the walk-run transition in humans. As implied above, the observation that human gait transitions reflect intralimb coordination transitions, while quadrupedal transitions have usually been quantified in terms of interlimb coordination, might be an explanation for the low correlation between anthropometric measures and walk-run transition speed in human gait.

Theoretical Orientations

One interesting question about the contributions to this book is whether there is a common theoretical thread. The short answer is "no!" This response might be interpreted negatively or, alternatively, it could be argued that the theme addressed in this book is of sufficient importance to be of interest to scientists of very different theoretical persuasions. Brener and Carnicom view the learning of economical responses from an operant conditioning perspective. Brener's work over the last ten years or more has focused on motor learning, economy of movement, production of criterion force-time responses, and number of related topics. But this work appears to have received little attention in the mainstream of motor behavior research. At some point in its history, motor behaviour took the information theory road and while some continue to follow it others have turned off to find answers in dynamical systems theory.

While there is clear evidence of the influence of dynamical systems theorising in many of the chapters, Holt and his colleagues are perhaps the strongest adherents to this position, a view supported by the homage paid to Bernstein in the quotation at the beginning of their chapter. As pointed out above, Holt's programme is oriented toward extending dynamical systems theorising to atypical gaits associated with impairments such as cerebral palsy. The test of a theory is, presumably, its success in explaining and predicting a wide range of phenomena.

As Caldwell and his collaborators indicated in their introduction, in addition to dynamical systems theory, traditional Newtonian mechanics is also widely used as a tool for analysing, to use their term, the "proficiency" of human movement. Zatsiorsky and Gregor's chapter is a good example of a contemporary biomechanical approach to analysing mechanical power using a linked-segment model based on Newtonian mechanics. It is interesting that the term "biomechanics" in the movement sciences is invariably used in the context of Newtonian mechanics. Linked-segment models of internal mechanical power have, for some time, been developed in order to measure the internal work associated with motor tasks, with much of the research focused on human gait. Zatsiorsky and Gregor provide a very useful update of this literature.

Measurement and Definition

One general contribution of the book is to provide extensive discussion of "efficiency," "economy," and related terms, such as "cost of transport." I am grateful to my colleague Peter LeRossignol who wrote the section in our chapter concerning measurement of the metabolic cost of exercise, issues concerning the denominator of the efficiency equation. Caldwell, van Emmerik, and Hamill, included a similar section at the start of their chapter but, in addition, discussed the efficiency equation numerator. They commented on Zatsiorsky and Gregor's speciality, measurement of the internal and external mechanical work done by the human body. They also highlighted the fact that using the "point-mass" model to represent total body mechanical energy takes no account of the internal mechanical work done to move the limbs. Measuring internal mechanical work is, however, a difficult biomechanical problem, one that is taken up in

Zatsiorsky and Gregor's excellent critical review of the strengths and limitations of various models of mechanical work.

Zatsiorsky and Gregor provide an extended discussion of the definition and calculation of mechanical work in human movement and for readers who find the mechanics hard going there is, nevertheless, much to be gained from the chapter. In an early paper Irizarry-Lopez and I (Sparrow and Irizarry-Lopez, 1987) calculated segmental rotational, translational, and potential kinetic energies, in an attempt to find out whether the summations of these energy components would change with practice at a novel task (hands and feet creeping). The fact that there was potential for metabolic energy savings via changes to the linked-system mechanics was encouraging, given our interest in metabolic energy changes with practice. The early encouragement that metabolic energy savings could be achieved by changes to the coordination and control of individual limbs and limb segments, was reinforced by reading Zatsiorsky and Gregor's chapter. A number of potential metabolic-energy saving mechanisms can be identified, such as energy exchanges between and within segments, storage and recovery of stored elastic energy, regulation of the rate of muscle contraction, and reduction of co-contractions. To date, however, there has been very little research linking segmental power analyses of internal work to metabolic energy cost as a function of practice. In principle, with external work rate held constant (via an ergometer), metabolic energy savings should be reflected in reductions in internal work due to practice-related refinements to the movement pattern.

Summary

This chapter has served to review the book's content by identifying common themes. Having done so, at this time, the challenge is to provide a further overriding perspective that might serve to unify the observations in this summary chapter. One way to summarise the various points of view on the metabolic energy minimisation hypothesis is to highlight an observation made by Caldwell and his colleagues on the first page of their chapter. They used the following quotation from the book's preface as the springboard for their discussion: ". . . economical movements are those that meet the *task demands* with relatively low metabolic energy expenditure." Their emphasis on task demands was made in support of the view that a single performance criterion such as minimum metabolic energy cost was unlikely to satisfy the task demands of a wide range of motor skills. Different skills, it was argued, have different task demands, and skilled performance is the process by which task-specific constraints are accommodated by the performer. In a 100-m sprint, for example, the task constraints are to traverse that distance in the least time, with no requirement to perform economically. Similarly, in the various discussions of human gait it has been argued that gait tasks have multiple demands or "criteria" and that minimising metabolic cost is likely to be only one of a number of competing objectives. O'Dwyer and his coauthors made a similar point in saying "the primary consideration in the execution of any movement is the fulfilment of the purpose or task goal." Energy expenditure, they argued, might become more of an influence later in practice, presumably as the skilled exponent not only meets the task goal but does so with low metabolic cost. This view that skilled motor behavior is reflected in the capacity to meet spatial, temporal, or other constraints of the task, while also being undertaken with relatively low metabolic energy cost, is entirely consistent with many traditional definitions of skill in the motor domain.

One way in which we can resolve the task constraints issue, however, is to suggest that all task constraints are, themselves, constraints on the individual's propensity to perform with the least metabolic cost. The essential problem in the coordination and control of action is not only to control degrees of freedom to achieve the task goal, but to do so in such a manner that the task goal is achieved economically. We can, therefore, take the position that there are not competing objectives of which metabolic economy is one, rather achieving the task goal economically is the single objective common to the coordination and control of all motor tasks. From this view, other objectives may be viewed as constraining the capacity to perform economically. In running 100 m, for example, the requirement to minimise movement time is a constraint on the capacity to cover that distance with minimum energy cost. Likewise, in stepping safely over an obstacle, safe clearance constrains the limb trajectory in such a way that the metabolic energy cost is likely to be higher than for unobstructed gait. Our tendency to walk around obstacles, to remove obstacles from the environment, and to traverse obstacles in such a way that safety is preserved with the least compromise to energy expenditure are good examples. The artificial or "contrived" constraints associated with work tasks and sports are those imposed upon an organism that has evolved to interact economically with the environment. Metabolic energy cost can, therefore, be viewed as a fundamental influence on coordination and control of action across all motor tasks, with specific speed, accuracy, and other tasks demands constraining the tendency to perform optimally in terms of energy expended to meet the task goal.

References

Diedrich, F.J., and W.H. Warren. 1995. Why change gaits? Dynamics of the walk-run transition. *Journal of Experimental Psychology* 21: 183-202.

Hoyt, D.F., and C.R. Taylor. 1981. Gait and the energetics of locomotion in horses. *Nature* 292: 239-240.

Hughes, K., B.S. Lay, and W.A Sparrow. 1999. Minimum principles in human motor control: the effects of practice on movement kinematics, metabolic energy expenditure, and muscle activation (EMG). Paper presented at the 26th Annual Experimental Psychology Conference, Macquarie University, April 9-11.

Kamon, E., and J. Gormley. 1968. Muscular activity pattern for skilled performance and during learning of a horizontal bar exercise. *Ergonomics* 11: 345-357.

Kram, R., and R. Taylor. 1990. Energetics of running: a new perspective. *Nature* 346: 265-267.

Newell, K.M. 1986. Constraints on the development of coordination. In *Motor development in children: aspects of coordination and control,* eds. M.G. Wade and H.T.A. Whiting, 341-361. Dordrecht, the Netherlands: Martinus Nijhoff.

Sparrow, W.A., and K.M. Newell. 1994 The coordination and control of human creeping with increases in speed. *Behavioural Brain Research* 63: 151-158.

Sparrow, W.A., and K.M. Newell. 1998. Metabolic energy expenditure and regulation of movement economy. *Psychonomic Bulletin and Review* 5: 173-196.

Taylor, C.R., and V.J. Rowntree. 1973. Running on two or four legs: which consumes more energy? *Science* 179: 186-187.

Winters, J.M., and A.H. Seif-Naraghi. 1991. Strategies for goal-directed fast movements are by products of satisfying performance criteria. *Behavioral and Brain Sciences* 14: 357-359.

Index

Note. The italicized f and t following page numbers refer to figures and tables, respectively.

About the Editor

W.A. Sparrow, PhD, is currently a senior lecturer in the School of Health Sciences at Deakin University, Melbourne, Australia. A major focus of his work has been metabolic energy expenditure and movement coordination and control.

Sparrow's work has been published in such scholarly journals as the *Journal of Motor Behavior* and the *Psychonomic Bulletin and Review.* The major theme of this book had its origins in a paper titled *The Efficiency of Skilled Performance,* which appeared in the *Journal of Motor Behavior* in 1983. This work proposed that references to "economy" or "efficiency" in traditional definitions of motor expertise could be studied experimentally by examining the effects of practice on the metabolic energy expended to achieve the motor task goal.

Sparrow received his PhD at the University of Illinois in Urbana-Champaign, where he also worked as a research assistant in the Motor Behavior Laboratory under the supervision of Karl Newell.

He and his wife, Helen, reside in Melbourne, Australia. His leisure time activities include reading and swimming.

About the Contributors

Bruce Abernethy is Professor and Head of the School of Human Movement Studies at the University of Queensland in Brisbane, Australia. He is co-editor of *The Creative Side of Experimentation* (Human Kinetics, 1992) and co-author of *The Biophysical Foundations of Human Movement* (Human Kinetics, 1996). His research interests are in the control and learning of skilled movement.

Bjørn Almåsbakk is in the Department of Sport Sciences at the University of Trondheim in Norway.

Jasper Brener is Professor of Psychology at the State University of New York at Stony Brook. His interest in behavioral energetics stemmed from his earlier research on sources of behaviorally related variations in cardiovascular performance. This work confirmed Paul Obrist's idea that variations in cardiovascular activity often attributed to psychological processes can be largely accounted for by associated variations in overall energy expenditure. The variations in metabolic rate are, in turn, caused primarily by striate muscular activity. Efficient regulation of the striate muscles is expressed by reduced rates of energy expenditure and cardiovascular performance. The current chapter explores the role of external feedback in generating efficient motor performance.

Robin Burgess-Limerick is senior lecturer in Occupational Biomechanics within the School of Human Movement Studies at the University of Queensland, Australia. His research interests bridge biomechanics and motor control with a particular focus on ergonomics and human factors, manual handling, office ergonomics, and gait.

Graham E. Caldwell is an Associate Professor in the Department of Exercise Science at the University of Massachusetts at Amherst. He holds degrees from the University of Waterloo (BSc, MSc) and Simon Fraser University (PhD). His work is focused on understanding the performance of skilled human movement, using inverse dynamics, simulation, and musculoskeletal modeling.

Scott Carnicom completed work toward this chapter while a doctoral student under the supervision of Dr. Jasper Brener in the Department of Psychology at the State University of New York at Stony Brook. Scott's doctoral work focused on the effects of various forms of feedback on operant force learning in rats. In August of 2000, Scott will begin as an Assistant Professor of Psychology at Marymount University in Arlington, Virginia.

Richard van Emmerik is an Assistant Professor at the Exercise Science Department, University of Massachusetts at Amherst. He received his Masters degree from the Vrije Universiteit in Amsterdam, the Netherlands, and his PhD from the University of Illinois at Urbana-Champaign. His research background is in motor control and learning, with a special emphasis on movement coordination issues in posture and gait. His research is directed to problems due to aging and movement disabilities (such as in Parkinson's disease, stroke, and Down syndrome).

Sergio T. Fonseca is an adjunct professor in the departmento de fisioterapia at the Universidade Federal de Minas Gerais in Belo Horizonte, Brazil.

Robert J. Gregor is currently Professor and Head of the Department of Health and Performance Sciences and Director of the Center for Human Movement Studies at Georgia Tech. He is past president of the American Society of Biomechanics and a member of the Sub-Commission on Biomechanics and Physiology, Medical Commission, IOC. Dr. Gregor's primary research interests focus on the use of skeletal muscle as a resource to the nervous system in the generation and control of movement.

Joseph Hamill is a professor in the Department of Exercise Science at the University of Massachusetts at Amherst. He holds undergraduate degrees from York University (BA) and Concordia University (BS) and graduate degrees from the University of Oregon (MS and PhD). His work focuses on lower extremity mechanics during locomotion, with particular emphasis on the mechanisms of overuse injuries.

Alastair Hanna is employed full-time as Sport Scientist (Biomechanics) by the Queensland Academy of Sport, based in Brisbane, Australia. He is currently completing a PhD through the School of Human Movement Studies at the University of Queensland in which he is investigating gait transitions in human locomotion.

Kenneth G. Holt received a PhD in biomechanics from the University of Massachusetts in 1989. He also received a Master of Science in Physical Therapy from Boston University in 1983 and a Master of Science in Physical Education (emphasis in Motor Control) from Pennsylvania State University in 1976. He is an Associate Professor in the Sargent College of Health and Rehabilitation Sciences at Boston University, Director of the Barreca Motion Analysis Laboratory at BU, and a Fellow of the Center for the Ecological Study of Perception and Action, University of Connecticut. He is happily married with two young children and would like to ride bicycles faster and more frequently.

Kirstie Hughes is currently a doctoral student under the supervision of Dr. William Sparrow in the School of Health Sciences at Deakin University, Australia. Her doctoral work focuses on the effects of practice and pacing on the metabolic energy expenditure and kinematics of motor tasks. She currently resides in Melbourne, Australia. Her leisure time activities include horse riding and reading.

Robert Neal is a Senior Lecturer in biomechanics within the School of Human Movement Studies at the University of Queensland. His research is in sport biomechanics, injury mechanics, and gait; he has a particular interest in golf.

Peter Neilson's competence as a systems and control engineer is meshed with a parallel career in neurophysiological and neurological research. He draws together his teaching in systems and control at the University of NSW and his continuing research activity at the Neuroengineering Laboratory with a strand of lectures on human movement control systems and projects that are attractive to many young engineers.

Colonel John P. Obusek, ScD is a research physical therapist and the Deputy Commander of the U.S. Army Research Institute of Environmental Medicine, Natick, Massachusetts. His research is focused on understanding the dynamics of human movement and its application to protecting soldier health and performance.

Nicholas O'Dwyer studied psychology at University College Dublin and obtained a PhD in motor control from the University of New South Wales in Sydney. He is currently an associate professor in the School of Physiotherapy at the University of Sydney. His research interests encompass information processing underlying motor control and learning, mechanisms of multijoint coordination, muscle servosystems and stretch reflex physiology, and analysis of neurological disorders (spasticity, stroke, and cerebral palsy).

Aftab Patla is a Professor in the Department of Kinesiology at the University of Waterloo in Canada. His research program has three major themes: understanding the roles of vision in the control of human locomotion; strategies for maintenance of dynamic stability during standing and walking; and aging and mobility.

Peter Le Rossignol is currently in the School of Human Movement at Deakin University in Australia.

A.P. Russell is currently at the Biochimie Medicale at Geneve University. His primary interests are physiology of exercise relating to human performance, as well as gene transcription and translation. Other interests include athletics, golf, and snowboarding.

Roland van den Tillaar was born in the Netherlands. He has studied physical education for four years, followed by three years of human movements science study in the Netherlands. He is currently a doctoral student at the Department of Sport Sciences at the University of Trondheim, Norway. Roland's doctoral work focuses on coordination and training of fast movements, such as overarm throwing. His hobbies are track and field (decathlon) and playing team handball.

John (HTA) Whiting, professor emeritus from the Free University in Amsterdam, the Netherlands, has just completed a five year appointment as Professor in the Department of Sport Sciences at the University of Trondheim in Norway. At the same time, he held an honorary professorship in the Department of Psychology at the University of York, an appointment which is ongoing. He was recently awarded an honorary doctor of science degree by the University of Waterloo, Canada, for his contribution to the development of the field of Human Movement Science and a similar award from The University of the Mediterranean, Marseille, France, for his contribution to functional neurosciences.

Vladimir M. Zatsiorsky has been a professor in the department of kinesiology at the Pennsylvania State University since 1991; he is also currently the director of the biomechanics laboratory at Penn State. He received his Doctor of Science degree from the Central Institute of Physical Culture in Moscow, where he later served for 18 years as professor and department chair of the Department of Biomechanics. He was a biomechanics and fitness consultant to the national Olympics teams of the USSR. He has authored more than 250 scientific journal articles and is a member of the American Society of Biomechanics and the International Society of Biomechanics.

DATE DUE